GUIDE TO AMERICA'S
FEDERAL JOBS

A Complete Directory of U.S. Government Career Opportunities

FOURTH EDITION

Karol Taylor and Janet M. Ruck

Works
America's Career Publisher

Guide to America's Federal Jobs, Fourth Edition

A Complete Directory of U.S. Government Career Opportunities

© 2009 by JIST Publishing

Published by JIST Works, an imprint of JIST Publishing
7321 Shadeland Station, Suite 200
Indianapolis, IN 46256-3923

Phone: 800-648-JIST   Fax: 877-454-7839
E-mail: info@jist.com   Web site: www.jist.com

Quantity discounts are available for JIST products. Please call our Sales Department at 800-648-JIST for a free catalog and more information.

Visit www.jist.com for information on JIST; free job search tips, tables of contents, and sample pages; and online ordering.

Acquisitions Editor: Susan Pines
Development Editor: Heather Stith
Cover Designer: Alan Evans
Interior Designer and Layout: Toi Davis
Proofreaders: Linda Seifert and Jeanne Clark
Indexer: Jeanne Clark

Printed in the United States of America

14 13 12 11 10   9 8 7 6 5 4 3 2

ISBN 978-1-59357-654-7

This Book Can Save You Many Hours of Frustration

With more than 1.8 million employees, the federal government is the country's largest employer. Yet untangling the terminology and procedures used in federal job hunting may leave you frustrated and discouraged.

Where do you start? Which departments and agencies have jobs that interest you? Are federal jobs available in your area? What's the best and easiest way to find out about federal openings? How do you make sense of vacancy announcements that ask for information such as KSAs?

Take heart! The federal government offers an average of 24,000 job openings a *day*, and you learn how to find and apply for them with this book's help. *Guide to America's Federal Jobs* is your best overall resource on federal employment and gives you the most current information, step-by-step guidance, and helpful tips throughout.

We conducted extensive research for the most useful details on federal employment and present them clearly in this book. We hope it saves you many hours of frustration, answers your questions, and leads you to a federal job.

Table of Contents

Summary of Major Sections

Introduction. The introduction explains how this book can help you and how to best use the information. The introduction begins on page xi.

Part I: Understanding, Finding, and Applying for Federal Jobs. The three chapters in this part unravel the complexities of federal job hunting. ***Chapter 1*** outlines the types of available jobs, describes the federal pay system, and explains how to explore federal careers by using the USAJOBS Web site. ***Chapter 2*** explains all the ins and outs of using the USAJOBS site to find a federal job. ***Chapter 3*** takes you step-by-step through the process of getting a federal job, everything from understanding federal hiring procedures to writing a federal-style resume. Part I begins on page 1.

Part II: Descriptions, URLs, and Sample Job Vacancies for Federal Agencies and Departments. The book's longest section provides details on the many federal agencies and departments. In addition, this part summarizes some agencies' actual job announcements to give you an excellent grasp of the types of jobs available and their application requirements. Uniform Resource Locators, or URLs, lead you to helpful Web sites. ***Chapter 4*** covers the legislative branch. ***Chapter 5*** highlights the judicial branch. ***Chapter 6*** profiles the executive branch and its many departments, agencies, and boards. Part II begins on page 55.

Part III: Special Federal Job Opportunities. ***Chapter 7*** explains federal job opportunities that veterans can receive. ***Chapter 8*** covers federal opportunities for people with disabilities. ***Chapter 9*** reviews federal job programs for students. Part III begins on page 317.

Part IV: Appendixes. The appendixes offer numerous helpful resources, including federal jobs listed by college major, a complete sample vacancy announcement, sample federal-style resumes and KSA responses, and a list of career resources. Part IV begins on page 335.

Detailed Table of Contents

Part III: Special Federal Job Opportunities 317

Chapter 7: Special Federal Job Opportunities for Veterans 319

Chapter 8: Special Federal Job Opportunities for People with Disabilities 325

Chapter 9: Special Federal Job Opportunities for Students 329

Part IV: Appendixes 335

Appendix A: Federal Jobs by College Major 337

© JIST Works

Introduction

Over the years, many myths have arisen about job opportunities with the federal government. Some of the most common are that the government hires only faceless bureaucrats to shuffle papers, federal jobs pay poorly, the jobs are unrewarding, and they're all located in Washington, DC.

This book should shatter those myths forever.

Most important, this book should help you navigate the federal employment maze by clearly explaining what you need to know—from how to research a targeted federal job to how to make your application stand out. Although the federal government has made serious efforts in recent years to improve its hiring process, in too many cases applying for a job remains a bewildering, complex, and frustrating experience. Don't be discouraged. In most cases, you'll find that the extra effort required to apply for a federal job is well worth your time and patience. Think of your long-term goals and how your persistence will help you to meet them.

How This Book Is Organized

Part I of this book disentangles the federal hiring process from beginning to end, using plain language (something the government generally isn't known for) to lead you step by step along the way. It also explains, in detail, how to use the USAJOBS Web site, which is the main source for information about federal jobs.

The federal government is a complex organization. To help you find the agencies that best match your talents and interests, the second part of this book profiles dozens of federal agencies and departments and then summarizes information about their major organizational components. Some of the information may surprise you. For example, did you know that the U.S. Forest Service (part of the Department of Agriculture) employs archeologists? URLs for the main Web site of each agency or department are listed, and for most departments you'll also commonly find URLs for Web sites that provide basic employment information, lists of job openings, descriptions of internship opportunities, and information about smaller components within the overall department. All URLs were current at press time.

In Part III, you'll find helpful information on special opportunities in the federal government for veterans, for people with disabilities, and for students.

A Few Helpful Notes About This Book

Before you start reading, it might be helpful for you to know the following:

★ To save you time, this book is not designed to be read from front to back (unless you really want to). You might want to start with the second part that describes actual federal jobs and then return to the first part to learn how to find and apply for similar jobs. Or you may want to browse through the book initially, looking for things that catch your eye. If you're looking for something specific, you may want to use the table of contents and the index to quickly find the relevant information.

★ Making generalizations about federal hiring and personnel management practices, as we do in this book, is a dangerous business. This is especially true today because selected agencies are obtaining permission to throw out the regular rules to improve the hiring process. Even in agencies that abide by the normal rules, many variations and exceptions exist that only the agency's personnel specialists fully understand. Once you find a federal job for which you'd like to apply, protect yourself by carefully reading every word in the vacancy announcement (more about this in Part I) and by checking the agency's Web site for information about its current hiring and personnel management practices.

★ Along with entries on the agencies of the executive, judicial, and legislative branches of government, Part II includes details on quasi-official agencies; international organizations in which the U.S. participates; and other boards, commissions, and committees.

★ This book touches briefly on opportunities at the U.S. Postal Service and the active-duty portion of the Department of Defense, but note that both of these agencies have their own hiring and personnel systems. A good resource is the *Occupational Outlook Handbook* (available from JIST Publishing). This book has statements on Postal Service workers and job opportunities in the Armed Forces.

★ We obtained virtually all the information in this book from federal government publications, Web sites, and databases. We examined an enormous amount of material, and we've included only the information we think will be directly useful in your federal job search. We also condensed and clarified the materials from federal sources to save you time and to make the information easier to understand.

★ We obtained all statistics in this book from databases and publications produced by the federal Office of Personnel Management (OPM) unless otherwise noted.

★ No one source exists for data covering *every* federal employee. The main sources we relied on were links to federal organizations from USA.gov; National Archives's U.S. Government Manual, 2007–2008 edition; and OPM's Central Personnel Data File, which provides data regarding selected civilian employees. When we cite statistics about "federal employees," they're from these sources, but each has its unique set of limitations. Numbers from these sources do not correlate, so we had to choose the most recent numbers when we could locate a date.

A few organizations had fact sheets, some of them had information on their "About" page, and many had relevant information on their strategic plans. A comparison of National Archive and USA.gov data resulted in the final information presented on these pages.

We've tried to include in this book the things you need to know to apply for federal jobs. We hope it answers your questions about the types of available jobs and about federal employment issues. It's impossible to answer every conceivable question in one book, but we've designed this one to point you toward additional information about a wide variety of subjects.

Good luck in your federal job hunt!

Part I

Understanding, Finding, and Applying for Federal Jobs

1

CHAPTER 1

Uncle Sam Wants You

With more than 1.8 million civilian employees (excluding the postal service), the federal government is the nation's largest employer (as of January 2007). In this chapter and Chapter 2, we will discuss the many opportunities available in the federal government and how you can take advantage of these opportunities. By considering your career aspirations and the skills you have to offer, you can most likely find a job that matches who you are with what the federal government needs.

What Factors Affect Federal Job Opportunities?

Staffing levels in federal government, while relatively stable in the short run, can be subject to change in the long run primarily because of changes in public policies as legislated by the Congress, which affect spending levels and hiring decisions for the various departments and agencies. In general, over the coming decade, domestic programs are likely to see cuts in their budgets as Congress seeks to reduce the federal budget deficit, but the cuts will likely affect some agencies more than others. Any employment declines, however, generally will be carried out through attrition—simply not replacing workers who retire or leave the federal government for other reasons. Layoffs, called *reductions in force,* have occurred in the past, but they are uncommon and usually affect relatively few workers.

Retirement Tsunami

In spite of legislative budget cuts, there still will be numerous employment opportunities in many agencies from the need to replace workers who leave the workforce, retire, or accept employment elsewhere. In fact, the need for replacement for workers will be significant in the coming years. Like other American employers, the federal government is facing the issue of the increasing age of the American workforce, which some have called a crisis. For example, the U.S. Office of Personnel Management (OPM) estimates that among all full-time permanent employees in the federal workforce as of October 2004, 58 percent of supervisory and 42 percent of nonsupervisory workers will be eligible to retire by the end of 2010.

Consider these Office of Personnel Management figures showing the top 10 agencies with highest percentages of employees projected to retire by 2012:

★ Federal Aviation Administration: 26 percent

★ Department of Housing and Urban Development: 26 percent

★ Social Security Administration: 23 percent

★ Education Department: 22 percent

★ Energy Department: 22 percent

★ National Science Foundation: 22 percent

3

★ General Services Administration: 22 percent

★ Interior Department: 21 percent

★ Labor Department: 21 percent

★ Treasury Department: 21 percent

The federal government also anticipates that it will need to fill 193,000 critical-need federal jobs in the near future because of its aging workforce and subsequent anticipated retirements. According to Partnership for Public Service, this number includes the following jobs:

★ 83,000 security and law enforcement jobs

★ 23,000 nurses and other health care workers

★ 21,000 Treasury Department employees

★ 15,000 air traffic controllers

To fill the gap left by what former director of the Office of Personnel Management Linda Springer calls a "retirement tsunami," the federal government is working to make the job recruitment, application, and selection process easier and less cumbersome. It is expected that streamlining the process will make the federal government a more attractive and more welcoming employer. A number of initiatives have taken place in order to expedite the application process and to spread the word that the federal government is hiring, that it is an attractive employer, and that it welcomes candidate applications.

Government Job Stability

Note, however, that although it may be easier to apply for a federal job, getting the job may be tough. Competition is expected for many federal positions, especially during times of economic uncertainty, when workers seek the stability of federal employment. In general, federal employment is considered to be relatively stable because it is not affected by cyclical fluctuations in the economy, as are employment levels in many private sector industries.

Partnership for Public Service

The Partnership for Public Service is a nonprofit organization that works to improve the federal government by helping them to attract talented employees and encouraging innovation. As part of its mission, the Partnership has created a number of initiatives designed to mitigate the sometimes unwieldy application process. (For more information, see the Web site at http://www.ourpublicservice.org.) As a result, the Office of Personnel Management (OPM) has created a number of hiring flexibilities (that is, exceptions to the often cumbersome government hiring regulations) designed to attract certain populations to the federal government.

What Kinds of Jobs Are Available in the Federal Government?

The federal government is an organization formed to produce public services. Its essential duties include defending the United States from foreign aggression and terrorism, representing U.S. interests abroad, enforcing laws and regulations, and administering domestic programs and agencies. Although U.S. citizens are particularly aware of the federal government when they pay their income taxes each year, they usually do not consider the government's role when they watch a weather forecast, purchase fresh and uncontaminated groceries, travel by highway or air, or make a deposit at their bank. Workers employed by the federal government play a vital role in these and many other aspects of our daily lives.

Although the federal government employs workers in every major occupational group, workers are not employed in the same proportions in which they are employed throughout the economy as a whole (see Table 1.1). The analytical and technical nature of many government duties translates into a much higher proportion of professional, management, business, and financial occupations in the federal government, compared with most industries. Conversely, the government sells very little, so it employs relatively few sales workers.

TABLE 1.1

Distribution of Employment in the Federal Government and for All Industries by Major Occupational Group

Occupational Group	Federal Government	All Industries
Management, business, and financial	33.2%	10.2%
Professional and related	32.8%	19.8%
Office and administrative support	14.3%	16.2%
Service	8.0%	19.2%
Installation, maintenance, and repair	4.7%	3.9%
Transportation and material moving	2.9%	6.8%
Construction and extraction	1.7%	5.5%
Production	1.5%	7.1%
Sales and related	0.5%	10.6%
Farming, fishing, and forestry	0.4%	0.7%

Note: These numbers reflect the most recent data available (2006) and do not include postal service jobs.

As you may note when looking the Tables 1.2 through 1.7, the rate of employment in many occupations is projected to decline over the next several years. Some of this projected slow growth or decline is due to governmental cost-cutting, the growing use of private contractors, and the practice of turning over the development, implementation, and management of some programs of the federal government to state and local governments. Employment declines will be the greatest among office and administrative support occupations and production occupations because of increasing office automation and contracting out of these jobs.

However, many job openings should arise from the need to replace workers who retire or leave the federal government for other reasons. In addition, some job growth will be generated by increased homeland security needs. Demand also will continue to grow for specialized workers in areas related to border and transportation security, emergency preparedness, public health, and information analysis.

A study by the Partnership for Public Service, which surveyed federal department and agency hiring needs through September 2009, found that most new hires in the federal government will come in five major areas:

★ Security, enforcement, and compliance, which includes inspectors, investigators, police officers, airport screeners, and prison guards

★ Medical and public health fields

★ Engineering and the sciences, including microbiologists, botanists, physicists, chemists, and veterinarians

★ Program management and administration

★ Accounting, budget, and business, which includes revenue agents and tax examiners needed mainly by the Internal Revenue Service

The Department of Health and Human Services also will need health insurance specialists and claims and customer service representatives to implement the Medicare Prescription Drug benefit. Patent examiners, foreign service officers, and lawyers also are in high demand.

Management, Business, and Financial Occupations

As Table 1.2 shows, management, business, and financial workers make up about 33 percent of federal employment and are primarily responsible for overseeing operations. Managerial workers include a broad range of officials who, at the highest levels, may head federal agencies or programs. Middle managers, on the other hand, usually oversee one activity or aspect of a program. One management occupation, legislators, is responsible for passing and amending laws and overseeing the executive branch of the government. Within the federal government, legislators are entirely found in Congress.

Other occupations in this occupational group are accountants and auditors, who prepare and analyze financial reports, review and record revenues and expenditures, and investigate operations for fraud and inefficiency. Management analysts study government operations and systems and suggest improvements. Purchasing agents handle federal purchases of supplies, and tax examiners, collectors, and revenue agents determine and collect taxes.

TABLE 1.2

Employment of Wage and Salary Workers in Federal Government Management, Business, and Financial Occupations and Projected Change

Occupation	Current Number of Workers	Percent of Total Federal Workforce	Projected Percent Change
All management, business, and financial occupations	650,000	33.2%	−2.9%
General and operations managers	29,000	1.5%	−0.4%
Financial managers	12,000	0.6%	−5.5%
Purchasing agents, except wholesale, retail, and farm products	30,000	1.5%	−14.9%
Claims adjusters, examiners, and investigators	42,000	2.2%	−5.5%
Compliance officers, except agriculture, construction, health and safety, and transportation	91,000	4.6%	−5.5%
Human resources, training, and labor relations specialists	23,000	1.2%	3.8%
Logisticians	23,000	1.2%	4.0%
Management analysts	45,000	2.3%	−5.5%
Accountants and auditors	24,000	1.2%	−14.9%
Budget analysts	14,000	0.7%	−5.5%
Tax examiners, collectors, and revenue agents	36,000	1.8%	1.2%

Note: Numbers reflect 2006 data; projections are for the period 2006–2016. Columns may not add to totals due to omission of occupations with small employment.

Source: Bureau of Labor Statistics, http://www.bls.gov

Professional and Related Occupations

Professional and related occupations account for about the same percentage (nearly 33 percent) of federal employment as management, business, and financial occupations do (see Table 1.3). The largest groups of professional workers are in life, physical, and social science occupations, such as biological scientists, conservation scientists and foresters, environmental scientists and geoscientists, and forest and conservation technicians. They perform tasks such as determining the effects of drugs on living organisms, preventing fires in the national forests, and predicting earthquakes and hurricanes.

Large numbers of federal workers also hold jobs as engineers, including aerospace, civil, computer hardware, electrical and electronics, environmental, industrial, mechanical, and nuclear engineers. Engineers are found in many departments of the executive branch, but the vast majority works in the Department of Defense. Other engineers work in the National Aeronautics and Space Administration as well as other agencies. In general, they solve problems and provide advice on technical programs, such as building highway bridges or implementing agency-wide computer systems.

The professional occupations category includes these other types of jobs as well:

★ Many health professionals, such as licensed practical and licensed vocational nurses, registered nurses, and physicians and surgeons, work for the Department of Veterans Affairs in VA hospitals.

★ Many lawyers, judges, and law clerks work for the federal government to write, administer, and enforce many of the country's laws and regulations.

★ Computer specialists, primarily computer software engineers, computer systems analysts, and network and computer systems administrators, are employed throughout the federal government. They write computer programs, analyze problems related to data processing, and keep computer systems running smoothly.

TABLE 1.3

Employment of Wage and Salary Workers in Federal Government Professional and Related Occupations and Projected Change

Occupation	Current Number of Workers	Percent of Total Federal Workforce	Projected Percent Change
All professional and related occupations	642,000	32.8%	−3.2%
Computer specialists	77,000	3.9%	2.0%
Engineers	90,000	4.6%	−4.4%
Engineering technicians, except drafters	29,000	1.5%	−5.1%
Biological scientists	23,000	1.2%	−5.5%
Conservation scientists	8,000	0.4%	12.2%
Chemists	6,000	0.3%	−5.5%

Occupation	Current Number of Workers	Percent of Total Federal Workforce	Projected Percent Change
Environmental scientists and specialists, including health	6,000	0.3%	−5.5%
Biological technicians	12,000	0.6%	−5.5%
Forest and conservation technicians	26,000	1.3%	−4.9%
Lawyers	31,000	1.6%	−5.5%
Paralegals and legal assistants	14,000	0.7%	5.5%
Education, training, and library occupations	32,000	1.6%	−5.5%
Physicians and surgeons	25,000	1.3%	−5.5%
Registered nurses	54,000	2.7%	4.0%
Health technologists and technicians	40,000	2.1%	−5.6%
Licensed practical and licensed vocational nurses	14,000	0.7%	−5.5%
Occupational health and safety specialists	7,000	0.3%	−5.5%

Note: Numbers reflect 2006 data; projections are for the period 2006–2016. Columns may not add to totals due to omission of occupations with small employment.

Source: Bureau of Labor Statistics, http://www.bls.gov

Office and Administrative Support Occupations

About 14 percent of federal workers are in office and administrative support occupations (see Table 1.4). These employees aid management staff with administrative duties. Administrative support workers in the federal government include information and record clerks, general office clerks, and secretaries and administrative assistants.

TABLE 1.4

Employment of Wage and Salary Workers in Federal Government Office and Administrative Support Occupations and Projected Change

Occupation	Current Number of Workers	Percent of Total Federal Workforce	Projected Percent Change
All office and administrative support occupations	279,000	14.3%	−15.5%
Bookkeeping, accounting, and auditing clerks	21,000	1.1%	−5.5%
Procurement clerks	15,000	0.7%	−14.9%
Eligibility interviewers, government programs	26,000	1.3%	6.3%
Human resources assistants, except payroll and timekeeping	14,000	0.7%	−5.5%
Secretaries and administrative assistants	34,000	1.7%	−15.4%
Word processors and typists	14,000	0.7%	−24.4%

Note: Numbers reflect 2006 data; projections are for the period 2006–2016. Columns may not add to totals due to omission of occupations with small employment.

Source: Bureau of Labor Statistics, http://www.bls.gov

Service Occupations

Compared with the economy as a whole, workers in service occupations are relatively scarce in the federal government, accounting for only 8 percent of the total federal workforce (see Table 1.5). About one out of two federal workers in service occupations are protective service workers, such as correctional officers and jailers, detectives and criminal investigators, and police officers. These workers protect the public from crime and oversee federal prisons.

© JIST Works

TABLE 1.5

Employment of Wage and Salary Workers in Federal Government Service Occupations and Projected Change

Occupation	Current Number of Workers	Percent of Total Federal Workforce	Projected Percent Change
All service occupations	157,000	8.0%	2.9%
Firefighters	8,000	0.4%	−5.5%
Correctional officers and jailers	16,000	0.8%	13.4%
Detectives and criminal investigators	39,000	2.0%	13.4%
Police and sheriff's patrol officers	12,000	0.6%	3.9%
Building cleaning workers	12,000	0.6%	−3.4%

Note: Numbers reflect 2006 data; projections are for the period 2006–2016. Columns may not add to totals due to omission of occupations with small employment.

Source: Bureau of Labor Statistics, http://www.bls.gov

Installation, Maintenance, and Repair Occupations

Federally employed workers in installation, maintenance, and repair occupations include aircraft mechanics and service technicians who fix and maintain all types of aircraft, and electrical and electronic equipment mechanics, installers, and repairers who inspect, adjust, and repair electronic equipment such as industrial controls, transmitters, antennas, radar, radio, and navigation systems (see Table 1.6).

TABLE 1.6

Employment of Wage and Salary Workers in Federal Government Installation, Maintenance, and Repair Occupations and Projected Change

Occupation	Current Number of Workers	Percent of Total Federal Workforce	Projected Percent Change
All installation, maintenance, and repair occupations	93,000	4.7%	−6.1%
Electrical and electronic equipment mechanics, installers, and repairers	15,000	0.8%	−2.0%
Aircraft mechanics and service technicians	19,000	1.0%	−14.9%

Note: Numbers reflect 2006 data; projections are for the period 2006–2016. Columns may not add to totals due to omission of occupations with small employment.

Source: Bureau of Labor Statistics, http://www.bls.gov

Other Occupational Groups

The federal government employs a relatively small number of workers in transportation; production; construction; sales and related; and farming, fishing, and forestry occupations. However, the government employs almost all or a significant number of some occupations, such as air traffic controllers, agricultural inspectors, and bridge and lock tenders (see Table 1.7).

TABLE 1.7

Employment of Wage and Salary Workers in Federal Government Farming and Transportation Occupations and Projected Change

Occupation	Current Number of Workers	Percent of Total Federal Workforce	Projected Percent Change
All farming, fishing, and forestry occupations	9,000	0.4%	−11.5%
Agricultural inspectors	6,000	0.3%	−14.7%

 © JIST Works

Occupation	Current Number of Workers	Percent of Total Federal Workforce	Projected Percent Change
All transportation and material moving occupations	56,000	2.9%	−1.0%
Air traffic controllers	22,000	1.1%	9.1%

Note: Numbers reflect 2006 data; projections are for the period 2006–2016. Columns may not add to totals due to omission of occupations with small employment.

Source: Bureau of Labor Statistics, http://www.bls.gov

Opportunities for Older Workers

The Partnership for Public Service has identified the baby boomer population from the private sector as a good source of federal candidates. One of the initiatives it has designed to make the federal government a desirable employer for the 50+ population is the FedExperience Transitions to Government program. In this program, the Partnership works with private sector employers to recruit and assist older workers who want to make a contribution in a second career in government and not necessarily prepare for a traditional retirement. In the pilot program launched in fall 2008, the program has focused on matching the talents and interests of IBM retirees and employees nearing retirement with staffing needs at the Department of Treasury.

What Kind of Pay Does the Federal Government Offer?

Most federal civilian employees (71 percent as of September 2004) are paid under the GS. GS or *General Schedule* is the name for a pay scale utilized by the majority of white-collar personnel in the civil service of the federal government. The GS includes most professional, technical, administrative, and clerical positions in the federal civil service. The rest of federal civilian employees (29 percent) are paid under several different pay scales. The following sections describe the GS and the other major pay scales used for civilian employees in the federal government.

The General Schedule

The GS is separated into 15 grades (GS-1, GS-2, and so on up to GS-15). Within each grade, there are 10 steps. Entry-level positions are generally in the GS-1 through GS-7 range. Grades GS-8 through GS-12 indicate a mid-level position, and GS-13, GS-14, and GS-15 are reserved for top-level positions. A new GS employee is normally employed in the first step of their assigned GS grade. As an incoming federal employee, it is possible to negotiate the step, but not grade. Each step higher than the first one is usually earned after serving a given period of service (at one-, two-, or three-year intervals). However, an employee can move to a higher step in a shorter amount of time based on outstanding work performance, which is called a "quality step increase."

The federal government pays competitively, with adjustments for locality pay and annual cost of living increases. *Locality pay* is a percentage of the base salary and differs depending on where you work. There are 32 different locality pay areas, most of which are major cities and the areas surrounding them and one that encompasses the rest of the United States. The locality pay percentage can range from 14.23 percent for employees working in the Indianapolis area to 34.35 percent for those who work in the San Francisco area (according to 2009 data).

To give you a general idea of what you can expect to make as a federal employee, Table 1.8 lists the salary range of each GS grade, including the locality pay rate for the rest of the United States (which was 13.86 percent in 2009). When you look at this table, keep in mind that each grade has 10 steps. To find the most recent salary table by grade, log on to the Web site for the Compensation Administration for the Office of Personnel Management (OPM) at http://www.opm.gov/oca/ and click on Salaries and Wages.

TABLE 1.8

Salary Ranges by GS Grade

Grade	Salary Range
1	$19,971–$24,985
2	$22,454–$28,254
3	$24,499–$31,847
4	$27,504–$35,753
5	$30,772–$40,005
6	$34,300–$44,589
7	$38,117–$49,553
8	$42,214– $54,879
9	$46,625–$60,612
10	$51,345–$66,747
11	$56,411–$73,329
12	$67,613–$87,893
13	$80,402–$104,525
14	$95,010–$123,519
15	$111,760–$145,290

Source: U.S. Office of Personnel Management, www.opm.gov, 2009 data.

Other Pay Scales

Several other pay scales are used in the federal government:

★ At one time, the GS included three "supergrades": GS-16, GS-17, and GS-18. These grades were eliminated under the provisions of the Civil Service Reform Act of 1978 and replaced by the Senior Executive Service and the more recent Senior Level (nonsupervisory) pay scales.

★ High-ranking federal employees are paid according to the Executive Schedule.

★ The Federal Wage System for federal blue-collar civilian employees who are paid by the hour ensures that federal trade, craft, and laboring workers receive the same pay for doing the same work as other federal and private employees in their area. The Wage Grade (WG) schedule includes most federal blue-collar workers.

Some federal agencies (for example, the United States Securities and Exchange Commission, the Federal Reserve System, and the Federal Deposit Insurance Corporation) have their own pay schedules, as do the United States Postal Service and the Foreign Service.

Volunteering for the Government

Generally speaking, federal agencies are prohibited by law (section 1342 of title 31, United States Code) from accepting volunteer service. No person may provide unpaid service to the government or provide service with the understanding that he or she will waive pay. Exceptions to this prohibition are provided only for employment in emergencies involving the protection of life or property, employment of assistants to handicapped employees, employment of experts and consultants, or employment of students in order to further their educational goals (see Chapter 9 for more information about this kind of volunteer service).

In addition, some federal agencies, such as the National Park Service and the Forest Service, have specific authorities to accept unpaid services for specific jobs or functions. Individuals who are interested in volunteering their services to the federal government should contact the agency of most interest to inquire about specific opportunities or log on to http://www.usafreedomcorps.gov.

What Kind of Benefits Does the Federal Government Offer?

The federal government is known for offering good benefits to its employees. These include the following:

★ 401(k) program

★ Thrift savings program

★ Dental and vision insurance

★ Long-term disability

- ★ Work/life programs

- ★ Business travel insurance

- ★ Federal employees' health benefits program

- ★ Federal employees' group life insurance program

- ★ Domestic partner benefits

- ★ Ten paid federal holidays

- ★ Flexible work schedules

- ★ Generous vacation and sick leave (13 vacation and 13 sick days during the first year of employment and more days thereafter)

- ★ Subsidized mass transit commute

- ★ On-site child care centers

- ★ Retirement benefits

- ★ Student loan repayment (some agencies)

The federal government is also a big supporter of many different ways of working and a variety of work schedules. For example, OPM and the General Services Administration (GSA) work together to support *telework* (work arrangements that use telecommunications technology to provide flexibility in work locations, such as working from home) in federal agencies. The joint OPM/GSA Web site http://www.telework.gov provides information to agencies, managers, and employees about how to effectively implement telework programs and arrangements. OPM and GSA also work directly with telework coordinators in each agency to provide guidance and assistance.

In addition, alternative work schedules (AWS) are popular in the federal government. Employees use them in a variety of ways: from avoiding peak rush hour traffic, to being able to see children off to school, to having non-weekend time to accomplish errands and other personal business. Organizations benefit by having more dedicated employees who are able to maximize their productive time and minimize the effects of outside responsibilities. In some cases, alternative work schedules can enable an organization to better serve customers, who may be in other time zones or have nontraditional schedules themselves.

Throughout the working life of any employee, different stages bring different responsibilities and demands at and outside of work. The federal government understands these changing lifecycle needs and utilizes tools such as part-time work and job sharing to create career flexibility and a diverse workforce of good people. For employees who have child care and/or elder care responsibilities, as well as those interested in phased retirement, job sharing and other part-time arrangements can be very attractive alternatives. They enable employees to continue their engagement with work, contribute to the family income, and progress in their careers. The organization benefits by retaining the talents of experienced people and enhancing their loyalty, as well as by being more attractive to potential employees. The federal government has a long history of encouraging these employment tools for its workforce. For more information about benefits, go to http://www.usajobs.gov/ei61.asp.

How Can You Use USAJOBS to Explore Careers in the Federal Government?

No matter what you want to do, there is most likely a federal job that will satisfy your career need. With more than 15 cabinet departments plus independent agencies, government corporations, and the Executive Office of the President, there is an excellent possibility that there is a job for you in the federal government.

Assessing Yourself

Before you begin your federal job search, the first thing to consider is what it is you want to do. What are your career goals? What is the career you've dreamed of having your entire life? What skills do you have that qualify you for a job? Did you graduate from college? Do you have special expertise that sets you apart from other candidates? Do you speak a foreign language? What is it you want to do with your life? What kinds of goals and dreams have you harbored that can lead you to a career that is fulfilling and satisfying and takes care of you and your family?

Part of the career exploration process involves self-assessment, in which you consider your skills, talents, abilities, and personality. There are many books and online resources that can help you conduct this self-assessment. Sometimes it is helpful to consult with a career counselor. To find one in your area, check out the National Career Development Association at http://www.ncda.org. If you are still in college, you may have access to a career center. If you are a college graduate, you have access to career resource services through your alumni association.

The many federal departments and agencies have diverse missions and goals, thus the opportunities for employment and the types of jobs available are also diverse. In many ways, a career with the federal government can be as unique as you and your talents and interests are! Take the time to consider the individual skills and qualifications that make you unique and marketable. It is worth the investment in yourself to find the best fit or match in a federal job so that you can be the most satisfied with your career.

Exploring Careers with USAJOBS

To make federal employment more accessible and demystify the federal application process, the Office of Personnel Management (OPM) has created a Web site that provides virtual one-stop shopping for federal jobs. USAJOBS is the federal government's recruitment and application Web site, which boasts many features designed to make the federal application process easier.

This section walks you through using the Career Exploration features at USAJOBS. If you already know the types of jobs you may be interested in applying for, you may skip this section and go immediately to Chapter 2. That chapter focuses on how to use USAJOBS to search for jobs. Chapter 3 discusses how to write a competitive federal application by using the USAJOBS site.

To explore careers with the USAJOBS site, follow these steps:

1. Go to http://www.usajobs.gov. Note the five tabbed sections at the top of the page.

2. Click on the Info Center tab of USAJOBS to bring up a screen with a great deal of information (see Figure 1.1). Note the section of this screen called Career Exploration.

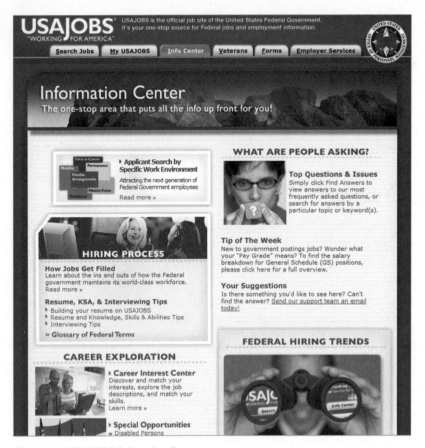

Figure 1.1. USAJOBS Information Center.

3. Click the Learn More link under the Career Interest Center heading to display the screen shown in Figure 1.2. Note that the Career Exploration screen offers four different ways to help you explore the different job opportunities in the federal government.

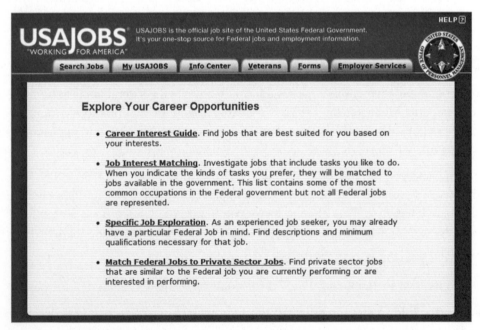

Figure 1.2. The Career Exploration screen.

To find federal jobs that correspond with your interests, click on the Career Interest Guide link to open a new window (see Figure 1.3). You have a choice of two ways to use this tool.

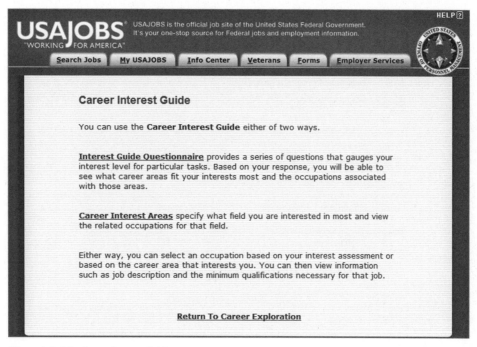

Figure 1.3. The Career Interest Guide.

If you click the Interest Guide Questionnaire link, a list of duties is displayed (see Figure 1.4). Choose your level of interest for each of the duties and click the Submit Questionnaire button. You will then see a results screen that shows you which interest area best suits you. Click on an interest area to see related occupations.

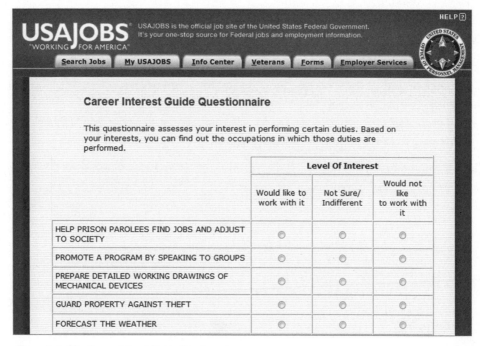

Figure 1.4. The Career Interest Guide Questionnaire.

If you click the Career Interest Areas link, a list of career areas is displayed (see Figure 1.5). Click on the interest area you want to explore to view a list of related occupations in that area.

Figure 1.5. Career Interest Areas.

Regardless of whether you choose the questionnaire or the list of interest areas, you will be presented with a list of occupations that are related to the interest area you selected. When you select a job title and click on the Find Occupation button, you can view information such as a job description and the minimum qualifications necessary for that job.

Another career exploration tool is the Job Interest Match. To access this tool, click the Job Interest Matching link on the Career Exploration screen (see Figure 1.2). The Job Interest Match screen presents three occupational groups (see Figure 1.6): clerical and technical; professional and administrative; and supervisory, managerial, and executive.

When you click on one of these occupational group links, you will see a long list of tasks that is broken down into several categories. Select the tasks that interest you and the Match button at the end of the list. The results screen presents a list of jobs that include the tasks you select. Click on the job title that interests you to find out more about that job.

Specific Job Exploration is another tool offered on the Career Exploration screen (see Figure 1.2). Just click the Specific Job Exploration link to view a list of federal job titles (see Figure 1.7).

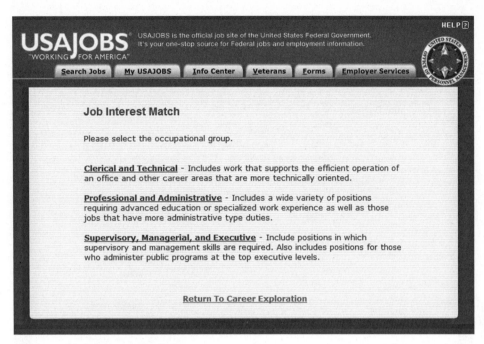

Figure 1.6. The Job Interest Match tool.

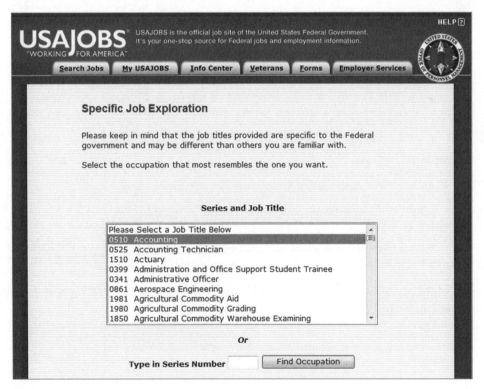

Figure 1.7. The Specific Job Exploration tool.

Find the title you are interested in and select it, keeping in mind that federal job titles may be different than others you are familiar with. Then click the Find Occupation button to access information such as a job description, minimum qualifications, and career progression for that job (see Figure 1.8). (You also may have to select a performance level for the job you choose.)

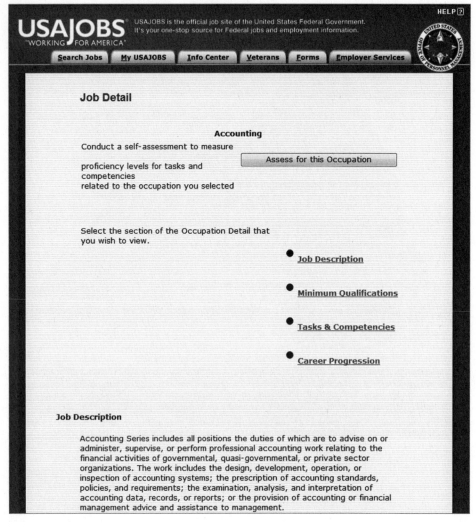

Figure 1.8. Job Detail screen.

If you are a current federal employee, there is a career exploration tool just for you. By clicking the Match Federal Jobs to Private Sector Jobs link on the Career Exploration screen (see Figure 1.2), you can access the Public/Private Sector Crosswalk (see Figure 1.9). Select a job from the list and click the Submit button to see a list of matching private sector job titles.

Now that you have assessed your interests, skills, and possible occupational path in the federal government, the next step is to start the job search process.

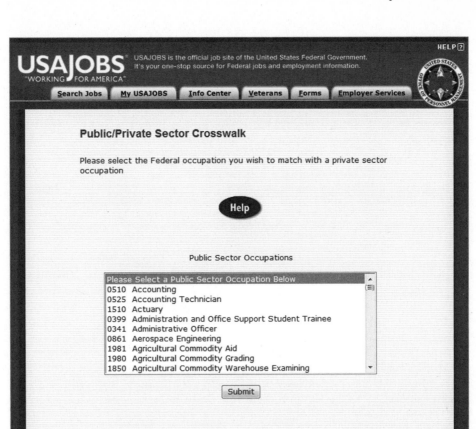

Figure 1.9. The Public/Private Sector Crosswalk.

CHAPTER 2

How to Find a Federal Job

Finding a federal job is very different from finding a job in the private sector. You've undoubtedly heard that the process can often be time-consuming and burdensome. However, not only has the USAJOBS Web site greatly simplified the federal job search, but you also have the advantage of being armed with the resources and the tools described in this book! By the end of this chapter, you will be ready and able to tackle the process of finding a federal job.

How to Search for a Federal Job on USAJOBS

USAJOBS, the federal government's employment information system, provides worldwide job vacancy information, employment information fact sheets, job applications, and forms in a variety of formats to ensure access for job seekers with differing physical and technological capabilities. Operated by OPM, the USAJOBS Web site at http://www.usajobs.gov is considered the one-stop source for federal jobs and employment information and is updated every business day. On any given day, about 49,000 federal jobs are posted on USAJOBS. Although not all federal government jobs are posted on USAJOBS, most are. Therefore, we will focus primarily on the USAJOBS site as the source of finding federal jobs.

USAJOBS by Phone

USAJOBS by Phone is an interactive voice response telephone system that job seekers can access by calling 1-703-724-1850 or TDD 1-978-461-8404. Like the USAJOBS Web site, USAJOBS by Phone is available 24 hours a day, 7 days a week. Through this service, job seekers can access current job vacancies, employment information fact sheets, applications, and forms and apply for some jobs.

The heart of USAJOBS is its database of federal job openings. That database provides powerful tools to narrow your search, yet it is quite user-friendly. USAJOBS gives you five different methods for searching the database:

★ Basic Search

★ Agency Search

★ Series Search

★ Advanced Search

★ Senior Executive Search

Using Basic Search

Because the Basic Search fits the needs of most users, we will start with it:

1. Go to http://www.usajobs.gov. Note the tabbed sections at the top of the page.

2. Click on the Search Jobs tab to display the Basic Search screen (see Figure 2.1).

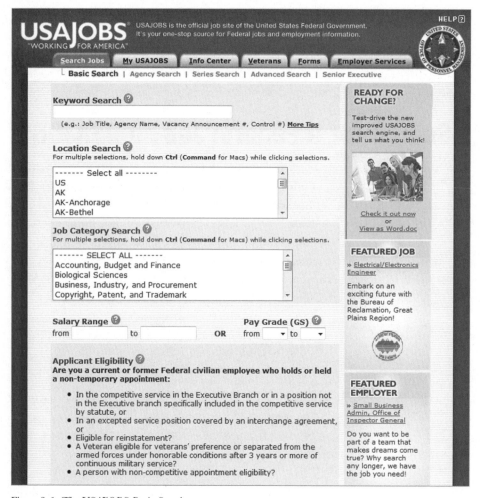

Figure 2.1. The USAJOBS Basic Search screen.

Like the other search methods, Basic Search provides multiple fields where you can type in information or select items from drop-down menus. And like the other search methods, you can use any or all of the fields to narrow your search. You're only required to complete one field of your choice. In Basic Search, you can search by keyword, location, job category, and salary range or pay grade.

In the Keyword box, you can type any words that you think might appear in a relevant vacancy announcement, such as the following:

★ A job title (such as archeologist)

★ Words that may appear in a job description (such as investigate)

★ The name of the agency where you'd like to work (such as Department of Education)

★ The job location (such as Omaha)

★ The number for a particular vacancy (if you know it)

Don't enter a lot of keywords. The more you use, the narrower your search will be because USAJOBS will look for vacancy announcements that contain all of the words you enter. You want to narrow your search, but you don't want to narrow it so far that you eliminate jobs that might be of interest to you. However, if you want to focus your search more precisely, Table 2.1 lists certain words or characters that you can use.

TABLE 2.1
Keyword Operators

Operator	Purpose	Example
OR	Broaden a search by including multiple keywords.	environment OR ecology
AND NOT	Narrow a search by eliminating certain common results.	clerk AND NOT mailroom
" "	Narrow a search to include only results containing a certain phrase.	"social work"
( )	Narrow a search by grouping keywords in order to specify multiple conditions that must be met.	(writer OR editor) AND NOT technical
*	Broaden a search to find results that contain variations on the root word you enter.	investigat*

The Location field lets you select a city, region, state, or foreign country where you would like to work. It offers a drop-down list that you scroll through. The location field is especially helpful if you don't intend to move from the city you currently live in or you're planning to move to a specific city. In either case, you can obtain announcements for all federal job openings in the area by clicking on the appropriate city or region. If you would like to work in a foreign country, the list includes many countries and areas of the world where the federal government has employees.

The Job Category field provides a drop-down list you can scroll through to select a particular occupational area or areas. The available choices are listed in Table 2.2.

TABLE 2.2

Job Categories at USAJOBS

Accounting, Budget, and Finance

Biological Sciences

Business, Industry, and Procurement

Copyright, Patent, and Trademark

Education

Engineering and Architecture

Equipment, Facilities, and Services

Human Resources

Information, Arts, and Public Affairs

Information Technology

Investigation and Inspection

Legal and Claims Inspecting

Library and Archives

Management, Administration, Clerical, and Office Services

Mathematics and Statistics

Medical, Dental, and Public Health

Physical Sciences

Postal Service

Quality Assurance and Grading

Safety, Health, Physical and Resource Protection

Social Science, Psychology, and Welfare

Supply

Trades and Labor

Transportation

Veterinary Medical Science

By typing in your desired salary in the Salary Range field, you can search for job announcements based on compensation. We recommend that you ignore the Salary Range field for the time being because it can limit your search. If you type in a salary range, you may miss out on good jobs that pay either more or less than you've listed. For a broader salary search, you can select numbers from the Pay Grade drop-down lists. Refer to Table 1.8 in Chapter 1 for an idea of what the salary range is for each grade.

You next have to answer one question and make two easy selections before you can search the jobs database. The Applicant Eligibility field asks whether you're one of the following:

★ A current or former federal civilian employee who holds or held a nontemporary appointment

★ A current permanent federal employee in the competitive service in the executive branch or in a position not in the executive branch but specifically included in the competitive service by statute

★ A current federal employee in an excepted service position covered by an interchange agreement

★ A person eligible for veterans' preference or a person separated from the armed forces under honorable conditions after three years or more of continuous military service

★ A person with noncompetitive appointment eligibility

If none of this terminology is familiar to you, you most likely do not qualify for any of the categories, and you should probably leave the No button selected (that's the default option). But if you fit one of the categories listed, be sure to click the Yes button. Your choice helps USAJOBS show you relevant job openings.

Next, you must decide whether to sort the job openings you'll receive by date or keyword relevance. If you expect to search the site frequently, you'll probably want to sort by date so you always see the newest jobs first. You want to make sure that you have ample time to apply for the job before the close date.

Next, you must choose whether to have the job openings listed in brief view or detailed view. The brief view is really brief: It just lists the date, job title, agency, and location for each job. The detailed view (which is the default choice) includes all of that information and the first couple lines of the job description, the job type, the job status (full-time, part-time, and so on), and the salary. Because the detailed view provides more information, it makes deciding whether to read the full vacancy announcement much easier.

Finally, click the Search for Jobs button to run your search. Your search will result in a list of jobs. When you find a job in your search results that looks good, click on the job title to get the full vacancy announcement. A *vacancy announcement* is the federal government's term for a document that describes a job opening. It lists the job title, the location, the salary, the duties, the required qualifications, application instructions, and the date by which you must submit your application materials.

Because vacancy announcements contain all of the information an applicant needs in order to prepare a competitive application, they are quite extensive and detailed and long. The shortest are usually 5 or 6 pages, but it's not uncommon for them to run 15 to 24 pages. Because of this length, it's best to first scan the announcement for highlights. Then if the job still looks good, you can go back and read the announcement more carefully. In the next chapter, we provide you with step-by-step instructions on how to use what you read in a vacancy announcement to help you write a winning federal resume.

Using Other USAJOBS Search Methods

In addition to Basic Search, four other search methods are available at USAJOBS. To use them, click the appropriate tab at the top of the search page (see Figure 2.1).

The Agency Search lets you search for jobs within a selected federal agency. You can type the agency or department's name in the appropriate field or select the name from a drop-down list. For many large departments, the list also includes individual components. For example, you can select the entire Department of the Interior or its individual components, such as the Bureau of Indian Affairs, the Bureau of Land Management, the National Park Service, the U.S. Fish and Wildlife Service, or the U.S. Geological Survey, among others. The Agency Search page also has fields for location, series number, occupational series, and salary or pay grade range.

The Series Search lets you look for jobs by occupational series number or name. You can type the series number in the appropriate field or select the series from a drop-down list. The Series Search page also has fields for location and salary or pay grade range. Brief descriptions of the occupations included in each series are available at http://www.opm.gov/fedclass/text/HdBkToC.htm in the *Handbook of Occupational Groups and Families.*

The Advanced Search lets you search for jobs by combining some or all of the fields available at USAJOBS, many of which offer drop-down lists. The fields include keyword, title, occupational series number, occupational series, location, agency, and salary or pay grade range.

The Senior Executive Search lets you search for high-level executive jobs. The Senior Executive Search page has fields for keywords and location.

How to Create USAJOBS Job Search Agents

A job hunt, whether in the federal government or the private sector, can take a while. Visiting USAJOBS every day to search for new job openings may become a chore. And who can remember which combination of keywords and search fields produced great results the other day? Wouldn't it be great if someone could search USAJOBS for you and send you e-mail alerts when new jobs were posted that met your precise criteria? You probably could hire someone to perform this task for you, but the job agents at USAJOBS will do it for free. You can create up to 10 agents to find jobs that perfectly match your selected criteria. Note that in order to set up a job search agent, you first must start an account with USAJOBS.

Starting a USAJOBS Account

To use the job search agents, you must have an account with USAJOBS. It doesn't cost anything to set up an account, just follow these steps:

1. Go to http://www.usajobs.gov and click on the My USAJOBS tab at the top of the page (see Figure 2.2).

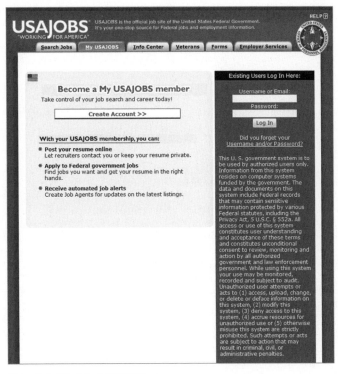

Figure 2.2. The My USAJOBS tab.

2. Click the Create Account button.

3. In the secure form, fill in your name, address, e-mail address, user name, and password. Also, select a password question and enter an answer (see Figure 2.3).

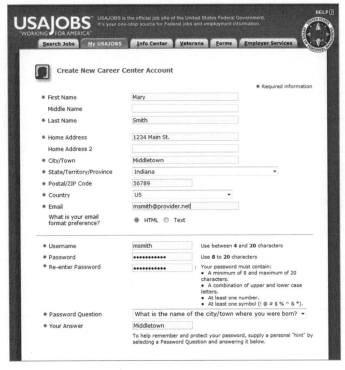

Figure 2.3. Creating a profile on USAJOBS.

4. Answer the questions about U.S. citizenship and veterans' preference by clicking the appropriate buttons.

5. Click the Submit button to set up your USAJOBS account. A welcome message is displayed to confirm that your account has been established.

You can now log in to your account from the My USAJOBS tab by entering the user name and password that you established and clicking the Log In button.

Creating a Job Search Agent

To create a job search agent, start by following these steps:

1. From the MY USAJOBS tab, log in to your USAJOBS account to go to your personal page.

2. Click the MY Job Search Agents link (see Figure 2.4).

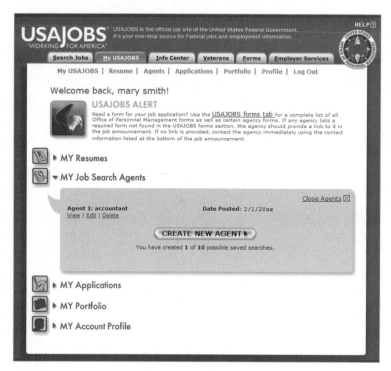

Figure 2.4. Using a USAJOBS account to create a job search agent.

3. Click the Create New Agent button in the box that appears to go to the page where you actually create agents.

This page will look familiar if you've previously searched the jobs database. Once again, you choose search criteria from fields. The first four fields—job locations, job categories, occupational series, and agencies—provide drop-down menus. To make multiple selections from a menu, hold down the Control key on a PC or the Command key on a Mac while clicking on your choices. For the remaining seven fields, you must click on a selection or type in information:

★ **Salary Range or Pay Grade Range.** If you wish, you can type numbers into this field or select pay grade numbers from the drop-down lists. However, as before, we recommend that you leave these blank to avoid missing out on great opportunities that may pay more or less than you expect.

★ **Senior Executive.** If you click this field's button, your agent will search only for jobs in the Senior Executive Service. These jobs are high-level executive positions, but there are only about 6,000 of them in the federal government.

★ **Applicant Eligibility.** This is the same field we discussed in the Basic Search section earlier in this chapter. Click the Yes button if you meet the listed eligibility criteria or the No button if you don't.

★ **How Often Do You Want to Receive Email Notification?** Five choices are available in this field: daily, weekly, biweekly, monthly, or none. We recommend choosing daily or weekly because some jobs would already be closed by the time you'd receive bi-weekly or monthly alerts. If you choose none, the agent will store searches in your personal account but not send you e-mail alerts when it finds new jobs.

★ **Position Type.** You can select part-time, full-time, or both.

★ **Title Search.** Enter keywords from job titles that interest you in this field.

★ **Search Keywords.** You can type words or phrases into this field that you think are likely to appear in relevant vacancy announcements. For example, you might use words that describe your educational and professional experiences and skills.

★ **Agent Title.** Type a name for your agent in this field. You must enter something in this field because it is a required field. Enter something distinctive so that you can easily keep track of multiple agents.

Finally, click the Save Agent button at the bottom of the page. You will be taken back to your personal account page. If you want to try out the job search agent, click on View to have the agent search for jobs based on the criteria you chose. If you want to change the agent, click on Edit. Clicking on Delete will remove the job search agent.

Once you find a vacancy announcement that looks promising, the next step is to apply for the job. In Chapter 3, you will learn exactly what you must do in order to present yourself and your qualifications in a manner that gets you the job.

Writing a Competitive Federal Application

Many years ago, federal job applicants had to pass a civil service test in order to be placed on registers of eligible applicants (called simply *eligibles*) maintained by the Office of Personnel Management (OPM). All applicants also had to complete a standard federal employment application form, the SF-171. The federal job application process has changed significantly in recent years. The SF-171 is now obsolete, and only a few positions require a written test. Instead, a federal job application consists of a resume, personal essays, and supplemental information. This chapter takes you through the whole federal job application process, from hiring procedures and vacancy announcements through federal resumes and KSAs and finally to job interviews and salary negotiations.

Understanding Federal Hiring Procedures

Because of the many laws, executive orders, and regulations that govern federal employment, the federal hiring process is more complicated than the hiring process in private industry. Most federal jobs are *competitive service* jobs, which means that the jobs are under OPM's jurisdiction and are subject to the civil service laws passed by Congress. Some agencies are allowed to bypass standard federal hiring procedures in order to fill certain jobs. These jobs are known as *excepted service* jobs. The following sections detail the differences between these two classes of federal jobs.

Competitive Service

Most federal government civilian positions are part of the competitive civil service. That means that applicants for these jobs must compete with other applicants in open competition. Also, competitive service jobs must be advertised. Agencies in the competitive service are required by law and OPM regulation to post jobs with OPM whenever they are seeking candidates from outside their own workforce for positions lasting more than 120 days. These jobs are posted on OPM's USAJOBS site. A job posting (that is, a *vacancy announcement*) is an agency's decision to seek qualified candidates for a particular position. The agency is under no obligation to make a selection. In some instances, an agency may cancel the posting and choose to reannounce the position later.

The general process for filling a competitive service job is as follows:

1. After the closing date on the vacancy announcement, all of the received applications are rated on the extent and quality of experience, education, and training relevant to the duties of the position.

2. Applicants are assigned a score and ranked on a list from best qualified to least qualified. Depending on the job and how the information was submitted, the score may be generated by

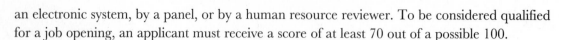

an electronic system, by a panel, or by a human resource reviewer. To be considered qualified for a job opening, an applicant must receive a score of at least 70 out of a possible 100.

3. Applicants who best meet the job qualifications are put on a list called the *certificate of eligibles* (also known as a *cert*). These are the applicants who are eligible to be interviewed for the position. Typically, this list is limited to the top three applicants.

4. A human resource specialist then conducts a review of the application package for all applicants who make the cert and, if necessary, may request additional information from the applicants to verify information.

5. Interviews are conducted if necessary, and a hiring decision is made. The whole hiring process, from receiving and application to hiring someone, can take as long as six months.

The civil service laws that govern competitive service jobs ensure that applicants and employees receive fair and equal treatment in the hiring process. They give hiring officials broad authority to review more than one applicant source before determining the best-qualified candidate based on job-related criteria.

U.S. Merit Systems Protection Board

The U.S. Merit Systems Protection Board (MSPB) serves as an independent guardian of the merit systems under which federal employees work. Merit-based civil service rules ensure that federal employees are well-qualified to perform their jobs and are able to serve the public free from management abuse and partisan political pressure. See http://www.mspb. gov for more information about this organization.

In filling competitive service jobs, agencies can generally choose from among three groups of candidates:

★ Applicants with no prior civil service who meet the qualification requirements for a specific vacancy announcement.

★ Applicants who are eligible for noncompetitive movement within the competitive service. These individuals presently or previously served under career-type appointments in the competitive service. They are selected under agency merit promotion procedures and can receive an appointment by promotion, reassignment, transfer, or reinstatement. These current or previous federal employees are called *status applicants*. Status applicants can be hired without having to compete with members of the general public.

★ Applicants who qualify for a special noncompetitive appointing authority established by law or executive order. Examples of special noncompetitive appointing authorities include the Peace Corps and the Veterans Recruitment Appointment (VRA). (See Chapter 7 for more information on hiring programs for veterans.)

Excepted Service

Sometimes federal jobs are available under special circumstances. These excepted service jobs consist of all positions in the executive branch that federal law, the president, or the OPM has designated as excepted from the competitive service or the senior executive service. For example, presidential exceptions include jobs overseas held by foreign nationals. Unlike competitive service jobs, excepted service jobs are not subject to the appointment, pay, and classification rules in Title 5, United States Code. Excepted service jobs do not have to be advertised, although some are posted on USAJOBS.

Agencies that offer excepted service jobs can set their own qualification requirements. Instead of using competitive civil service procedures, these agencies have their own hiring system that establishes the evaluation criteria they use in filling their internal vacancies. However, they are subject to veterans' preference. (For more information on veteran's preference, see Chapter 7.)

Some agencies may have specific jobs or even entire divisions that are classified as excepted service. For example, certain employees of the Veterans Health Administration in the Department of Veterans Affairs work in excepted service positions. Legal statute also has excepted entire agencies from civil service hiring procedures. These agencies include the following:

★ Foreign Service

★ Federal Bureau of Investigation (FBI)

★ Central Intelligence Agency (CIA)

★ Tennessee Valley Authority

★ General Accounting Office

★ Postal Service

Excepted agencies such as these are not required to post their job announcements in USAJOBS. To learn about their job opportunities, you must go to their Web sites. (Chapter 6 provides contact information for all the agencies in the executive branch of the government.) Also, most of these positions are protected under separate merit systems and are not subject to change during transitions (such as the election of a new president). The following sections provide details about excepted service appointments listed under OPM Schedules A, B, and C.

Schedule A Appointing Authorities

The federal government typically has a difficult time filling positions that require highly technical or specialized skills because individuals with these skills can earn much more in the private sector than they can under the general service pay schedules. One way the federal government attracts and retains people with highly developed skills is to pay competitive salaries under OPM's Schedule A hiring authorities. These authorities describe special jobs and situations for which it is impractical to use standard qualification requirements and to rate applicants using traditional competitive procedures.

Schedule A exceptions are also used to hire attorneys because, by law, OPM cannot develop qualification standards or examinations for attorney jobs. Other special jobs that are excepted include chaplain, law clerk trainee, medical doctor, dentist, certain interpreters, experts for consultation purposes, teachers in military dependent schools overseas, and faculty positions of service academies.

Additional Schedule A exceptions allow for the filling of any job under special or unique circumstances, such as the following:

★ Filling a critical short-term job or continuing job pending completion of examinations, clearances, or other procedures

★ Filling a temporary or part-time job in a remote or isolated location

★ Hiring a noncitizen because no qualified citizen is available

★ Quickly staffing a temporary federal board or commission

★ Hiring applicants with mental retardation or a severe physical or psychiatric disability to fill any job in which the person is able to perform with or without reasonable accommodation (for more information on this exception, refer to Chapter 8)

Schedule B Appointing Authorities

Schedule B authorities apply to jobs and situations for which it is impractical to rate applicants using competitive procedures. However, under Schedule B authorities, applicants must meet specific qualification criteria for the job. Schedule B includes hiring authorities for the Student Temporary Employment Program, the Student Career Experience Program, and the Federal Career Intern Program. Students are the only ones who qualify for these programs, so it is not practical to use competitive procedures to hire them. (For more information on these and other federal programs for students, refer to Chapter 9.)

Schedule C Appointing Authorities

Employees in the excepted service who are subject to change at the discretion of a new administration are commonly referred to as Schedule C employees. Schedule C employees are excepted from the competitive service because they have a confidential or policy-determining relationship with their supervisor and agency head. Most Schedule C positions are at the GS-15 level and below. Appointments to Schedule C positions require advance approval from the White House Office of Presidential Personnel and OPM, but appointments may be made without competition. The president can also authorize individual exemptions under Schedule C. Interestingly, OPM does not review the qualifications of a Schedule C appointee; final authority on this matter rests solely with the appointing official.

Generally, the authority to fill a Schedule C position is revoked by OPM when the person who was appointed leaves or the confidential or policy-determining relationship between the person appointed and his/her superior ends. Agencies then need specific approval from OPM to establish or reestablish the position. Schedule C appointees are not covered by federal employment rules and regulations for removal procedures and generally have no rights to appeal these actions to the Merit Systems Protection Board, which monitors such activities. This is true, regardless of veteran's preference or length of service in the position.

To help with transitions, OPM has delegated authority to agencies to establish a limited number of temporary transitional Schedule C positions. Agencies can use this delegated authority during the first year of a new presidential administration and during a one-year period immediately following the appointment of a new head of an agency or the designation of an "acting" one. A list of Schedule C positions is published annually in the Federal Register, for transparency purposes.

Expert and Consultant Appointments

Schedule C enables agencies to appoint experts and consultants without regard to competitive civil service requirements to positions that primarily require performance of advisory services, rather than performance of operating functions. If the individual meets the definitions of expert or consultant under federal regulations, and if the work assigned requires expert or consultant services, agencies may use expert and consultant appointments for individuals who have been nominated by the president, but not yet confirmed, or for individuals whose permanent excepted appointments are pending approval from OPM.

Agencies may not use expert and consultant appointments to avoid following employment procedures or solely in anticipation of a competitive career-conditional appointment. An expert and consultant appointment authority may not be used to fill positions in the senior executive service. However, if a position meets the criteria for placement in the senior executive service, OPM may authorize limited authority to appoint an individual during the transition period.

Analyzing a Vacancy Announcement

A vacancy announcement is the equivalent of a job posting. You can find vacancy announcements primarily on federal agency Web sites and on USAJOBS. (Appendix B shows a sample vacancy announcement that may be helpful to refer to as you are reading this section.) The vacancy announcement is your guide to creating and submitting a high quality application. Everything you need to know regarding the content of your materials as well as what materials to provide are spelled out in detail.

In this section, you will learn how to analyze a vacancy announcement, which is your key to writing a competitive federal application. The first step is to read through the entire announcement, making note of relevant information that will help you prepare a competitive application.

At the beginning of a vacancy announcement (and the top of each tabbed section) is some important information:

★ **Department:** A federal department is headed by a cabinet-level position and includes the following 15 executive departments: Agriculture, Commerce, Defense, Education, Energy, Health and Human Services, Homeland Security, Housing and Urban Development, Interior, Labor, State, Transportation, Treasury, Veterans' Affairs, and Attorney General.

★ **Agency:** This can be any department or independent establishment of the federal government, including a government-owned or controlled corporation, that has the authority to hire employees in the competitive, excepted, and senior executive service.

★ **Job Announcement Number:** Each job opening has a unique announcement number. You should always include the announcement number on your resume and any other materials you submit.

★ **Position Title:** The position title is listed in bold letters at the top of each section of the vacancy announcement. The federal government uses a standardized list of job titles. This is helpful because when you find a job you like, you can go back to the search screen and plug the title into the keywords field to find similar positions.

Vacancy announcements are organized into five sections that you can access by clicking on the appropriate tab:

★ Overview

★ Duties

★ Qualifications and evaluations

★ Benefits and other info

★ How to apply

We will study each section individually.

Overview

The Overview section provides a summary of the job so that you can determine whether you are eligible to apply for the job (see Figure 3.1). To determine whether you are qualified for the job, you will need to analyze the information in the Qualifications and Evaluations section of the vacancy announcement.

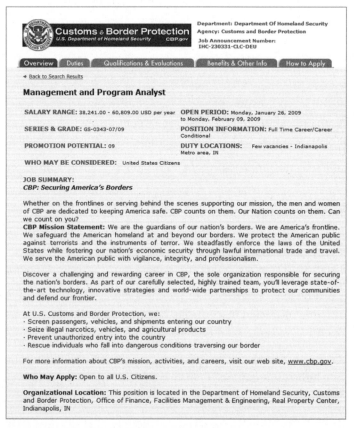

Figure 3.1. The Overview section of a vacancy announcement.

The Overview section includes the following information:

★ **Salary Range:** This line provides the salary, in dollars, which includes locality pay. If the vacancy announcement lists just one grade for the job, your education and experience will determine where you fall in the range. Many jobs are listed at multiple grades. In these cases, the salary range runs from the lowest grade to the highest (including steps and locality pay). Your education and experience will determine the grade for which you qualify.

★ **Series and Grade:** Most announcements start this line with a GS, which indicates that the job is part of the General Schedule pay system. Next is the four-digit series number that identifies the federal occupational series assigned to this job. The government groups similar jobs together in an occupational series. For example, all secretarial jobs are in the 0318 occupational series. The series number is most helpful if you want to run another search at USAJOBS to find similar jobs. (Descriptions of the occupations included in each series are available in the *Handbook of Occupational Groups and Families* at http://www.opm.gov/fedclass/text/HdBkToC.htm.) The last set of numbers indicates where the job falls among the 15 grades in the General Schedule pay system, which we discussed in Chapter 1.

★ **Promotion Potential:** This number indicates the top grade level you can achieve in the job with promotions.

★ **Who May Be Considered:** This description specifies what constitutes the pool of applicants. Some common terms that may be listed here are as follows:

  • *All U.S. Citizens:* Anyone who is a U.S. citizen can apply. The announcement might instead list "non-status candidates," which is another term for all U.S. citizens.

  • *All U.S. Citizens in the Local Commuting Area:* Only U.S. citizens who live within a reasonable driving distance of the job are eligible.

  • *Status Applicants Only:* Only current federal employees may apply.

  • *[Agency] Employees Only:* Only current employees of the named agency may apply.

★ **Open Period:** This timeframe starts when the job is announced and lasts through the closing date, which is the final date that applications will be accepted. It's usually a period of two to four weeks. Pay special attention to the closing date because you won't be considered for the job if your application is late. If you apply electronically, all application materials must be submitted by 11:59 p.m. (EST) of the closing date. If you're mailing your application materials, check to see whether your application must arrive at the agency by the closing date or be postmarked by the closing date. In this situation, the closing date is 5:00 p.m. EST. Vacancy announcements are usually removed from USAJOBS on the closing date.

★ **Position Information:** This item may indicate whether the job is full-time or part-time or whether it's permanent or temporary. Permanent employees are generally hired into the federal government under a career-conditional appointment. A career-conditional employee must complete three years of substantially continuous service (that is, must not include any break in service of more than 30 calendar days) before becoming a full career employee. The first year of service of an employee who is given a career-conditional appointment is considered a probationary period.

★ **Duty Location:** This item states where the job is located. The place could be a city and state or even a foreign country.

★ **Job Summary:** The posting agency typically uses this spot to sell itself to applicants. You also may find an overview of the requirements of the position here.

★ **Key Requirements:** Highlights important information to consider when preparing and submitting an application. This information is also often provided in the Benefits and Other Information section of the announcement.

Duties

The Duties section describes in detail what work the successful applicant will perform in the position (see Figure 3.2). You should review this section very carefully to determine whether you are able to perform the duties. You may want to print out this section and read it again with a pen or highlighter, marking the important job-related terminology or expertise that you need to include in your application materials.

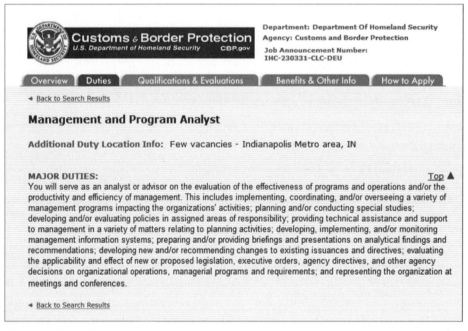

Figure 3.2. The Duties section of a vacancy announcement.

Qualifications and Evaluations

After reading the Overview section of a vacancy announcement, you may conclude that you are eligible to apply for the job. However, you must also be *qualified* to apply for the job in order to receive enough points to make the *cert* (certificate of eligibles). A basic principle of federal employment is that all candidates must meet the qualification requirements for the position for which they receive an appointment. To determine whether you are qualified for a certain job, you must read the Qualifications and Evaluations section carefully.

The Qualifications and Evaluations section gives detailed information about the qualifications that the successful candidate must possess in order to be considered qualified for the position (see Figure 3.3). Education requirements as well as specific work experience, certifications, and licensure are included in this section. This section also is the part of the announcement where you would typically find the KSAs (knowledge, skill, and ability statements) that you need to write responses to as part of your application.

In addition, this section provides guidelines for how an application will be evaluated. Review this section very carefully to determine whether you are qualified for the position and whether you will be able to substantiate your qualifications. If you are not qualified for the job, it is in your best interest not to apply. As with the Duties section, you may want to print out the Qualifications and Evaluations section and highlight the information you need to use in preparing your application materials.

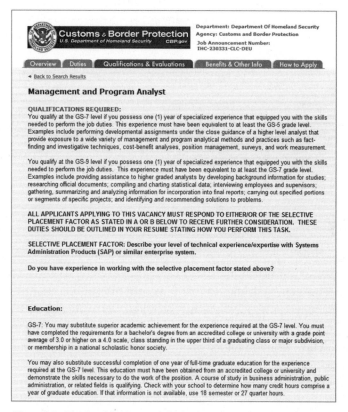

Figure 3.3. The Qualifications and Evaluations section of a vacancy announcement.

Benefits and Other Info

The Benefits and Other Info section lists the many benefits that a federal position offers, as well as other information that is important to the position. Figure 3.4 shows an example of this section of a vacancy announcement.

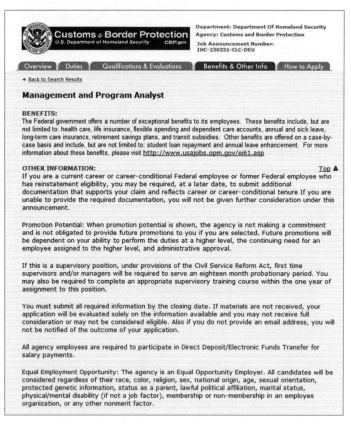

Figure 3.4. The Benefits and Other Info tab of a vacancy announcement.

How to Apply

Do not overlook the How to Apply section! In the federal government, your application materials must adhere to very strict standards in order to get you to the interview stage. The How to Apply section provides step-by-step guidelines to follow in order to submit your application (see Figure 3.5). This section will state whether applications are accepted electronically and/or by hard copy, how and whether to submit application essays, and so on. You must follow the instructions exactly indicated in this section. How well you follow these instructions will determine whether your application lands you on the certificate of eligibles.

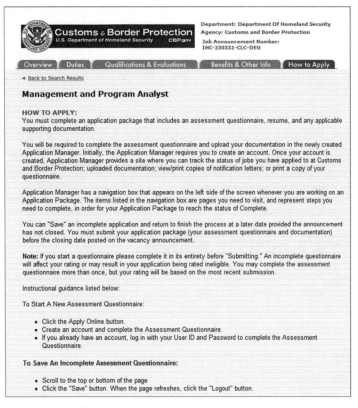

Figure 3.5. The How to Apply section of a vacancy announcement.

Make sure that you note any required supplemental information listed in this section. This information could include your transcripts (if you are a recent college graduate), DD-214 (separation papers from the military), or a performance appraisal. The human resource specialist who is reviewing your material will not remind you to send supplemental information if you happen to omit it from your application materials.

Following instructions, as indicated by the requirements of the vacancy announcement, is as important to demonstrating your value as a candidate as the content of the materials that you submit. Some vacancy announcements require that you submit the materials by fax; for others you may upload the documents that you have scanned into your computer. You must read the instructions in the How to Apply section to determine what you should send and how you should send it!

Creating a Winning Federal Resume

When you apply for a federal job, you must submit a federal-style resume. Private sector resumes do not contain all of the information that the federal application process requires. For this reason, the average federal resume is three to five pages long. This section provides information on creating federal-style resumes. (Refer to Appendix C for samples of federal-style resumes.)

An Optional Application for Federal Employment

The OF-612 is a job application form that appeared between the demise of the SF-171 application form and the inception of the federal resume. The OF-612 is not obsolete, and some agencies permit its use. However, read the How to Apply tab on the vacancy announcement to determine whether the OF-612 is allowable for the job for which you are applying. (You can find the OF-612 online on the Forms tab of the USAJOBS site at http://www.usajobs.gov.) If you have a choice between the OF-612 and the federal resume, the resume is the better choice. It is more flexible and allows you ample opportunity to better showcase and highlight your qualifications.

Using USAJOBS's Resume Builder

An easy way to write a federal resume is to use the USAJOBS Resume Builder feature, which permits you to create a resume, field by field, in the proper federal resume format. In order for you to use this feature, you first need to create an account on USAJOBS. (Chapter 2 explains how to do this.)

To access the USAJOBS Resume Builder, follow these steps:

1. From the USAJOBS Web site (http://www.usajobs.gov), click on the My USAJOBS tab.

2. Enter your user name and password to log in to your account and go to your personal page.

3. Click the MY Resumes link.

4. Click the Create New Resume button to open the Resume Builder form. Note that you must complete all fields that are marked with a red asterisk. All other information requested is optional.

5. To create content for your federal resume targeted to a specific job vacancy announcement, refer to the information you gathered while analyzing the vacancy announcement. If you have ever performed similar work, be sure to include the terminology (keywords) used in the Duties and Qualifications and Evaluations sections of the vacancy announcement in your resume.

Many of the hiring agencies will accept electronic submissions of resumes created through USAJOBS for vacancies listed on the Web site. You can also mail or fax the resume you create in USAJOBS. Make sure that you follow the instructions in the How to Apply section of the vacancy announcement *exactly*.

Including the Necessary Information

Whether you use the USAJOBS Resume Builder feature, add to an existing resume in a word processing program, or use an agency's application program, you must include certain information.

First, your federal resume must include information on the job for which you are applying. You can find this information on the vacancy announcement:

- ★ The announcement number.

- ★ The position title.

- ★ The job's grade (GS-5, GS-7, and so on). If the announcement lists more than one grade, list the lowest grade you would accept. For example, if the announcement describes the job as GS-5/7, decide whether you would take the GS-5 or if you would only accept a GS-7.

Next, include your personal information:

- ★ Your full name.

- ★ Mailing address with ZIP code.

- ★ Day and evening telephone numbers (with the area code).

- ★ E-mail address.

- ★ Social Security number (required).

- ★ Country of citizenship.

- ★ Veteran's preference (if applicable).

- ★ Reinstatement eligibility (if applicable; for former federal employees only).

- ★ Highest federal civilian grade held (if you've previously worked for the federal government). Also provide the job series number and the dates you were employed. If you have not been a federal employee, and this information does not apply to you, make sure you note that fact.

A key part of the resume is, of course, your work experience. Include experience that is relevant to your targeted position. Note that a federal resume format requires that you list your experience in reverse chronological order. Do not go back further than 10 years in your work experience, unless some of your relevant work experience is older than 10 years. If you have volunteer experience that's relevant to the job for which you're applying, you should include it on your resume as well.

For each job you've held, provide the following information:

- ★ Job title.

- ★ The starting and ending dates (including month and year).

- ★ The employer's name, city, and state.

- ★ The average number of hours worked per week (or just say "full-time").

- ★ Your supervisor's name and telephone number. (Also indicate whether your most recent supervisor can be contacted.)

- ★ If you've previously worked for the federal government, the occupational series numbers and the starting and ending grades of those positions.

After you list these details, make sure you effectively describe your duties and accomplishments for each job. Give examples that shed additional light on the scope of your experience. Be specific. If you won an award, say what it was for. If you helped your employer save money or streamline a process, describe how you did it and the results. Use numbers to quantify your accomplishments whenever possible.

Study the vacancy announcement and emphasize the parts of your work history that match the qualifications listed there. Also check the vacancy announcement for any keywords you can repeat in your descriptions. Note that conducting an adequate analysis of the vacancy announcement with substantiation of your experience can result in 8 to 10 hours of time invested per application.

The Importance of Keywords

Keywords are those words that contain the most important and significant elements of a job description. Using keywords appropriately in your application materials indicates that you have qualifying experience (which is particularly helpful if a computer is initially screening your application). Just be sure the keywords accurately match your skills. An excellent resource to help you pinpoint the correct industry and occupational language is O*NET OnLine at http://online.onetcenter.org. Developed by the Department of Labor, this source of occupational information provides descriptions for hundreds of jobs.

You also need to provide details about your education on your resume. If you have no college experience, include the name, city, and state of your high school and the date you received a diploma or GED. If you have completed college coursework, you do not need to include information about high school because a high school education is implied.

List the name, city, and state of the college or university where you have studied. Make sure you include your majors, the type and year of any degrees, and specific courses you've taken that relate to the job. If you are working toward a degree, list the number of credits you've earned and include the month and year you expect to graduate.

Some automated forms also require you to enter your grade point average. Even if it's not required, you may want to include it if it's high enough to help. College graduates with GPAs of at least 3.0 sometimes qualify for higher starting pay and expedited hiring programs. (See Chapter 9 for more information about these programs.)

Finally, explain your other qualifications on your resume. These may include the following:

★ Any other skills relevant to the job that are not immediately obvious from other parts of your resume. These skills might include experience with specific computer software or knowledge of a foreign language.

★ Job-related training courses (include title and year).

★ Job-related honors or special accomplishments such as publications, memberships in professional or honor societies, speaking appearances, and performance awards (include dates).

You might want to consider including a separate section in your resume that summarizes your qualifications. Summaries can be especially helpful in explaining long or varied work histories. Whenever possible, use the summaries to focus on the qualifications listed in the vacancy announcement.

Converting a Resume in Word to a Plain Text Document

When you submit an online resume, you will need to take precautions to ensure that your document is readable by the recipient. Some word processing programs transmit to others with unwanted characters (such as squiggles, question marks, and so on) that indicate incompatibility between programs. Therefore, you want to remove all formatting from your resume that could convert into strange markings. The following instructions will ensure that you remove any possible errors from your Word document.

1. Open the resume into a Word document.

2. Choose Edit, Select All from the menu bar to highlight the whole document.

3. Click the Bold button on the toolbar several times until nothing is bolded. Do the same with the Italics and Underline buttons if anything on the resume is italicized or underlined.

4. Click outside the highlighted area.

5. Remove all the tabs, making sure anything aligned to the right is now aligned to the left. If you need a comma to separate such things as dates, be sure to insert them.

6. Go to each bulleted section of the resume and remove the bullets one section at time.

7. Add new bullets using a hyphen, asterisk, or tilde. The new bullet must be located on the keyboard.

8. Save as a .txt (Text) document, making sure the original document still exists as a Word document.

9. Open the document in WordPad and review it thoroughly to ensure it does not have any question marks or strange markings.

Highlighting Your Strengths with Application Essays

Some vacancy announcements require that you submit personal essays, sometimes called KSAs (knowledge, skills, and abilities), application essays, competency statements, or quality rating factors. These one-page essays are included with your federal government application and address your individual knowledge, skills, and abilities as they relate to the vacancy announcement for which you are applying. They are never optional, despite what might be stated in the announcement.

If the job you are applying for requires essays, you have a tremendous opportunity to showcase your accomplishments, highlight your qualifications, and target your expertise to the job! Use your answers to persuade the agency to hire you by showing how well your experience and training connects with the requirements of the job. KSAs alone will not qualify you for a federal job, but they are essential to receiving a high proficiency rating.

Organizing Your Information

Review the Duties and Qualifications and Evaluations sections of the vacancy announcement carefully, paying particular attention to keywords or phrases describing the position responsibilities.

(If you followed our earlier advice in "Analyzing a Vacancy Announcement," you should already have these printed out and highlighted.)

Note the questions or statements that you have to address in your application essays. Make sure you differentiate between and among knowledge, skill, and ability:

★ **Knowledge:** An organized body of information, usually of a factual or procedural nature, that, when applied, makes adequate job performance possible.

★ **Skill:** The proficient manual, verbal, or mental utilization of data, people, or things. Skills are observable, quantifiable, and measurable.

★ **Ability:** The power to perform a given activity.

Go back to your resume and list the experiences you've had that address each KSA. Review each list and select the items that best illustrate a link between your experience and each KSA.

Next, add information relevant to each KSA that may not be included in your resume, such as any specialized training, publications, leadership roles, student activities, and awards. Make sure you acknowledge and include the entire range of experiences, including volunteer work, internships, school projects, and extracurricular activities.

Link all these different examples explicitly to the KSA questions. Whatever work you have done, in the private sector for pay or as a volunteer, the key is to tie these experiences back to the KSAs in a way that demonstrates that you are the best candidate for the job. Think of the KSAs as a set of interview questions. The goal is to market yourself and your experiences in such a way as to convey to the hiring manager that you are the best person for the job.

Consider the CCAR formula provided by OPM that all federal agencies use when advising employees on how to write these essays:

★ **Context:** What issue did you have to resolve? State the problem.

★ **Challenge:** What conditions did you have to consider when dealing with the issue? Describe the budget constraints, new regulations, or other factors that affected the decisions you made.

★ **Action:** How did you use your skills to address the situation? Provide a step-by step description.

★ **Result:** What did you accomplish? Quantify your achievements in terms of time or money saved or other measures used to evaluate your work.

Using an Effective Writing Style

When you write your application answers, consider your audience. The people reading your application have other jobs to perform; they do not have time to sift through your application, searching for salient points. Find the right balance between providing compelling information and information overload.

Use concrete examples to illustrate your skills. Examples are much more compelling than simple statements. In other words, show, don't just tell, about your skills and experience. Use examples to paint a picture of you in action, so the reader sees you successfully completing the job. Be sure to include examples that demonstrate your ability to take initiative, as well as any other personal management skills that are important to the position.

Keep these style guidelines in mind while you are writing federal application essays:

★ Tailor each answer to read between half a page and a page in length.

★ Use the active voice.

★ Write in the first person, using personal pronouns.

★ Proofread your work and correct any spelling or grammar mistakes.

★ Always use plain language and don't use acronyms.

★ Use keywords from the vacancy announcement whenever it's appropriate.

★ Be concise.

★ Make sure you answer the question that is asked.

★ Cite quantitative data where possible. Use data that measure how much (such as how much money or time you generated or saved) or how many (such as how many people attended, how many units you produced) and point to positive change (percentage growth or savings) to which you directly contributed wherever possible.

★ Make sure your answers reflect your level of responsibility. Clearly identify whom you interacted with and how (for example, providing key information to a manager, working with a group of peers, or supervising a team).

★ Focus on examples of your experience from the last five years, if possible. Each answer should include one example; try to use different examples for each answer. However, it is okay to use the same example and to go back beyond five years if the example is powerful.

When you have finished writing your answers, ask an objective third party (such as a career counselor) to read them. Provide your reviewer with the vacancy announcement as well for evaluation purposes. Ask your reader to ensure that you have included all of your relevant experiences, that your responses flow well, and that the answers don't contain any typographical or grammatical errors.

Appendix C provides some KSA examples for you to review. You can find additional information on writing a federal resume and application essays at the following Web sites:

★ **Resume and KSA Tips:** http://www.usajobs.gov/infocenter/resumetips.asp

★ **A Guide to KSA Writing:** http://www.ourpublicservice.org/OPS/programs/calltoserve/toolkit/KSAs.pdf

★ **Writing a KSA:** http://www.makingthedifference.org/federaljobs/ksawriting.shtml

★ **The Importance of KSAs in the Federal Application Process:** http://www.cdc.gov/hrmo/KSAhowto.htm

★ **All About KSAOs:** http://www.archives.gov/careers/jobs/ksas.pdf

Preparing for an Interview

Like most managers, federal managers usually interview applicants before deciding whom to hire. There are no special rules for federal interviews. You can prepare for them as you would any others. Learn more about the job by visiting the agency Web site (these are listed in Chapters 4, 5, and 6), skimming its publications and mission statements, and reviewing its organizational chart. You also should review the job announcement and your application.

On the day of the interview, take a notepad and pen and copies of the materials you submitted. Take two copies of your resume, in case the interviewer does not have a copy. Give yourself enough time to find the correct office and navigate security procedures. You probably need to bring photo identification as well as any materials that the hiring manager requests. Be prepared to enter a highly secure federal building. You may walk through a scanner and need to place your belongings on a belt that moves through an X-ray machine (like at the airport). While you are waiting to see the interviewer, review your application materials (resume, application essays) to familiarize yourself with the contents. Knowing what you have to offer is a great way to boost your self-confidence!

You might meet with the hiring manager alone or with a panel of managers and coworkers. The standard advice about interviews applies, including listening well, being ready with specific examples of your skills, and sending thank-you notes. Ask those who interview you for their business cards so you have accurate names and job titles.

Thank-You Notes

As in the private sector, it is considered standard practice to send thank-you notes within 24 hours following a job interview. Because of the anthrax scare a number of years ago, the mailrooms of many federal agencies irradiate incoming mail. As a result, your thank-you note may be delayed in reaching its destination, diminishing its effectiveness. It is recommended, therefore, that you send your thank-you note electronically.

Negotiating Salary and Accepting the Job

When you are selected for a job in the federal government, a human resources specialist will telephone you with an offer. This is a good time to ask questions about pay and benefits. Negotiating for pay is not as common in federal work as it is in the private sector because pay ranges are set by law. You cannot negotiate grade, but you can negotiate step (refer back to Chapter 1 for a discussion about the steps within each grade or go online to http://www.opm.gov/oca/08tables). You have the most leverage when you are offered the job. So do your research and know how much your skills are worth, so you can negotiate adequately during the job offer. Agencies have some flexibility in pay and can start experienced workers at the high end of the pay range, based on qualifications, market conditions, the applicant's past salary, and agency regulations. Some agencies can also offer signing bonuses, student loan repayment, and relocation assistance.

In addition to answering questions about pay and benefits, the human resources specialist will explain the process of getting a security clearance or other background check, if such checks are required for the job. If you need time to decide whether to accept the job, ask for it. If you do accept, the specialist will give you a start date and tell the hiring manager—who will probably be your new boss.

Part II

Descriptions, URLs, and Sample Job Vacancies for Federal Agencies and Departments

CHAPTER 4

Legislative Branch

More than 200 years ago, the founders of the United States gathered in Philadelphia, Pennsylvania, to create a constitution for a new national government and lay the foundation for self-governance. The Constitution of the United States, ratified by the last of the 13 original States in 1791, created the three branches of the federal government and granted certain powers and responsibilities to each. The legislative, judicial, and executive branches were created with equal powers but very different responsibilities that act to keep their powers in balance.

The legislative branch is responsible for forming and amending the legal structure of the nation. Its largest component is Congress, the primary U.S. legislative body, which is made up of the Senate and the House of Representatives. This body includes senators, representatives, their staffs, and various support workers. The legislative branch employs only about one percent of federal workers, nearly all of whom work in the Washington, DC, area. This chapter describes the organizations within the legislative branch and lists Web addresses, contact information, and sample job vacancies for them as well.

Architect of the Capitol

U.S. Capitol Building, SB15
Washington, DC 20515
202-228-1793

★ Web site: http://www.aoc.gov

★ Job vacancies: http://www.aoc.gov/employment/apply.cfm

The Architect of the Capitol is responsible for the care and maintenance of the U.S. Capitol and the buildings and grounds across the Capitol complex. The agency is charged with implementing construction, renovation, conservation, and landscape improvement projects as authorized by the Congress. The Capitol complex includes the Capitol, the congressional office buildings, the Library of Congress buildings, the Supreme Court building, the Thurgood Marshall Federal Judiciary Building, the U.S. Botanic Garden, the Capitol Power Plant, the Capitol Police Headquarters, the Robert A. Taft Memorial, and other facilities. Duties include mechanical and structural maintenance of the buildings, the upkeep and improvement of the Capitol grounds, the arrangement of inaugural ceremonies and other events and ceremonies held in the building or on the grounds, the care and repair of all works of art in the Capitol, and the maintenance and restoration of murals and other architectural elements throughout the Capitol complex. It employs approximately 2,200 people.

Select Facility

The **U.S. Botanic Garden** informs visitors about the aesthetic, cultural, economic, therapeutic, and ecological importance of plants to the well-being of humankind. The garden has artistic displays of plants, exhibits, and educational programs promoting botanical knowledge through the cultivation of an ordered collection of plants; fostering plant conservation by acting as a repository for endangered species; and growing plants for the beautification of the Capitol complex. Uniquely situated at the heart of the U.S. Capitol, the U.S. Botanic Garden seeks to promote the exchange of ideas and information relevant to its mission among national and international visitors and policymakers. It employs approximately 60 people.

★ Web site: http://www.usbg.gov/

★ Career information: http://www.usbg.gov/education/get-involved.cfm

Sample Job Vacancies

Electrician
Agency: Capitol Building/Capitol Visitor Center
Salary: $26.00 to $30.37/hour
Location: Washington, DC

Duties: The incumbent performs electrician duties in support of equipment and electrical systems in the Capitol Building. Installs, assembles, troubleshoots, modifies, repairs, and maintains routine and standard electrical lines, circuits, systems, and associated fixtures, controls, and equipment. Responsibilities include troubleshooting electrical devices containing electronic components in order to isolate the cause of the malfunction of electrical control systems, analog/digital controls, and solid-state motor control circuits in equipment. Examples of these are fire alarm systems, variable speed drives and electric motor starters for the air conditioning systems, cafeteria and kitchen equipment (ovens, ranges, and so on), replacement of resisters and repair of circuit boards on the lighting dimmer banks, and automatic door opening systems.

How to apply: Position is being filled through an online application system. Application submitted by any form of mail delivery will not be accepted. Do not e-mail, fax, or deliver applications or forms for this vacancy. All applications must be submitted, and forms attached through online services. Any required forms must be attached as text or image files to your job application; forms received by e-mail will not be accepted. If you are unable to apply online, you may contact the employing office for alternative application procedures.

Information Technology Specialist
Agency: Information Technology Division
Salary: $102,721 to $133,543
Location: Washington, DC

Duties: Manages, administers, and ensures security, maintenance, and operations of database systems, such as MS SQL Server and Oracle. Maintains functional knowledge of the data itself. Manipulates and maintains the data as necessary to meet user and system requirements. Manages the lifecycle of an information technology project from concept development through implementation. Provides consultation and instruction to other specialists on database and file accessing techniques, search strategies, processing and space utilization efficiencies, database security procedures, backup and program recovery techniques, and testing techniques. Works collaboratively with ITD staff to ensure that tasks are completed effectively and efficiently.

Wellness Center Attendant
Agency: Wellness Center
Salary: $41,210 to $53,574
Location: Washington, DC

Duties: Maintains the gymnasium area, sports conditioning equipment, saunas, and therapeutic pools in a clean and orderly manner. Plans and performs general property management support services, such as disposal of equipment. Performs general maintenance and repair on a variety of exercise equipment. Maintains accountability for turn-in and issue of linen and other items. Assists members of Congress, other congressional staff, and visitors requesting information, guidance, or referral for special assistance. Sets up and adjusts specialized equipment with multiple features based on the specific fitness and/or individualized health goal criteria. Ensures that all safety rules and regulations for the gymnasium facility and conditioning equipment are observed. Monitors the physical activity and treatment of senators and provides Cardiopulmonary Resuscitation if required. Determines the scope and nature of actions required to resolve customer service problems and process transactions, based on experience and past practice.

Congressional Budget Office

Second and D Streets SW
Washington, DC 20515
202-226-2600

★ Web site: http://www.cbo.gov/

★ Job vacancies: http://www.cbo.gov/Employment/jobs.cfm

★ Internships: http://www.cbo.gov/Employment/intern.cfm

★ Fellowships: http://www.cbo.gov/Employment/fellowships.shtml

The Congressional Budget Office (CBO) provides the Congress with economic analyses of alternative fiscal, budgetary, and programmatic policy issues and with information and estimates required for the congressional budget process. CBO is a small, nonpartisan agency that produces policy analyses, cost estimates, and budget and economic projections that serve as a basis for the Congress's decisions about spending and taxes. Every piece of legislation affecting the use of the nation's resources undergoes CBO's scrutiny. The Congress depends on CBO to help it find its way each year through the intricate maze of programs competing for funds and to serve as a "reality check" for partisan advocacy.

CBO is a public-sector "think tank" that employs more than 230 people at levels ranging from undergraduate and graduate interns to seasoned researchers with doctorates and substantial experience. Well over half of its staff has advanced degrees in economics, public administration, or a wide variety of other disciplines.

Selected CBO Divisions

The **Macroeconomic Analysis Division** is responsible for preparing CBO's economic projections, analyzing the effects of fiscal policy on the economy, and advising Congress on general macroeconomic issues. *Macroeconomics,* the study of the economy as a whole, focuses on key economic indicators, such as employment, production, income, saving, investment, trade, interest rates, and inflation.

The Macroeconomic Analysis Division employs approximately 26 Ph.D.-level economists. It also offers opportunities to a few assistant analysts. The division gives economists who are interested in public policy a unique opportunity to apply their training in economics. Its staff members write CBO studies, draft testimony to be delivered at congressional hearings, and carry out original research for publication in academic journals.

★ Web site: http://www.cbo.gov/aboutcbo/organization/mad.htm

The **National Security Division** analyzes budgetary issues related to national defense and international security. Its research focuses on defense budgets, military forces and weapon systems, the demand for and supply of military personnel, the military's industrial and support facilities, and U.S. foreign assistance programs. The division's analyses examine the budgetary effects of proposed legislation, the cost-effectiveness of current and potential defense programs, and the impact on the private sector of legislative initiatives concerning defense.

Analysts in the National Security Division bring the tools of rigorous quantitative analysis to their work. Many of the division's 17 staff members hold Ph.D.s, and others have master's degrees. Division members have backgrounds spanning a number of disciplines including economics, engineering, physics, mathematics, operations research, and international affairs. Some analysts have served in the military, but most gained their knowledge of defense issues as civilians while working at CBO, nonprofit research organizations, or the Department of Defense.

★ Web site: http://www.cbo.gov/aboutcbo/organization/nsd.htm

Other CBO Divisions

Budget Analysis Division

http://www.cbo.gov/aboutcbo/organization/bad.htm

Health and Human Resources Division

http://www.cbo.gov/aboutcbo/organization/hhrd.htm

Management, Business, and Information Services Division

http://www.cbo.gov/aboutcbo/organization/mbisd.htm

Microeconomic Studies Division

http://www.cbo.gov/aboutcbo/organization/msd.htm

Tax Analysis Division

http://www.cbo.gov/aboutcbo/organization/tad.htm

Sample Job Vacancies

Assistant Analyst
Agency: Congressional Budget Office
Salary: $36,000 to $42,000
Location: Washington, DC

Duties: The candidate would be responsible for monitoring bills as they move through the legislative process and analyzing the impact of federal legislation on the private sector. In addition, the analyst would work with senior economists in preparing studies to analyze the economic and budgetary impact of issues before the Congress. The successful candidate will provide the division's analysts with spreadsheet and statistical analyses, graphics, literature reviews, and other research assistance.

Qualifications: The position requires a person who can accurately interpret and analyze legislative proposals and take initiative to gather suitable data to address policy questions. The candidate should have the ability to handle several analytic issues simultaneously and complete projects in a timely manner. The position also requires a person who can work well as a part of a team. Candidates also should have strong quantitative and writing skills and a desire to work on issues of current interest to the Congress.

Candidates should have a bachelor's degree in economics, public policy, or a related field of study. Training or experience in industry or regulatory analysis, or experience with the legislative process, is desirable but not required. To qualify based on education, submit copy of transcript or list of courses with credit hours, major(s), and grade-point average or class ranking.

Programmer/Analyst
Agency: Health and Human Resources Division
Salary: $39,000 to $90,000. Salary is commensurate with experience, education, and other qualifications.
Location: Washington, DC

Duties: The successful candidate will work with senior economists on a range of specific projects. Responsibilities include assembling databases, performing analyses using large micro-data files, modeling proposed changes in federal programs and policies, and creating and operating micro-simulation models. Commonly used databases include the Current Population Survey, the Survey of Income and Program Participation, the Medical Expenditure Panel Survey, and Medicare and Medicaid claims files.

Qualifications: Candidates should have a Bachelor's or Master's degree in Economics, Public Policy, or a related discipline. They should also be proficient in SAS and/or STATA. Prior experience with the above-mentioned data sets would be a definite advantage. Candidates should have a strong interest in federal policies and programs related to health care, income support, and education. Upon employment, new employees are required to submit paperwork to obtain a National Agency Check Investigation clearance.

Government Accountability Office

441 G Street NW
Washington, DC 20548
202-512-3000

★ Web site: http://www.gao.gov/

★ Job vacancies: http://www.gao.gov/careers/apply.html

★ Student internships: http://www.gao.gov/careers/student.html

★ Career information: http://www.gao.gov/careers/career.html

★ Strategic plan: http://www.gao.gov/sp/d071sp.pdf

Named the 2006 Best Place to Work in the federal government and one of the Best Places in 2007, the Government Accountability Office (GAO) is an independent, nonpartisan agency. Often called the "congressional watchdog," GAO is the investigative arm of the Congress and is charged with examining all matters relating to the receipt and disbursement of public funds. It has offices in Atlanta, Georgia; Boston, Massachusetts; Chicago, Illinois; Dallas, Texas; Dayton, Ohio; Denver, Colorado; Huntsville, Alabama; Los Angeles, California; Norfolk, Virginia; San Francisco, California; and Seattle, Washington. GAO is organized into 13 teams that work on specific subject areas.

The ability to review practically any governmental function requires a multidisciplined staff. More than half of GAO's employees have doctoral or master's degrees from leading universities in such areas as public administration, public policy, law, business, computer science, accounting, economics, and the social sciences. GAO has more than 3,000 employees from coast-to-coast, two-thirds of whom work at GAO headquarters in Washington, DC. Major career tracks include analyst, financial auditor, and specialist (including information technology specialist, economist, actuary, and communications analyst).

The **Office of the General Counsel** (OGC) provides a wide variety of legal services that help ensure efficient, effective, and economical government operations. OGC attorneys assist the Congress, federal agencies, and GAO analysts in interpreting the laws that govern the expenditure of public funds and the many government programs and activities.

★ Web site: http://www.gao.gov/about/workforce/ogc.html

Selected GAO Teams

More than 200 billion tax dollars are spent each year buying sophisticated weaponry, complex space and satellite systems, advanced technologies, and a broad range of goods and services needed to make the federal government run. This sum comprises the largest element of discretionary spending in the federal budget. The **Acquisition and Sourcing Management Team** examines whether this money is being spent efficiently and effectively and whether acquisitions maximize agencies' ability to meet their mission objectives. The team also analyzes commercial practices and how they can be applied to government.

★ Web site: http://www.gao.gov/jobs/asm.pdf

The **Defense Capabilities and Management Team** leads GAO's efforts to support congressional oversight of the Department of Defense. It studies a wide range of current and future defense issues, including assessing defense plans and force capabilities to deal with adversaries who are more likely to strike in nontraditional ways.

★ Web site: http://www.gao.gov/jobs/dcm.pdf

The **Natural Resources and Environment Team** provides Congress with fact-based analyses on a variety of issues, including the safety of the food supply, farm income, management of national lands, quality of water and air, and hazardous waste cleanup and storage.

★ Web site: http://www.gao.gov/jobs/nre.pdf

★ Careers: http://www.gao.gov/careers/nre.html

The **Physical Infrastructure Team** helps Congress address the challenge of maintaining a safe, secure, and effective national physical infrastructure (transportation, postal and telecommunications networks, oil and gas pipelines, and federal buildings and facilities) by identifying best practices and assessing improvement efforts and alternative options.

★ Web site: http://www.gao.gov/jobs/pi.pdf

Other GAO Teams

Applied Research and Methods Team

http://www.gao.gov/jobs/arm.pdf

Education, Workforce, and Income Security Team

http://www.gao.gov/jobs/ewi.pdf

Financial Management and Assurance Team

http://www.gao.gov/jobs/fma.pdf

Financial Markets and Community Investment Team

http://www.gao.gov/jobs/fmci.pdf

Health Care Team

http://www.gao.gov/jobs/hc.pdf

Homeland Security and Justice Team

http://www.gao.gov/jobs/hsj.pdf

Information Technology Team

http://www.gao.gov/jobs/it.pdf

International Affairs and Trade Team

http://www.gao.gov/jobs/iat.pdf

Strategic Issues Team

http://www.gao.gov/jobs/si.pdf

Sample Job Vacancy

Analyst
Agency: Health Care Team
Salary: $44,402 to $81,719
Location: Washington, DC

Duties: The incumbent of this position will perform entry-level analyst duties, which consist of developing research methods, reviewing documents, conducting interviews, summarizing facts, interpreting data, performing program evaluations, drafting segments of reports and testimonies, and delivering oral briefings.

Qualifications: Applicants must have successfully completed a full four-year course of study from an accredited college or university leading to a bachelor's or higher degree and must have superior academic achievement, which may be substituted for experience.

Alternatively, applicants may qualify with a bachelor's degree and at least one year of full-time graduate education. Such education must demonstrate the knowledge, skills, and abilities necessary to do the work of the position.

Applicants may also qualify based on experience. Applicants must have one year of directly related full-time experience conducting program analysis or professional experience in a team-based environment that clearly demonstrates analytical, data gathering, writing, and research skills.

Government Printing Office

732 North Capitol Street NW
Washington, DC 20401
202-512-0000

★ Web site: http://www.gpo.gov/

★ Job vacancies: http://www.gpo.gov/careers/jobs.htm

★ Career information: http://www.gpo.gov/careers/index.html

The Government Printing Office (GPO) keeps America informed by producing, procuring, and disseminating printed and electronic publications of the Congress as well as the executive departments and establishments of the federal government. Created initially to satisfy the printing needs of Congress, the GPO today is the focal point for printing and information dissemination for the entire federal community. In addition to Congress and the White House, approximately 130 federal departments and agencies rely on the GPO's services. Congressional publications, federal regulations and reports, census and tax forms, and U.S. passports are among the documents produced by or through the GPO. The GPO provides government information in a wide range of formats, including print, microfiche, CD-ROM, and online through GPO Access. GPO sells approximately 9,000 different printed and electronic publications that originate in various government agencies. It administers the federal depository library program through which a comprehensive range of government publications are made available for the free use of the public in approximately 1,300 libraries throughout the country. GPO also provides online access to more than 200,000 federal government titles, including the Congressional Record and the Federal Register.

GPO employs about 2,250 people nationwide, about half of them in the graphics arts and related blue-collar occupations. Most are based at the GPO's central office facility in Washington, DC, making the GPO the largest industrial employer in the District of Columbia. GPO also operates a printing plant in Denver, Colorado; a technical documentation facility in Atlantic City, New Jersey; a publication distribution facility in Pueblo, Colorado; and regional and satellite procurement offices throughout the country.

Sample Job Vacancy

Photographer
Agency: Government Printing Office
Salary: $50,408 to $65,531
Location: Washington, DC

Duties: The primary role of GPO's photographer is to produce photographs for internal publications. All new work is digital, and there is some work scanning historical images to convert them to digital format. The photographer takes official portraits of all executives and covers visiting dignitaries and related special events, coordinating directly with the Executive Offices on these events to understand itineraries and objectives. From information that the client provides and conversations with the subjects(s), the photographer determines the ideal location, setting, lighting, and poses that will convey the needed messages. The photographer also has to interact with subjects from all levels of the agency to help them relax and pose in the appropriate manner.

How you will be evaluated: If you meet the listed qualifications, you will be further evaluated on the following knowledge, skills, and abilities (KSAs) in the occupational questionnaire:

★ Skill in understanding the communication objectives of each project and delivering creative solutions.

★ Skill in taking digital photographs and modifying, editing, and saving them using Photoshop.

★ Skill in taking well-composed images.

A review of your resume and supporting documentation will be made and compared against your responses to the occupational questionnaire. The score you receive is a measure of the degree to which your background matches the KSAs required of this position. Your narrative responses should explain how your experience, education, training, awards, and appraisals demonstrate that you possess the given KSA. Failure to respond or fully explain your experience may result in your score being lowered or you being found ineligible for this position.

Those applicants who are considered qualified based on their questionnaire score will be forwarded to a subject matter expert (a creative services manager in this case). The subject matter expert will score your online portfolio. The portfolio score will form the ordering of the competitive certificate of eligibles. This portfolio evaluation will focus primarily on your photos of people and will rate your technical and composition skills as well as your creativity.

Library of Congress

101 Independence Avenue SE
Washington, DC 20540
202-707-5000

* Web site: http://www.loc.gov/

* Job vacancies: http://www.loc.gov/hr/employment/index.php?action=cMain.showJobs

* Internships, fellowships, and volunteer programs: http://www.loc.gov/hr/employment/index.php?action=cMain.showFellowships

* Special employment programs: http://www.loc.gov/hr/employment/index.php?action=cMain.showEmploymentPrograms

* Career information: http://www.loc.gov/hr/employment/index.php?action=cMain.showHome

* Frequently asked questions: http://www.loc.gov/hr/employment/index.php?action=cInstructions.showInstructionsFaq

The Library of Congress (LOC) is the nation's oldest federal cultural institution and serves as the research arm of Congress. It is also the largest library in the world, with more than 138 million items on approximately 530 miles of bookshelves. The collections include more than 32 million books and other printed materials, 2.9 million recordings, 12.5 million photographs, 5.3 million maps, and 61.4 million manuscripts. The library's mission is to make its resources available and useful to Congress and the American people and to sustain and preserve a universal collection of knowledge and creativity for future generations. LOC employs approximately 3,900 staff.

Selected LOC Agencies

The **Congressional Research Service** is where members of Congress turn for the nonpartisan research, analysis, and information they need to make informed decisions. The CRS staff comprises nationally recognized experts in a range of issues and disciplines, including law; economics; foreign affairs; public administration; defense and homeland security; and the information, social, political, and natural sciences. The breadth and depth of this expertise enables CRS staff to come together quickly to provide integrated analyses of complex issues that span multiple legislative and program areas.

★ Job vacancies: http://www.loc.gov/crsinfo/

★ Internships and special hiring programs: http://www.loc.gov/crsinfo/internships/

★ Law recruit program: http://www.loc.gov/crsinfo/lawrecruit.html

The **Copyright Office** is an office of record, the place where claims to copyright are registered and where documents relating to copyright may be recorded when the requirements of the copyright law are met. The Copyright Office furnishes information about the provisions of the copyright law and the procedures for making registration, explains the operations and practices of the Copyright Office, and reports on facts found in the public records of the office. The Copyright Office also administers various compulsory licensing provisions of the law, which include collecting royalties. Additionally, the Copyright Office and the Library of Congress administer the Copyright Arbitration Royalty Panels, which meet for limited times for the purpose of adjusting rates and distributing royalties. The Copyright Office also provides expert analysis, advice, and assistance to Congress on national and international intellectual property matters.

★ Web site: http://www.copyright.gov/

Other LOC Agencies

American Folklife Center

http://www.loc.gov/folklife/

Business Reference Services

http://www.loc.gov/rr/business/

Center for the Book

http://www.loc.gov/loc/cfbook/

Children's Literature Center

http://www.loc.gov/rr/child/

John W. Kluge Center

http://www.loc.gov/loc/kluge/

Law Library

http://www.loc.gov/law/public/law.html

Motion Picture Conservation Center

http://www.loc.gov/rr/mopic/mpcc.html

National Film Preservation Board

http://www.loc.gov/film/

National Recording Preservation Board

http://www.loc.gov/rr/record/nrpb/

Poetry and Literature Center

http://www.loc.gov/poetry/

Recorded Sound Reference Center

http://www.loc.gov/rr/record/

Sample Job Vacancy

Supervisory Public Program Specialist
Agency: Office of the Librarian
Salary: $73,100 to $95,026
Location: Washington, DC

Duties: Makes arrangements for special events, ceremonies, exhibition openings, seminars, conferences, receptions, and other official functions. Coordinates details related to guest lists, seating, space planning, event budgets, menus, food service, outside vendors and contractors, personnel, security, cleaning, setup, and equipment. Plans, schedules, and assigns work to subordinates. Establishes guidelines and performance expectations for staff members; provides feedback and periodically evaluates employee performance.

Qualifications: Applicants must have had progressively responsible experience and training sufficient in scope and quality to furnish them with an acceptable level of the following knowledge, skills, and abilities to perform the duties of the position without more than normal supervision:

★ Ability to communicate in writing.

★ Skill in planning, organizing, and coordinating special events and public programs.

★ Ability to supervise, plan, and execute work through others.

★ Ability to analyze organizational and operational problems and develop solutions using analytical methods to improve programs and processes.

★ Ability to adapt.

★ Ability to negotiate and monitor contracts.

★ Ability to communicate effectively other than in writing.

U.S. Capitol Police

119 D Street NE
Washington, DC 20510
1-866-561-USCP (toll-free)

The U.S. Capitol Police protects and supports the Congress in meeting its constitutional responsibilities. They protect life and property; prevent, detect, and investigate criminal acts; and enforce traffic regulations throughout the large complex of congressional buildings, parks, and thoroughfares. Additionally, they protect members of Congress, officers of the United States Senate and United

States House of Representatives, and the families of these members and officers. The U.S. Capitol Police are located throughout the entire United States, its territories and possessions, and the District of Columbia.

★ Web site: http://www.uscapitolpolice.gov/home.php

★ How to apply: http://www.uscapitolpolice.gov/apply.php

★ How to register for the examination: http://www.usajobs.gov/ei51.asp

Sample Job Vacancy

United States Capitol Police Officer
Agency: U.S. Capitol Police
Salary: $51,859 to $60,187
Location: Washington, DC

Qualifications: You must be 21 years of age on date of appointment, but not have reached your 37th birthday on date of appointment (age may be waived with prior qualifying federal civilian law enforcement experience). You also must be a U.S. citizen and possess a valid driver's license. You must possess a high school diploma or GED and submit a copy of your high school transcript along with any college transcript if it applies. You cannot be involved in any pending criminal or civil litigation.

You must be in excellent health and pass a pre-employment medical examination. After appointment, you will be subject to random testing for illegal drug use. You may need to stand for prolonged periods on concrete floors and walk over rough and uneven terrain. You also will be required to maintain firearm proficiency and carry a firearm while performing duties of this position. Lastly, you must be a mature, responsible individual with a high degree of tact.

How you will be evaluated: You will be evaluated based upon the score you achieve on the written test required for this position. In order to take the written test, you must meet the minimum requirements for the position. Once you pass the written test, the selection process consists of several stages of processing; you must be successful at each stage in order to proceed to the next. These stages are application review, personal interview, extensive background investigation, polygraph evaluation, physical examination, and psychological evaluation. If you are not chosen to continue in the selection process, you will be notified in writing of this decision. You are encouraged to establish a personal physical conditioning program as you will be required to participate in a rigorous physical conditioning program throughout your 28 weeks of training should you be selected for appointment.

United States House of Representatives

Washington, DC 20515
202-224-3121
TTY: 202-225-1904

★ Web site: http://www.house.gov/Welcome.html

★ Employment: http://www.house.gov/cao-hr/

★ Job line: 202-226-4504

★ Pages: http://pageprogram.house.gov

★ Internships (information located on each representative's Web site): http://dcjobsource.com/houseinterns.html (provides a link to each site by state)

★ Committee directory: http://www.house.gov/house/CommitteeWWW.shtml

As the largest part of Congress, the House of Representatives comprises 435 representatives and employs 6,700 people. It also has 22 committees and 106 subcommittees.

Population determines how many representatives each state has, but every state is entitled to at least one representative. Representatives must be residents of the state from which they are chosen. Members of the House of Representatives, who are elected for a term of two years, may hire up to 18 permanent employees for their congressional and district offices to assist them during their term in office.

Other Members of Congress

In addition to senators and representatives, Congress also includes a resident commissioner from Puerto Rico (elected for a four-year term) and delegates from American Samoa, the District of Columbia, Guam, and the Virgin Islands. Delegates are elected for a two-year term. The resident commissioner and delegates may take part in the floor discussions but have no vote in the full House or in the Committee of the Whole House on the state of the Union. They do, however, vote in the committees to which they are assigned.

Selected House of Representatives Committees

The **Committee on Education and Labor** has jurisdiction over federal programs dealing with education at all levels, as well as workforce initiatives aimed at strengthening health care, job training, and retirement security for workers. The committee and its five subcommittees oversee education and workforce programs that affect all Americans, from early learning through secondary education, from job training through retirement.

★ Web site: http://edworkforce.house.gov/

★ Internships: http://edworkforce.house.gov/about/internships/

The **Transportation and Infrastructure Committee** currently has jurisdiction over all modes of transportation: aviation, maritime and waterborne transportation, roads, bridges, mass transit, and railroads. The committee and its six subcommittees also have jurisdiction over other aspects of national infrastructure, including the following: clean water and waste management; the transport of resources by pipeline; flood damage reduction; the economic development of depressed rural and urban areas; disaster preparedness and response; and activities of the Army Corps of Engineers and various missions of the Coast Guard. The committee monitors the emerging role of satellites as a fundamental part of the transportation infrastructure, affecting all modes of travel.

★ Web site: http://transportation.house.gov/

The **Committee on Ways and Means** is the chief tax writing committee. It has jurisdiction over all taxation, tariffs, and other revenue-raising measures, including customs, collection districts, and ports of entry and delivery; reciprocal trade agreements; revenue measures; bonded debt of the United States; deposit of public monies; transportation of dutiable goods; tax-exempt foundations and charitable trusts; and Social Security.

★ Web site: http://waysandmeans.house.gov/

The **Committee on Homeland Security** provides congressional oversight over the development of the Department of Homeland Security. It holds hearings and studies issues related to protecting the country from future terrorist attacks.

★ Web site: http://homeland.house.gov/

Other House Committees

Agriculture

http://agriculture.house.gov/

Appropriations

http://appropriations.house.gov/

Armed Services

http://armedservices.house.gov/

Budget

http://budget.house.gov/

Energy and Commerce

http://energycommerce.house.gov/

Financial Services

http://financialservices.house.gov/

House Administration

http://cha.house.gov/

Intelligence

http://intelligence.house.gov/

Joint Committee on Taxation

http://www.house.gov/jct/

Joint Economic Committee

http://www.jec.senate.gov/

Judiciary

http://judiciary.house.gov/

Natural Resources

http://resourcescommittee.house.gov/

Oversight and Government Reform

http://oversight.house.gov/

Rules

http://www.rules.house.gov/

Science and Technology

http://science.house.gov/

Small Business

http://www.house.gov/smbiz/

Standards of Official Conduct

http://ethics.house.gov/

Veterans' Affairs

http://veterans.house.gov/

Sample Job Vacancy

Security Engineer
Agency: House Information Resources
Salary: $77,630 to $99,214
Location: Washington, DC

Duties: Provides technical support to the U.S. House of Representatives information security compliance and audit program. Conducts technical security reviews and audits of software applications and the network devices and databases that support each application. Manages the application audit and remediation schedule. Provides technical assistance to member, committee, and support offices to mitigate security vulnerabilities. Conducts security awareness training for system owners and developers. This position may require the ability to work shifts and be on-call on a rotating basis in order to provide 24 hours a day, 7 days a week technical support for the Information Systems Security Office.

United States Senate

Washington, DC 20510
202-224-3121

★ Web site: http://www.senate.gov/

★ Job line: 202-228-JOBS (5627)

★ Employment: http://www.senate.gov/visiting/common/generic/placement_office.htm

★ Employment bulletin: http://www.senate.gov/visiting/resources/pdf/seb.pdf

★ Placement office: 202-224-9167

★ Pages: http://www.senate.gov/reference/reference_index_subjects/Pages_vrd.htm

★ Internships: http://www.senate.gov, go to your senator's Web site for internship applications

★ Committee directory: http://www.senate.gov/pagelayout/committees/ d_three_sections_with_teasers/committees_home.htm

The Senate is part of Congress and is composed of 100 members, two from each state, who are elected to serve for a term of six years. Senators must be residents of the state from which they are chosen. Each senator has staff to assist him/her during a term in office. Unlike representatives, senators do not have a limit on the number of staff they can hire. The Senate employs approximately 17,400 people and has 20 committees and 68 subcommittees.

Because Senate jobs (and those in the House of Representatives) are considered to be excepted service positions, they are not listed on USAJOBS. Excepted service positions typically are not listed on that site. You can find Senate job postings on the employment bulletin site listed above. Excepted service organizations are listed on the following link: http://www.usajobs.gov/ei6.asp.

Congressional Committees and Subcommittees

Due to the high volume and complexity of the Congress's work, its tasks are divided among committees and subcommittees. Committees generally have legislative jurisdiction. Subcommittees handle specific areas of the committee's work. The House of Representatives and Senate each have their own committees and subcommittees in addition to sharing four joint committees. Committees receive varying levels of operating funds and employ varying numbers of aides. Each hires its own staff. The majority party controls most committee staff and resources, but a portion is shared with the minority.

Selected Senate Committees

The **Committee on Banking, Housing, and Urban Affairs** handles legislation related to financial institutions; control of prices of commodities, rents and services; deposit insurance; economic stabilization and defense production; export and foreign trade promotion; export controls; federal monetary policy, including the federal reserve system; financial aid to commerce and industry; issuance and redemption of notes; money and credit, including currency and coinage; nursing home construction; public and private housing (including veterans' housing); renegotiation of government contracts; urban development and urban mass transit. It has five subcommittees: Security and International Trade and Finance; Security, Insurance, and Investment; Financial Institutions; Housing, Transportation, and Community Development; and Financial Institutions.

★ Web site: http://banking.senate.gov/

The **Committee on Finance** handles legislation related to the following: bonded debt of the United States; customs, collection districts, and ports of entry and delivery; deposit of public moneys; general revenue sharing; health programs under the Social Security Act and health programs financed by a specific tax or trust fund; Social Security; national social security; reciprocal trade agreements; revenue measures; tariffs and import quotas; and transportation of dutiable goods.

★ Web site: http://finance.senate.gov/

The **Committee on Foreign Relations** is responsible for the foreign policy activities of the U.S. Senate. It evaluates all treaties with foreign governments; approves all diplomatic nominations; and writes legislation pertaining to U.S. foreign policy, national security policy, international economic policy, the State Department, foreign assistance programs, and many associated topics.

★ Web site: http://foreign.senate.gov/

The **Committee on Homeland Security and Governmental Affairs** is the chief oversight committee for the United States Senate. It created the Department of Homeland Security, for which it provides primary oversight. The committee also handles legislation related to the following: the United States archives, budget and accounting other than appropriations, the census and the collection of statistics, congressional organization, federal civil service, government information, intergovernmental relations, municipal affairs of the District of Columbia, oversight for the U.S. nuclear export policy, organization of the executive branch, postal service, and the status of officers and employees of the United States (including classification, compensation, and benefits). It has five subcommittees: Federal Financial Management; Disaster Recovery; State, Local, and Private Sector Preparedness and Integration; and Oversight of Government Management and Investigations.

★ Web site: http://hsgac.senate.gov/public/

The duty of the **Committee on Indian Affairs** is to conduct a study of any and all matters pertaining to problems and opportunities of Indians, including Indian land management and trust responsibilities; Indian education, health, special services, and loan programs; and Indian claims against the United States.

★ Web site: http://indian.senate.gov/public/

★ Internships: http://indian.senate.gov/intern.htm

The **Special Committee on Aging** was granted permanent status on February 1, 1977. Although special committees have no legislative authority, they can study issues, conduct oversight of programs, and investigate reports of fraud and waste. Throughout its existence, the Special Committee on Aging has served as a focal point in the Senate for discussion and debate on matters relating to older Americans. Often, the committee will submit its findings and recommendations for legislation to the Senate. In addition, the committee publishes materials of assistance to those interested in public policies that relate to the elderly.

★ Web site: http://aging.senate.gov/

Other Senate Committees

Agriculture, Nutrition, and Forestry

http://agriculture.senate.gov/

Appropriations

http://appropriations.senate.gov/

Armed Services

http://armed-services.senate.gov/

Budget

http://budget.senate.gov/

Commerce, Science, and Transportation

http://commerce.senate.gov/public/

Energy and Natural Resources

http://energy.senate.gov/public/

Environment and Public Works

http://epw.senate.gov/public/

Ethics

http://ethics.senate.gov/

Health, Education, Labor, and Pensions

http://help.senate.gov/

Intelligence

http://intelligence.senate.gov/

Judiciary

http://judiciary.senate.gov/

Rules and Administration

http://rules.senate.gov/

Small Business and Entrepreneurship

http://sbc.senate.gov/

Veterans' Affairs

http://veterans.senate.gov/public/

Sample Job Vacancies

Counsel
Agency: Judiciary Committee
Salary: Commensurate with experience
Location: Washington, DC

Duties: Senior Democratic senator is looking for a proactive, knowledgeable counsel to work on Judiciary Committee staff. Responsibilities to include developing, monitoring, and managing Judiciary legislation, preparing for hearings and assisting in all matters related to the jurisdiction of the Judiciary Committee. Candidates must possess no less than two years of substantive legal and related policy experience, excellent research and writing skills, and strong analytical and communication skills. Must also have a sense of humor, be a team player, and able to work well under pressure and with quick deadlines. Hill experience preferred; Senate or committee experience is a plus.

Qualifications: J.D. is required; please no recent graduates.

How to apply: Please e-mail resume and cover letter for consideration.

Economist
Agency: Joint Economic Committee
Salary: Commensurate with experience
Location: Washington, DC

Duties: The Democratic staff of the Joint Economic Committee of the U.S. Congress seeks staff economists with a serious interest in public policy research. Subject areas of interest include macroeconomics, the federal budget and tax policy, health care policy, energy markets, the U.S. labor market, and work-life issues. Successful candidates will have strong communication skills. The position requires independent research as well as working closely with other economists on the staff, in the federal government, and academics throughout the country.

Qualifications: A Ph.D. in economics or a related field, or commensurate work experience, is required. Capitol Hill experience is also a plus.

How to apply: If interested, please submit a resume, references, and two writing samples.

Executive Assistant

Agency: U.S. Senate
Salary: Commensurate with experience
Location: Washington, DC

Duties: Senior Democratic senator seeks organized, detail-oriented individual to fill executive assistant position. Individual will be responsible for acting as a liaison and doorkeeper to the senator with constituents, staff, and other senators. In addition, the executive assistant will monitor incoming telephone calls, take messages and return calls as requested, and be responsible for coordinating all of the senator's travel arrangements.

Qualifications: The ideal candidate for this position will possess strong oral and written communication skills, be able to exercise discretion and maintain the confidentiality of information, work well under pressure and in an extremely fast-paced environment, and be available to work long hours as necessary. Northeast ties a plus, Hill experience a must.

How to apply: Interested applicants should e-mail cover letter and resume. No calls please.

Legislative Assistant

Agency: U.S. Senate
Salary: Commensurate with experience
Location: Washington, DC

Duties: Democratic senator seeks an experienced legislative assistant to handle a host of issues possibly including, but not limited to, banking, budget, taxes, labor and pensions. Individual will be responsible for monitoring pending legislation in their assigned issue areas, drafting amendments and bills, meeting with constituents and preparing briefing materials for the senator.

Qualifications: Knowledge of Senate floor procedures and Hill experience very strongly preferred. Qualified applicants must have excellent oral and written communication skills, as well as an ability to function effectively in a fast-paced environment. Pennsylvania ties a plus.

How to apply: Interested applicants should e-mail a resume, cover letter, and two short writing samples, with the subject "Legislative Assistant."

CHAPTER 5

Judicial Branch

The judicial branch is responsible for interpreting the laws that the legislative branch enacts. The Supreme Court, the nation's definitive judicial body, makes the highest rulings. Its decisions usually follow the appeal of a decision made by the one of the regional courts of appeal, which hear cases appealed from U.S. district courts, the Court of Appeals for the Federal Circuit, or the state supreme courts. U.S. district courts are located in each state and are the first to hear most cases under federal jurisdiction. The judicial branch employs approximately 33,000 people. Unlike the legislative branch, the judicial branch's offices and employees are dispersed throughout the country.

Administrative Office of the United States Courts

One Columbus Circle NE
Washington, DC 20544
202-502-2600

★ Web site: http://www.uscourts.gov/adminoff.html

★ Job vacancies: http://www.uscourts.gov/employment.html

The Administrative Office of the U.S. Courts (AO) is charged with the nonjudicial, administrative business of the United States courts, including the maintenance of workload statistics and the disbursement of funds appropriated for the maintenance of the U.S. judicial system. The office provides service to the federal courts in three essential areas: administrative support, program management, and policy development. The office is charged with implementing the policies of the Judicial Conference of the United States and supporting the network of conference committees. It is also the focal point for judiciary communication, information, program leadership, and administrative reform.

The agency is a unique entity in government. Neither the executive branch nor the legislative branch has any one comparable organization that provides the broad range of services and functions that the AO does for the judicial branch. The agency's lawyers, public administrators, accountants, systems engineers, analysts, architects, statisticians, and other staff provide a broad array of professional services to meet the needs of judges and others working in federal courts nationwide.

Sample Job Vacancies

Management Analyst
Agency: Magistrate Judges Division
Salary: $37,084 to $67,190
Location: Washington, DC

Duties: The incumbent of this position, performing independently or as part of a team, advises magistrate judges and other court officers on a wide range of administrative subjects affecting magistrate judges, such as statistical reporting and chambers staffing. The duties of the position include applying analytical and evaluative methods and techniques in order to plan, analyze, and evaluate the effectiveness of operating programs. Candidates for this position must be able to use knowledge that has been acquired through formal training or extensive on-the-job experience to perform the job; work with, understand, and evaluate technical information related to the job; and advise others on technical issues.

Qualifications: Completion of four-year course of study leading to a bachelor's degree or at least one year of work experience in analyzing and evaluating the effectiveness of management or administrative operations. A combination of some college coursework and related work experience is also acceptable. Applicants must provide transcripts or other documentation to support their educational claims.

Secretary
Agency: Article III Judges Division
Salary: $33,269 to $60,825
Location: Washington, DC

Duties: Receive and direct telephone calls from United States judges, members and staff of Congress, executives of other federal agencies, AO staff, and others to appropriate division staff members. Provide secretarial and administrative support to division staff members. Assist the chief and deputy chief of the division, in the absence of the senior secretary, in providing direct support to United States judges and the designated committees of the Judicial Conference. Review all incoming and outgoing correspondence and reports submitted to the chief and deputy chief for signature and/or concurrence. Assist in developing proposed division administrative controls, procedures, policies, and practices affecting the service and support to Article III judges. Assist in maintaining an extensive follow-up control system to ensure that prompt consideration is given to pending matters and that required deadlines are met. Maintain filing systems, electronic and paper, within the division, including updating judges' biographical profiles. Assist in the production of manuals, guides, articles, books, and other materials. Assist in coordinating meetings and programs sponsored by the division, including providing administrative and logistical support for Judicial Conference committee meetings, orientation programs, and other training programs, and coordinate travel and related arrangements for division staff members.

Qualifications: Applicants must have one year of specialized experience that is in or directly related to the line of work of this position. Specialized experience is experience in organizing and carrying out office management and administrative responsibilities. Applicants must be able to type at least 40 words per minute.

Federal Judicial Center

Thurgood Marshall Federal Judiciary Building
One Columbus Circle NE
Washington, DC 20002-8003
202-502-4000

★ Web site: http://www.fjc.gov/

★ Job vacancies: http://www.fjc.gov/public/home.nsf/autoframe?openform&url_r=/public/
fjchr.nsf/ByPageNumber/1

The Federal Judicial Center is the judicial branch's agency for policy research and continuing education. The center's basic policies and activities are determined by its board, which is composed of the Chief Justice of the United States, who is permanent Chair of the Board by statute, and two judges of the U.S. courts of appeals, three judges of the U.S. district courts, one bankruptcy judge, and one magistrate judge. The Director of the Administrative Office of the United States Courts is also a permanent member of the board.

Lower Courts

★ Web site: http://www.uscourts.gov/

★ Job vacancies: http://www.uscourts.gov/employment.html

★ *Comparing Federal and State Court Systems:* http://www.uscourts.gov/outreach/resources/
comparefedstate.html

★ Information about administrative law judge positions: http://www.opm.gov/qualifications/alj/
alj.asp

http://www.usajobs.gov/ei28.asp

★ *Attorneys in the Federal Service:* http://www.usajobs.gov/EI24.asp

Article III of the Constitution declares, in section 1, that the judicial power of the United States shall be invested in one Supreme Court and in "such inferior courts as the Congress may from time to time ordain and establish." The "inferior" or lower courts consist of the United States courts of appeals, the United States district courts, territorial courts, the United States Court of International Trade, and the Judicial Panel on Multidistrict Litigation.

Selected Lower Courts

The **United States courts of appeals** are intermediate appellate courts created to relieve the Supreme Court of considering all appeals in cases originally decided by the federal trial courts. They are empowered to review all final decisions and certain interlocutory decisions of district courts. They also are empowered to review and enforce orders of many federal administrative bodies. The decisions of the courts of appeals are final except as the records of the decisions are subject to review by the Supreme Court.

The United States is divided geographically into 12 judicial circuits. Each circuit has a court of appeals. Each of the 50 states is assigned to at least one of the circuits. The territories and the Commonwealth of Puerto Rico are assigned variously to the first, third, and ninth circuits. In addition, the Court of Appeals for the Federal Circuit has nationwide jurisdiction to hear appeals in specialized cases, such as those involving patent laws and cases decided by the Court of International Trade and the Court of Federal Claims.

★ Web site: http://www.uscourts.gov/courtsofappeals.html

★ Web site with links to the circuit courts: http://www.uscourts.gov/courtlinks/

The **United States district courts** are the trial courts of general federal jurisdiction. Each state and territory has at least one district court; the larger states have as many as four. Altogether there are 94 district courts in the 50 states, plus one in Washington, DC. In addition, the Commonwealth of Puerto Rico has a district court with jurisdiction corresponding to that of district courts in the various states. Each district court has from 2 to 28 federal district judgeships, depending upon the amount of judicial work within its territory. Each district court has one or more United States magistrate judges and bankruptcy judges, a clerk, a United States attorney, a United States marshal, probation officers, court reporters, and their staffs. Cases from the district courts are reviewable on appeal by the applicable court of appeals.

★ Web site: http://www.uscourts.gov/districtcourts.html

★ Web site with links to the district courts: http://www.uscourts.gov/courtlinks/

Other Lower Courts

Judicial Panel on Multidistrict Litigation
http://www.jpml.uscourts.gov/

Territorial District Courts
Guam: http://www.gud.uscourts.gov/
Virgin Islands: http://www.vid.uscourts.gov/
Northern Mariana Islands: http://www.nmid.uscourts.gov/

United States Court of International Trade
http://www.cit.uscourts.gov/

Special Courts

United States Court of Appeals for the Armed Forces
http://www.armfor.uscourts.gov/

United States Court of Appeals for Veterans Claims
http://www.vetapp.gov/

United States Tax Court
http://www.ustaxcourt.gov/

Sample Job Vacancies

Chief Probation Officer

Agency: U.S. District Court for the Eastern District of Louisiana
Salary: $91,781 to $157,999
Location: New Orleans, Louisiana

Duties: Organizes the probation office to ensure expeditious handling of investigative work for the courts, institutions, and parole authorities to include effective case supervision of probationers and parolees. Reviews, analyzes, and interprets requirements for the administration of probation and parole services; promulgates policies, procedures, and guidelines necessary to meet these requirements. Provides specific recommendations to the court in personnel matters, including promotions, salary increases, disciplinary actions, and dismissals; determines that all personnel are carefully selected and adequately trained; makes certain the work of all subordinates is systematically evaluated. Manages the staff of the office. Makes estimates of personnel, space allocation, and operating allowance needs; approves requisitions; certifies vouchers for payment; and maintains appropriate fiscal controls in all matters pertaining to travel expenses and purchases of services, equipment, and supplies. Establishes and maintains cooperative relationships with all components of the criminal justice system to include federal, state, and local law enforcement, correction, and social service agencies.

Qualifications: Applicants must have a bachelor's degree from an accredited college or university. A master's degree is preferred. Applicants must also possess substantial management experience, along with organizational, administrative, and leadership skills. In addition, applicants must possess at least three years of progressively responsible experience in investigation, supervision, counseling, and guidance of offenders in community correction or pretrial programs.

Prior to appointment, the applicant chosen for this position must pass a full FBI background investigation and drug screening. Additionally, the applicant will be subject to random drug screening, as well as an updated FBI background investigation every five years. The chosen applicant must be a U.S. citizen or eligible to work in the United States.

Federal Judicial Staff Attorney

Agency: U.S. Court of Appeals Eleventh Circuit
Salary: $58,734
Location: Atlanta, Georgia

Duties: Assist in the disposition of appeals through the preparation of legal memoranda. The types of cases the office presently handles include direct criminal appeals involving sentencing guidelines and guilt/innocence issues, employment discrimination cases, immigration cases, and Social Security appeals. Staff attorneys work in a highly collegial environment with other recent law school graduates and lawyers coming from judicial clerkships or private practice, as well as with more experienced supervisory staff attorneys and senior management. Employment with the office offers a generous benefits package, civil and criminal law experience at the federal court level, and an environment providing significant responsibility and challenge.

Qualifications: Applicants must possess a Juris Doctor from a law school accredited by the American Bar Association and have excellent academic credentials. They must also have superior analytical, research, and writing skills and be proficient in computer-assisted research and WordPerfect. Good communication and interpersonal skills are essential. You must be a U.S. citizen to qualify for this position.

How to apply: Submit a resume (including law school class rank and/or percentile if available), cover letter, law school transcript, self-edited writing sample, and a list of at least three professional references. Third-year law students are encouraged to apply.

Intake/Customer Services Deputy Clerk
Agency: U.S. District Court of Arizona
Salary: $33,770 to $54,879
Location: Tucson, Arizona

Duties: The Intake/Customer Services Deputy Clerk receives and reviews incoming court documents to determine conformity with appropriate rules, practices and/or requirements; assures assignment of case numbers and randomly assigns cases to judges; routes documents to proper offices/persons after acceptance; scans documents; initiates civil cases on the court's electronic filing system; performs quality review of attorney filings; verifies attorneys' authority to practice before the court; handles sensitive and sealed information; assists attorneys and agencies with electronic filing procedures; maintains several automated case management logs; processes incoming and outgoing mail; updates and maintains paper filings; furnishes information to a wide variety of people within and outside of the court.

Qualifications: Preference will be given to applicants who have a bachelor's degree, preferably in business or public administration or court administration; Spanish speaking ability; experience using automated systems to perform tasks and manage information; strong customer service experience involving significant public contact and personal interaction; excellent oral and written communications skills; attention to detail and ability to independently prioritize and complete multiple tasks in a timely manner; ability to exercise sound judgment and work independently in challenging situations; strong work ethic and ability to work extended hours if needed.

How to apply: Go to our Web site to submit an online application. To be considered for the position, you will need to attach a cover letter, resume, and copy of your last performance evaluation to the online application.

Supreme Court of the United States

One First Street NE
Washington, DC 20543
202-479-3000

★ Web site: http://www.supremecourtus.gov/

★ Job vacancies: http://www.supremecourtus.gov/jobs/career/career.html

★ Internship information: http://www.supremecourtus.gov/jobs/jip/jip.html

★ Fellows program: http://www.fellows.supremecourtus.gov/index.html

★ Volunteer docent program: http://www.supremecourtus.gov/jobs/docentprogram.pdf

The Supreme Court has original jurisdiction in cases involving two or more states; actions or proceedings to which ambassadors, other public ministers, or vice consuls of foreign states are parties; those between the U.S. government and one or more states; and those between states and non-U.S. citizens. In all other cases, it is the court of last resort. The court consists of the chief justice and eight associate judges. Power to appoint a justice is under the jurisdiction of the President of the United States; appointments are made with the advice and consent of the Senate. Court officers assist the court in the performance of its functions.

Sample Job Vacancy

Building Support Specialist
Agency: Supreme Court of the United States
Salary: $37,084 to $53,574
Location: Washington, DC

Duties: Serves on the day shift for Building Support. Oversees building support service programs, including performing cleaning inspections, supervising carpet installation and repair as well as drapery installation and cleaning; and small office moves. Keeps stock records and reorders as necessary. Monitors assigned service contracts. Other duties as assigned.

Qualifications: High school diploma and at least five years building support service required. College education desirable. Familiarity with purchasing equipment, supplies, and other materials associated with cleaning service programs and ability to write concise and accurate reports required. Knowledge of administrative policies covering all areas of cleaning management and the ability to exercise judgment. Employment is subject to successful completion of a security background check.

How to apply: To apply, please fax the following required forms: OF-306 (Declaration for Federal Employment), OF-612 (Optional Application for Federal Employment), and a resume and cover letter. Applications mailed using government postage or through an internal federal government mail system will not be considered.

United States Sentencing Commission

One Columbus Circle NE, South Lobby Suite 2-500
Washington, DC 20002-8002
202-502-4500

★ Web site: http://www.ussc.gov/

★ Job vacancies: http://www.ussc.gov/Jobs.htm

The United States Sentencing Commission establishes sentencing guidelines and policies for the federal courts, advising them as to the appropriate form and severity of punishment for offenders convicted of federal crimes. The commission is composed of seven voting members appointed by the president with the advice and consent of the Senate and two nonvoting members. One of the voting members is appointed chairperson.

The commission promulgates and distributes to federal courts and to the U.S. probation system guidelines to be consulted in determining sentences to be imposed in criminal cases, general policy statements regarding the application of guidelines, and policy statements on the appropriate use of probation and supervised release revocation provisions. In addition, the commission provides training, conducts research on sentencing-related issues, and serves as an information resource for Congress, criminal justice practitioners, and the public.

Sample Job Vacancies

Assistant General Counsel

Agency: Office of General Counsel
Salary: $102,721 to $153,200
Location: Washington, DC

Duties: Responsibilities include, but are not limited to, the following: in-depth legal research related to sentencing and other issues involving analysis of statutes, proposed legislation, case law, and governmental and other reports; preparation of legal memoranda and analytical reports; preparation of oral and written responses to inquiries from commissioners, commission staff, prosecutors, defense attorneys, probation officers, judges, and the public generally; training of practitioners and judges in sentencing and guidelines practice; preparation of memoranda and draft language of proposed amendments to the federal sentencing guidelines; participating or leading staff working groups that focus on new legislation, guideline amendments, and other sentencing issues; and participating as a commission representative in professional conferences.

Qualifications: Applicants must have a minimum of five years of extensive legal experience which is in or directly related to the line of work of this position and which has equipped the applicant with the particular knowledge, skills, and abilities to successfully perform the duties of this position. Applicants must possess excellent oral and written communication skills and the ability to interact successfully with staff at all levels. Good organization and planning skills a must. Applicants must possess a law degree (JD) from a law school accredited by the American Bar Association and be a member of the bar of a state, territory, the District of Columbia, the Commonwealth of Puerto Rico, or a federal court of general jurisdiction.

Research Associate

Agency: Office of Research and Data Collection
Salary: $39,330 to $90,698
Location: Washington, DC

Duties: The incumbent will work with research staff to compile, organize, and document research-related data files and assist in the preparation of data file documentation, statistical tables, and graphic displays and presentations; analyze qualitative and quantitative data and contribute to reports and publications based on that data; review existing data for errors and perform edits and data cleaning of research data files; assist in the production of sentencing statistics; assist in the preparation of reports assessing the sentencing impact of judicial and/or congressional sentencing modifications to the guideline structure and process; assist in the preparation of databases, writing and executing computer program code and working with large data files; research, review, and analyze social science research literature; assist in evaluating research problems and applying or adapting available research methods to solve research problems; assist in the design and development of spreadsheets; and perform support or administrative tasks as needed.

Qualifications: Applicants must have an undergraduate degree from an accredited university or college, and a minimum of one year of experience working in a research environment as either an intern or a paid employee. In order to be considered for this position, applicants must address the following KSAs in a cover letter or separate written narrative statement: experience using a personal computer in a Windows environment; proficiency in using word processing software; experience using a spreadsheet software program; ability to work well in a team setting; ability to communicate effectively orally and in writing. Preference will be given to applicants with one or more of the following areas of experience: academic training in criminal justice, sociology, or a related empirical social science; satisfactory completion of coursework in statistics and/or methodology; experience programming with statistical software packages; experience in the collection of original data and the editing of micro data files; experience with database software packages.

CHAPTER 6

Executive Branch

Of the three branches of the federal government, the executive branch—through the power vested by the U.S. Constitution in the office of the president—has the widest range of responsibilities. Consequently, it employs about 98 percent of all federal civilian employees (excluding Postal Service workers), according to the latest data (2005). The executive branch is composed of the Executive Office of the President, 15 executive cabinet departments and nearly 90 independent agencies, each of which has clearly defined duties. The Executive Office of the President is composed of several offices and councils that aid the president in policy decisions. These include the Office of Management and Budget, which oversees the administration of the federal budget; the National Security Council, which advises the president on matters of national defense; and the Council of Economic Advisers, which makes economic policy recommendations.

Each of the 15 executive cabinet departments administers programs that oversee an aspect of life in the United States. The highest departmental official of each cabinet department, the secretary, is a member of the president's cabinet. These departments are listed by employment size in both Table 6.1 and the following descriptions:

★ **Defense.** This department manages the military forces that protect our country and its interests, including the departments of the Army, Navy, and Air Force and a number of smaller agencies. The civilian workforce employed by the Department of Defense performs various support activities, such as payroll and public relations.

★ **Veterans Affairs.** This department administers programs to aid U.S. veterans and their families, runs the veterans' hospital system, and operates our national cemeteries.

★ **Homeland Security.** This department works to prevent terrorist attacks within the United States, reduce vulnerability to terrorism, and minimize the damage from potential attacks and natural disasters. It also administers the country's immigration policies and oversees the Coast Guard.

★ **Treasury.** This department regulates banks and other financial institutions, administers the public debt, prints currency, and collects federal income taxes.

★ **Justice.** This department works with state and local governments and other agencies to prevent and control crime and ensure public safety against threats both domestic and foreign. It also enforces federal laws, prosecutes cases in federal courts, and runs federal prisons.

★ **Agriculture.** This department promotes U.S. agriculture domestically and internationally, manages forests, researches new ways to grow crops and conserve natural resources, ensures safe meat and poultry products, and leads the federal anti-hunger programs, such as food stamps and free school lunches.

★ **Interior.** This department manages federal lands, including the national parks; runs hydroelectric power systems; and promotes conservation of natural resources.

★ **Health and Human Services.** This department performs health and social science research, assures the safety of drugs and foods other than meat and poultry, and administers Medicare, Medicaid, and numerous other social service programs.

★ **Transportation.** This department sets national transportation policy; plans and funds the construction of highways and mass transit systems; and regulates railroad, aviation, and maritime operations.

★ **Commerce.** This department forecasts the weather, charts the oceans, regulates patents and trademarks, conducts the census, compiles statistics, and promotes U.S. economic growth by encouraging international trade.

★ **State.** This department oversees the nation's embassies and consulates, issues passports, monitors U.S. interests abroad, and represents the United States before international organizations.

★ **Labor.** This department enforces laws guaranteeing fair pay, workplace safety, and equal job opportunity; administers unemployment insurance; regulates pension funds; and collects and analyzes economic data.

★ **Energy.** This department coordinates the national use and provision of energy, oversees the production and disposal of nuclear weapons, and plans for future energy needs.

★ **Housing and Urban Development.** This department funds public housing projects, enforces equal housing laws, and insures and finances mortgages.

★ **Education.** This department monitors and distributes financial aid to schools and students, collects and disseminates data on schools and other education matters, and prohibits discrimination in education.

Numerous independent agencies perform tasks that fall between the jurisdictions of the executive departments and are more efficiently executed by an autonomous agency. Some smaller, but well-known, independent agencies include the Peace Corps, the Securities and Exchange Commission, and the Federal Communications Commission. Although the majority of these agencies are fairly small, employing fewer than 1,000 workers (many employ fewer than 100 workers), some are quite large. The largest independent agencies are the following:

★ **Social Security Administration.** This agency operates various old age, survivor, and disability insurance programs.

★ **National Aeronautics and Space Administration.** This agency oversees aviation research and conducts exploration and research beyond the Earth's atmosphere.

★ **Environmental Protection Agency.** This agency runs programs to control and reduce pollution of the nation's water, air, and lands.

★ **Tennessee Valley Authority.** This agency operates the hydroelectric power system in the Tennessee River Valley.

★ **General Services Administration.** This agency manages and protects federal government property and records.

★ **Federal Deposit Insurance Corporation.** This agency maintains stability of and public confidence in the nation's financial system by insuring deposits and promoting sound banking practices.

Even though the headquarters of most federal departments and agencies are based in the Washington, DC, area, only 16 percent of federal employees worked in the vicinity of the nation's capital in 2007 (see Table 6.1). In addition to federal employees working throughout the United States, about 92,000 (which includes foreign nationals) are assigned overseas, mostly in embassies or defense installations.

TABLE 6.1
Executive Branch Civilian Employment Locations

Agency	Employees in the United States	Employees in Washington, DC, Area
Total	1,774,000	284,000
Executive departments	1,593,000	234,000
Defense, total	623,000	65,000
Army	223,000	19,000
Navy	168,000	24,000
Air Force	152,000	6,000
Other Defense	80,000	16,000
Veterans Affairs	239,000	7,000
Homeland Security	149,000	20,000
Treasury	109,000	14,000
Justice	105,000	23,000
Agriculture	92,000	11,000
Interior	66,000	7,000
Health and Human Services	60,000	28,000
Transportation	53,000	9,000
Commerce	39,000	21,000
Labor	16,000	6,000
Energy	15,000	5,000
State	14,000	12,000
Housing and Urban Development	10,000	3,000

(continued)

(continued)

Agency	Employees in the United States	Employees in Washington, DC, Area
Education	4,000	3,000
Independent agencies	179,000	48,000
Social Security Administration	62,000	2,000
National Aeronautics and Space Administration	18,000	4,000
Environmental Protection Agency	18,000	5,000
Tennessee Valley Authority	12,000	0
General Services Administration	12,000	4,000
Small Business Administration	6,000	1,000
Office of Personnel Management	5,000	2,000
Other	45,000	30,000

Note: This table is based on January 2007 data from U.S. Office of Personnel Management and does not include workers for the U.S. Postal Service. This table and other labor information is available online from the U.S. Bureau of Labor Statistics at http://www.bls.gov.

This chapter describes the organizations within the executive branch and lists street addresses and phone numbers for them as well as listing Web addresses for both general and career information. In order to provide an overview of the kinds of jobs that are available, this chapter also lists sample job vacancies for each of the cabinet departments and the largest independent agencies.

Advisory Council on Historic Preservation

1100 Pennsylvania Avenue NW, Suite 803
Old Post Office Building
Washington, DC 20004
202-606-8503

★ Web site: http://www.achp.gov/

The Advisory Council on Historic Preservation (ACHP) is an independent federal agency that promotes the preservation, enhancement, and productive use of our nation's historic resources, and advises the president and Congress on national historic preservation policy. It employs approximately 45 people.

American Battle Monuments Commission

Courthouse Plaza II, Suite 500
2300 Clarendon Boulevard
Arlington, VA 22201
703-696-6900

★ Web site: http://www.abmc.gov/home.php

★ Job vacancies: http://www.abmc.gov/employment.php

The American Battle Monuments Commission, guardian of the United States' overseas commemorative cemeteries and memorials, honors the service, achievements, and sacrifice of United States
Armed Forces. This small, independent agency commemorates the services of the American Armed
Forces since the U.S. entry into World War I. It establishes suitable memorial shrines and designs,
constructs, operates, and maintains permanent American military burial grounds in foreign countries. The commission also controls the design and construction of U.S. military monuments and
markers in foreign countries by other U.S. citizens and organizations and encourages the maintenance of such monuments and markers by their sponsors.

The American Battle Monuments Commission has two major subordinate regions: the European
Region in Paris, France, and the Mediterranean Region in Rome, Italy. The Washington Office
directs the operations of three separate cemeteries: the Mexico City National Cemetery, the Corozal
American Cemetery in Panama, and the Manila American Cemetery in the Republic of the
Philippines.

The policy-making body of the commission consists of 11 commissioners who are appointed by the
president for an indefinite term and serve without compensation. They meet with the professional
staff of the commission twice annually. The commission has about 400 full-time civilian employees,
most of whom are foreign nationals from the countries where the commission installations are located. Of the 69 full-time civilian employees who are U.S. citizens, only 18 work in the United States.

Broadcasting Board of Governors

330 Independence Avenue SW
Washington, DC 20237
202-203-4400

★ Web site: http://www.bbg.gov/

★ Job opportunities: http://www.bbg.gov/about/jobs/index.html

★ Strategic plan: http://www.bbg.gov/bbg_plan.cfm

Every week, more than 155 million listeners, viewers, and Internet users around the world turn on,
tune in, and log on to U.S. international broadcasting programs. The independent, autonomous
entity that is responsible for all this U.S. government and government-sponsored, nonmilitary,
international broadcasting is the Broadcasting Board of Governors (BBG). The mission of the
BBG is to ensure and safeguard the integrity, quality, and effectiveness of the nation's international

broadcasters. By broadcasting accurate, objective, and balanced news and information about the United States and the world to audiences abroad, the BBG enhances understanding and promotes open communication of information and ideas in support of democracy and the freedom to seek, receive, and impart information worldwide.

The board is composed of nine members appointed by the president and the Secretary of State or a designee. The day-to-day broadcasting activities are carried out by the individual BBG international broadcasters: the Voice of America (VOA), Alhurra, Radio Sawa, Radio Farda, Radio Free Europe/Radio Liberty (RFE/RL), Radio Free Asia (RFA), and Radio and TV Martí, with the assistance of the International Broadcasting Bureau (IBB). BBG employs more than 2,000 people.

Selected BBG Agencies

Radio Free Europe/Radio Liberty (RFE/RL) is a private, nonprofit, U.S. government-funded radio broadcaster to Central, Southeastern, and Eastern Europe; the Caucasus; and Central and Southwestern Asia. RFE/RL broadcasts more than 1,000 hours of programming in 28 languages every week. All RFE/RL broadcasts are also streamed live and on-demand over the Internet. Audio, video, and text in English and the broadcast languages are available from its Web site. Headquartered in Prague, RFE/RL maintains 19 local bureaus and hires more than 750 freelancers.

★ Web site: http://www.rferl.org/

★ Job vacancies and internships: http://www.rferl.org/jobs/

The **Voice of America** broadcasts on radio and television in 44 languages to an estimated 134 million people each week. VOA radio provides around-the-clock news and features. It focuses on countries that lack a strong, independent media. VOA-TV produces programs in more than 44 languages, including news reports, feature magazines, and live call-in shows. There are 22 domestic and 16 overseas correspondents, in addition to more than 90 part-time reporters, called *stringers*.

TV broadcasts include original and acquired programs that reflect American life along with discussions on U.S. foreign and domestic policies. VOA's Web site provides continually updated news and information with photos, audio, and video.

★ Web site: http://www.voanews.com/

★ Internships: http://www.voanews.com/english/About/2006-08-09-interns.cfm

Other BBG Agencies

Alhurra

http://www.alhurra.com/index.aspx

Office of Cuba Broadcasting (Radio and TV Martí)

http://www.martinoticias.com/

Radio Farda

http://www.radiofarda.com/

Radio Free Asia

http://www.rfa.org/english/

Radio Sawa

http://www.radiosawa.com//

Central Intelligence Agency

Washington, DC 20505
703-482-0623

★ Web site: http://www.cia.gov/

★ Job vacancies: https://www.cia.gov/careers/jobs/view-all-jobs/index.html

★ Student opportunities: https://www.cia.gov/careers/student-opportunities/index.html

★ Career information: https://www.cia.gov/careers/index.html

★ How to apply: https://www.cia.gov/careers/jobs/how-to-apply.html

★ Strategic intent: https://www.cia.gov/about-cia/strategic-intent-2007-2011.html

The Central Intelligence Agency (CIA) collects, evaluates, and disseminates vital information on political, military, economic, scientific, and other developments abroad needed to safeguard national security. Under the direction of the president or the National Security Council, the CIA advises the National Security Council in matters concerning intelligence activities and conducts counterintelligence activities outside the United States. The CIA has no police, subpoena, or law enforcement powers or internal security functions.

In addition to "spies" (clandestine service), the CIA employs a wide variety of professionals and support staff, including attorneys, auditors, bookbinders, cartographers, cost analysts, counterterrorism analysts, crime and counternarcotics analysts, digital imaging technicians, electrical engineers, electronics specialists, fitness specialists, foreign language instructors, foreign media analysts, geographers, graphic designers, librarians, materials engineers, medical officers, multimedia designers, polygraph examiners, prepress specialists, psychologists, security professionals, software specialists, and video production specialists. Although the exact number of CIA employees is classified information, it is estimated that 20,000 people work for the CIA.

Selected CIA Agencies

The **Directorate of Intelligence and Analysis** is the analytical branch of the CIA and is responsible for the production and dissemination of all source intelligence analysis on key foreign issues. It coordinates the relationships between elements of the intelligence community and the intelligence or security services of foreign governments or international organizations on all matters involving intelligence related to national security or involving intelligence acquired through clandestine means.

★ Web site: https://www.cia.gov/offices-of-cia/intelligence-analysis/index.html

The **Directorate of Science and Technology** brings technical power and expertise to clandestine collection and analysis on the most pressing intelligence problems. It creates and applies innovative technology in support of the intelligence collection mission.

★ Web site: https://www.cia.gov/offices-of-cia/science-technology/index.html

★ Internships: https://www.cia.gov/offices-of-cia/science-technology/internship-program.html

★ Career information: https://www.cia.gov/offices-of-cia/science-technology/careers.html

The **Directorate of Support** builds and operates facilities. It ensures robust, secure communications over multiple networks connecting officers sitting in dispersed locations; acquires and ships a full range of critical equipment; secures buildings, people, data, and networks; and helps hire, train, and assign CIA officers for each directorate. It also manages the "businesses" within the CIA: contracts and acquisitions, financial services, administrative support, and the CIA phone company.

★ Web site: https://www.cia.gov/offices-of-cia/mission-support/index.html

The **National Clandestine Service** operates as the clandestine arm of the CIA and serves as the national authority for the coordination and evaluation of clandestine human intelligence operations across the intelligence community. The NCS supports our country's security and foreign policy interests by conducting clandestine activities to collect information that is not obtainable through other means. The NCS also conducts counterintelligence and special activities as authorized by the president.

★ Web site: https://www.cia.gov/offices-of-cia/clandestine-service/index.html

Other CIA Agency

Center for the Study of Intelligence

https://www.cia.gov/library/center-for-the-study-of-intelligence/index.html

Commodity Futures Trading Commission

Three Lafayette Centre
1155 Twenty-first Street NW
Washington, DC 20581
202-418-5000

★ Web site: http://www.cftc.gov/

★ Job vacancies: http://www.cftc.gov/aboutthecftc/careers/currentopenings/index.htm

★ How to apply/internships: http://www.cftc.gov/aboutthecftc/careers/howtoapply.html

★ Career information: http://www.cftc.gov/aboutthecftc/careers/index.htm

★ Strategic plan: http://www.cftc.gov/aboutthecftc/2009strategicplan-txt.html

The Commodity Futures Trading Commission (CFTC) protects market users and the public from fraud, manipulation, and abusive practices related to the sale of commodity futures and options in order to foster open, competitive, and financially sound commodity futures and option markets. CFTC regulates commodity futures trading and option markets in the United States. The CFTC monitors markets and market participants closely and, in addition to its headquarters office in Washington, DC, maintains offices in Chicago, Kansas City, and New York, cities where futures exchanges are located.

The commission has six major operating components: the Divisions of Market Oversight, Clearing and Intermediary Oversight, and Enforcement, and the Offices of the Executive Director, General Counsel, and Chief Economist. The commission consists of five commissioners who are appointed by the president, with the advice and consent of the Senate. The president designates one commissioner to serve as chairperson. CFTC employs approximately 400 people as attorneys, auditors, economists, futures trading specialists and investigators, and management professionals.

Consumer Product Safety Commission

4330 East-West Highway
Bethesda, MD 20814
301-504-7923

★ Web site: http://www.cpsc.gov/

★ Job vacancies: https://jobs1.quickhire.com/scripts/cpsc.exe

★ Student jobs: http://www.cpsc.gov/about/student.html

★ Student volunteer programs: http://www.cpsc.gov/about/volunteer.html

★ How to apply: http://www.cpsc.gov/about/howto.html

The Consumer Product Safety Commission (CPSC) protects the public against unreasonable risks of injury from consumer products; assists consumers in evaluating the comparative safety of consumer products; develops uniform safety standards for consumer products and minimizes conflicting state and local regulations; and promotes research and investigation into the causes and prevention of product-related deaths, illnesses, and injuries. CPSC employs about 400 people as engineers, compliance officers, toxicologists/chemists, mathematicians/statisticians, product safety investigators, pharmacologists, attorneys, computer specialists, and administrative and support staff. In addition to its headquarters, the CPSC has three regional offices in New York, New York; Chicago, Illinois; and Oakland, California. The CPSC product-testing laboratory is in Gaithersburg, Maryland.

Corporation for National and Community Service

1201 New York Avenue NW
Washington, DC 20525
202-606-5000

★ Web site: http://www.nationalservice.org/

★ Job vacancies: http://www.nationalservice.org/about/employment/index.asp

★ Strategic plan: http://www.nationalservice.org/about/focus_areas/index.asp

The Corporation for National and Community Service (CNCS) fosters civic responsibility, strengthens the ties that bind us together as a people, and provides educational opportunity for those who make a substantial commitment to service. CNCS administers the Senior Corps, AmeriCorps, and Learn and Serve America programs. It improves lives, strengthens communities, and fosters civic engagement through service and volunteering. CNCS employs approximately 400 people.

Selected CNCS Agency

AmeriCorps, the domestic Peace Corps, engages more than 75,000 Americans each year in intensive results-oriented service. AmeriCorps members recruit, train, and supervise community volunteers, tutor and mentor youth, build affordable housing, teach computer skills, clean parks and streams, run after-school programs, and help communities to respond to disasters and nonprofit groups to become self-sustaining. In exchange for a year of full-time service, AmeriCorps members earn an education award of $4,725 that they can use to pay for college or graduate school or to pay back qualified student loans.

AmeriCorps state and national members are selected by and serve with local and national organizations like Habitat for Humanity, the American Red Cross, Big Brothers/Big Sisters, and Boys and Girls Clubs. Others serve in AmeriCorps VISTA (Volunteers in Service to America) and AmeriCorps NCCC (the National Civilian Community Corps).

★ Web site: http://www.americorps.org/

★ Volunteering for Americorps: http://www.americorps.org/about/programs/index.asp

Other CNCS Agencies

Learn and Serve America

http://www.learnandserve.org/

Senior Corps

http://www.seniorcorps.org/

Council of Economic Advisers

G Street NW
Washington, DC 20502
202-395-5084

★ Web site: http://www.whitehouse.gov/cea/

★ Internships: http://www.whitehouse.gov/administration/eop/cea/internships/

The Council of Economic Advisers analyzes the national economy and its various segments, advises the president on economic developments, appraises economic programs and policies of the federal government, recommends policies for economic growth and stability to the president, assists in preparing the president's economic reports to the Congress, and prepares an annual report. The council consists of three members appointed by the president with the advice and consent of the Senate. The president designates one council member to be chairperson. The council employs about 25 people.

Council on Environmental Quality

722 Jackson Place NW
Washington, DC 20503
202-395-5750

★ Web site: http://www.whitehouse.gov/ceq/

The Council on Environmental Quality (CEQ) develops policies addressing the nation's social, economic, and environmental priorities, with the goal of improving the quality of federal decision making. CEQ evaluates, coordinates, and mediates federal activities; and advises and assists the president on both national and international environmental policy matters. The council employs about 20 people.

Court Services and Offender Supervision Agency for the District of Columbia

633 Indiana Avenue NW
Washington, DC 20004-2902
202-220-5300

★ Web site: http://www.csosa.gov/

The mission of Court Services and Offender Supervision Agency for the District of Columbia (CSOSA) is to increase public safety, prevent crime, reduce recidivism, and support the fair administration of justice in close collaboration with the community. This agency employs approximately 1,150 people. To find out about job vacancies at this agency, click the Employment link on its Web site.

Defense Nuclear Facilities Safety Board

625 Indiana Avenue NW, Suite 700
Washington, DC 20004
202-694-7000

★ Web site: http://www.dnfsb.gov

The Defense Nuclear Facilities Safety Board reviews and evaluates the content and implementation of standards for defense nuclear facilities of the Department of Energy (DOE); investigates any event or practice at these facilities that may adversely affect public health and safety; and reviews and monitors the design, construction, and operation of facilities. The board is composed of five members appointed by the president with the advice and consent of the Senate. Members of the board are appointed from among U.S. citizens who are respected experts in the field of nuclear safety.

The board makes recommendations to the Secretary of Energy concerning DOE defense nuclear facilities to ensure adequate protection of public health and safety. In the event that any aspect of operations, practices, or occurrences reviewed by the board is determined to present an imminent or severe threat to public health and safety, the board transmits its recommendations directly to the president. The board employs more than 90 people.

Department of Agriculture

1400 Independence Avenue SW
Washington, DC 20250
202-720-4623

★ Web site: http://www.usda.gov

★ Internships: http://www.usda.gov/da/employ/intern.htm

★ Job categories: http://www.usda.gov/da/employ/careergr.pdf

★ Career information: http://www.usda.gov/wps/portal/!ut/p/_s.7_0_A/
7_0_1OB?navtype=MA&navid=CAREERS

★ Strategic plan: http://www.ocfo.usda.gov/usdasp/usdasp.htm

Through its 17 agencies and more than 300 programs worldwide, the Department of Agriculture (USDA) helps develop rural areas; assists Americans in rural areas to rent or purchase housing through loan and guarantee programs; helps feed hungry Americans by providing food stamps and free or reduced-cost school meals; and inspects meat, poultry, and egg products for safety. It also works to improve and maintain farm income and to develop and expand markets abroad for U.S. agricultural products.

The USDA also serves as steward of the nation's 192 million acres of national forests and rangelands through the Forest Service, encourages voluntary efforts to protect natural resources on land that is privately owned, conducts research on everything from human nutrition to new crop technologies, and publishes dietary guidelines for Americans in conjunction with the Department of Health and Human Services.

The USDA offers careers in dozens of areas, including agricultural business, agricultural marketing, agronomy, animal sciences, archaeology, chemistry, consumer safety, economics, engineering, food program management, food technology, forestry, geology and hydrology, international trade economics, landscape architecture, mathematics and statistics, nutrition, plant pathology and physiology, soil sciences and conservation, veterinary medicine, and wildlife biology, among others. The administrative side of the USDA offers opportunities in areas such as accounting and auditing, computer sciences, contracting procurement, criminal justice, management and program analysis, personnel management, and public affairs. Jobs should be plentiful at the USDA in coming years because it anticipates the retirement or the eligibility for retirement of a substantial portion of its more than 103,300 employees within the next few years.

Students who are looking for work can find many opportunities at the USDA. In a typical year, the USDA employs 7,500 or more students in a variety of work and internship positions. Most students are paid between $10 and $11 per hour. Selected positions can lead directly into full-time federal employment, and in some cases new graduates are reimbursed for tuition, books, and incidental educational costs if they agree to work at the USDA for a certain period of time. The Forest Service employs more students and interns than any other agency at the USDA.

Selected USDA Agencies

The **Agricultural Marketing Service** provides standardization, grading, and market news for six commodity programs: cotton, dairy, fruit and vegetable, livestock and seed, poultry, and tobacco. It also purchases commodities for federal food programs, collects and analyzes data about pesticide residue levels in agricultural commodities, and helps solve problems affecting U.S. and world agricultural transportation. To find information about job vacancies with this agency, click on the Opportunities link on the following Web site:

★ Web site: http://www.ams.usda.gov

The **Agricultural Research Service** is the main in-house scientific research agency for the USDA. It conducts research in areas such as protecting crops and livestock from pests and disease, improving the quality and safety of agricultural products, determining the best nutrition for people of all ages, and sustaining soil and other natural resources. With 2,100 scientists and 6,000 other employees, the ARS conducts 1,200 research projects within 22 national programs. It has offices in Albany, California; Fort Collins, Colorado; Athens, Georgia; Peoria, Illinois; Beltsville, Maryland; Stoneville, Mississippi; Wyndmoor, Pennsylvania; and College Station, Texas.

★ Web site: http://www.ars.usda.gov

★ Job vacancies: http://www.ars.usda.gov/careers/docs.htm?docid=11797

★ Student and summer employment: http://www.ars.usda.gov/careers/docs.htm?docid=1345

★ Career information: http://www.ars.usda.gov/Careers/Careers.htm

★ Receive new job vacancies by e-mail: http://www.ars.usda.gov/Careers/docs.htm?docid=1358

★ Recruitment calendar: http://www.ars.usda.gov/Careers/docs.htm?docid=1364

The **Farm Service Agency** (FSA) administers farm commodity, disaster, and conservation programs for farmers and ranchers through its offices across the country. These programs include farm emergency, ownership, marketing, and operating loans; price support programs; financial incentives for farmers and ranchers to employ sound land conservation practices; and assistance for farmers and ranchers whose crops and livestock are harmed by the weather.

★ Web site: http://www.fsa.usda.gov

★ Job vacancies: http://jobsearch.usajobs.opm.gov/a9agfsa.asp

★ Service Center locator: http://offices.sc.egov.usda.gov/locator/app?state=us&agency=fsa

The **Food and Nutrition Service** (FNS) administers federal food assistance programs that serve one in six Americans, primarily low-income adults and children. It provides food stamps to buy food at retail stores, free or reduced-price school breakfasts and lunches for children from low-income families, commodities for distribution to food banks and soup kitchens, cash and commodities for food delivered to senior citizens through senior citizen centers or meals-on-wheels programs, and nutritious food supplements for low-income women who are pregnant or postpartum and their infants and children up to five years of age. The FNS also supports nutrition education efforts and coordinates nutrition policy within the USDA.

★ Web site: http://www.fns.usda.gov/fns

★ Job opportunities: http://www.fns.usda.gov/hr/

★ Career information: http://www.fns.usda.gov/hr/careers.htm

The **Forest Service** manages 193 million acres of the nation's forests and grasslands. It employs more than 30,000 people in careers that include forestry, biology, education, firefighting, accounting, computer science, law enforcement, recreation, geographic information, and more. Many temporary employees are required for seasonal work such as fighting wildfires and conducting recreation programs. The Forest Service also employs more students and interns than any other agency in the Department of Agriculture. The Forest Service has offices in Juneau, Alaska; Albany, California; San Francisco, California; Fort Collins, Colorado; Lakewood, Colorado; Atlanta, Georgia; St. Paul, Minnesota; Missoula, Montana; Albuquerque, New Mexico; Asheville, North Carolina; Portland, Oregon; Radnor, Pennsylvania; Ogden, Utah; Madison, Wisconsin; Milwaukee, Wisconsin; and Rio Piedras, Puerto Rico.

★ Web site: http://www.fs.fed.us

★ Job vacancies: http://jobsearch.usajobs.opm.gov/a9fs.asp

★ Student employment programs: http://www.fs.fed.us/fsjobs/jobs_students.shtml

★ Volunteer information: http://www.fs.fed.us/volunteer/volunteer-opportunities/index.shtml

★ Career information: http://www.fs.fed.us/fsjobs/

★ How to apply: http://www.fs.fed.us/fsjobs/employ/asap/User_Guide_applicant.doc

★ Strategic plan: http://www.fs.fed.us/plan/

Other USDA Agencies

Animal and Plant Health Inspection Service

http://www.aphis.usda.gov

Center for Nutrition Policy and Promotion

http://www.cnpp.usda.gov/

Cooperative State Research, Education, and Extension Service

http://www.csrees.usda.gov

Economic Research Service

http://www.ers.usda.gov

Food Safety and Inspection Service

http://www.fsis.usda.gov

Foreign Agricultural Service

http://www.fas.usda.gov

Grain Inspection, Packers, and Stockyards Administration

http://www.usda.gov/gipsa

Marketing and Regulatory Programs Business Services

http://www.aphis.usda.gov/mrpbs/

National Agricultural Library

http://www.nalusda.gov

National Agricultural Statistics Service

http://www.nass.usda.gov/index.asp

Natural Resources Conservation Service

http://www.nrcs.usda.gov

Research, Education, and Economics

http://www.ree.usda.gov/

Risk Management Agency

http://www.rma.usda.gov

Rural Development

http://www.rurdev.usda.gov

Sample Job Vacancies

Animal Health Technician
Agency: Animal and Plant Health Inspection Service
Salary: $30,772 to $54,879
Location: Atlanta, Michigan

Duties: Assists Veterinary Medical Officers (VMO) with inspection and testing of livestock, poultry, and other avian species to detect animal diseases and parasites. Supervises cleaning and disinfecting of vehicles and premises that are contaminated by disease organisms or as a precautionary measure. Assists with conducting primary investigations, issuing warning notices, and executing violation notices. Contacts owners of diseased or exposed animals or poultry. As required, collects data for the National Animal Health Monitoring System, trains and/or provides technical supervision to lower graded technicians, and serves as a member of a Regional Emergency Animal Disease Eradication Organization taskforce.

Special conditions: As a condition of employment, a background investigation may be required for this position. Valid state driver's license is required at time of hiring. The names and numbers of two professional and two character references are required with application package. This position is subject to unscheduled overnight details of undetermined lengths in the event of animal health emergencies or other conditions requiring immediate response. Selectees will be required to attend a veterinary services orientation session and at least three formal veterinary services courses within the span of nine months to one year. Selectees will be subject to a mobility agreement that will be in effect for three years from the date of their appointment.

Ecologist
Agency: Forest Service
Salary: $46,625 to $73,329
Location: New Ellenton, South Carolina

Duties: Performs duties related to the evaluation and management of ecosystems. Analyzes biological components and processes in the context of ecosystems including environmental factors, physical-chemical relationships, and social relationships. Uses quantitative and systems analysis techniques to predict effects of planned or natural changes in ecosystems and to develop understanding of and solutions to ecological problems. Prepares a variety of written reports, plans, agreements and/or environmental impact statements that assess environmental conditions and impacts. Performs duties such as surveying for threatened, endangered, sensitive, and rare plants; recommending mitigation measures; monitoring selected populations; or developing conservation plans.

Qualifications: Successful completion of full four-year course of study in an accredited college or university leading to a bachelor's or higher degree that included a major field of study in biology or a related field of science underlying ecological research.

How to apply: Applications for this position are being processed through an on-line applicant assessment system that has been specifically configured for USDA Forest Service applicants. Even if you have already developed a resume in USAJOBS, you will need to access this online system to complete the application process.

Department of the Air Force

1690 Air Force Pentagon
Washington, DC 20330-1670
703-697-6061

★ Web site: http://www.af.mil/

★ Job vacancies: http://jobsearch.usajobs.opm.gov/a9af.asp

★ Air Force Personnel Center: http://ask.afpc.randolph.af.mil/

★ Air Force civilian employment: https://ww2.afpc.randolph.af.mil/resweb/

★ Internships: http://gum.afpc.randolph.af.mil/cgi-bin/askafpc.cfg/php/enduser/
std_adp.php?p_faqid=7707

★ Summer employment: https://ww2.afpc.randolph.af.mil/resweb/summer/summer.htm

★ Civilian application guide "job kit:" http://ask.afpc.randolph.af.mil/docs/civemploy/resweb/
jobkit/5240_JobKit.pdf

★ Resume writer: https://ww2.afpc.randolph.af.mil/resweb/resume/resume.htm

★ Receive job information via e-mail: https://ww2.afpc.randolph.af.mil/resweb/cans.htm

The Department of the Air Force defends the United States through control and exploitation of air, space, and cyberspace. It is administered by a civilian secretary appointed by the president and is supervised by a military chief of staff. The U.S. Air Force employs more than 150,000 civilians in a full range of fields, including financial management, information management, public affairs, engineering, computers/communications, sports/fitness recreation management, contracting, logistics, education, human resource management, child development, science, technical training, lodging management, community planning, architecture, manpower management, safety, security, occupational health, family matters, history, and special investigation.

Selected Air Force Agencies

The **Air Education and Training Command** (AETC) recruits, trains, and educates quality people for the aerospace force and the nation. It provides basic military training, initial and advanced technical training, flying training, and professional military and degree-granting professional education. AETC also conducts joint, medical service, readiness, and Air Force security assistance training. It employs more than 60,000 active duty members, 14,000 civilians, 7,300 reservists, and 11,500 contractors.

★ Web site: http://www.aetc.af.mil/

★ Air Force ROTC: http://www.afrotc.com/

The **Air Force Academy** offers degrees in basic sciences, humanities, engineering, social sciences, and in interdisciplinary studies. The faculty consists of approximately 565 professors and instructors, of whom 70 percent are military and 30 percent are civilian. Each summer, through the Cadet

Summer Research Program, approximately 190 selected cadets spend five weeks at various Air Force, Department of Defense, and other research facilities around the world.

★ Web site: http://www.usafa.af.mil/index.cfm?catname=AFA%20Homepage

★ Job vacancies: http://www.usafa.af.mil/10abw/10msg/mss/dpc/?catname=dpc

The **Air Force Special Operations Command** (AFSOC) is the nation's specialized air power. The command provides combat search and rescue, agile combat support, information warfare, precision aerospace fires, airborne radio and television broadcasts for psychological operations, specialized aerospace mobility, and refueling to unified commands. It delivers foreign aviation instructors who provide other governments with military expertise for their internal development. AFSOC employs approximately 12,900 active-duty, Air Force Reserve, Air National Guard, and civilian personnel.

★ Web site: http://www2.afsoc.af.mil/

Other Air Force Agencies

Air Combat Command

http://www.acc.af.mil/

Air Force Cyber Command

http://www.afcyber.af.mil/

Air Force Materiel Command

http://www.afmc.af.mil/

Air Force Reserve Command

http://www.afrc.af.mil/

Air Force Space Command

http://www.afspc.af.mil/

Air Mobility Command

http://www.amc.af.mil/

Air National Guard

http://www.ang.af.mil/

Pacific Air Forces

http://www.pacaf.af.mil/

U.S. Air Forces in Europe

http://www.usafe.af.mil/

Department of the Army

1500 Army Pentagon
Washington, DC 20310
703-695-6518

★ Web site: http://www.army.mil/

★ Civilian job vacancies: http://www.cpol.army.mil/

★ Student information: http://acpol.army.mil/employment/student_overview.htm

★ Internships and fellowships: http://acpol.army.mil/employment/intern_overview.htm

★ Civilian career intern program: https://ncweb.ria.army.mil/dainterns/default.htm

★ Career information: http://acpol.army.mil/employment/index.htm

★ Army job application kit: http://cpol.army.mil/library/employment/jobkit

The Department of the Army organizes, trains, and equips active duty and reserve forces for the preservation of peace, security, and the defense of the country. The U.S. Army focuses on military land operations; its soldiers must be trained with modern arms and equipment and be ready to respond quickly. It also administers programs aimed at protecting the environment, improving waterway navigation, flood and beach erosion control, and water resource development. It provides military assistance to federal, state, and local government agencies, including natural disaster relief assistance. The U.S. Army generally moves in to an area, secures it, and instills order before it leaves. It has approximately 250,000 civilians serving in nearly 80 countries.

The U.S. Army conducts both operational and institutional missions. The operational army consists of numbered armies, corps, divisions, brigades, and battalions that conduct full-spectrum operations around the world. The institutional army supports the operational army. Institutional organizations provide the infrastructure necessary to raise, train, equip, deploy, and ensure the readiness of all army forces. The training base provides military skills and professional education to every soldier as well as members of sister services and allied forces. It also allows the army to expand rapidly in time of war. The industrial base provides world-class equipment and logistics, and U.S. Army installations provide the power-projection platforms required to deploy land forces promptly to support combatant commanders. Once those forces are deployed, the institutional army provides the logistics needed to support them.

Selected Army Agencies

The **U.S. Army Forces Command** trains, mobilizes, deploys, sustains, transforms, and reconstitutes conventional forces, providing relevant and ready land power to combatant commanders worldwide in defense of the nation at home and abroad. Commands include: U.S. Army Materiel Command, U.S. Army Training and Doctrine Command, Eighth U.S. Army, U.S. Army Europe and 7th Army, U.S. Army Pacific, U.S. Army Special Operations Command, U.S. Army Space and Missile Defense Command, U.S. Army Military Surface Deployment and Distribution Command, U.S. Army South, U.S. Army Central, and U.S. Army North. Specific information on each of these commands can be obtained from the Military Links tab on the following Web site:

★ Web site: www.forscom.army.mil/

★ Job vacancies: http://www.goarmy.com/JobCatList.do?redirect=true&fw=careerindex&bl=

The **U.S. Army Corps of Engineers** (USACE) is made up of approximately 22,000 civilian and 650 military men and women who work hand in hand as leaders in engineering and environmental matters. Its diverse workforce of biologists, engineers, geologists, hydrologists, natural resource managers, and other professionals provide quality responsive engineering services to the country, including planning, designing, building, and operating water resources and other civil works projects (navigation, flood control, environmental protection, disaster response, and so on); designing and managing the construction of military facilities for the U.S. Army and Air Force; and providing design and construction management support for other defense and federal agencies.

★ Web site: http://www.usace.army.mil/

★ Job vacancies: http://www.usace.army.mil/CEHR/Pages/WorkforUSACE.aspx

U.S. Army Europe and 7th Army (USAREUR) is the U.S. European Command's primary land component. It monitors armed conflicts and potential flashpoints throughout a 98-nation area. The U.S. Army's largest forward-deployed command, USAREUR supports NATO and U.S. bilateral, multinational, and unilateral objectives. It supports U.S. Army forces in the European Command area; receives and assists in the reception, staging, and onward movement and integration of U.S. forces; establishes, operates, and expands operational lines of communication; and supports U.S. combat commanders and joint and combined commanders.

★ Web site: http://www.hqusareur.army.mil/

★ Civilian employment: http://cpolrhp.belvoir.army.mil/eur/

The **U.S. Military Academy** is located in West Point, New York. The course lasts for four years, during which the cadets receive a general education and theoretical and practical training as junior officers. Cadets who complete the course satisfactorily receive the degree of Bachelor of Science and a commission as second lieutenant in the U.S. Army. West Point employs approximately 500 faculty.

★ Web site: http://www.usma.edu/

★ Civilian employment: http://www.usma.edu/cpac/

Other Army Agencies

Army Criminal Investigation Command

http://www.cid.army.mil/

Army Intelligence and Security Command

http://www.inscom.army.mil/

Army Medical Department

http://www.armymedicine.army.mil/

Army National Guard

http://www.arng.army.mil/

Army Reserve

http://www.armyreserve.army.mil/ARWEB

Military District of Washington

http://www.mdw.army.mil/

Training and Doctrine Command

http://www-tradoc.army.mil/

Department of Commerce

1401 Constitution Avenue NW
Washington, DC 20230
202-482-2000

★ Web site: http://www.doc.gov/

★ Job vacancies: http://jobsearch.usajobs.opm.gov/a9cm.asp

★ Student career opportunities: http://hr.commerce.gov/Careers/StudentCareerOpportunities/
index.htm

★ Senior professional opportunities: http://hr.commerce.gov/Careers/
SeniorProfessionalOpportunities/index.htm

★ Career information: http://www.commerce.gov/JobsCareerOpportunities/index.htm

The Department of Commerce (DOC) promotes the nation's international trade, economic growth, and technological advancement. The department provides a wide variety of programs. It offers assistance and information to increase America's competitiveness in the world economy; administers programs to prevent unfair foreign trade competition; provides social and economic statistics and analyses for business and government planners; provides research and support for the increased use of scientific, engineering, and technological development; works to improve our understanding of the Earth's physical environment and oceanic resources; grants patents and registers trademarks; develops policies and conducts research on telecommunications; provides assistance to promote domestic economic development; and assists in the growth of minority businesses.

The DOC employed approximately 50,000 civilians in 2007, 20,000 of them in the Washington, DC, metropolitan area, according to the U.S. Office of Personnel Management. The DOC employs a wide variety of people, including accountants, agriculture engineers, attorneys, auditors, budget analysts, business development specialists, cartographers, chemical or material engineers, chemists, computer hardware and software engineers, computer scientists, computer specialists, criminal investigators, economists, electrical engineers, electronic engineers, engineering technicians, export compliance specialists, financial analysts, fishery or wildlife biologists, geodesists, geographers, geophysicists, international trade specialists, mathematicians, mechanical engineers, metallurgy engineers, meteorologists, oceanographers, physical scientists, physicists, program analysts and management analysts, statisticians, telecommunications policy analysts, textile engineers, and transportation and construction engineers.

Selected DOC Agencies

The **Bureau of Economic Analysis** is the nation's economic accountant, integrating and interpreting a variety of source data to draw a complete picture of the U.S. economy. It provides information on such key issues as economic growth, regional development, and the nation's position in the world economy.

★ Web site: http://www.bea.gov/

★ Job vacancies: http://www.bea.gov/jobs/index.htm

The **Census Bureau** serves as the leading source of quality data about the nation's people and economy. It compiles and disseminates current statistics on population, housing, U.S. foreign trade, state and local governments, manufacturers, and transportation, among others. The bureau employs more than 6,000 employees.

★ Web site: http://www.census.gov/

★ Job vacancies: http://jobsearch.usajobs.opm.gov/a9census.asp

★ Student information: http://www.census.gov/hrd/www/jobs/student.html

★ Postdoctoral research programs: http://www.census.gov/hrd/www/jobs/prp.html

★ Census field jobs (temporary): http://www.census.gov/hrd/www/jobs/fo.html

★ Career information: http://www.census.gov/hrd/www/jobs/emp_opp.html

The **Economics and Statistics Administration** advises the government on matters relating to economic developments and forecasts and on the development of macroeconomic and microeconomic policy. ESA provides broad and targeted economic data, analyses and forecasts for use by government agencies, businesses, and others, as well as develops domestic and international economic policy. This agency includes the Census Bureau and the Bureau of Economic Analysis.

★ Web site: http://www.esa.doc.gov/

★ Job vacancies: http://www.esa.doc.gov/employment.cfm

★ Student internships: http://www.esa.doc.gov/employment.cfm#internships

The **National Oceanic and Atmospheric Administration** (NOAA) conducts research, collects data, and makes predictions about our environment. NOAA works on a global scale, over a wide spectrum of disciplines. It also serves as the steward of the nation's oceans and coasts while assisting their economic development.

Unknown to many, NOAA has its own commissioned officer corps, NOAA Corps, the smallest of the seven uniformed services. NOAA Corps officers operate ships, fly aircraft, lead mobile field parties, conduct diving operations, manage research projects, and serve in staff positions throughout NOAA. Sea duty is common, and there is a two-year service obligation after successful completion of a basic officer training class.

★ Web site: http://www.noaa.gov/

★ Job vacancies: http://jobsearch.usajobs.opm.gov/a9noaa.asp

★ NOAA Commissioned Officer Corps: http://www.noaacorps.noaa.gov/

★ NOAA Marine Operations: http://www.moc.noaa.gov/shipjobs/index.htm

★ NOAA Fisheries Law Enforcement: http://www.nmfs.noaa.gov/ole/

The **U.S. Patent and Trademark Office** (USPTO) promotes the progress of science and the arts by giving inventors exclusive rights to their inventions for a specific period of time. By issuing patents, the USPTO encourages technological advancement through incentives to invent, invest in, and disclose new technology worldwide. By registering trademarks, the agency assists businesses in protecting their investments, promoting goods and services, and safeguarding consumers against deception in the marketplace. Approximately 8,916 people are employed in this agency. In 2006, the employees included 4,883 patent examiners and 413 trademark examiners. Patent examiners are generally scientists and engineers who do not necessarily hold law degrees. In contrast, all trademark examiners must be licensed attorneys.

★ Web address: http://www.uspto.gov/

★ Job vacancies: http://jobsearch.usajobs.opm.gov/a9pto.asp

Other DOC Agencies

Bureau of Industry and Security

http://www.bis.doc.gov/

Economic Development Administration

http://www.eda.gov/

International Trade Administration

http://trade.gov/index.asp

Marine and Aviation Operations

http://www.omao.noaa.gov/

Minority Business Development Agency

http://www.mbda.gov/

National Environmental Satellite, Data, and Information Service

http://www.nesdis.noaa.gov/

National Institute of Standards and Technology

http://www.nist.gov/

National Marine Fisheries Service

http://www.nmfs.noaa.gov/

National Ocean Service

http://oceanservice.noaa.gov/

National Technical Information Service

http://www.ntis.gov/

National Telecommunications and Information Administration

http://www.ntia.doc.gov/

National Weather Service

http://www.nws.noaa.gov/

Sample Job Vacancies

Meteorologist

Agency: National Weather Service
Salary: $31,934 to $91,212
Location: Oberlin, Ohio

Duties: Makes independent meteorological decisions in an accurate and timely manner; conveys complex meteorological information in an understandable manner, both verbally and in writing. Provides meteorological consultation and advice to senior level air traffic controllers concerning forecast or actual adverse weather conditions that affect air traffic operations or aircraft safety. Conducts weather training sessions for controllers with the facility and ensures the efficient collection and distribution of pilot reports. Must have a strong working knowledge of computer principles to implement or modify applications software, manage files and databases, and operate advanced meteorological workstations.

Qualifications: Bachelor's degree in meteorology, atmospheric science, or other natural science major. Applicants also must have one year of specialized experience equivalent to the next lower grade level. Specialized experience must have equipped the applicant with the following knowledge, skills, and abilities:

★ Knowledge of operational meteorology, hydrology and NWS service programs

★ The ability to develop or improve programs and services as they relate to external and internal customers of an operational hydro-meteorological office

★ The ability to contribute to the understanding of hydro-meteorological knowledge through effectively communicating applied research

★ The ability to work effectively in a team environment

Supervisory Telephone Interviewer

Agency: Bureau of the Census
Salary: $17.77 to $23.10 per hour
Location: Frederick County, Maryland

Duties: The incumbent provides technical supervision and assigns work to telephone interviewers involved in data capture for various surveys. Provides answers to survey-specific questions and general questions about the computer system. Conducts interviewer training sessions. Instructs interviewers in the proper use of interviewing procedures. Conducts recruiting sessions. Monitors interviewing staff and provides feedback to improve performance. Keys interviewer monitoring forms and prepares report to summarize the results. Responds to and documents all inquiry calls from survey respondents to verify or clarify survey goals and purposes. Conducts pre-shift meetings to communicate information to the staff. Performs routine computer activities to monitor survey progress and performance. Documents unusual problems that arise during survey training or production interviewing. Reviews progress reports and ensures work is completed within specified time limits.

Qualifications: Specialized experience in a position requiring knowledge of telephone interviewing techniques or data collection for a variety of surveys/projects in a computer-assisted telephone interviewing environment. Candidates also must have demonstrated in their work experience or training that they possess, or have the potential to develop, the qualities of successful supervision. Selectee may be required to serve a supervisory/managerial probationary period. You must be a U.S. citizen or national to qualify for this position.

How to apply: All applicants must submit their quality of experience factors with their resume or Optional Application for Federal Employment (OF-612) and the last four digits of their Social Security number. Application forms may be hand-delivered, mailed, or faxed. E-mailed applications will not be accepted.

Department of Defense

Office of the Secretary
1400 Defense Pentagon
Washington, DC 20301
703-545-6700

★ Web site: http://www.defenselink.mil

★ Civilian jobs: http://www.godefense.com/

★ Student internships: http://www.dfas.mil/careers2/college/internships.html

★ Student information: http://www.godefense.com/students.html

★ Military spouse employment: http://www.nmfa.org/site/
PageServer?pagename=home_spouseemployment

★ Delegated Examining Unit (this site includes a resume builder, a job kit, and information on resume preparation): http://www.dfas.mil/careers/post/deubuilderinfo.html

The Department of Defense (DoD) coordinates and supervises all agencies and functions of the U.S. government relating directly to national security and the military. DoD provides the military forces needed to deter war and protect the security of our country. The major elements of DoD's forces are the Army, Navy, and Air Force, consisting of about 1.3 million men and women on active duty. They are backed, in case of emergency, by the 1.1 million members of the Reserve and National Guard. In addition, there are approximately 700,000 civilian employees in the DoD.

Reporting to the DoD are the three military departments and 17 defense agencies. The three military departments are the Army, Navy, and Air Force. The Marine Corps is a branch of the Department of the Navy, and the Coast Guard is under the Department of Homeland Security. These military departments are responsible for recruiting, training, and equipping their forces, but operational control of those forces is assigned to one of the Unified Combatant Commands, a branch of DoD. Under the President of the United States, who is also Commander in Chief, the Secretary of Defense exercises authority, direction, and control over the Department of Defense, which includes the separately organized military departments, the Joint Chiefs of Staff providing military advice, the combatant commands, defense agencies, and field activities established in support of military departments. The defense agencies serve under the authority of the various undersecretaries for defense. There are approximately 80,000 civilian employees working in these agencies.

Selected DoD Agencies

Viewed as the civilian human resources center of excellence within the federal government, the **Civilian Personnel Management Service** develops and implements human resource management initiatives to support military leaders throughout the DoD in maintaining a strong civilian workforce to effectively support its mission and goals.

★ Web site: http://www.cpms.osd.mil/

★ Civilian Assistance and Reemployment Division: http://www.cpms.osd.mil/care/

The **Defense Advanced Research Projects Agency** (DARPA) is the central research and development organization of the DoD, charged with maintaining U.S. technological superiority over potential adversaries. Its research programs include advanced technology, defense sciences, information processing and exploitation, microsystems, tactical technology, and unmanned combat air systems. DARPA has job opportunities for scientists and engineers as well as security, administrative, budget, and management professionals. DARPA employs approximately 240 people.

★ Web site: http://www.darpa.mil/

★ Submit your resume and cover letter: http://www.darpa.mil/hrd/index.htm

★ Other employment opportunities: http://www.darpa.mil/hrd/opportunities.htm

The **Defense Commissary Agency** (DCA) provides an efficient and effective worldwide system of commissaries that sell quality groceries and household supplies at low prices to members of the armed services community. DCA has a worldwide system of nearly 280 commissaries. DCA employs more than 17,000 people throughout 14 countries.

★ Web site: http://www.commissaries.com/

★ Job vacancies and career information: http://www.commissaries.com/inside_deca/HR/employment_opportunities.cfm

The **Defense Contract Audit Agency** (DCAA) performs all contract audit functions for DoD and provides accounting and financial advisory services to all DoD components responsible for procurement and contract administration. In addition to its headquarters, DCAA has five regional offices and more than 300 field audit offices and suboffices throughout the United States and overseas. DCAA employs more than 4,000 people, almost 3,500 of them auditors.

★ Web site: http://www.dcaa.mil/

★ Career information: http://www.dcaa.mil/careercenter/index.htm

The **Defense Finance and Accounting Service** (DFAS) delivers professional finance and accounting services to the defense community. In addition to its headquarters in Arlington, Virginia, DFAS has sites in Denver, Colorado; Indianapolis, Indiana; Columbus, Ohio; Cleveland, Ohio; Limestone, Maine; and Rome, New York. It also has offices overseas in Japan and Germany. This agency offers job opportunities in the areas of accounting, auditing, financial management, human resources, and information technology.

★ Web site: http://www.dfas.mil/

★ Job vacancies: http://www.dfas.mil/careers/search.html

★ Career information: http://www.dfas.mil/careers.html

★ Strategic plan: http://www.dfas.mil/about/StrategyVision/2008-2013STRATEGICPLAN.pdf

The **Defense Information Systems Agency** (DISA) is responsible for planning, developing, fielding, operating, and supporting command, control, communications, and information systems that serve the needs of the president, vice president, the secretary of defense, the Joint Chiefs of Staff, the combatant commanders, and other DoD components under all conditions of peace and war. DISA employs about 8,200 people, of which 6,200 are civilians.

★ Web site: http://www.disa.mil/

★ Career information: http://www.disa.mil/audience/jobseekers.html

The **Defense Intelligence Agency** (DIA) provides timely, objective, all-source military intelligence to policymakers, war fighters, and force planners. DIA collects and produces foreign military intelligence; coordinates DoD intelligence collection requirements; operates the Central Measurement and Signature Intelligence Organization; manages the Defense Human Intelligence Service and the Defense Attaché System; and operates the Joint Intelligence Task Force for Combating Terrorism and the Joint Military Intelligence College.

Most of DIA's activities are performed at the Defense Intelligence Analysis Center at Bolling Air Force Base in Washington, DC. The agency's headquarters are located at the Pentagon. There are additional locations in Arlington, Virginia; Fort Detrick in Frederick, Maryland; and Redstone Arsenal in Huntsville, Alabama. DIA has more than 7,000 military and civilian employees worldwide. DIA employs more than 11,000 combined military (30 percent) and civilian (70 percent) people worldwide.

★ Web site: http://www.dia.mil/

★ Job vacancies: http://diajobs.dia.mil/

★ Internships: http://www.dia.mil/employment/student/index.htm

The **Defense Logistics Agency** (DLA) is DoD's largest combat support agency, providing world-wide logistics support in both peacetime and wartime to the military services as well as several civilian agencies and foreign countries. DLA supports both the logistics requirements of the military services and the military services' acquisition of weapons and other materiel. Agency supply centers consolidate the requirements of the military services and procure the supplies in sufficient quantities to meet their projected needs. The agency manages supplies in eight commodity areas: fuel, food, clothing, construction material, electronic supplies, general supplies, industrial supplies, and medical supplies. DLA employs approximately 22,000 civilians.

★ Web site: http://www.dla.mil/

★ Internships: http://www.hr.dla.mil/prospective/interns/

★ Automated Staffing Program: http://www.hr.dla.mil/prospective/howtoapply/

★ Career information: http://www.hr.dla.mil/prospective/

The **Defense Security Service** (DSS), formerly the Defense Investigative Service, conducts background investigations on individuals being considered for a security clearance, a sensitive position, or entry into the U.S. Armed Forces. It safeguards classified information used by contractors under the defense portion of the National Industrial Security Program; protects conventional arms, munitions, and explosives in custody of DoD contractors; protects and assures DoD's private sector critical assets and infrastructures throughout the world; and provides security education, training, and awareness programs. DSS also has a counter-intelligence office to support the national counterintelligence strategy. DSS has approximately 621 civilian employees.

★ Web site: http://www.dss.mil/

★ Employment information: https://www.dss.mil/GW/ShowBinary/DSS/about_dss/employmentinfo.html

The **Defense Threat Reduction Agency** (DTRA) reduces the threat posed by weapons of mass destruction (chemical, biological, nuclear, radiological, and high explosive) by implementing arms control treaties and by executing the Cooperative Threat Reduction Program. It uses combat support, technology development, and chemical-biological defense to deter the use of and reduce the impact of such weapons. It prepares for future threats by developing the technology and concepts needed to counter the new weapons of mass destruction threats and adversaries.

DTRA employs 2,000 civilian and military personnel at more than 14 locations around the world. Most employees work in the Washington, DC, area; other locations are Albuquerque, New Mexico; Darmstadt, Germany; Moscow, Russia; and Yokota Air Base, Japan. DTRA employees have a variety of skills and include nuclear physicists; policy analysts and treaty experts; mechanical, civil, electrical, and computer engineers; chemists; biologists; linguists; accountants; program analysts; and financial and logistics management specialists.

★ Web site: http://www.dtra.mil/

★ Career information: http://www.dtra.mil/be/employment_opp/civilian/index.cfm

The **Department of Defense Education Activity** (DoDEA) is a civilian agency of the U.S. Department of Defense that manages a system of schools for the children of military service members and Department of Defense civilian employees throughout the world. It operates 222 public schools in 15 districts located in 13 foreign countries, 7 states, Guam, and Puerto Rico. Headquartered in Arlington, Virginia, the DoDEA has divided its schools into three areas, each of which is managed by a director. Within each area, schools are organized into districts headed by superintendents. Approximately 8,785 teachers serve DoDEA's 102,600 students. Children of enlisted military personnel represent 85 percent of the total enrollment in DoDEA schools.

The DoDEA instructional program provides a comprehensive prekindergarten through twelfth grade curriculum that is competitive with that of any school system in the United States. All schools within DoDEA are fully accredited by U.S. accreditation agencies. DoDEA maintains a high school graduation rate of approximately 97 percent.

★ Web site: http://www.dodea.edu/home/index.cfm

★ Job vacancies: http://jobsearch.usajobs.opm.gov/a9dd16.asp

★ Educator's online application: http://www.dodea.edu/offices/hr/onlineapplication/default.htm

★ Teaching categories and requirements: http://www.dodea.edu/offices/hr/categories/default.htm

★ Troops to teachers: http://www.dantes.doded.mil/dantes_Web/troopstoteachers/index.asp

The **National Security Agency** (NSA) and the **Central Security Service** (CSS) together comprise the country's largest cryptologic organization. NSA employs the country's premier code makers and code breakers and ensures an informed, alert, and secure environment for U.S. war fighters and policymakers. CSS promotes full partnership between NSA and the cryptologic elements of the U.S. Armed Forces.

NSA, CSS, and military cryptologic elements employ individuals in the following career fields: acquisition and business management, computer/electrical engineering, computer science, cryptanalysis, foreign languages, human resources, intelligence analysis, mathematics, occupational health, research security (police), and signals analysis. The number of employees who work for these organizations is classified information.

★ Web site: http://www.nsa.gov/

★ Career information, student programs, and internships: http://www.nsa.gov/careers/

The **Office of Economic Adjustment** (OEA) assists communities adversely impacted by DoD program changes, including base closures or realignments, base expansions, and contract or program cancellations. Within OEA, the primary tool for DoD's economic adjustment projects is the Defense Economic Adjustment program for base realignment and closure (BRAC).

★ Web site: http://www.oea.gov

The **Unified Combatant Commands** are 10 military commands with broad continuing missions maintaining the security and defense of the United States against attack; supporting and advancing the national policies and interests of the United States; discharging U.S. military responsibilities; and preparing plans, conducting operations, and coordinating activities of the forces assigned to them in accordance with the directives of higher authority. The operational chain of command runs from the president to the secretary of defense to the commanders of the combatant commands. The Chairperson of the Joint Chiefs of Staff serves as the spokesman for the commanders of the combatant commands, especially on the operational requirements.

★ Central Command: http://www.centcom.mil/

★ Pacific Command: http://www.pacom.mil/

★ Southern Command: http://www.southcom.mil/home/

★ Northern Command: http://www.northcom.mil/

★ European Command: http://www.eucom.mil/english/index.asp

★ Joint Forces Command: http://www.jfcom.mil/

★ Special Operations Command: http://www.socom.mil/

★ Strategic Command: http://www.stratcom.mil/

★ Transportation Command: http://www.transcom.mil/

★ U.S. Africa Command: http://www.africom.mil/

Other DoD Agencies

American Forces Information Service

http://www.defenselink.mil/home/news_products.html

Business Transformation Agency

http://www.defenselink.mil/bta/

Defense Contract Management Agency

http://www.dcma.mil/

Defense Prisoner of War/Missing Personnel Office

http://www.dtic.mil/dpmo

Defense Security Cooperation Agency

http://www.dsca.osd.mil/

Defense Technical Information Center

http://www.dtic.mil/dtic/

Missile Defense Agency

http://www.mda.mil/

National Geospatial Intelligence Agency

http://www.nga.mil/

Office of the General Counsel

http://www.dod.mil/dodgc/

Pentagon Force Protection Agency

http://www.pfpa.mil/index2.html

Joint Service Schools

The joint service schools serve as the DoD centers for acquisition, technology, and logistics training; performance support; continuous learning; and knowledge sharing.

The **Defense Acquisition University** is a corporate university serving the Department of Defense Acquisition, Technology, and Logistics workforce, a total of more than 134,000 people. It provides basic, intermediate, and advanced certification training, assignment-specific training, performance support, job-relevant applied research, and continuous learning opportunities. It has six campuses nationwide, including its headquarters in Fort Belvoir, Virginia.

★ Web site: http://www.dau.mil/

★ Job vacancies: http://www.dau.mil/about-dau/jobs.aspx

The **Defense Language Institute**: **Foreign Language Center** (DLIFLC) provides culturally based foreign language education and training. Instruction is provided in approximately 23 languages and several dialects and administered through 31 language departments.

★ Web site: http://www.dliflc.edu/

★ Job vacancies: http://www.dliflc.edu/employment/employment_index.html

The central focus of all educational programs conducted by **Defense Resources Management Institute** is analytical decision making. The emphasis is not on training in job-specific skills, but rather on the concepts, techniques, and issues that pervade defense resources management decision making in most mid-management through executive level positions.

★ Web site: http://www.nps.edu/drmi/subPages/aboutDRMI.html

★ Job vacancies: http://www.nps.edu/drmi/subPages/positionsAvailable.html

The **National Defense University** incorporates the following colleges: the Industrial College of the Armed Forces, the National War College, the Joint Forces Staff College, the Information Resources Management College, and the College of International Security Affairs. The mission of the National Defense University is to educate military and civilian leaders through teaching, research, and outreach in national security, military, and national resource strategy; joint and multinational operations; information strategies, operations and resource management; acquisition; and regional defense studies.

★ Web site: http://www.ndu.edu/

★ Job vacancies and internships: http://www.ndu.edu/info/employment.cfm

★ Joint Forces Staff College: http://www.jfsc.ndu.edu

★ Industrial College of the Armed Forces: http://www.ndu.edu/ICAF/

★ Information Resources Management College: http://www.ndu.edu/irmc

★ National War College: http://www.ndu.edu/nwc/

★ College of International Security Affairs: http://www.ndu.edu/snsee/index.cfm

The **National Defense Intelligence College** (sometimes called Joint Military Intelligence College) serves the intelligence community and operates under the authority of the director of the Defense Intelligence Agency. Its mission is to educate military and civilian intelligence professionals, and conduct and disseminate relevant intelligence research. The college awards the Bachelor of Science in Intelligence (BSI) and Master of Science of Strategic Intelligence (MSSI) degrees and also offers two diploma intelligence programs at the undergraduate and postgraduate levels. Evening and weekend programs are available as well, one of which is specifically for military reservists and is taught by reserve faculty.

★ Web site: http://www.dia.mil/college/about.htm

★ Job vacancies: http://www.dia.mil/employment/index.html

The **Uniformed Services University of the Health Sciences** educates career-oriented medical officers for the military departments and the Public Health Service. The university currently incorporates the F. Edward Hébert School of Medicine (including graduate and continuing education programs) and the Graduate School of Nursing. Medical school matriculants must be commissioned officers in one of the uniformed services. They must meet the physical and personal qualifications for such a commission and must give evidence of a strong commitment to serving as a uniformed medical officer. The graduating medical student is required to serve for seven years, excluding graduate medical education. Students of the Graduate School of Nursing must be commissioned officers of the Army, Navy, Air Force, or Public Health Service prior to application. Graduate nursing students must serve a commitment determined by their respective service. The university employs 100 full-time faculty and 3,500 adjunct faculty.

★ Web site: http://www.usuhs.edu/

★ Job vacancies: http://www.usuhs.mil/chr/vacancies.shtml

★ F. Edward Hébert School of Medicine: http://www.usuhs.mil/medschool/fehsom.html

★ Graduate School of Nursing: http://www.usuhs.mil/gsn/

Sample Job Vacancies

Associate Professor

Agency: National Defense University
Salary: $95,043 to $153,200
Location: Washington, DC

Duties: Serves as a recognized expert and professor of government management and leadership at the Information Resources Management College (IRMC) contributing expertise in government financial management and leadership, in such areas as strategic planning, leadership, and oversight of federal agency budgeting and financial operations; development and maintenance of integrated financial and accounting management systems, including financial reporting and internal controls; and monitoring agency financial performance. Recommends course topics and content, instructional methods, and other aspects of educational programs. Serves as research advisor to individual students on topics related to national security. Provides analyses of management and leadership issues to develop new concepts and approaches to issues of significant national security. Conducts studies, prepares papers, and gives presentations in relevant areas of government financial management and leadership.

Qualifications: Applicants should have progressive professional experience in a relevant area and evidence of potential as a scholar. Teaching experience at the university level is preferred. Applicants will be rated on the basis of the listed criteria and the potential to accomplish the duties by subject matter experts appointed with the purpose of identifying the best-qualified candidate. You must be a U.S. citizen to qualify for this position. Selected applicant will be subject to random drug testing. You also must be able to obtain and maintain a Top Secret security clearance. Travel requirement for this position is occasional. You may be required to travel up to 20 to 30 percent of the time.

Lead Store Associate

Agency: Defense Commissary Agency
Salary: $33,507 to $43,560
Location: Bedford, Massachusetts

Duties: Distributes and balances workload among employees in accordance with established work-flow, monitors status and progress of work, and makes day-to-day adjustments in accordance with established priorities. Ensures written instructions, reference materials, and supplies are available and assists with problems. Maintains records of work accomplishments and time expended, and prepares production reports as required. Recommends changes in work methods that will improve the timeliness or quality of work performed by employees. When requested, provides input to supervisor on employee performance and disciplinary problems. As necessary, conducts on-the-job training covering all aspects of the work performed in the various functional retail areas of the store, including front-end operations, shelf stocking, inventory, merchandising, housekeeping, and security and safety methods. Ensures that safety, sanitation, security and housekeeping rules are followed.

Qualifications: Applicants must have at least one full year of specialized experience equivalent to at least the GS-4 level in the federal service. Specialized experience is defined as experience that demonstrates possession of practical knowledge of various commissary duties and responsibilities in order to instruct lower graded associates on how to perform their assigned tasks. Or applicants must have successfully completed at least four years of education above the high school level in an accredited business, secretarial, or technical school; junior college; or college or university. If you do not meet in full the experience or education requirements, you may qualify based on an equivalent combination of your experience and education.

Work involves frequent lifting, pushing, pulling, carrying and handling of commissary products weighing up to 50 pounds without assistance; heavier products are moved with assistance from other workers or by using weight-handling equipment. Work also involves prolonged standing, stooping, kneeling, bending, and climbing.

Security Specialist

Agency: Defense Finance and Accounting Service
Salary: $67,833 to $88,179
Location: Indianapolis, Indiana

Duties: Conducts required assessments and inspections. Conducts overall planning and implementation of security policies and procedures. Provides for the safeguarding of information, personnel, property, assets, and material from theft, loss, misuse, fraud, disclosure, espionage, or sabotage. Develops and implements security policy for the agency. Provides guidance to functional managers on annual assessments as they pertain to security matters. Conducts inspections of security operations at the DFAS sites and assists in security training and instruction programs. Reviews and advises on design and inspects facilities where sensitive material will be located. Ascertains the use of such material in the DFAS sites, who will have access to it, and how it should be protected. Establishes procedures to prevent unauthorized access to classified information. Develops special contingency plans, as necessary, for the safeguarding of classified information. Oversees preliminary inquiries of security incidents.

Qualifications: One year of specialized experience. Examples of specialized experience include reviewing, analyzing, and resolving difficult and complex security problems; developing and implementing procedures and practices to meet security objectives; and using vulnerability and risk assessment products to develop operational and physical vulnerability and risk assessments. Candidates must clearly demonstrate the possession of knowledge, skills, and abilities, or competencies necessary to successfully perform the work of the position at the appropriate level to be qualified for the position. Applicants must describe how their experience meets the competencies within the body of the resume. No separate statements addressing KSAs or competencies are required.

Department of Education

400 Maryland Avenue SW
Washington, DC 20202
202-401-2000
800-USA-LEARN (800-872-5327) (toll-free)

★ Web site: http://www.ed.gov/

★ Job vacancies: http://jobsearch.edhires.ed.gov/

★ EdHIRES (online job application): http://www.ed.gov/about/jobs/open/edhires/

★ Internship application: http://www.ed.gov/students/prep/job/intern/

★ Hispanic employment: http://www.ed.gov/about/jobs/work/RHhispanics.html

★ National Security Education Program Fellowships: http://www.nsep.gov/index.html

★ Strategic plan: http://www.ed.gov/about/reports/strat/index.html?src=ln

The Department of Education (ED) establishes policy; administers and coordinates most federal funding to education; collects data on America's schools and disseminates research; focuses national attention on key education issues; enforces federal statutes prohibiting discrimination in programs and activities receiving federal funds; and ensures equal access to education for everyone. ED has approximately 5,000 employees and a budget of more than $68.6 billion. The majority of the staff works at the various ED buildings in Washington, DC. Additionally, about 4,200 ED employees work in 10 regional offices around the country.

Selected ED Agencies

The **Institute of Education Sciences** (IES) is ED's main research arm. It compiles statistics, conducts and funds research, and provides guidance to others researching education policy and practice. Its three operational divisions are the National Center for Education Research, the National Center for Education Evaluation and Regional Assistance, and the National Center for Education Statistics.

The **National Center for Education Research** (NCER) researches topics in education related to teaching methods, the impact of technology, and the way children learn. The center's Division of Teaching and Learning researches topics related to literacy, math and science, readiness, and socialization. The center's Division of Policy and Systems researches topics related to rural and distance schooling, school reform, assessment and accountability, education workforce, and adult and post-secondary education.

The **National Center for Education Evaluation and Regional Assistance** (NCEE) evaluates and disseminates information on educational studies, especially those relating to reading, mathematics, science, closing the achievement gap, educational practices, and education technology. It also manages the National Library of Education.

The **National Center for Education Statistics** (NCES) collects and analyses data related to education in the United States and other countries. The National Center for Special Education Research (NCSER) conducts special education research designed to expand the knowledge and understanding of infants, toddlers, and children with disabilities.

★ Web site: http://www.ed.gov/about/offices/list/ies/

★ Web site for NCER: http://ies.ed.gov/ncer/

★ Web site for NCEE: http://ies.ed.gov/ncee/

★ Web site for NCES: http://nces.ed.gov/

★ Web site for NCSER: http://ies.ed.gov/ncser/

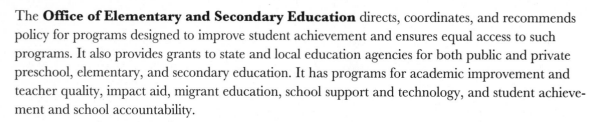

The **Office of Elementary and Secondary Education** directs, coordinates, and recommends policy for programs designed to improve student achievement and ensures equal access to such programs. It also provides grants to state and local education agencies for both public and private preschool, elementary, and secondary education. It has programs for academic improvement and teacher quality, impact aid, migrant education, school support and technology, and student achievement and school accountability.

★ Web site: http://www.ed.gov/about/offices/list/oese/

The **Office of Federal Student Aid** works to ensure that all eligible individuals can benefit from federally funded or federally guaranteed financial assistance for postsecondary education. It administers Pell grants, Stafford loans, PLUS loans, and the "campus-based" programs: federal work study, Perkins loans, and Federal Supplemental Educational Opportunity grants. These programs provide almost $91 billion of financial aid a year to college students. Before any of these funds can be issued, a determination of eligibility must be made. The Free Application for Federal Student Aid (FAFSA) is the required application form.

★ Web site: http://www.ed.gov/about/offices/list/fsa/

★ Web site: http://www.fafsa.ed.gov/

The **Office for Civil Rights** (OCR) serves student populations facing discrimination and their advocates and is responsible for ensuring that recipients of federal education funds are abiding by civil rights laws. As one of the largest federal civil rights agencies in the United States, OCR employs about 650 attorneys, investigators, and staff. The agency is headquartered in Washington, DC, and has 12 regional offices.

★ Web site: http://www.ed.gov/about/offices/list/ocr/

The **Office of Vocational and Adult Education** works to ensure that all Americans have the knowledge and technical skills necessary to succeed in postsecondary education, the workforce, and life. Through its comprehensive policies, programs, and activities, OVAE is helping reform America's high schools, supporting America's community colleges, and expanding America's adult education programs.

★ Web site: http://www.ed.gov/about/offices/list/ovae/

Other ED Agencies

Center for Faith-Based and Community Initiatives

http://www.ed.gov/about/inits/list/fbci/

International Affairs Office

http://www.ed.gov/about/inits/ed/internationaled/

Office of English Language Acquisition

http://www.ed.gov/about/offices/list/oela/

Office of Innovation and Improvement

http://www.ed.gov/about/offices/list/oii/

Office of Postsecondary Education

http://www.ed.gov/about/offices/list/ope/

Office of Safe and Drug-Free Schools

http://www.ed.gov/about/offices/list/osdfs/

Office of Special Education and Rehabilitative Services

http://www.ed.gov/about/offices/list/osers/

White House Initiative on Educational Excellence for Hispanic Americans

http://www.yic.gov/

White House Initiative on Historically Black Colleges and Universities

http://www.ed.gov/about/inits/list/whhbcu/edlite-index.html

White House Initiative on Tribal Colleges and Universities

http://www.ed.gov/about/inits/list/whtc/edlite-index.html

Sample Job Vacancies

Education Program Specialist
Agency: Office of Innovation and Improvement
Salary: $28.45 to $36.99/hour
Location: 20 vacancies throughout the country

Duties: As part of the Teaching Ambassador Fellowship program, these classroom fellows will function as paid, part-time consulting advisors to the U.S. Department of Education for one year. As practicing classroom teachers, fellows will share an important perspective for education policy and program discussions. Fellows will spend the majority of their time at the school and local level(s) and will share these experiences with other fellows and with the U.S. Department of Education at designated times throughout the year. These positions are located throughout the United States within the classroom fellows' school districts.

Qualifications: Be a currently practicing teacher or instructional coach/specialist in a United States Pre-K–12 public school (including public charter schools). Have a minimum of three years of teaching experience (experience may include private and public schools, as long as you are currently teaching in a public school). Be a certified teacher according to the state in which you are teaching. Be able to obtain support from your administrator and district to sign an Intergovernmental Personnel Act (IPA) agreement for your participation in the program. This support will be verified by telephone for candidates selected as finalists for the positions. Be able to successfully obtain a federal security clearance, which includes a background investigation and a credit check.

How to apply: Application to this announcement requires the online submission of basic applicant information, including a resume and responses to vacancy-specific questions. Your responses to the vacancy questions must be substantiated by your resume. Be sure that the experience/education as described on your resume contains accurate and sufficient information that clearly supports your responses to all of the questions by addressing experience and education relevant to the position. If you exaggerate or falsify your experience, education, and/or your responses to questions, your ratings can/will be changed, or you may be removed from employment consideration. Applicants who do not respond to the application questions will be rated ineligible.

Research Scientist/Specialist

Agency: Institute of Education Sciences
Salary: $85,000 to $130,000
Location: Washington, DC

Duties: Incumbents will develop, implement, and manage research, evaluation, and statistics activities and programs carried out or funded by the agency; monitor research, evaluation, and statistics activities carried out by grantees and contractors; conduct scientific reviews of research, evaluation, and statistics plans and products; analyze data and synthesize information from education research and related areas; prepare written products to convey research-based knowledge and information to a variety of audiences; conduct evaluations of agency activities; engage in dissemination and outreach activities, such as publishing scholarly work and attending scientific conferences; and collaborate and consult with staff.

Qualifications: This position requires a doctoral degree or equivalent experience in an appropriate field and at least five years of research experience in education-related fields (such as cognitive, developmental, educational, or social psychology; economics; education; statistics). You must demonstrate strong research skills and knowledge in an area of specialization and have experience publishing in scientific peer-reviewed journals and reviewing for such journals. You will need to successfully complete a background security investigation before you can be appointed into this position.

How to apply: Curriculum vitae or resume and a letter of interest should be submitted electronically to the deputy director. If applying electronically is not possible, applicants should contact the director by phone. All applications must be received or postmarked by the closing date of this announcement. All documents will be retained by the Institute of Education Sciences as part of the record of this action. Documents received in franked government envelopes will be returned without consideration. Please do not include your Social Security number on your application when emailing or faxing documents. If selected, you will be required to provide this information under the authority of Executive Order 9397 to uniquely identify you from other applicants who may have the same name.

Department of Energy

1000 Independence Avenue SW
Washington, DC 20585
202-586-5000

★ Web site: http://www.energy.gov

★ Job vacancies: http://humancapital.doe.gov/jobs/

★ Internships: http://humancapital.doe.gov/jobs/student.htm

★ Career information: http://www.energy.gov/about/employment.htm

The Department of Energy's (DOE) mission is to foster a secure and reliable energy system that is environmentally and economically sustainable; to be a responsible steward of the nation's nuclear weapons; to clean up the department's facilities; to lead in the physical sciences and advance the biological, environmental, and computational sciences; and to provide premier scientific instruments for the nation's research enterprise.

In addition to its headquarters in Washington, DC, DOE has operations offices located throughout the country. In addition, DOE's laboratories and technology centers house world-class facilities where more than 30,000 scientists and engineers perform cutting-edge research.

Selected DOE Agencies

The **Federal Energy Regulatory Commission** (FERC) regulates and oversees energy industries in the economic, environmental, and safety interests of the American public. FERC is an independent agency that regulates the interstate transmission of natural gas, oil, and electricity. FERC also regulates natural gas and hydropower projects.

★ Web site: http://www.ferc.gov/

★ Job vacancies: http://www.ferc.gov/careers/job-search.asp

★ Internships and student information: http://www.ferc.gov/careers/student-rel/intern.asp

The **Office of Fossil Energy** is made up of about 1,000 scientists, engineers, technicians, and administrative staff. Its headquarters offices are in downtown Washington, DC, and in Germantown, Maryland. The organization also has field offices in Morgantown, West Virginia; Pittsburgh, Pennsylvania; Tulsa, Oklahoma; New Orleans, Louisiana; Casper, Wyoming; and Albany, Oregon.

The Office of Fossil Energy is responsible for several high-priority presidential initiatives, including implementation of the administration's $2 billion, 10-year initiative to develop a new generation of environmentally sound clean coal technologies and the nation's Strategic Petroleum Reserve and Northeast Home Heating Oil Reserve. Both of these initiatives are key emergency response tools available to the president to protect Americans from energy supply disruptions.

★ Web site: http://www.fe.doe.gov/

★ Job vacancies: http://fossil.energy.gov/aboutus/jobs/index.html

★ Student information: http://fossil.energy.gov/education/index.html

★ Laboratories and facilities: http://fossil.energy.gov/facilities/index.html

The **Office of Nuclear Energy's** Nuclear Energy Program represents the core of the U.S. government's expertise in nuclear engineering and technology. Its activities benefit the American people by helping to maintain the nation's access to diverse and environmentally responsible sources of energy and by advancing the country's economic and technological competitiveness.

★ Web site: http://www.ne.doe.gov/

★ Job vacancies: http://www.ne.doe.gov/neJobs2.html

★ Special programs: http://www.ne.doe.gov/nePrograms2.html

The **Office of Science** manages fundamental research programs in basic energy sciences, biological and environmental sciences, and computational science. In addition, the Office of Science is the federal government's largest single funder of materials and chemical sciences, and it supports unique and vital parts of U.S. research in climate change, geophysics, genomics, life sciences, and science education. The office employs approximately 16,000 employees.

★ Web site: http://www.sc.doe.gov/

★ Internships and fellowships: http://www.science.gov/internships/

★ Workforce development for students and teachers: http://www.sc.doe.gov/Program_Offices/Workforce_Development.htm

★ National laboratories: http://www.sc.doe.gov/National_Laboratories/index.htm

★ Grants and contracts: http://www.sc.doe.gov/grants/grants.html

Power produced at federal water projects in excess of project needs is marketed by the **Power Marketing Administrations** to consumers. Each of the four power marketing administrations is a distinct and self-contained entity within the Department of Energy, much like a wholly owned subsidiary of a corporation.

★ Web site: http://www.energy.gov/organization/powermarketingadmin.htm

Other DOE Agencies

Energy Information Administration

http://www.eia.doe.gov/

Laboratories and Technology Centers

http://www.energy.gov/organization/labs-techcenters.htm

National Nuclear Security Administration

http://nnsa.energy.gov/

Office of Civilian Radioactive Waste Management

http://www.ocrwm.doe.gov/

Office of Energy Efficiency and Renewable Energy

http://www.eere.energy.gov/

Office of Environmental Management

http://www.em.doe.gov/pages/emhome.aspx

Office of Health, Safety, and Security

http://www.hss.energy.gov/index.html

Office of Legacy Management

http://www.lm.doe.gov/

Office of Scientific and Technical Information

http://www.osti.gov/

Sample Job Vacancies

Chemist/Physical Scientist
Agency: Radiological and Environmental Sciences Laboratory (RESL)
Salary: $46,625 to $104,525
Location: Idaho Falls, Idaho

Duties: Have or acquire a thorough knowledge of counting statistics, error propagation, the different types of counting techniques and instruments used to determine the beta-emitting radionuclides, and be able to interpret complex counting data and spectra. Participate as an assessor for DOE, Nuclear Regulatory Commission (NRC), or other contract laboratories and provide technical expertise on measurement science and expert advice to representatives of DOE, NRC, contractor laboratories, and international organizations. Represent RESL at national and international scientific meetings, conferences, and committees on analytical measurement technology and performance testing. Conduct research and development to improve analytical methods and report scientific findings in professional journals, reports, and at technical meetings. Have the education, career direction, communication skills, and technical ability to perform as an expert in radioanalytical measurements. Be self-motivated and work well in a cooperative team environment and have good oral and written communication skills.

How you will be evaluated: Rating and selection for this position is a five-step process. First, your application will be reviewed to determine if you meet basic eligibility requirements for hire into federal service, such as U.S. citizenship. Next, your application will be reviewed to determine if you have the qualifying, specialized experience for this position. You must sufficiently describe your specialized experience so we may determine the quality of your experience, or you will be disqualified. If you meet the specialized experience requirement, your responses to the written competency-based questions will be reviewed and scored by a panel of subject matter experts who will review your resume/application, transcripts (if applicable), and your responses to the competency-based questions. Upon receiving a passing score on your written responses to the competency-based questions, you will be invited to an assessment interview. Immediately after the interview, you will be required to do a 10–15 minute presentation and have a prepared one-page handout on a problem that you have encountered when conducting an experiment or working on a project. Qualified candidates will then be placed for selection consideration into either the Best Qualified or Qualified category. The selecting official has the option to conduct further interviews after referral.

General Engineer

Agency: Natural Gas and Oil Project Management Division
Salary: $53,234 to $87,893
Location: Morgantown, West Virginia

Duties: Duties of the position include serving as contracting officer's representative in planning, organizing, and managing extensive research, development, and demonstration efforts. The incumbent prepares procurement documentation, administers funding, and coordinates, as appropriate, the use of resources for project activities. The incumbent also assists management, division teams, and technology managers in developing individual projects and programs as well as developing budget needs for assigned projects and program areas.

Qualifications: Degree in professional engineering. For the GS-9, a master's degree or one year of professional scientific or engineering experience is required. For the GS-11, you must have a Ph.D. or one year of experience at or equivalent to the GS-9 level. For the GS-12 level, you must have one year of project management or research experience in the natural gas and oil industry. You must be a U.S. citizen to qualify for this position.

How you will be evaluated: Qualified applicants will be rated against the established quality ranking factors (QRF):

★ Knowledge of engineering and scientific concepts, principles, and practices related to the natural gas and oil industry with special emphasis in the areas of naturally occurring methane hydrates or carbon dioxide enhanced oil recovery (50 percent).

★ Ability to plan, organize, and manage complex technical projects (30 percent).

★ Skill in written communication in order to prepare technical reports/information (10 percent).

★ Skill in communicating orally with management and peers within the scientific community (10 percent).

Department of Health and Human Services

200 Independence Avenue SW
Washington, DC 20201
202-619-0257

★ Web site: http://www.hhs.gov/

★ Job vacancies: http://jobsearch.usajobs.opm.gov/a9hhs.asp

★ Student employment and internships: http://www.hhs.gov/careers/student/index.html

★ Emerging Leaders program: http://hhsu.learning.hhs.gov/elp/

★ Presidential Management Fellows program: http://learning.hhs.gov/development/pmf.asp

★ Commissioned Corps: http://dcp.psc.gov/vats/rept_select.htm

★ Strategic plan: http://aspe.hhs.gov/hhsplan/2007/

The Department of Health and Human Services (DHHS) is most involved with the nation's human service concerns. DHHS is the principal agency for protecting the health of all Americans and for providing essential human services, especially to those who are least able to help themselves. In one way or another, DHHS touches the lives of more Americans than any other federal agency. It is an organization of people serving people, from newborn infants to persons requiring health services to our most elderly citizens.

DHHS represents almost a quarter of all federal outlays, and it administers more grant dollars than all other federal agencies combined. DHHS works closely with state and local governments, and many HHS-funded services are provided at the local level by state or county agencies or through private sector grantees. The department's programs are administered by 11 operating divisions, including 8 agencies in the U.S. Public Health Service and 3 human services agencies. Approximately 62,500 people work for DHHS.

Selected HHS Agencies

The **Centers for Disease Control and Prevention** (CDC), a branch of the Public Health Service, provides a system of health surveillance to monitor and prevent disease outbreaks (including bioterrorism), implement disease prevention strategies, and maintain national health statistics. CDC provides for immunization services, workplace safety, and environmental disease prevention. Working with the World Health Organization, CDC also guards against international disease transmission, with personnel stationed in more than 40 foreign countries. The CDC director is also the administrator of the Agency for Toxic Substances and Disease Registry, which helps prevent exposure to hazardous substances from waste sites on the U.S. Environmental Protection Agency's National Priorities List and develops toxicological profiles of chemicals at these sites. CDC employs more than 15,000 people in 170 occupations. It is composed of the Office of the Director, the National Institute for Occupational Safety and Health, and six coordinating centers.

★ Web site: http://www.cdc.gov/

★ Job vacancies: http://www.cdc.gov/employment/findcareer.htm

★ Career information, internships, and student information: http://www.cdc.gov/employment/

★ Commissioned Corps: http://www.cdc.gov/employment/pdf/ Commissioned_Corps_and_CDC_Fact_Sheet.pdf

The **Centers for Medicare and Medicaid Services** (CMS) administers the Medicare and Medicaid programs, which provide health care to about one in every four Americans. Medicare provides health insurance for more than 41 million elderly and disabled Americans. Medicaid, a joint federal-state program, provides health coverage for some 44 million low-income persons, including 19 million children, and nursing home coverage for low-income elderly. CMS also administers the State Children's Health Insurance Program that covers more than 4.2 million children. CMS employs more than 4,500 people.

★ Web site: http://www.cms.gov/

★ Job vacancies: http://www.cms.hhs.gov/CareersatCMS/

★ Special hiring programs, including student programs: http://www.cms.hhs.gov/ CareersatCMS/02_SpecialHiringPrograms.asp#TopOfPage

★ Career information: http://www.cms.hhs.gov/CareersatCMS/04_Positions.asp#TopOfPage

The **Food and Drug Administration** (FDA) protects the public health by assuring the safety, efficacy, and security of human and veterinary drugs, biological products, medical devices, the national food supply, cosmetics, and products that emit radiation. FDA is also responsible for speeding innovations that make medicines and foods more effective, safer, and more affordable. It provides public access to accurate, scientifically proven information needed to use medicine effectively and to choose foods that improve health. FDA employs approximately 9,000 people who work in various locations around the country.

★ Web site: http://www.fda.gov/

★ Job vacancies: http://www.fda.gov/jobs/positions08.html

The **Health Resources and Services Administration** (HRSA) provides access to essential health care services for people who are low-income, uninsured, or live in rural areas or urban neighborhoods where health care is scarce. HRSA-funded health centers provide medical care to more than 13 million patients each year at more than 3,600 sites nationwide. The agency helps prepare the nation's health care system and providers to respond to bioterrorism and other public health emergencies, maintains the National Health Service Corps, and helps build the health care workforce through many training and education programs. HRSA administers a variety of programs to improve the health of mothers and children and serves people living with HIV/AIDS through the Ryan White CARE Act programs. HRSA also oversees the nation's organ transplantation system. HRSA employs more than 1,600 people.

★ Web site: http://www.hrsa.gov/

★ Job vacancies: http://www.hrsa.gov/about/jobs.htm

The **National Institutes of Health** (NIH) is the primary federal agency for conducting and supporting medical research. Helping to lead the way toward important medical discoveries that improve people's health and save lives, NIH scientists investigate ways to prevent disease as well as the causes, treatments, and even cures for common and rare diseases. Composed of 27 institutes and centers, the NIH provides leadership and financial support to researchers in every state and throughout the world. NIH supports some 50,000 research projects nationwide in diseases including cancer, Alzheimer's, diabetes, arthritis, heart ailments, and AIDS. The NIH employs more than 17,000 people, including 6,000 scientists.

★ Web site: http://www.nih.gov

★ Job vacancies and career information: http://www.jobs.nih.gov/

★ Internships and research opportunities: http://www.jobs.nih.gov/vacancies/student/default.htm

Other HHS Agencies

Administration for Children and Families

http://www.acf.hhs.gov/

Administration for Native Americans

http://www.acf.hhs.gov/programs/ana/

Administration on Aging

http://www.aoa.gov/

Administration on Developmental Disabilities

http://www.acf.hhs.gov/programs/add/

Agency for Healthcare Research and Quality

http://www.ahrq.gov/

Agency for Toxic Substances and Disease Registry

http://www.atsdr.cdc.gov/

Indian Health Service

http://www.ihs.gov/

Office of Refugee Resettlement

http://www.acf.hhs.gov/programs/orr/

Substance Abuse and Mental Health Services Administration

http://www.samhsa.gov/

U.S. Public Health Service Commissioned Corps

http://www.usphs.gov/

Sample Job Vacancies

Dental Assistant
Agency: Indian Health Service
Salary: $29,499 to $31,847
Location: Shiprock, New Mexico

Duties: The incumbent provides a variety of clerical, housekeeping, preventive, and clinical dental assisting functions allowing the dental team to function efficiently and better serve the intended population in the provision of the preventive, restorative, and acute oral health treatment needs of patients ranging from pediatric to geriatric age groups. Provides routine maintenance and clean up procedures on all dental equipment and their proper storage when not in use. Decontaminates the work environment. Properly stores supplies and replenishes when necessary. Schedules and seats dental patients, sets up proper instruments for dental procedures, and accurately records treatment rendered on patient records. Provides assistance during routine examination and restorative, periodontal, and surgical procedures as well as other dental specialties. Exposes, processes, and mounts intra and extra oral diagnostic radiographs. Is responsible for supportive laboratory procedures, properly filling out laboratory requisition, pouring study models, and trimming models under supervision of the dentist. Provides oral prophylaxis treatment. Provides sealants where appropriate. Participates in community prevention outreach. Takes and records vital signs and glucose levels.

Qualifications: Successful completion of one year of an accredited dental hygiene program. All persons born after 12-31-56 must provide proof of immunity to rubella and measles. The position requires long periods of standing, walking, sitting, and bending. Work involves exposures to communicable diseases, radiation, and flying debris; therefore, masks, lead aprons, and protective eyewear are often needed. You must be a U.S. citizen to qualify for this position. You will need to successfully complete a background security investigation before you can be appointed into this position.

Health Communications Specialist
Agency: Center for Disease Control and Prevention
Salary: $83,714 to $108,830
Location: Atlanta, Georgia

Duties: Incumbent serves as a health communication and Web content expert and advisor for the National Center for Immunization and Respiratory Diseases and Influenza Division. Plans, analyzes, evaluates, writes, and implements health communication messages and materials that are accurate and accessible to diverse scientific and nonscientific audiences to promote and support influenza information via the Web and other channels. Evaluates various communication science and marketing techniques to achieve optimal program results and positive health outcomes. Coordinates and conducts activities related to long and short-range planning; program and project development, implementation, and evaluation; audience research; and translation and dissemination of science to a variety of audiences and in a variety of formats, with special emphasis on Web communications. Develops, implements, and manages national influenza communication and marketing programs, projects, or initiatives for various audiences, including demonstration projects.

Qualifications: At least one year of experience utilizing communication science and marketing techniques in planning, implementing, managing, and evaluating public health communication and marketing programs and strategies related to influenza.

How to apply: First, register at USAJOBS. Then respond to the online application and assessment questions. Lastly, select and print fax cover sheets and fax the required documentation.

Department of Homeland Security

Washington, DC 20528
202-282-8000

★ Web site: http://www.dhs.gov/

★ Job vacancies: http://www.usajobs.opm.gov/homeland.asp

★ Career opportunities: http://www.dhs.gov/xabout/careers/

★ Career information: http://www.dhs.gov/xabout/careers/content_multi_image_0014.shtm

★ Strategic plan: http://www.dhs.gov/xabout/strategicplan/

The Department of Homeland Security (DHS) leads the unified national effort to secure the United States. DHS will prevent and deter terrorist attacks and protect against and respond to threats and hazards to the nation. The department will ensure safe and secure borders, welcome lawful immigrants and visitors, and promote the free flow of commerce.

Component agencies analyze threats and intelligence, guard borders and airports, protect critical infrastructure, and coordinate the response of the country to future emergencies. Besides providing a better-coordinated defense of the homeland, DHS is also dedicated to protecting the rights of American citizens and enhancing public services, such as natural disaster assistance and citizenship services, by dedicating offices to these important missions. DHS employs approximately 160,000 people.

Selected DHS Agencies

The **Federal Emergency Management Agency** (FEMA) reduces the loss of life and property and protects the nation from all hazards, including natural disasters, acts of terrorism, and other man-made disasters, by leading and supporting the nation in a risk-based, comprehensive emergency management system of preparedness, protection, response, recovery, and lessening of loss. FEMA has more than 2,600 employees working at headquarters, regional, and area offices. FEMA has 4,000 disaster assistance employees. It partners with 27 other federal agencies and the Red Cross.

★ Web site: http://www.fema.gov/

★ Job vacancies: http://www.fema.gov/career/publicSearch.do?action=Init

The **Transportation Security Administration** (TSA) is comprised of 43,000 security officers, inspectors, directors, air marshals, and managers who protect the nation's transportation systems so that people can travel safely. They look for bombs at checkpoints in airports, inspect rail cars, patrol subways with law enforcement partners, and work to make all modes of transportation safe.

★ Web site: http://www.tsa.gov/index.shtm

★ Job vacancies: http://jobsearch.usajobs.opm.gov/a9tsa.asp

★ Federal Air Marshal Service careers: http://www.tsa.gov/lawenforcement/people/fams_join.shtm

★ Career information: http://www.tsa.gov/join/careers/index.shtm

On March 1, 2003, services formerly provided by the Immigration and Naturalization Service (INS) transitioned into the Department of Homeland Security (DHS) under **U.S. Citizenship and Immigration Services** (USCIS). In support of the DHS overall mission, the priorities of the USCIS are to promote national security, continue to eliminate immigration case backlogs, and improve customer services. This new bureau includes approximately 15,000 employees and contractors working in approximately 250 headquarters and field offices around the world. Through a network of local offices, application support centers, service centers, local area immigration services field offices, national customer service call (NCSC) centers, forms centers, and the Internet, USCIS processes all immigrant and nonimmigrant benefits provided to visitors of the United States. To find out about career opportunities at USCIS, click the Careers at USCIS link on the following Web site:

★ Web site: http://www.uscis.gov/portal/site/uscis

The **U.S. Coast Guard** (USCG) is a military branch of the United States involved in maritime law, mariner assistance, and search and rescue, among other duties. One of the seven uniformed services and the smallest armed service of the United States, its stated mission is to protect the public, the environment, and the U.S. economic and security interests in any maritime region where those interests may be at risk. USCG has a broad and important role in homeland security, law enforcement, search and rescue, marine environmental pollution response, and the maintenance of river, intracoastal and offshore aids to navigation. It lays claim to being the United States' oldest continuous seagoing service.

In order to accomplish the Coast Guard's missions, its 40,150 active-duty men and women, 8,000 reservists, and 35,000 auxiliarists serve in a variety of job fields, ranging from operation specialists and small-boat operators and maintenance specialists to electronic technicians and aviation mechanics. In addition, the Coast Guard has more than 7,000 civilian positions in more than 200 types of jobs in more than 100 locations across the country.

★ Web site: http://www.uscg.mil/

★ Job vacancies (civilian): http://jobsearch.usajobs.opm.gov/a9uscg.asp

★ Civilian employment information: http://www.uscg.mil/hq/cgpc/cpm/home/geninfo.htm

The **U.S. Customs and Border Protection** (CBP) is the unified border agency within the DHS. CBP protects our nation's borders from terrorism, human and drug smuggling, illegal migration, and agricultural pests while facilitating the flow of legitimate trade and travel. CBP includes more than 44,000 employees to manage, control, and protect the country's borders at and between the official ports of entry. CBP employs more than 13,000 border patrol and air and marine agents and approximately 20,000 officers and agriculture specialists. It also has the nation's largest law enforcement canine program.

★ Web site: http://www.customs.gov/xp/cgov/home.xml

★ Job vacancies: http://jobsearch.usajobs.opm.gov/a9ins.asp

★ Customs careers: http://www.customs.gov/xp/cgov/careers/

★ Study guides and preparation manuals: http://www.customs.gov/xp/cgov/careers/study_guides/

★ Contact information: http://www.customs.gov/xp/cgov/toolbox/contacts/

The **U.S. Immigration and Customs Enforcement** (ICE) is the largest investigative arm of the Department of Homeland Security (DHS). The ICE organization is composed of four law enforcement divisions and several support divisions. These divisions combine to form a new investigative approach with new resources to provide unparalleled investigation, interdiction, and security services to the public and law enforcement partners in the federal and local sectors.

★ Web site: http://www.ice.gov/about/operations.htm

★ Job vacancies, career information, and internships: http://www.ice.gov/careers/index.htm

The **U.S. Secret Service** protects the president and vice president, their families, heads of state, and other designated individuals; investigates threats against these protectees; protects the White House, vice president's residence, foreign missions, and other buildings within Washington, DC; and plans and implements security designs for designated national special security events. The Secret Service also investigates violations of laws relating to counterfeiting of obligations and securities of the United States; financial crimes that include access device fraud, financial institution fraud, identity theft, and computer fraud; and computer-based attacks on the country's financial, banking, and telecommunications infrastructure. The uniformed division employs more than 1,300 officers.

★ Web site: http://www.secretservice.gov/

★ Job vacancies, internships, and student employment: http://www.secretservice.gov/opportunities.shtml

★ Testing locations: http://www.secretservice.gov/opportunities_exams.shtml

★ Special agents: http://www.secretservice.gov/whoweare_sa.shtml

★ Uniformed division: http://www.secretservice.gov/whoweare_ud.shtml

★ Application forms: http://www.secretservice.gov/opportunities_forms.shtml

★ Career fairs: http://www.secretservice.gov/opportunities_fairs.shtml

Other DHS Agencies

Computer Emergency Readiness Team

http://www.us-cert.gov/

Directorate for Science and Technology

http://www.dhs.gov/xabout/structure/editorial_0531.shtm

Domestic Nuclear Detection Office

http://www.dhs.gov/xabout/structure/editorial_0766.shtm

Federal Law Enforcement Training Center

http://www.fletc.gov/

Global Security Principal Directorate

https://www-gs.llnl.gov/

National Protection and Programs Directorate

http://www.dhs.gov/xabout/structure/editorial_0794.shtm

Office of Health Affairs

http://www.dhs.gov/xabout/structure/editorial_0880.shtm

Office of Operations Coordination

http://www.dhs.gov/xabout/structure/editorial_0797.shtm

Office of Policy

http://www.dhs.gov/xabout/structure/editorial_0870.shtm

Sample Job Vacancies

Electronics Mechanic
Agency: U.S. Coast Guard
Salary: $22.08 to $25.77/hour
Location: New Haven, Connecticut

Duties: Is responsible for maintaining and repairing electronic lighthouses and associated equipment. Also performs system testing, calibration, and maintenance for a variety of electronic systems including radar, HF/VHF/UHF radio, radio location, and nationwide differential global positioning system. Is responsible for coordinating, collaborating, and communicating with the Maintenance Logistics Commands regarding fiscal year funding required to meet operational requirements and performance/cost goals. Work is performed both indoors and outdoors in a variety of weather conditions. The work involves considerable agility in working in close and cramped spaces, working on buoys, and climbing ship's ladders and towers. Work requires lifting of 75 pounds. The position will require some overnight travel in the New England area. The mechanic must possess a valid driver's license.

Qualifications: Applicants will be evaluated on their ability to perform the duties of the position rather than the length of experience. Eligibility will be determined by the relevance, scope, and quality of all experience and training, regardless of where or how acquired. Applicants will be rated and ranked based on their knowledge of the following job elements: ability to perform the work of the position without more than normal supervision; knowledge of electronic theory; troubleshooting (electronics); and electronic equipment installation, repair, and alignment.

How you will be evaluated: The U.S. Coast Guard system simplifies the federal application process by replacing the former KSA/job element statements with on-line self-assessment questions. Your resume and responses to the self-assessment questions are an integral part of the process for determining your qualifications for the position. Therefore, it is important to support your responses to the self-assessment questions by providing examples of past and present experience when requested.

Transportation Security Officer (TSO)
Agency: Transportation Security Administration
Salary: $30,222 to $45,322
Location: West Palm Beach, Florida

Duties: You will perform a variety of duties related to providing security and protection of air travelers, airports, and aircraft. As a TSO, you may be required to perform passenger screening, which includes tasks such as hand-wanding, pat-down searches, and monitoring walk-through metal detector screening equipment. You also may be required to perform baggage screening, including the operation of X-ray machines to identify dangerous objects in baggage and cargo and on passengers and prevent those objects from being transported onto aircraft. TSOs communicate with the public, giving directions and responding to inquiries in a professional and courteous manner. TSOs also must maintain focus and awareness and work within a stressful environment that includes noise from alarms, machinery, and people; distractions; time pressure; disruptive and angry passengers; and the requirement to identify and locate potentially life-threatening devices and devices intended on creating massive destruction and make effective decisions in both crisis and routine situations.

Qualifications: Applicants must be proficient in English and have a high school diploma, GED, or equivalent; or have at least one year of full-time work experience in security work, aviation screener work, or X-ray technician work. They also must be able to repeatedly lift and carry up to 70 pounds, continuously stand between one to four hours without a break in order to carry out screening functions, and walk up to two miles during a shift. All TSOs must meet job-related medical standards that will be assessed in a pre-employment medical evaluation. To be considered for initial employment, applicants must also pass a pre-employment drug screening test and a background investigation, including a criminal check and a credit check.

Department of Housing and Urban Development

451 Seventh Street SW
Washington, DC 20410
202-708-1422

★ Web site: http://www.hud.gov/

★ Job vacancies: http://jobsearch.usajobs.opm.gov/a9hudp.asp

★ Internships and contracting opportunities: http://www.hud.gov/jobs/index.cfm

★ Strategic plan: http://www.hud.gov/offices/cfo/stratplan.cfm

The Department of Housing and Urban Development (HUD) is the principal federal agency responsible for programs concerned with the country's housing needs, fair housing opportunities, and improvement and development of the nation's communities. HUD's mission is to increase homeownership, support community development, and increase access to affordable housing free from discrimination. HUD has about 9,500 employees and is organized into 10 regions that oversee approximately 81 field offices located in every state; in Washington, DC; and in Puerto Rico.

Selected HUD Agencies

Ginnie Mae guarantees investors the timely payment of principal and interest on mortgage-backed securities (MBS) backed by federally insured or guaranteed loans, mainly loans insured by the Federal Housing Administration (FHA) or guaranteed by the Department of Veterans Affairs (VA). Other guarantors or issuers of loans eligible as collateral for Ginnie Mae MBS include the Department of Agriculture's Rural Housing Service (RHS) and the Department of Housing and Urban Development's Office of Public and Indian Housing (PIH).

Web site: http://www.ginniemae.gov/

The **Office of Housing** oversees the Federal Housing Administration (FHA), the largest mortgage insurer in the world, and regulates housing industry business. The mission of the Office of Housing is to contribute to building and preserving healthy neighborhoods and communities; maintain and expand homeownership, rental housing, and health care opportunities; and stabilize credit markets in times of economic disruption.

★ Web site: http://www.hud.gov/offices/hsg/

★ Job vacancies: http://jobsearch.usajobs.opm.gov/a9hudp.asp

★ Federal Housing Administration: http://www.hud.gov/offices/hsg/fhahistory.cfm

★ Office of Affordable Housing Preservation: http://www.hud.gov/offices/hsg/omhar/index.cfm

The **Office of Public and Indian Housing** (PIH) ensures safe, decent, and affordable housing; creates opportunities for residents' self-sufficiency and economic independence; and assures the fiscal integrity of all program participants. PIH manages several programs, including the Capital Fund, which provides funds for the development, financing, and modernization of public housing developments and for management improvements; the HOPE VI Program, which addresses severely distressed public housing by helping with physical improvements, management improvements, and social and community services to address resident needs; and Housing choice vouchers, which allow very low-income families to choose and lease or purchase safe, decent, and affordable privately owned rental housing.

★ Web site: http://www.hud.gov/offices/pih

Other HUD Agencies

Center for Faith-Based and Community Initiatives

http://www.hud.gov/offices/fbci/index.cfm

Office of Community Planning and Development

http://www.hud.gov/offices/cpd/

Office of Fair Housing and Equal Opportunity

http://www.hud.gov/offices/fheo/

Office of Healthy Homes and Lead Hazard Control

http://www.hud.gov/offices/lead/

Policy Development and Research Information Service

http://www.huduser.org/

Real Estate Assessment Center

http://www.hud.gov/offices/reac/

Small and Disadvantaged Business Utilization

http://www.hud.gov/offices/osdbu/

Sample Job Vacancies

Community Planning and Development Representative

Agency: Assistant Secretary for Community Planning and Development
Salary: $49,020 to $59,309
Location: Portland, OR

Duties: The incumbent serves as a point of contact between HUD and assigned communities for a variety of Community Planning and Development (CPD) programs. The incumbent has extensive knowledge of CPD's programs, legislation, regulations and policies; and provides information, advice, and technical assistance to elected officials, senior level staff, managers, and other officials in local governmental as well as private not-for-profit organizations and the business sector. Uses judgment and initiative to overcome obstacles to program management, provides support and assistance to grantees in meeting their local community development, affordable housing, and homeless assistance needs. Utilizes a variety of automated data systems in preparing reports, tracking information, and performing monitoring functions. Safeguards the public trust in CPD programs. At the GS-09 level, the incumbent will perform these duties under the guidance of a senior staff member, with on-the-job training and developmental assignments in order to prepare for more complex, independent responsibilities.

How you will be evaluated: Once the application process is complete, a review of your application will be made to ensure you meet the job requirements. To determine if you are qualified for this job, a review of your resume and supporting documentation will be made and compared against your responses to the occupational questionnaire. The numeric rating you receive is based on your responses to the questionnaire. The occupational questionnaire measures your ability to demonstrate the following knowledge, skills, and abilities: knowledge of community development programs, policies, and procedures; ability to deal effectively with HUD clients, local government officials, citizen groups, or the public at large on programmatic or technical issues; ability to gather and analyze facts and data and draw conclusions; ability to communicate clearly, concisely, and informatively in writing; and ability to use automated systems such as Excel and other database management systems to retrieve, analyze and manage program data.

Public Affairs Specialist

Agency: Office of Field Policy and Management
Salary: $98,924 to $128,607
Location: Boston, Massachusetts

Duties: Oversee all aspects of the media and communication programs in the region in conjunction with the regional director; function as the official means of informing the press, specific groups, and the general public of Housing and Urban Development activities and goals; compile information and material for use by the assistant secretary for public affairs, and/or the regional director; maintain a constant awareness of sensitive issues; set up media events, funding announcements, press conferences, and public forums; recommend case-by-case and/or systemic strategies for addressing problems; provide responses to the public, the news media and government officials on behalf of the agency that are professionally accurate, pertinent, tactful, and completely harmonious with established policies and purposes of the department; contact members of the press to clarify issues on articles and stories; maintain and update media contacts in the region.

Qualifications: You must have one year of specialized experience equivalent to at least the GS-13 level in the federal service or comparable pay band system. For this position, specialized experience is defined as experience applying public affairs principles, methods, practices, and techniques in order to administer a comprehensive public information program. Such experience also includes formulating innovative approaches to resolve highly complex and sensitive community relations problems and issues that affect public housing authorities, local communities, and state and local governments.

Department of the Interior

1849 C Street NW
Washington, DC 20240
202-208-3100

★ Web site: http://www.doi.gov/

★ Job vacancies: http://www.doi.gov/doijobs/jobs.html

★ Internships: http://www.doi.gov/doijobs/employ5.html

★ Strategic plan: http://www.doi.gov/ppp/Strategic%20Plan%20FY07-12/
  strat_plan_fy2007_2012.pdf

The Department of the Interior (DOI) manages the country's public lands and minerals, national parks, national wildlife refuges, and western water resources and upholds federal trust responsibilities to Indian tribes and commitments to island communities. It is responsible for migratory wildlife conservation; historic preservation; endangered species; surface-mined lands protection and restoration; mapping; geological, hydrological, and biological science; and assistance for insular areas.

DOI is a large, decentralized agency with more than 72,000 employees and 180,000 volunteers in approximately 2,400 operating locations across the United States, Puerto Rico, U.S. territories, and freely associated states. It employs people in more than 90 career fields, including accounting, animal care, archaeology, biological sciences, cartography, chemistry, construction engineering, ecology, firefighting, geology, landscape architecture, curating, petroleum engineering, public affairs, surface mining reclamation, telecommunications, vocational training, and water management.

Selected DOI Agencies

Established in 1824, the **Bureau of Indian Affairs** (BIA) is the oldest bureau of the DOI. BIA currently provides services (directly or through contracts, grants, or compacts) to approximately 1.7 million American Indians and Alaska Natives. There are 561 federally recognized American Indian tribes and Alaska Natives in the United States. BIA is responsible for the administration and management of 56 million acres of land held in trust by the United States for American Indians, their tribes, and Alaska Natives. The Bureau of Indian Education (BIE) provides education services to approximately 48,000 Indian students. It employs approximately 9,000 people.

★ Web site: http://www.doi.gov/bia/

★ Bureau of Indian Education: http://www.bia.edu/

The **Bureau of Land Management** (BLM) is responsible for managing 262 million acres of land (13 percent of the land in the United States) and about 700 million additional acres of subsurface mineral resources. The bureau is also responsible for wildfire management and suppression. Most of the lands the BLM manages are located in the western United States, including Alaska, and are dominated by extensive grasslands, forests, high mountains, arctic tundra, and deserts. The BLM manages a wide variety of resources and uses, including energy and minerals; timber; forage; wild horse and burro populations; fish and wildlife habitat; wilderness areas; and archaeological, pale-ontological, and historical sites. BLM employs more than 10,000 people who are assisted by 20,000 volunteers.

★ Web site: http://www.blm.gov/

★ Job vacancies: http://jobsearch.usajobs.opm.gov/a9blm.asp

★ Firefighting jobs: http://www.firejobs.doi.gov/

★ Internships and student employment: http://www.blm.gov/wo/st/en/res/blm_jobs/national_recruitment1/internship_opportunities.html

★ Volunteer information: http://www.blm.gov/volunteer/

★ Career information: http://www.blm.gov/wo/st/en/res/blm_jobs.html

The **National Park Service** (NPS) preserves the natural and cultural resources and values of the national park system for the enjoyment, education, and inspiration of this and future generations. The Park Service cooperates with partners to extend the benefits of natural and cultural resource conservation and outdoor recreation throughout this country and the world. The National Park System of the United States comprises 384 areas covering more than 83 million acres in 49 states, the District of Columbia, American Samoa, Guam, Puerto Rico, Saipan, and the Virgin Islands. The National Park Service employs more than 15,000 full-time employees and 5,000 seasonal workers.

★ Web site: http://www.nps.gov

★ Job vacancies: http://data2.itc.nps.gov/digest/usajobs.cfm

★ Seasonal employment: http://www.sep.nps.gov/

★ Internships: http://www.nps.gov/gettinginvolved/internships/index.htm

★ Volunteer information: http://www.nps.gov/volunteer/

The **U.S. Fish and Wildlife Service** manages more than 95 million acres of land and water consisting of more than 544 national wildlife refuges, thousands of small wetlands, and other special management areas. It also operates 70 national fish hatcheries, 69 fish and wildlife management assistance offices, 63 fishery resource offices, and 81 ecological services field stations. The service is responsible for migratory birds, endangered species, certain marine mammals, and inland sport fish-eries. The Fish and Wildlife Service employs about 7,900 people.

★ Web site: http://www.fws.gov

★ Job vacancies: http://jobsearch.usajobs.opm.gov/a9fws.asp

★ Student programs: http://www.fws.gov/jobs/wwd_student.html

★ Career information: http://www.fws.gov/jobs/

★ National programs and functions: http://info.fws.gov/function.html

Other DOI Agencies

Bureau of Reclamation

http://www.usbr.gov

Minerals Management Service

http://www.mms.gov

National Interagency Fire Center

http://www.nifc.gov/

Office of Surface Mining Reclamation and Enforcement

http://www.osmre.gov

United States Geological Survey

http://www.usgs.gov

Sample Job Vacancies

Visitor Use Assistant
Agency: National Park Service
Salary: $24,156 to $31,401
Location: St. John, Virgin Islands

Duties: As a uniformed employee of the National Park Service (NPS), the incumbent serves as a front line representative of the agency. In many instances, the incumbent is the first and only contact the visiting public has with a NPS employee. The incumbent works at an entrance station, visitor center, campground, or other visitor contact station. The incumbent is responsible for providing answers to recurring visitor questions concerning the specific park area. The incumbent explains the area's recreational opportunities, including NPS interpretive service, concession-operated facilities and services, and campground availability; distributes maps, brochures, and other printed material; provides directions and routes of travel through the park; and informs visitors of potential safety hazards. The incumbent is responsible for collecting appropriate fees at park entrance station, visitor center, mooring pay station, or other visitor contact stations following established accountability guidelines for handling government funds. The incumbent operates an electronic cash register; performs opening and closing shift functions; issues entrance receipts, park passes, and federal recreation passports in accordance with established guidelines; and verifies entrance receipts and various passes for validity dates.

Qualifications: Have at least one year of progressively responsible clerical or office experience such as communicating orally with staff and the public; working independently and organizing material; prioritizing work; operating an electronic cash register, credit card machine, money counter, calculator, photocopy machine; and using a typewriter or computer. Or have successfully completed at least two years of education above high school. Or have an equivalent combination of successfully completed postsecondary education and experience.

Conditions of employment: Selectee must possess or be able to obtain a valid state driver's license. Selectee must wear the agency uniform and comply with established standards. Selectee may work weekends, holidays, and/or varied shifts. Some travel is required. Selectee may work on vessels to aid in mooring fee collection. Housing is not available, and relocation expenses will not be paid. A Cost of Living Allowance (COLA) of 25 percent will be added to the base salary. Special Agency Check (SAC) and background investigation is required.

Wildlife Biologist
Agency: U.S. Fish and Wildlife Service
Salary: $50,367 to $65,478
Location: Fairbanks, Alaska

Duties: With principal investigator oversight, the employee plans projects and oversees logistics; oversees field crew and conducts fieldwork; analyzes data and produces accurate field reports and presentations; and assists other staff biologists with other writing assignments. Leads a small group of lower graded technicians and volunteers in gathering field data and provides training in techniques and procedures, plans work, and provides input to supervisor concerning performance of lower graded technicians and volunteers. Primary fieldwork consists of conducting surveys, nest searches, and nest monitoring of threatened Steller's and spectacled eiders near Barrow, Alaska. Operates cars, trucks, and ATVs. A valid state's driver's license is required. Within capabilities, may service or repair equipment.

Qualifications: Applicants must have a degree in biological science or have a combination of education and experience equivalent to a major in biological science. In addition, applicants must have completed at least one year of full-time professional specialized experience, such as providing technical support to professional biologists in completing all phases of a biological study or project on waterfowl. Or they must have earned a master's degree in wildlife biology or have a combination of graduate education and experience. To receive full credit for your educational background in determining qualifications, submit a copy of your college transcript with your application.

Conditions of employment: Travel to study sites is by commercial aircraft, motor vehicle, and ATV. Fieldwork occurs in a remote and isolated environment without access to the road system and possibly without telephones or the Internet. Fieldwork is physically demanding and requires hiking through wet uneven tundra areas, as well as conducting stationary observations in cold and windy weather. Weather is usually cold and windy and can be wet or buggy. Bending, lifting objects, and carrying equipment of variable weights will be required; position requires the ability to carry sampling equipment and supplies weighing 40 pounds or more for extended distance in tundra. You will be required to safely carry, handle, and use firearms for bear defense of self and others.

Department of Justice

950 Pennsylvania Avenue NW
Washington, DC 20530
202-514-2000

- ★ Web site: http://www.usdoj.gov/

- ★ Job vacancies: http://www.usdoj.gov/06employment/06_1.html

- ★ Attorney vacancies: http://www.usdoj.gov/oarm/attvacancies.html

- ★ Student information: http://www.usdoj.gov/careers/

- ★ Summer law intern program: http://www.usdoj.gov/oarm/arm/sp/sp.htm

- ★ Volunteer internships: http://www.usdoj.gov/oarm/arm/int/legalinternjq.htm

- ★ Career information: http://www.usdoj.gov/06employment/06_2.html

- ★ Strategic plan: http://www.usdoj.gov/jmd/mps/strategic2007-2012/index.html

Ranked the 2007 fifth best place to work, the Department of Justice (DOJ), led by the U.S. Attorney General, enforces the law and defends the interests of the United States according to the law, ensures public safety against threats foreign and domestic, provides federal leadership in preventing and controlling crime, seeks just punishment for those guilty of unlawful behavior, and ensures fair and impartial counsel for its citizens. The DOJ represents citizens in enforcing the law in the public interest. Through its thousands of lawyers, investigators, and agents, the DOJ plays the key role in protection against criminals and subversion, ensuring healthy business competition, safeguarding the consumer, and enforcing drug, immigration, and naturalization laws. The DOJ has more than 107,000 employees located both in the United States and overseas.

Selected DOJ Agencies

The **Bureau of Alcohol, Tobacco, Firearms, and Explosives** (ATF) is a law enforcement agency within the DOJ. Its unique responsibilities include preventing terrorism, reducing violent crime, and protecting our nation. The men and women of ATF perform the dual responsibilities of enforcing federal criminal laws and regulating the firearms and explosives industries. They work directly, and through partnerships, to investigate and reduce crimes involving firearms and explosives, acts of arson, and illegal trafficking of alcohol and tobacco products. ATF works to suppress and prevent crime and violence through enforcement, regulation, and community outreach; ensure fair and proper revenue collection; provide fair and effective industry regulation; assist federal, state, local, and international law enforcement; and provide innovative training programs in support of criminal and regulatory enforcement functions.

ATF has employees at headquarters and in 23 field offices. In addition, the ATF's Office of Laboratory Services employs more than 120 chemists, document analysts, fingerprint specialists, firearm and toolmark examiners, firearm technicians, and administrative support personnel. Other types of jobs at ATF include: security administration, intelligence, and classification specialists. ATF employs approximately 4,500 workers.

★ Web site: http://www.atf.gov/

★ Conditions of employment: http://www.atf.gov/careers/special-agents/qualifications.htm

★ Career information: http://www.atf.gov/careers/index.htm

The **Criminal Division** develops, enforces, and supervises the application of all federal criminal laws except those specifically assigned to other divisions. The division and the 93 U.S. attorneys have the responsibility for overseeing criminal matters under more than 900 statutes as well as certain civil litigation. Criminal Division attorneys prosecute many nationally significant cases. In addition to its direct litigation responsibilities, the division formulates and implements criminal enforcement policy and provides advice and assistance. For example, the division approves or monitors sensitive areas of law enforcement, such as participation in the Witness Security Program and the use of electronic surveillance; advises the attorney general, Congress, the Office of Management Budget, and the White House on matters of criminal law; provides legal advice and assistance to federal prosecutors and investigative agencies; and provides leadership for coordinating international as well as federal, state, and local law enforcement matters.

★ Web site: http://www.usdoj.gov/criminal/

★ Job vacancies: http://www.usdoj.gov/criminal/employment/vacancies.html

The **Drug Enforcement Administration** (DEA) enforces controlled substances laws and regulations of the United States and brings to the criminal and civil justice system of the United States (or any other competent jurisdiction) organizations and principal members of organizations that are involved in the growing, manufacture, or distribution of controlled substances appearing in or destined for illicit traffic in the United States. The DEA recommends and supports non-enforcement programs aimed at reducing the availability of illicit controlled substances on the domestic and international markets. DEA employs approximately 10,000 workers.

★ Web site: http://www.usdoj.gov/dea/

★ Job vacancies: http://jobsearch.usajobs.opm.gov/a9dea.asp

★ Career and internship information: http://www.usdoj.gov/dea/resources/job_applicants.html

The **Federal Bureau of Investigation** (FBI) is the investigative arm of DOJ. Its priorities are to protect the United States from terrorist attacks, from foreign intelligence operations, and from cyber-based attacks and high-technology crimes; combat public corruption at all levels; protect civil rights; combat international and national organized crime, major white-collar crime, and significant violent crime; support law enforcement and intelligence partners; and upgrade FBI technology.

The best-known career at FBI is the special agent. Other positions include computer specialist, crime scene specialist, linguist, fingerprint expert, intelligence research specialist, laboratory technician, accounting professional, laborer, and secretary. The FBI employs more than 30,000 personnel.

★ Web site: http://www.fbi.gov/

★ Job vacancies: http://www.fbijobs.gov/03.asp

★ Internships: http://www.fbijobs.gov/23.asp

★ FBI Honors Internship Program: http://www.fbijobs.gov/231.asp

★ Career information: http://www.fbijobs.gov/1.asp

★ Employment FAQs: http://www.fbijobs.gov/61.asp

The **Office of Justice Programs** (OJP) provides federal leadership in developing the country's capacity to prevent and control crime, improve the criminal and juvenile justice systems, increase knowledge about crime and related issues, and assist crime victims. It is organized into five bureaus: the Bureau of Justice Assistance, the Bureau of Justice Statistics, the National Institute of Justice, the Office of Juvenile Justice and Delinquency Prevention, and the Office for Victims of Crime.

★ Web site: http://www.ojp.usdoj.gov/

★ Job vacancies: http://www.ojp.usdoj.gov/about/jobs.htm

The **Tax Division** handles or supervises civil and criminal matters that arise under the internal revenue laws. In order to promote compliance with the tax laws and maintain confidence in the integrity of the tax system, the division strives to ensure consistent application and uniform enforcement of the internal revenue code. More than 350 attorneys work for the Tax Division in 14 civil, criminal, and appellate sections. These sections are based in Washington, DC, except for the Southwestern Civil Trial Section, which is located in Dallas, Texas. Tax Division attorneys work closely with the Internal Revenue Service and U.S. attorneys to develop tax administration policies, handle civil trial and appellate litigation in federal and state courts, pursue federal grand jury investigations, and handle criminal prosecutions and appeals.

★ Web site: http://www.usdoj.gov/tax/

★ Job vacancies: http://www.usdoj.gov/tax/vacancies.htm

★ Student employment programs: http://www.usdoj.gov/tax/career_lawstu.htm

The **U.S. Marshals Service** is the nation's oldest and most versatile federal law enforcement agency. Since 1789, federal marshals have served the nation through a variety of vital law enforcement activities. Ninety-five U.S. marshals, appointed by the president or the U.S. attorney general, direct the activities of 94 district offices and personnel stationed at more than 350 locations throughout the country, Guam, Northern Mariana Islands, Puerto Rico, and the Virgin Islands. The geographical structure of the U.S. Marshals Service mirrors the structure of the U.S. district courts.

The Marshals Service is involved in virtually every federal law enforcement initiative. Approximately 3,200 deputy marshals and criminal investigators perform the following nationwide, day-to-day missions: protection of federal judicial officials, which includes judges, attorneys, and jurors; apprehension of federal fugitives; insurance of the safety of witnesses who risk their lives testifying for the government; transportation of prisoners and illegal aliens; and management and disposal of seized and forfeited properties acquired by criminals through illegal activities.

★ Web site: http://www.usdoj.gov/marshals/

★ Centralized student career experience program: http://www.usmarshals.gov/careers/cscep.html

★ Career opportunities: http://www.usmarshals.gov/careers/index.html

The **U.S. Trustee Program** oversees the administration of bankruptcy cases and private trustees. There are 88 judicial districts comprised of 21 regional offices nationwide and an executive office for U.S. Trustees in Washington, DC. Program operations are carried out by 95 field offices that report to regional trustees. The program works to secure the just, speedy, and economical resolution of bankruptcy cases; monitors the conduct of parties and takes action to ensure compliance with applicable laws and procedures; identifies and investigates bankruptcy fraud and abuse; and oversees administrative functions in bankruptcy cases.

★ Web site: http://www.usdoj.gov/ust/

★ Job vacancies: http://www.usdoj.gov/ust/eo/private_trustee/vacancies/

Other DOJ Agencies

Antitrust Division

http://www.usdoj.gov/atr/

Asset Forfeiture Program

http://www.usdoj.gov/jmd/afp/

Civil Division

http://www.usdoj.gov/civil/

Civil Rights Division

http://www.usdoj.gov/crt/crt-home.html

Community Oriented Policing Services

http://www.cops.usdoj.gov/

Environment and Natural Resources Division

http://www.usdoj.gov/enrd/

Executive Office for Immigration Review

http://www.usdoj.gov/eoir/

Executive Office for U.S. Attorneys

http://www.usdoj.gov/usao/eousa/index.html

Federal Bureau of Prisons

http://www.usdoj.gov/bop

Foreign Claims Settlement Commission

http://www.usdoj.gov/fcsc/

National Drug Intelligence Center

http://www.usdoj.gov/ndic/index.htm

Office of Information Policy

http://www.usdoj.gov/oip/oip.html

Office of Sex Offender Sentencing, Monitoring, Apprehending, Registering, and Tracking

http://www.ojp.usdoj.gov/smart/

Office of the Pardon Attorney

http://www.usdoj.gov/pardon/index.html

Office on Violence Against Women

http://www.ovw.usdoj.gov/

United States National Central Bureau of INTERPOL

http://www.usdoj.gov/usncb/

United States Parole Commission

http://www.usdoj.gov/uspc/

Sample Job Vacancies

Cook Foreman

Agency: Bureau of Prisons
Salary: $23.38 to $27.29/hour
Location: Talledega, Alabama

Duties: The incumbent's primary responsibility is to provide supervision and instruction to 25–30 inmate workers who are assigned the duties of cooks, butchers, bakers, dining and dish workers, vegetable preparation workers, and pot and pan washers. Incumbent provides continual training to the inmate workers in order to update their knowledge in all phases of production, presentation, and sanitation of food items. The incumbent is responsible for training inmates in the safe operation of a variety of food service equipment in the preparation and delivery of meals.

Incumbent oversees the receiving, storing, and issuing of all food and nonfood items. The incumbent is fully involved in maintaining total compliance with the standards of food operations as set by the American Correctional Association, Bureau of Prisons Program Statements, Operation Memorandums, and local institution supplements.

Incumbent is responsible for security operations such as key control, yeast control, knife and blade control, and inmate accountability and conducts routine contraband searches throughout the work area. Incumbent is responsible for his/her crew and crew kit throughout the workday. Incumbent is responsible for timely and accurate counts.

Along with all other correctional institution employees, incumbent is charged with responsibility for maintaining security of the institution. The staff correctional responsibilities precede all others required by this position and are performed on a regular and recurring basis.

Qualifications: To qualify for this position, you must meet the Barely Acceptable level on both screen-out elements (ability to supervise and aptitude for work with prisoners), receive at least one half of the total possible points, and you must furnish detailed information on your resume to support your KSA responses and to demonstrate that you possess the knowledge, skills, abilities, and the level of work to successfully perform the duties of this position at the journeyman level.

For this level of work, you must independently prepare all types of meats, poultry, seafood, vegetables, fruits, sauces, and gravies for regular and modified diet menus. Prepare, cook, season, and portion food for all meals by following standardized recipes at different levels of difficulty and plan, regulate, and schedule cooking procedures so that numerous completed food products are ready at the appropriate temperature and time. Plan and prepare or coordinate the preparation of entire meals. Prepare and present food so that it is visually appealing to customers and conforms to established food standards in terms of shape, size, texture, color, and flavor. Prepare foods for such modified diets as diabetic, sodium restricted, and low-cholesterol. Prepare menu items using special or difficult recipes that require numerous interrelated steps, many ingredients, and lengthy preparation time. Prepare a variety of menu items using several different and complex methods of preparation such as cook/chill.

Examine all food for quality and freshness before preparation, prepare, season, and cook braised and sauteed meats, poached fish, steamed or fricasseed poultry, creamed soups, and casserole dishes. Monitor temperatures and steam pressures, evaluate the condition of food being cooked at frequent intervals, and turn and baste meat to add flavor and to prevent uneven cooking and drying out. Make substitutions and adjustments in food preparation procedures and seasoning to make the food more attractive and to improve taste, and make modifications to recipes for ingredient quantities, the number of servings, and the size of the equipment available. Test and evaluate new food products and develop and modify standardized recipes, including detailed equipment lists. In some work situations, cooks at this level may coordinate the work of lower graded cooks engaged in a variety of standard cooking operations simultaneously at one or more work centers. Direct and monitor the preparation of menu items by lower grade cooks, and review menus and standardized recipes with them to assure that food items are made correctly.

This position requires a thorough knowledge of the full range of food preparation principles including the techniques and procedures necessary to develop new or revise current recipes. Know the procedures related to cooking in large quantities. Have skills necessary to overcome practical production problems, evaluate final food products, and initiate corrective action when an item does not meet established quality standards. Develop standardized recipes for quantity cooking and are able to expand and modify recipes according to the capacity of the equipment in the kitchen as well as in response to adjustments in the number of servings needed. Have a thorough understanding of the importance of flavoring materials such as vanilla, herbs, and spices and the special rules that apply to the use of seasonings when modifying or extending recipes for large quantities of food. Plan and coordinate a full range of food preparation activities involving quantity food production where a number of items are cooked simultaneously and require varied cooking methods, timing requirements, many ingredients, and numerous interrelated steps. Manage various cooking processes so that food items are served at their peak taste, texture, and appearance with minimum holding periods and so that safe and critical temperature and time control points are met.

Criminal Investigator

Agency: Office of the Inspector General
Salary: $70,339 to $117,469
Location: Ewing, New Jersey

Duties: Serves as a special agent performing a variety of criminal investigative and analytical assignments. Analyzes initial allegations and recommends the extent of required investigative resources, and the necessity for collateral support; plans, organizes and personally conducts investigations with regard to a wide variety of allegations; and plans and conducts surveillance or undercover work. Apprehends and arrests persons violating U.S. laws and conducts searches and seizures incident to the arrest or when appropriate, by warrant. Coordinates investigations that involve multiple subjects. Plans workload and, as necessary, trains and directs lower-graded criminal investigators in investigative methods and techniques. Provides technical assistance to other law enforcement personnel by evaluating and discussing investigative problems and making suggestions. Investigates allegations of crimes and crime scenes. Performs pre-and post investigation analysis and makes recommendations of appropriate actions. Prepares reports and present findings orally and in writing to managers, prosecutors, and other high-level officials. Participates in the formulation, interpretation, application, and execution of plans, policies, standards, and procedures affecting the conduct of investigations. Testifies as a government witness before grand juries and in courts in criminal cases and testifies at administrative hearings in noncriminal cases. Works on cases involving a variety of or a specific investigative function. Researches and analyzes information, determines actions to be taken, documents cases, formalizes reports, and/or makes recommendations. Performs other duties as assigned.

Knowledge, skills, and abilities required: Knowledge of criminal laws; federal rules of procedure; rules of evidence; investigative principles, techniques, and precedent court decisions; and laws and decisions relating to search, seizure, and arrest. Ability to plan, organize, and conduct sensitive and complex criminal investigations, including those related to bribery of government officials, larceny, embezzlement, contract/grant fraud, and conflicts of interest. Skill in effectively communicating, in both oral and written form, complex facts, circumstances, and evidence in a fashion that is easily understandable by a variety of audiences, such as supervisors, prosecutors, judges/juries, and agency decision makers. Skill in conducting search warrants, performing arrests, handling informants, and working/organizing undercover operations. Ability to conduct physical and electronic surveillance utilizing a variety of audio, video, and photographic equipment to record evidence.

Other information: All applicants must apply through the AVUE online system for consideration. Applicants should submit supporting documentation such as SF-50s, recent performance appraisals issued within the past 12 months, and, if applicable, DD-214s. These documents may be scanned in and submitted with your online application, faxed, e-mailed, or mailed/delivered to the U.S. Department of Justice. Please ensure that the vacancy announcement number appears on all documents.

Applicants selected for this position are required to submit to a drug test and receive a negative drug test prior to appointment. In addition, this position is a drug-testing designated position subject to random testing for illegal drug use. A background security investigation will be required for all new hires. The selectee must be able to obtain and keep a Top Secret clearance. Proficiency in English required.

The position requires that the incumbent must possess and maintain a valid state driver's license. Moderate travel is required. Selectee must sign a mobility agreement to accept relocation to other geographic areas if required by the agency.

The Attorney General has established a maximum entry age of the day before your 37th birthday for original entry into law enforcement officer positions. Prior to appointment, the person selected for this position must be determined physically fit by an authorized government physician to perform strenuous and physically demanding duties, and also pass a medical examination (which includes vision, hearing, cardiovascular, and mobility of extremities) given by an authorized government physician. The incumbent will be required to carry a firearm while performing duties and to maintain firearm proficiency.

Evidence and Transportation Assistant

Agency: Drug Enforcement Administration
Salary: $38,117 to $49,553
Location: Orlando, Florida

Duties: Performs administrative and technical duties associated with receiving, logging, storing, securing, and disposing of seized drug and non-drug evidence. Provides clerical and technical support for an asset seizure program. Reviews and processes seizures or forfeitures. Coordinates efforts with appropriate offices. Performs duties related to managing government-owned or leased passenger cars, trucks, or special purpose vehicles. Performs office automation work requiring the use of software applications and computer equipment. Prepares correspondence, reports, technical documents, graphs/charts, forms, and other office support materials.

Qualifications: Applicant must be able to type 40 words per minute. Qualifying experience for the GS-5 level includes one year of specialized experience equivalent to the GS-4 level. Examples of specialized experience are providing general clerical support (such as greeting visitors, maintaining files, and typing routine correspondence) or gathering program data or information following routine search procedures. The experience requirements for the GS-5 level may be met by completion of a bachelor's degree or four years of education above high school. Equivalent combinations of successfully completed post high school education and specialized experience may be used to meet the total experience requirements.

Qualifying experience for the GS-6 level includes one year of specialized experience equivalent to the GS-5 level. Examples of specialized experience are receiving and processing documents and data/statistical information in accordance with established procedures, reviewing documents and reports for completeness, entering information into an automated tracking system, and performing database file searches. The experience requirements for the GS-6 level may be met by the completion of six months of graduate level education that is directly related to the work of the position.

Qualifying experience for the GS-7 level includes one year of specialized experience equivalent to the GS-6 level. Examples of specialized experience are assisting in the development and/or implementation of clerical or administrative procedures for application within an organization; or selecting and arranging data and information from files and other resources for use by others in completing larger reports and projects. The experience requirements for the GS-7 level may be met by completion of one year of graduate level education that is directly related to the work of the position.

Education Technician

Agency: Federal Bureau of Prisons
Salary: $38,693 to $55,701
Location: Phoenix, Arizona

Duties: Assists with the maintenance and control of the Education Department records and files and assists with ensuring that all reporting requirements are met. Creates, maintains, and files education records for each inmate. Coordinates/corresponds with previous schools attended by inmates and with schools and colleges where inmates may be seeking admission upon release. Is responsible for the proper care, maintenance, storage, and security of all equipment and supplies belonging to the Education Department. Maintains inventory and submits requisitions for ordering supplies and equipment. Records and maintains budgetary data and financial records, and is able to provide statistical information to supervisors and staff members.

Incumbent may have responsibility for assisting with the inmate leisure and/or law library services, which includes maintaining books and equipment in a usable and orderly manner; monitoring procurement and receipt of materials for the library; ensuring proper check-out and exchange procedures; and may oversee the recruiting and training of inmate library clerks.

Incumbent may be assigned other miscellaneous duties which are not a regular and recurring part of the job, some of which include: conducting initial education interviews, completing necessary paperwork for verification of GED/HS criteria, providing coverage in education classes in the temporary absence of an instructor or program coordinator, and assisting and/or monitoring certain educational testing.

Along with all other correctional institution employees, incumbent is charged with responsibility for maintaining security of the institution. The staff correctional responsibilities precede all others required by this position and are performed on a regular and recurring basis.

How to apply: First, you must create a user account and at least one federal resume in USAJOBS. Information you provide in USAJOBS is general information completed by all applicants. The information you provide and your Federal resume will become part of your application and will automatically be transferred to the BOP-Careers system when you apply online. Second, in BOP-Careers, you will answer vacancy specific questions used to evaluate your qualifications for the specific job to which you are applying. When completed, the information you provided at USAJOBS and the answers to the vacancy questions will become your application. Third, submit required supporting documentation via mail, fax or e-mail. BOP-Careers does not accept documents uploaded to USAJOBS.

Operations and Communications Center Specialist

Agency: Federal Bureau of Investigation
Salary: $51,805 to $97,658
Location: Los Angeles, California

Duties: At the full performance level, serves as a point of contact for the general public, other law enforcement organizations, other government agencies, and various FBI entities for any situation that may rise in which LAFO, the Operational Command Center of the FBI has jurisdiction or interest. Manipulates a wide variety of highly complex specialized automated information sources, including FBI, local, and state law enforcement databases and commercial computerized information systems. Receives, analyzes, and disseminates information pertaining to potential and actual emergencies or national security situations. Implements plans, policies, and procedures to ensure timely and accurate FBI notification and mobilization actions in civil emergency situations. Conducts complex short-term and long-term research projects. Applies methods and techniques to handle difficult telephone and face-to-face complaints and inquiries from the public. Operates, monitors, and tests all communications systems within OCC. Responsible for physical security of office premises including any storage areas, offsite locations, or auxiliary parking facilities. Secures evidence delivered after hours and weekends. Must maintain numerous security clearances. Maintains the OCC in a high state of readiness 24 hours, 7 days a week. Works all shifts on a rotating basis, and prepares comprehensive logs after each shift.

How to apply: To be considered for this position, you are required to submit the information listed below online at USAJOBS before midnight Eastern Time on the closing date of the announcement.

★ Your resume

★ Your responses to the questionnaire that follows the on-line resume submission which can include narrative responses to the job-related questions.

★ Applicable supporting documentation (i.e., SF-50, any veteran's preference documentation, etc.) by attaching your documents with your resume on USAJOBS (see instructions below), by FAX. Please include your name, the vacancy announcement number, and a daytime telephone number on all supporting documentation. To ensure your information is secure, please block out any Social Security numbers (SSNs). Clean copies may be requested if you are hired.

Trial Attorney

Agency: U.S. Trustee Program
Salary: $120,830 to $153,200
Location: Washington, DC

Duties: The incumbent serves in the Office of General Counsel. The office is responsible for coordinating, directing, and developing legal policies, procedures, and litigation positions for the United States Trustee Program (Program) in enforcing the Bankruptcy Code. Its staff provides assistance to senior managers in Washington and to the program's substantial field office staff. The program's field attorneys filed more than 17,000 motions and complaints in 2008.

The incumbent provides legal advice and guidance on litigation strategy, evidentiary issues, procedural questions, discovery disputes, and other issues as they arise in the trial court and on appeal. The incumbent is responsible for performing legal research on complex factual, legal, and policy issues and providing legal and practical conclusions and recommendations in the form of oral advice, briefings, presentations, and legal memoranda for the use of the general counsel, senior management, and program field offices. The incumbent prepares pleadings, motions, interrogatories, appellate briefs, and other legal documents; conducts research of files and records; and assembles and correlates material to be used as evidence in the course of proceedings.

The incumbent leads trial teams in high profile cases, serves as a resource to litigation teams and to the program's 400 trial attorneys, crafts litigation strategy in major cases and represents the program in court and in settlement negotiations. Some travel to program offices, courts, and training around the country is required.

Qualifications: Applicants must possess a Juris Doctorate degree and be an active member of the bar (any jurisdiction). Applicants must have at least seven years of post legal experience. Outstanding academic credentials are essential.

Applicants should have superior analytical and research skills; outstanding communication and advocacy skills, both orally and in writing; a broad legal background; the ability to master new areas quickly; the ability to meet short deadlines and function effectively in time-sensitive situations; and proficiency in fostering and maintaining working relationships for the coordination and development of litigation strategy and procedures. Extensive litigation and trial experience of a minimum of five years, with at least three years of experience representing the federal government, is highly preferred. Current salary and years of experience will determine the appropriate salary level.

Department of Labor

200 Constitution Avenue NW
Washington, DC 20210
866-4-USA-DOL (toll-free)
202-693-5000

★ Web site: http://www.dol.gov/

★ Job vacancies: http://www.doors.dol.gov/

★ Internships: http://www.dol.gov/_sec/media/internprogram.htm

★ College student guide: http://www.dol.gov/oasam/doljobs/college-guide.htm

★ Career and fellowship information: http://www.dol.gov/dol/jobs.htm

★ State labor offices: http://www.dol.gov/esa/contacts/state_of.htm

★ Strategic plan: http://www.dol.gov/_sec/stratplan/strat_plan_2006-2011.htm#sg

The Department of Labor (DOL) fosters, promotes, and develops the welfare of the wage earners of the United States to improve their working conditions and to advance their opportunities for profitable employment. In carrying out this mission, the DOL works to ensure safe and healthful working conditions, a minimum hourly wage and overtime pay, freedom from employment discrimination, unemployment insurance, and workers' compensation. The DOL also protects workers' retirement and health care benefits; provides for job training programs; helps workers find jobs; works to strengthen free collective bargaining; and keeps track of changes in employment, prices, and other national economic measurements. Special efforts are made to meet the unique job market problems of older workers, youths, minority group members, women, individuals with disabilities, and other groups. The DOL employs more than 12,300 workers.

Selected DOL Agencies

The **Bureau of International Labor Affairs** (ILAB) conducts research on and formulates international economic, trade, immigration, and labor policies in collaboration with other U.S. government agencies and provides international technical assistance in support of U.S. foreign labor policy objectives. ILAB works together with other U.S. government agencies to create a more stable, secure, and prosperous international economic system in which all workers can achieve greater economic security, share in the benefits of increased international trade, and have safer and healthier workplaces where the basic rights of workers and children are respected and protected.

ILAB also helps administer the U.S. labor attaché program at embassies abroad; carries out overseas technical assistance projects; monitors internationally recognized worker rights; and conducts labor study programs for foreign visitors to the United States. ILAB has established itself as one of the most important and reliable sources of information on the exploitation of child labor around the world.

★ Web site: http://www.dol.gov/ilab/

The **Bureau of Labor Statistics** (BLS) is the principal fact-finding agency for the federal government in the broad field of labor economics and statistics. The BLS is an independent national statistical agency that collects, processes, analyzes, and disseminates essential statistical data to the American public, the U.S. Congress, other federal agencies, state and local governments, and businesses. The BLS also serves as a statistical resource to the Department of Labor. BLS hires economists, mathematical statisticians, and computer programmers.

★ Web site: http://www.bls.gov/

★ Student employment: http://www.bls.gov/jobs/student.htm

★ Career information: http://www.bls.gov/jobs/

The **Mine Safety and Health Administration** (MSHA) enforces compliance with mandatory safety and health standards as a means to eliminate fatal accidents, to reduce the frequency and severity of nonfatal accidents, to minimize health hazards, and to promote improved safety and health conditions in the country's mines. MSHA hires mining, chemical, and electrical engineers; mine safety and health inspectors; and industrial hygienists, among others.

★ Web site: http://www.msha.gov/

The **Occupational Safety and Health Administration's** (OSHA) mission is to save lives, prevent injuries, and protect the health of America's workers. To accomplish this, federal and state governments must work in partnership with more than 100 million working men and women and their six and a half million employers who are covered by the Occupational Safety and Health Act of 1970. OSHA's staff establishes protective standards, enforces those standards, and reaches out to employers and employees through technical assistance and consultation programs. OSHA hires industrial hygienists, safety engineers, and safety and health specialists, along with administrative and support staff.

★ Web site: http://www.osha.gov/

The **Office of Job Corps** is a no-cost education and vocational training program administered by the U.S. Department of Labor that helps people ages 16 through 24 get a better job, make more money, and take control of their lives. Students enroll to learn a trade, earn a high school diploma or GED, and get help finding a good job. Students participating in the program are paid a monthly allowance that increases as they continue through the program. Job Corps provides career counseling and transition support to its students for up to 12 months after they graduate from the program.

★ http://jobcorps.dol.gov/

The **Office of Workforce Investment** (OWI) provides national leadership, oversight, policy guidance, and technical assistance to the nation's workforce investment system, including the one-stop career center systems, the youth and adult employment and training programs, and national programs for targeted populations. OWI oversees the Business Relations Group, which focuses on high-growth/high-demand industries and innovative workforce solutions. OWI also oversees the development and dissemination of tools and information related to workforce and economic data, career guidance, skills, and competencies.

Within OWI, the **Employment and Training Administration** (ETA) provides quality job training, employment, labor market information, and income maintenance services primarily through state and local workforce development systems. ETA also administers programs to enhance employment opportunities and business prosperity. ETA provides information and services to help workers manage their careers and employers to find skilled workers. These services include a toll-free telephone help line and the online CareerOne Stop and O*NET, an important tool to assist in resume writing.

★ Web site: http://www.doleta.gov/

★ Job vacancies and career information: http://www.doleta.gov/jobseekers/

★ CareerOne Stop: http://www.careeronestop.org/

★ O*NET: http://online.onetcenter.org/

The **U.S. Women's Bureau** promotes the well-being of wage-earning women, improves their working conditions, increases their efficiency, and advances their opportunities for profitable employment.

★ http://www.dol.gov/wb/

The **Veterans' Employment and Training Service** (VETS) provides veterans and transitioning service members with the resources and services to succeed in the 21st century workforce by maximizing their employment opportunities, protecting their employment rights, and meeting labor-market demands with qualified veterans. VETS offers employment and training services to eligible veterans through a noncompetitive Jobs for Veterans state grants program. Under this grant program, funds are allocated to state workforce agencies in direct proportion to the number of veterans seeking employment within their state.

★ http://www.dol.gov/vets/

Other DOL Agencies

Center for Faith-Based and Community Initiatives

http://www.dol.gov/cfbci/

Employee Benefits Security Administration

http://www.dol.gov/ebsa/

Office of Disability Employment Policy

http://www.dol.gov/odep/

Office of Small Business Programs

http://www.dol.gov/osbp/welcome.html

Pension Benefit Guaranty Corporation

http://www.pbgc.gov/

Sample Job Vacancies

Economic Assistant
Agency: Bureau of Labor Statistics
Salary: $15.35 to $19.66/hour
Location: Yuma, Arizona

Job summary: This position is a permanent part-time position. Some weekend or evening hours may be required. The weekly hours of work vary, but are expected to average 16 to 32 hours per week. The average weekly and/or total hours may increase or decrease.

Duties: The incumbent of this position is responsible for the collection of primary data for the Consumer Price Index (CPI). Assignments require pricing a wide variety of outlet and product types in establishments that provide retail goods and services to the public. Assignments require the incumbent to monitor and report on local economic conditions affecting retail transactions and trends. Incumbent is responsible for securing initial voluntary cooperation from housing unit inhabitants and is responsible for repricing rental units for the CPI.

The incumbent regularly conducts visits to stores, offices, and housing units. He/she must be able to inspect a wide array of commodities and quality features. The position requires travel throughout a pricing area (city and adjacent counties) including neighborhoods of all economic types.

During the first year, travel to Washington office is necessary for training. There will be a two-week trip and a one-week trip. Additional travel outside of local area may be necessary, as needed, for training.

Qualifications: Applicants must have one year of specialized experience equivalent to the GS-4 level, or successful completion of a full four-year course study with major study in economics, or 24 semester hours in any combination of courses such as business law, statistics, algebra, precalculus, or economics. Specialized experience must demonstrate the applicant's ability to perform research or related work that involved collecting, compiling, verifying, analyzing, or reporting data. Direct contact with, and direct sales to, the public is a plus.

How to apply: Your application and all required supplemental documents must be submitted in the manner specified in this section. Applications and supplemental documents that are submitted in any other manner will be handled as incomplete and will not be considered. First, You must create a user account and at least one federal resume at USAJOBS. After you finish submitting your resume from USAJOBS, you will automatically be taken to DOORS where you will be asked to complete the next step of the application process. In DOORS, you will answer vacancy-specific questions necessary to evaluate your qualifications for the specific job to which you are applying. After the vacancy closes the HR office uses the application package to automatically rate, rank, and certify candidates. The last step of the application process is to fax all of the required supplemental documentation that is specified in the "Required Documents" section of this vacancy announcement. For example, applicants are required to submit a copy of their college transcript (in English) as part of their application package if using education as a basis for qualifying for this position. The fax cover sheets with fax instructions are displayed in DOORS after you finish answering all vacancy-related questions. You must use a separate fax cover sheet for each type of supporting document.

Economist
Agency: Bureau of Labor Statistics
Salary: $31,751 to $51,124
Location: Detroit, Michigan

Duties: As a BLS economist, your duties may include visiting establishments to collect economic data; reviewing data for consistency and accuracy; analyzing and interpreting data; planning and conducting surveys; preparing internal reports, press releases, or articles on economic trends and activities; interacting with outside customers on economic trends; assisting in the development and application of computer software; helping to develop measurement techniques for economic analysis; and writing and editing articles, reports, and other communications published by BLS. At BLS, you will receive specific assignments in a variety of directly or indirectly collected BLS surveys. Typically, your assignments will be designed to develop basic competence in the collection, reporting, and evaluation of data. The developmental nature of the assignments will prepare you for higher level work. As you progress, you are expected to reach the point of undertaking work of greater than average difficulty in at least one of the program areas. In addition, you are expected to develop a general understanding of BLS data and to be able to consult with users or establishments on routine problems concerning the collection, uses, and limitations of published statistics.

Economists working in the BLS regions are concerned primarily with the data collection activities. These activities frequently include interviewing establishment officials to acquire needed data, analyzing data for conformance to program procedures, and preparing periodic reports on survey processes and problems. Economists working in the BLS Headquarters in Washington, DC, are concerned primarily with the consolidation, reporting, and evaluation of the collected data. Initial assignments are performed in accordance with precise instructions. In both headquarters and regional offices, some positions in the federal/state programs may require the incumbent to provide limited technical guidance to participating state agencies.

Qualifications: Degree in economics or in any related field that included at least 21 semester hours in economics and three semester hours in statistics, accounting, or calculus. Or a combination of courses equivalent to a major in economics, plus appropriate experience or additional education. Examples of qualifying experience include individual economic research assignments, supervisory or project coordination assignments, or teaching assignments in a college or university. For GS-07, applicants also must have either one year of economic-related specialized experience comparable in level of difficulty and responsibility to the GS-5 level in the federal service or superior academic achievement (upper third of graduating class, 3.0 or better grade point average, or membership in a national honor society).

Education Campaign Coordinator
Agency: Employee Benefits Security Administration
Salary: $86,927 to $113,007
Location: Washington, DC

Duties: Provides leadership in the development, recommendation, and implementation of a communications strategy and action plan that promotes the agency's health benefits and fiduciary education initiatives. Gives speeches and coordinates and participates in outreach activities and other meetings/discussions. Works with office senior staff in developing informational products, such as brochures, pamphlets, videos, public service announcements, reports to Congress, etc., in support of campaign communication strategy and action plan. Writes articles, speeches, and talking points for senior officials. Maintains an inventory of booklets, pamphlets, and other materials produced by the agency to assist in making them available for agency outreach and for use by other government and private concerns. Establishes and maintains partnerships/liaisons with other government agencies and private concerns to implement campaign plan including developing and distributing materials and participating in outreach activities. Maintains campaign budget. Ensures program coverage and editorial balance in terms of articles and publication/issuances released by the agency. Serves as spokesperson/representative for the campaign in meetings, outreach activities, and work with partners.

How you will be evaluated: Applicants meeting the minimum qualification requirements for this position are further evaluated against the evaluation factors to determine who will be referred to the selecting official. The rating and ranking of candidates to determine the best qualified will be accomplished by comparing the candidate's responses to the evaluation factors (KSA questions) against the evaluation criteria. Applicants will be scored on a scale of 70 to 100. In order to receive consideration, applicants must separately address each of the evaluation factors. Evaluation factors should be prepared in clear and concise paragraphs, not exceeding one page for each factor. Current and/or past supervisors may be contacted unless specified otherwise. A panel and/or the selecting official or his/her designee may interview applicants.

Evaluation Factors (KSAs):

1. Describe your skill in communications principles, methods, and techniques.

2. Describe your knowledge of workers and employers and others seeking assistance in complying with the law, including their levels of knowledge about the law, government programs or industry, their concerns, and their need for information.

3. Describe your ability to develop written and web-based materials and tools to disseminate worker/consumer and/or compliance assistance information about the law, government programs, or industry.

4. Describe your ability to effectively communicate orally and disseminate information about the law, government programs, and industry.

5. Describe your knowledge of health or retirement related legal requirements, government programs or industry.

In the event of tied ratings, applicants will be further evaluated based on the following:

Knowledge of media markets, research tools, and ability to evaluate program effectiveness.

Industrial Hygienist

Agency: Occupational Safety and Health Administration
Salary: $38,117 to $73,329
Location: Mobile, Alabama

Duties: For GS-07, Performs industrial hygiene inspections of a limited nature in a variety of workplaces and may perform portions of inspections that are being conducted by higher graded industrial hygienists. Maintains, calibrates, operates, reads and may select a wide variety of sampling and measuring devices. Performs selected laboratory analyses and/or interprets laboratory results. Writes limited reports or portions of inspection data collected and analytical results.

For GS-09 and GS-11, performs industrial hygiene inspections of a routine nature in a variety of workplaces noting hazardous conditions and unsafe work practices. May or may not work as auxiliary to higher-graded industrial hygienist(s) in performing segments of more complex and difficult inspections. Selects, sets up, calibrates, monitors and reads a wide variety of sampling and measuring devices. Prepares technical reports based on findings of studies, inspections, analysis of laboratory results, etc. Recommends and reviews corrective action to ensure hazard abatement is accomplished. Promotes sound industrial hygiene practices by working with employers and employees and by participating in public information activities. Provides justification for findings to third parties when appropriate.

Qualifications: A bachelor's or higher degree from an accredited college or university in industrial hygiene or a branch of engineering, physical science, or life science that included 12 semester hours in chemistry (including organic chemistry) and 18 additional semester hours of courses in any combination of chemistry, physics, engineering, health physics, environmental health, biostatistics, biology, physiology, toxicology, epidemiology, or industrial hygiene. Courses in the history or teaching of chemistry are not acceptable.

For GS-07, one year of graduate level education or superior academic achievement at the undergraduate level (upper third of graduating class, 3.0 GPA for all coursework during the last two years, 3.5 GPA in required courses completed in major field during the final two years, or membership in a national scholastic honor society). For GS-9, two years of progressively higher level graduate education leading to a master's degree or equivalent graduate degree at an accredited college or university in a field of study described above. For GS-11, three years of progressively higher level graduate education leading to a Ph.D. degree or equivalent doctoral degree from an accredited college or university in a field of study described above.

A combination of education and experience is also acceptable. The education must include at least 12 semester hours of course work in chemistry (including organic chemistry) and 18 additional semester hours as specified above, plus additional education and/or experience. Qualifying experience may have been obtained in field, laboratory, engineering, or other environment if the work provided a means of obtaining a professional knowledge of the theory and application of the principles of industrial hygiene and closely related sciences such as physics and engineering controls.

Any combination of graduate level education and professional work experience that equals 2 years is qualifying for GS-9. Any such combination that equals three years is qualifying for GS-11.

Spanish-speaking applicants are desired, but not required. All applicants are required to submit a copy of their college transcript (in English) as part of their application package.

Metal/Nonmetal Mine Safety and Health Inspector
Agency: Mine Safety and Health Administration
Salary: $38,117 to $73,329
Location: Warrendale, Pennsylvania

Job summary: This job screening will be held at the Ramada Inn. MSHA will test and interview eligible candidates for MSHA's Inspector Career Intern Program. Candidates will be evaluated on basic math and writing skills, and the necessary technical and general competencies required for inspection work. Prepare for the math and writing tests now. Math and writing guides are available on MSHA's Inspector Career Intern Program Web site. Review the guides and practice. You will be given 60 minutes to complete the tests, so we recommend practicing in a timed environment. Please be aware that although formulas will be provided to you during the math test, you will not be permitted to use a calculator.

Candidates who have previously passed the math and writing tests within the last two years can register for an interview only by applying to this vacancy announcement. Applicants whose test results are scheduled to expire within six months are strongly encouraged to re-test in order to maintain their eligibility for consideration.

All applicants must first pass both the math and writing tests in order to be interviewed for possible employment. All interviews are conducted onsite and candidates must appear in person.

Key requirements: Frequent travel (some inspector positions require 5 to 15 nights per month), possession of a valid state driver's license, pre- and post-employment drug testing and medical examinations, pre- and post-employment background and suitability check, and, for males between 18 and 25, registration with the Selective Service System.

Duties: MSHA Inspector job responsibilities include conducting on-site inspections or investigations of underground and surface mines, mills, and quarries in order to identify potential hazardous conditions to the safety and health of workers, ensure proper mining equipment maintenance and use, check mining practices for conformance with safety and health laws and regulations, issue citations when violations and hazards are identified, determine how accidents and disasters are caused and prevented, help direct rescue and firefighting operations after fires or explosions, investigate safety and health complaints from mine personnel, and discuss inspection/investigation findings and provide technical advice and assistance to mine management and personnel.

What to expect next: Selected candidates will participate in a formal training program, and may be converted to a permanent position after successfully completing the program. The formal training program at the GS-7 level is three years; and at the GS-9 and GS-11 levels, two years.

Department of the Navy

1200 Navy Pentagon
Washington, DC 20350
703-697-7391

★ Web site: http://www.navy.mil/

★ Civilian employment: https://chart.donhr.navy.mil/

★ How to apply for a civilian job: https://www.donhr.navy.mil/Jobs/default.asp

The Department of the Navy recruits military and civilian personnel. It organizes, supplies, equips, trains, mobilizes, and demobilizes the U.S. Navy and Marine Corps, including their human capital and physical assets. The department oversees the construction, outfitting, and repair of naval ships, aircraft, equipment, and facilities. The department protects the United States by the effective prosecution of war at sea, including (with its Marine Corps component) the seizure or defense of advanced naval bases, to support, as required, the forces of all military departments of the United States and to maintain freedom of the seas.

The Department of the Navy has three principal components: the Navy Department, consisting of executive offices mostly in Washington, DC; the operating forces, including the Marine Corps, the reserve components, and, in time of war, the U.S. Coast Guard (in peace, a component of the Department of Homeland Security); and the shore establishment. The shore establishment provides support to the operating forces (known as "the fleet") in the form of facilities for the repair of machinery and electronics; communications centers; training areas and simulators; ship and aircraft repair; intelligence and meteorological support; storage areas for repair parts, fuel, and munitions; medical and dental facilities; and air bases. The Department of the Navy employs approximately 176,000 civilians.

Selected Navy Agencies

The **Naval Air Systems Command** (NAVAIR) provides materiel support for naval and marine aircraft and airborne weapon systems, such as guided missiles. NAVAIR provides engineering, development, testing, and evaluation of airborne weapons systems. In addition to its work with manned aircraft, NAVAIR works to enhance the intelligence, surveillance, and reconnaissance capabilities of unmanned systems. NAVAIR develops, delivers, and sustains aircraft, weapons, and systems. It maintains the operational forces of the U.S. Navy in a state of battle readiness.

★ Web site: http://www.navy.mil/local/navair/

★ Job vacancies: http://www.navair.navy.mil/tfsmd/staffing/STFCLS.HTM

The **Naval Sea Systems Command** (NAVSEA) is the largest of the Navy's five systems commands. It provides materiel support to the U.S. Navy, Marine Corps, and the Defense and Transportation departments for ships, submarines, other sea platforms, shipboard combat systems and components, other surface and undersea warfare and weapons systems, and ordnance expendables not specifically assigned to other system commands. NAVSEA employs nearly 50,000 NAVSEA military and civilian team members.

★ Web site: http://www.navsea.navy.mil/

★ Job vacancies: http://www.navsea.navy.mil/content/Careers/NAVSEA_Jobs.aspx

The **Naval Special Warfare Command** (NSW) is the naval component to the United States Special Operations Command headquartered in Tampa, Florida. NSW provides a versatile, responsive, and offensively focused force with a continuous overseas presence. The major operational components of NSW include Naval Special Warfare Groups. These components deploy Sea, Air, Land (SEAL) Teams, SEAL Delivery Vehicle Teams, and Special Boat Teams worldwide to meet the training, exercise, contingency, and wartime requirements of theater commanders. NSW employs approximate 775 civilian support personnel.

★ Web site: http://www.navsoc.navy.mil/

Based in San Diego, the **Space and Naval Warfare Systems Command** (SPAWAR) provides technical and material support to the Department of the Navy for space systems; command, control, communications, and intelligence systems; and electronic warfare and undersea surveillance. It develops, delivers, and maintains effective, capable, and integrated command, control, communications, computer, intelligence, and surveillance systems.

★ Web site: http://enterprise.spawar.navy.mil

★ Career information: http://enterprise.spawar.navy.mil/body.cfm?Type=C&category=18&subcat=5

The **U.S. Marine Corps** (USMC) mainly provides force protection for the sea. USMC is the only forward-deployed force designed for expeditionary operations by air, land, or sea. Marines are trained to be first on the scene to respond to attacks on the United States or its interests, acts of political violence against Americans abroad, disaster relief, humanitarian assistance, or evacuation of Americans from foreign countries. The Marine Corps has a civilian workforce of approximately 25,000 employees.

★ Web site: http://www.marines.mil/units/hqmc/Pages/default.aspx

★ Employment application tools: https://lnweb1.manpower.usmc.mil/CCLD/employment/employment_opportunities_employee_applicant_tools.htm

The **U.S. Naval Observatory** (USNO) is one of the oldest scientific agencies in the country. Established in 1830 as the Depot of Charts and Instruments, its primary mission was to care for the U.S. Navy's chronometers, charts, and other navigational equipment. Today, the U.S. Naval Observatory is the preeminent authority in the areas of precise time and astrometry, and distributes earth orientation parameters and other astronomical data required for accurate navigation and fundamental astronomy.

★ Web site: http://www.usno.navy.mil/USNO

Other Navy Agencies

Bureau of Medicine and Surgery

http://navymedicine.med.navy.mil/

Commander Navy Installations Command

https://www.cnic.navy.mil/

Commander Operational Test and Evaluation Forces

http://www.cotf.navy.mil/

Military Sealift Command

http://www.msc.navy.mil/

Naval Facilities Engineering Command

https://portal.navfac.navy.mil/portal/page/portal/navfac/

Naval Network Warfare Command

http://www.netwarcom.navy.mil/

Naval Postgraduate School

http://www.nps.edu/

Naval Reserve

http://www.navyreserve.com/

Naval Safety Center

http://www.safetycenter.navy.mil/

Naval Supply Systems Command

https://www.navsup.navy.mil/navsup

Program Executive Office, Ships

http://peoships.crane.navy.mil/

U.S. Fleet Forces Command

http://www.cffc.navy.mil/

U.S. Naval Academy

http://www.usna.edu/

U.S. Naval Forces Central Command and Fifth Fleet

http://www.cusnc.navy.mil/

U.S. Pacific Fleet

http://www.cpf.navy.mil/

Department of State

2201 C Street NW
Washington, DC 20520
202-647-4000
877-487-2778 (passport information—toll-free)
202-663-1225 (visa information)
202-647-5225 (American traveler hotline)

★ Web site: http://www.state.gov/

★ Job vacancies: http://jobsearch.usajobs.opm.gov/a9st00.asp

★ Franklin Fellows program: http://www.careers.state.gov/FF/index.html

★ Fulbright program: http://fulbright.state.gov/

★ Student employment: http://www.careers.state.gov/student/

★ Student career programs: http://www.careers.state.gov/students/programs.html

★ Youth and education: http://www.state.gov/youthandeducation/

★ Career options: http://www.careers.state.gov/resources/career-nav.html

★ Career information: http://www.state.gov/careers/

★ Foreign service officer program: http://www.careers.state.gov/officer/index.html

★ Strategic plan: http://www.state.gov/s/d/rm/rls/dosstrat/

Ranked the 2007 number six best place to work, the U.S. Department of State (State) manages U.S. relationships with foreign governments, international organizations, and people of other countries. The Department of State advises the president in the formulation and execution of foreign policy and promotes the long-range security and well-being of the United States. This department determines and analyzes the facts relating to American overseas interests, makes recommendations on policy and future action, and takes the necessary steps to carry out established policy. The Department of State engages in continuous consultations with the American public, Congress, other U.S. departments and agencies, and foreign governments. It negotiates treaties and agreements with foreign nations, speaks for the United States in the United Nations and other international organizations in which the United States participates, and represents the United States at international conferences.

The United States maintains diplomatic relations with nearly 180 of the 191 countries in the world, as well as with many international organizations. The Department of State maintains nearly 260 diplomatic and consular posts around the world, including embassies, consulates, and missions to international organizations.

The Foreign Service employs approximately 21,000 people internationally and an additional 14,000 civil service employees located in Washington, DC, to achieve the goals and implement the initiatives of American foreign policy. A Foreign Service career is a way of life that offers unique rewards, opportunities, and sometimes hardships. Members of the Foreign Service can be sent to any embassy, consulate, or other diplomatic mission anywhere in the world to serve the diplomatic needs of the United States. The Foreign Service selection process is lengthy, multistaged, and highly competitive. For detailed information about the process, see the link "Steps to becoming a Foreign Service Specialist."

About 65,000 civil service employees, headquartered primarily in Washington, DC, are involved in Department of State areas ranging from human rights to narcotics control to trade to environmental issues. These employees are the domestic counterparts to consular officers abroad, issuing passports and assisting U.S. citizens in trouble overseas.

Selected Department of State Agencies

The **Bureau of Diplomatic Security** (DS) protects the secretary of state and other senior government officials, residents, and visiting foreign dignitaries and foreign missions in the United States. DS conducts criminal, counterintelligence, and personnel security investigations; and ensures the integrity of international travel documents, sensitive information, classified processing equipment, and management information systems. It physically and technically protects domestic and overseas facilities of the Department of State; provides professional law enforcement and security training to U.S. and foreign personnel; and oversees a comprehensive, multifaceted overseas security program servicing the needs of U.S. missions and the resident U.S. citizens and business communities. Through the Office of Foreign Missions, the bureau regulates domestic activities of the foreign diplomatic community in the areas of taxation, real property acquisitions, motor vehicle operation, domestic travel, and customs processing. It also manages reciprocity and immunity issues for foreign diplomats in the United States.

In the United States, DS investigates passport and visa fraud and conducts personnel security investigations. DS trains foreign civilian law enforcement officers in disciplines designed to reduce the threat and repercussions of terrorism throughout the world. With more than 486 special agents assigned to diplomatic missions in 157 countries, DS is the most widely represented American security and law enforcement organization around the world.

★ Web site: http://www.state.gov/m/ds/

★ Career information: http://www.state.gov/m/ds/career/

The **Bureau of International Narcotics and Law Enforcement Affairs** (INL) develops, coordinates, and implements the international narcotics control and anticrime assistance activities of the Department of State. It provides advice on international narcotics control matters for OMB, the National Security Council, and the White House Office of National Drug Control Policy and ensures implementation of U.S. policy in international narcotics matters. The bureau also provides guidance on narcotics control and anticrime matters to chiefs of missions and directs narcotics control coordinators at posts abroad. It communicates or authorizes communication, as appropriate, with foreign governments on drug control and anticrime matters, including negotiating, concluding, and terminating agreements relating to international narcotics control and anticrime programs.

★ Web site: http://www.state.gov/p/inl/

The **Bureau of International Organization Affairs** (IO) provides guidance and support for U.S. participation in international organizations and conferences and formulates and implements U.S. policy toward international organizations, with particular emphasis on those organizations that make up the United Nations (UN) system. It provides direction in the development, coordination, and implementation of U.S. multilateral policy. IO works to advance U.S. policies and interests through multilateral diplomacy and to ensure that the UN and other international organizations remain viable and effective.

★ Web site: http://www.state.gov/p/io/

★ Job vacancies: http://www.state.gov/p/io/empl/

★ U.S. Mission to the United Nations: http://www.un.int/usa/

The **Bureau of Population, Refugees, and Migration** (PRM) formulates policies on population, refugees, and migration and administers U.S. refugee assistance and admissions programs. It works closely with the U.S. Agency for International Development, which administers U.S. international population programs. The bureau also coordinates U.S. international migration policy and oversees admissions of refugees to the United States for permanent resettlement. PRM administers and monitors U.S. contributions to international and nongovernmental organizations to assist and protect refugees abroad.

★ Web site: http://www.state.gov/g/prm/

The **Foreign Service Institute** (FSI) is the federal government's primary training institution for officers and support personnel of the U.S. foreign affairs community, preparing American diplomats and other professionals to advance U.S. foreign affairs interests overseas and in Washington. At the George P. Shultz National Foreign Affairs Training Center, FSI provides more than 450 courses, including some 70 foreign languages, to more than 50,000 enrollees a year from the Department of State and more than 40 other government agencies and the military service branches.

★ Web site: http://www.state.gov/m/fsi/

★ Transition center: http://www.state.gov/m/fsi/tc/

The **Bureau of Oceans, Environment, and Science** (OES) serves as the foreign policy focal point for international oceans, environmental, and scientific efforts. Nearly 200 employees further these goals through programs and activities concerning infectious diseases, biodiversity, climate change, access to water and energy, oceans affairs, science and technology cooperation, management of toxic chemicals, environmental components of trade agreements, and the exploration of space. In addition, the bureau represents the United States at major international negotiations.

Located within OES, the **Health, Space, and Science Directorate** includes the **Office of International Health Affairs,** which works with U.S. agencies to facilitate policy-making regarding international bioterrorism, infectious disease, surveillance and response, environmental health, and health in post-conflict situations. The **Office of Space and Advanced Technology** handles issues arising from our exploration of space to assure global security regarding this new frontier, and the **Office of Science and Technology Cooperation** promotes the interests of the U.S. science and technology communities in the international policy arena.

★ Web site: http://www.state.gov/g/oes/

The **Office of the Chief of Protocol** directly advises, assists, and supports the president, the vice president, and the secretary of state on official matters of national and international protocol, and in the planning, hosting, and officiating of related ceremonial events and activities for visiting heads of state. The office also is the administrator of Blair House, the president's official guesthouse. The Office of Protocol serves as the coordinator within and between the State Department and the White House on all protocol matters for presidential or vice presidential travel abroad. The chief of protocol, the deputy chief, and four assistant chiefs share responsibility for officiating the swearing in of senior State Department officials, selection boards, and incoming Foreign Service and Civil Service employees.

★ Web site: http://www.state.gov/s/cpr/

Other Agencies in the Department of State

Arms Control and International Security

http://www.state.gov/t/

Bureau of African Affairs

http://www.state.gov/p/af/

Bureau of Consular Affairs

http://travel.state.gov/

Bureau of Democracy, Human Rights, and Labor

http://www.state.gov/g/drl/

Bureau of East Asian and Pacific Affairs

http://www.state.gov/p/eap/

Bureau of Economic, Energy, and Business Affairs

http://www.state.gov/e/eeb/

Bureau of Educational and Cultural Affairs

http://exchanges.state.gov/

Bureau of European and Eurasian Affairs

http://www.state.gov/p/eur/

Bureau of Intelligence and Research

http://www.state.gov/s/inr/

Bureau of International Information Programs

http://www.state.gov/r/iip/

Bureau of International Security and Nonproliferation

http://www.state.gov/t/isn/

Bureau of Near Eastern Affairs

http://www.state.gov/p/nea/

Bureau of Overseas Buildings Operations

http://www.state.gov/obo/

Bureau of Political-Military Affairs

http://www.state.gov/t/pm/

Bureau of South and Central Asian Affairs

http://www.state.gov/p/sca/

Bureau of Verification, Compliance, and Implementation

http://www.state.gov/t/vci/

Bureau of Western Hemisphere Affairs

http://www.state.gov/p/wha/

Office of International Women's Issues

http://www.state.gov/g/wi/

Office of the U.S. Global AIDS Coordinator

http://www.state.gov/s/gac/

Office of War Crimes Issues

http://www.state.gov/s/wci/

Office to Monitor and Combat Trafficking in Persons

http://www.state.gov/g/tip/

Public Diplomacy and Public Affairs

http://www.state.gov/r/

U.S. Mission to the United Nations

http://www.usunnewyork.usmission.gov/

Sample Job Vacancies

Financial Management Specialist
Agency: Washington Liaison Office for Global Financial Services
Salary: $50,408 to $79,280
Location: Washington, DC

Duties: At both the full performance level, GS-11, and the GS-09 level, the incumbent is responsible for evaluating financial policies, systems and procedures; reviewing financial controls; designing and preparing financial reports; performing reconciliation of accounts and associated subsidiary records; conducting analytical or program work pertaining to payroll or benefit systems; and developing and implementing financial procedures.

Typical duties performed at the GS-11 level include: evaluating the effectiveness of operating financial systems in relation to meeting established financial practices and standards and organizational needs; assuring the proper documentation of transactions and the proper entry of transactions in accounts and for preparation of balance sheets and income statements; developing statistical charts, comparative analyses, financial statements, and summary statements; and identifying and resolving financial and operational irregularities and problems with records, subsidiary ledgers, appropriations, and obligations.

Typical duties performed at the GS-09 level include: identifying financial and operational irregularities and problems in records, subsidiary ledgers, appropriations, and/or obligations that do not comply with established policies and practices, or that adversely affect funds; providing solutions when well-established principles and practices apply; verifying that obligations and expenditures occur in a timely manner in accordance with work plans and regulatory and procedural controls; recommending the transfer of funds between object classes and line item accounts under the same allotment when funds are needed to cover increases in obligations or expenditures fall within established limits; and preparing data summaries for inclusion in special and recurring financial reports covering the status of funds, expenses, and obligations.

Qualifications: U.S. Citizenship is required. Must be able to obtain/maintain a Top Secret security clearance.

At the GS-09 level, must have at least one year of experience (equivalent to at least the GS-07 or higher levels in the federal service) performing routine fundamental financial management tasks or a Master's degree, or at least two years (or 36 semester hours) of graduate-level education towards such a degree, in finance or another field directly related to this position. When an applicant has less than one year of specialized experience, he or she may combine successfully completed graduate-level education with experience to meet the total qualification requirements.

At the GS-11 level, must have at least one or more years of responsible experience (equivalent to at least the GS-09 or higher levels in the federal service) identifying and resolving moderately complex financial management tasks or have a Ph.D., or at least three years of graduate-level education towards such a degree, in finance or another field directly related to this position. Combinations of successfully completed education and experience may be used to meet the total qualification requirements.

Foreign Service Regional Medical Technologist
Agency: Office of Medical Services
Salary: $42,314 to $62,140
Location: Many vacancies throughout the world

Job summary: The Office of Medical Services in the Department of State maintains and promotes the health of employees and their accompanying family members who represent United States government agencies abroad. The department assigns Foreign Service medical technologists, medical officers, medical officers/psychiatrists, and health practitioners to selected posts overseas. Many of these posts have significant health risks and local medical care that is inadequate by U.S. standards. The foreign service medical technologist performs a wide variety of unusual and specialized tests and procedures ranging from difficult to more complex in nature in a variety of fields, such as parasitology, microbiology, mycology, chemistry, hematology, blood banking, and urinalysis. Duties also include training contract medical technologists and developing quality control standards. Regional medical technologists are presently serving in Beijing; Cairo; Dakar; Jakarta; Lagos; Mexico City; Moscow; New Delhi; and Washington, DC. While the preference of an applicant for a particular post or area of assignment is given every possible consideration, assignments are dictated by the needs of the service.

Duties: Serving as a Regional Medical Technologist (RMT) in support of the employees of the United States' government and their eligible family members, a medical technologist may work in conjunction with other Foreign Service medical personnel. At each post of responsibility, the RMT manages the health unit laboratory, supervises the locally hired medical technologist, and performs testing in hematology, chemistry, parasitology, immunology, microbiology, and urinalysis. The RMT also oversees the performance of locally hired medical technologists in health unit laboratories at regional posts to assure delivery of reliable laboratory services. These regional posts are within and outside of the country of assigned post. In addition, the RMT assures that Clinical Laboratory Improvements Amendment (CLIA) laboratory standards for operation and Occupational Safety and Health Administration (OSHA) standards for safety are maintained at assigned and regional posts; provides training on these laboratory and safety standards; performs routine visitations to regional posts to teach and instruct on laboratory science and food safety, to act as liaison with local laboratories, and to address all laboratory-related issues; and assures implementation of programs developed by the Office of Medical Services. Foreign Service Medical Technologists are considered "essential personnel" and are therefore on call to provide services 24 hours a day, 7 days a week.

Qualifications: Applicant must have a minimum of a bachelor's degree in medical technology, clinical laboratory science or chemistry, physical science, or biological science from a recognized institution and four years of laboratory experience with at least two years generalist training/experience and two years experience in a designated specialty/subspecialty. Four years of experience must be within the last five years. Applicant must possess a current registration as a medical technologist or clinical laboratory scientist with either the American Society for Clinical Pathology (ASCP), the National Credentialing Agency for Laboratory Personnel, Inc. (NCA), the American Medical Technologist (AMT), or Health Education and Welfare (HEW).

Applicant must have demonstrated skill in performing tests with detail and accuracy and providing information to appropriate individuals as necessary. The work involves exercising a high degree of laboratory management expertise. Applicant must have knowledge of general anatomy, medical terminology and laboratory science, quality control procedures and quality assurance plans, and laboratory equipment used in performing a variety of laboratory tests; skill in maintaining and troubleshooting laboratory equipment; and the ability to train other medical professionals in laboratory techniques.

The patient population covered is unique because of background and lifestyle as part of a diplomatic community overseas. This population also differs in terms of clinical and administrative needs and the national security concerns inherent in their employment. Applicant must be a skilled and experienced medical technologist who recognizes and understands the problems of delivering laboratory services to a large group of Americans posted in widely scattered groups of varying size, most often where local medical resources are limited or nonexistent. Experience in providing laboratory results and assistance via electronic communication such as fax, telephone, telegram, and e-mail is preferable. Experience in performing laboratory techniques to diagnose infectious and tropical diseases is required.

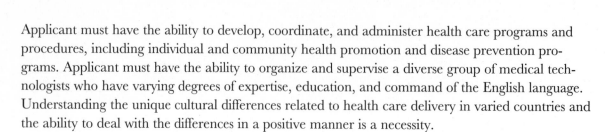

Applicant must have the ability to develop, coordinate, and administer health care programs and procedures, including individual and community health promotion and disease prevention programs. Applicant must have the ability to organize and supervise a diverse group of medical technologists who have varying degrees of expertise, education, and command of the English language. Understanding the unique cultural differences related to health care delivery in varied countries and the ability to deal with the differences in a positive manner is a necessity.

Candidates must have the capacity to gain the cooperation and confidence of patients, co-workers, supervisors, and subordinates. Individuals must have experience in working in a multidisciplinary practice as well as experience in team building. Effective written and oral communications skills and the ability to present laboratory findings in a clear and concise manner to medical and nonmedical personnel are essential. The demonstrated ability to teach or lecture to groups on laboratory issues is preferred. Computer skills are required.

Purchasing Agent

Agency: Harry S Truman Division, Office of Global Publishing Solutions, Information Sharing Services, Bureau of Administration
Salary: $33,269 to $43,251
Location: Washington, DC

Duties: The incumbent will be responsible for responding to internal requests for outsourced goods and services, office supplies, miscellaneous production consumables, repair and/or servicing of production equipment, parts; assisting managers in preparing specifications and/or scope of work for the needed requirements; reviewing requests, soliciting suppliers/vendors, and preparing bids for approval; recommending alternatives and substitutes if items requested are not available; procuring items with government credit card or preparing corresponding purchase request for approval; and establishing and creating Blanket Purchase Agreements (BPA) as needed. If required, incumbent will maintain official time and attendance databases and prepare official time and attendance reports and issue and review timecards for accuracy in monitoring of shift and night differentials, overtime, and tardiness.

Qualifications: Have one or more years of related experience (experience that is equivalent to at least the GS-4 level in the federal service), or have bachelor's or higher degree in any field of study, or have a combination of related work experience and undergraduate education. Related experience is demonstrated experience in purchasing regulations, policies, and procedures, including solicitation and methods such as oral solicitations, credit card purchasing, and calls against Blanket Purchase Agreements. Related experience also involves utilizing knowledge of common business practices, including price evaluation, in order to ensure that expenditures are reasonable and to identify better purchasing opportunities and knowing the characteristics of printing supplies and other commodities (sizes, brand names, packaging, quality, etc.) in order to advise others on various sources and the quality of requested items.

How to apply: You must submit your application so that it will be received by the closing date of the announcement. To apply for this position, you must provide a complete application package, which includes your responses to the assessment questionnaire, and your resume and any other documents specified in the Required Documents section of this job announcement. Use Application Manager for convenience and quickest processing. Track your progress to a complete application package using the My Application Packages checklist and status displays in Application Manager.

Special Assistant for Executive Operations
Agency: Iraq Transition Assistance Office
Salary: $73,100 to $113,007
Location: Baghdad, Iraq

Job summary: The U.S. Department of State is the lead U.S. foreign affairs agency. To facilitate this mission, the Iraq Transition Assistance Office (ITAO) was established by National Security Presidential Directive (NSPD) 36. ITAO's purpose is to perform the specific project of supporting executive departments and agencies in concluding remaining large infrastructure projects expeditiously in Iraq, in facilitating Iraq's transition to self-sufficiency, and in maintaining an effective diplomatic presence in Iraq. ITAO operates under the direction of the Chief of Mission, U.S. Embassy Baghdad.

Under this temporary appointment, compensation includes salary plus danger pay and post differentials paid at the rate of 35 percent each. Please see benefits section for specific details.

Duties: As directed by the chief of staff, supports the ITAO director by preparing or coordinating responses to assignments that are required by the front office of the embassy. Provides expert advice and program assistance in the coordination and management of a wide variety of the most sensitive and complex projects, keeping the supervisor informed of critical developments and providing expert advice on the subjects of civil affairs and economic operations. Drafts and supervises key policy and program initiatives for ITAO; conducts analysis of reconstruction developments, political-economic linkages, and infrastructure security for key principals; and utilizes that analysis in advice and presentations. Assists the director and others in the executive office with the preparation of documents related to the strategy for U.S. government assistance. Coordinates agenda items and presentations for the Joint Executive Steering Committee (Mission Task Force on Reconstruction, Development, and Assistance) to join military and civilian efforts in support of reconstruction objectives, including local governance, capacity building, and delivery of essential services. Undertakes research projects that require the identification of sources of information, fact-finding research and investigation, analysis, report writing, correspondence preparation, and follow-up. These assignments are typically of a highly sensitive and controversial nature and involve contact and coordination with key civilian and military officials within ITAO, U.S. Mission, MNF-I, and other governmental and nongovernmental organizations.

Qualifications: Know the principles and methodologies of program and project management and management reporting. Know the organization and functional interrelationships within the Department of State and Defense and their relationships with other cabinet-level agencies involved in the formation of national security policy and plans. Must be extremely effective in negotiating conflicting views to develop policy and major program aspects in pursuit of national policies and goals. Be able to manage large-scale study efforts requiring coordination across agencies of the U.S. government and other nations. Have extensive knowledge of requisite nature of background information and data, format of presentation, levels of coordination, etc. Possess highly developed written and oral communication skills and ability to complete tasks efficiently. Have strong interpersonal skills to effectively communicate and interact with all levels within and outside the organization.

All candidates for employment must obtain a minimum of a Secret security clearance from the Diplomatic Security Service (DSS). Even if the candidate has previously held a government security clearance or still holds one, the candidate must complete a Questionnaire for National Security

Positions (SF-86), a credit/consumer report release form, and two sets of fingerprint cards for adjudication by the Diplomatic Security Service. Full disclosure and candor is imperative when completing this paperwork.

All employees assigned to or deployed to Iraq under Chief of Mission authority and working for agencies that participate in the Department of State Medical Program are required to receive a medical clearance from the State Department's Office of Medical Services (MED) before departure to post. Employees must be free of a medical or mental condition that would require follow-up treatment or care not currently available in Iraq or that may be exacerbated by service in Iraq. A review of vaccination status and update is also required.

Employees also must receive an ethics clearance, which may require completing and executing the Executive Branch Public Financial Disclosure Form (SF-278). Ethics clearances are required to help ensure that employees do not violate or participate in any actions creating the appearance that they are violating the law or standards governing ethical conduct for employees of the executive branch.

Supervisory Language Training Specialist

Agency: Foreign Service Institute
Salary: $73,100 to $113,007
Location: Arlington, Virginia

Duties: Manages and directs a foreign language training program or programs that vary widely by numbers of Language and Culture Instructors (LCIs) and students, frequency of course presentations, and lengths of courses. Recruits, trains, and develops LCIs to teach language and culture of assigned language(s). Exercises professional linguistic skills to develop language training program(s) that bring students to high levels of language proficiency. May manage several linguistic sections where languages taught differ from own areas of linguistic expertise. Designs new courses and/or makes extensive revisions in existing training course(s). May manage groups of LCIs and students whose political, cultural, and religious differences make coordinative and counseling efforts difficult and challenging.

Provides complete range of resources and inputs to language program(s) assigned, including design of curriculum and course content; supervision and management of LCIs; and supervision, counseling, and evaluation of students. Performs needs analyses in determining need for course design and development, and monitors course presentations to assess usability of courses in terms of teacher effectiveness and student reactions. Develops educational and technological materials for use with existing language materials, and develops supplementary materials to accompany basic text materials as required. Introduces training techniques into language program(s). Utilizes developmental teams in the School of Language Studies to design and develop course materials and oversees work of teams in course preparation efforts.

Makes presentations and briefings, and develops and conducts workshops in areas of expertise. Personally conducts demonstration training classes and works with problem classes to improve student performance. Tailors training to individual needs of students as required, and may design programs for special needs of ambassadors and other high-ranking officials. Establishes special language training programs for other federal departments and agencies. Participates in significant pilot projects to test efficacy of new course materials that may reduce length and cost of training program(s). Delegates various testing, staffing, and routine counseling duties to LCIs as required to manage high volume courses. Utilizes LCIs to coordinate various program functions, such as materials development, testing, reading, educational technology, and administrative functions.

Qualifications: Must be a speaker of a language other than English and have language teaching experience at the postsecondary level or to adult students. Applicants who do not meet this selective placement factor will not be considered qualified for this vacancy.

Must also have a degree that included or was supplemented by major duty in education or in a subject-matter field appropriate to the position. Or must have completed courses equivalent to a major in education, or in a subject-matter field appropriate to the position, plus appropriate experience or additional course work that provided knowledge comparable to that normally acquired through the successful completion of a four-year course of study.

To qualify based on education, submit a copy of your transcript or list of courses with credit hours, major(s), and grade-point average or class ranking. Application materials will not be returned. You can receive credit for education received outside the United States if you provide evidence that it is comparable to an accredited educational institution in the United States when you apply.

Additionally, all applicants who apply to GG-12 grade level must have one year of specialized experience equivalent to the GS/GG-11 grade level. All applicants who apply to GG-13 grade level must have one year of specialized experience equivalent to the GS/GG-12 grade level.

In addition, applicant's experience must also demonstrate that the applicant possesses the following qualities:

★ Ability to assign, review, and supervise the work of others

★ Objectivity and fairness in judging people on their ability and situations on the facts and circumstances

★ Ability to adjust to change, work pressures, or difficult situations without undue stress

★ Willingness to consider new ideas or divergent points of view

★ Capacity to see the job through

You must be a U.S. citizen to qualify for this position. After appointment, you will be subject to random testing for illegal drug use. In order to qualify for this position, you must be able to obtain and maintain a secret security clearance. You must serve a one-year supervisory probationary period, unless excepted by regulation.

Application checklist: Is your application complete? Have you included the following?

1. Resume or OF-612 form sent electronically or faxed? The form must list work performed, the dates (month and year for start and end of each position), and hours worked per week.

2. Educational transcripts from any and all schools and/or universities attended (copies are acceptable). If you have education from a non-U.S. institution, did you include a copy of your certified transcript that gives the U.S. equivalent of your education?

3. Ranking factors/knowledge, skills, and abilities. Write statements addressing each KSA individually.

4. Citizenship. Did you list it on your resume/OF-612/or other resume form?

5. Did you write the announcement number and title and grade of the position you are applying for, as well as your name, on top of each page of your application? (**Include this information on any faxed and e-mailed documents as well.**)

6. Did you include your Social Security number in the application (front page only please)?

7. Current government employees, did you include your most recent performance appraisal and your most recent SF-50 form?

8. All additional documentation should be faxed by the closing date on the announcement.

Department of Transportation

1200 New Jersey Avenue SE
Washington, DC 20590
866-377-8642 (toll-free)
202-366-4000

★ Web site: http://www.dot.gov/

★ Job vacancies: http://jobsearch.dot.gov/

★ Internships: http://careers.dot.gov/stu_intern.html

★ Student information: http://careers.dot.gov/stuopp.html

★ Co-op program: http://careers.dot.gov/stu_coop.html

★ Fellowships: http://careers.dot.gov/stu_scholar.html

★ Career entry-level programs: http://careers.dot.gov/stu_entryprog.html

★ Career information: http://careers.dot.gov/

★ How to apply: http://careers.dot.gov/js_apply.html

★ Strategic plan: http://www.dot.gov/stratplan2011/

The U.S. Department of Transportation (DOT) establishes the country's overall transportation policy. Under the DOT umbrella are 11 administrations whose jurisdictions include highway planning, development, and construction; motor carrier safety; urban mass transit; railroads; aviation; and the safety of waterways, ports, highways, and oil and gas pipelines. Decisions made by the DOT in conjunction with the appropriate state and local officials strongly affect other programs such as land planning, energy conservation, scarce resource utilization, and technological change. DOT employs more than 54,000 people across the country.

Selected DOT Agencies

The **Federal Aviation Administration** (FAA) regulates civil aviation and U.S. commercial space transportation, maintains and operates air traffic control and navigation systems for both civil and military aircrafts, and develops and administers programs relating to aviation safety and the National Airspace System. FAA's major roles include regulating civil aviation to promote safety;

encouraging and developing civil aeronautics, including new aviation technology; developing and operating a system of air traffic control and navigation for both civil and military aircraft; researching and developing the National Airspace System and civil aeronautics; developing and carrying out programs to control aircraft noise and other environmental effects of civil aviation; and regulating U.S. commercial space transportation.

In addition to its headquarters in Washington, DC, FAA has nine geographical regions and two major centers, the Mike Monroney Aeronautical Center in Oklahoma City, Oklahoma, and the William J. Hughes Technical Center in Atlantic City, New Jersey. FAA employs aviation professionals such as air traffic controllers, airway transportation specialists, aerospace engineers, aviation safety inspectors, and civil aviation security specialists, as well as administrators, support staff, and technical specialists.

★ Web site: http://www.faa.gov/

★ Job vacancies: http://jobs.faa.gov/Allfaajobs.htm

★ Career information: http://www.faa.gov/jobs/

★ FAA Academy: http://www.faa.gov/about/office_org/headquarters_offices/arc/programs/academy/

★ FAA education offices and events: http://www.faa.gov/education_research/education/

The **Federal Highway Administration** (FHWA) ensures America's roads and highways continue to be as safe and as technologically up-to-date as possible. FHWA disseminates and enforces highway safety regulations, administers highway transportation programs, and conducts research and development in support of improving and preserving America's highway system. Although state, local, and tribal governments own most of the nation's highways, FHWA provides financial and technical support for constructing, improving, and preserving America's highway system. The $30 billion annual budget is funded by fuel and motor vehicle excise taxes. The budget is primarily divided between two programs: federal-aid funding to state and local governments and Federal Lands Highways funding for national parks, national forests, American Indian lands, and other land under federal stewardship. FHWA employs more than 2,800 professionals and consists of a headquarters office in Washington, DC; a division office in each state (including four metropolitan offices), the District of Columbia, and Puerto Rico; a resource center (with four locations); and three Federal Lands Highways division offices.

★ Web site: http://www.fhwa.dot.gov/

★ Career information: http://www.fhwa.dot.gov/vacancy/index.htm

The **Maritime Administration** manages programs to aid in the development, promotion, and operation of the U.S. Merchant Marine. It is also charged with organizing and directing emergency merchant ship operations. The Maritime Administration administers subsidy programs to pay the difference between certain costs of operating ships under the U.S. flag and operating them under foreign competitive flags on essential services and the difference between the costs of constructing ships in U.S. shipyards and constructing them in foreign shipyards.

★ Web site: http://www.marad.dot.gov/

The **National Highway Traffic Safety Administration** (NHTSA) carries out programs relating to the safety performance of motor vehicles and related equipment. It administers state and community highway safety programs with the Federal Highway Administration, including the corporate average fuel economy program, and the federal odometer law. NHTSA carries out the National Driver Register Program to facilitate the interstate exchange of state records on problem drivers, conducts studies and operates programs aimed at reducing economic losses in motor vehicle crashes and repairs, and issues theft prevention standards for passenger and nonpassenger motor vehicles.

NHTSA is responsible for reducing deaths, injuries, and economic losses resulting from motor vehicle crashes; regulating the motor vehicle industry; investigating safety defects in motor vehicles; setting and enforcing fuel economy standards; helping states and local communities reduce the threat of drunk drivers; promoting the use of safety belts, child safety seats, and air bags; investigating odometer fraud; establishing and enforcing vehicle antitheft regulations; and providing consumer information on motor vehicle safety topics. The administration employs approximately 600 people and has 10 regional offices. To view career opportunities at NHTSA, visit the following Web site, click on the About NHSTA link, and then click on the Career Opportunities link.

★ Web site: http://www.nhtsa.dot.gov/

The mission of the **Saint Lawrence Seaway Development Commission** is to serve the marine transportation industries by providing a safe, secure, reliable, efficient, and competitive deep draft international waterway in cooperation with the Canadian St. Lawrence Seaway Management Corporation.

★ Web site: http://www.seaway.dot.gov/

★ Job vacancies: http://www.greatlakes-seaway.com/en/careers/index.html

Other DOT Agencies

Bureau of Transportation Statistics

http://www.bts.gov/

Federal Motor Carrier Safety Administration

http://www.fmcsa.dot.gov/

Federal Railroad Administration

http://www.fra.dot.gov/

Federal Transit Administration

http://www.fta.dot.gov/

Pipeline and Hazardous Materials Safety Administration

http://www.phmsa.dot.gov/

Research and Innovative Technology Administration

http://www.rita.dot.gov/

Surface Transportation Board

http://www.stb.dot.gov/

Sample Job Vacancies

Administrative Coordinator
Agency: Federal Aviation Administration
Salary: $33,475 to $50,212
Location: Orlando, Florida

Duties: Serves as the administrative coordinator for the System Support Center (SCC). Performs administrative and logistics support for the SSC. Uses a computer to perform office automation duties. Provides administrative support services for the manager and local personnel on time and attendance, travel, file maintenance, supplies, motor vehicles, and so on. Establishes and maintains databases for the SSC such as procurement actions, property records, and store credit. Establishes and maintains subject files for administrative and logistics programs in accordance with agency guidelines. May provide clerical support, preparing memorandums or reports as required in the administrative and logistics program areas. Works independently in accordance with overall objectives set by the manager. Carries out assignments with a minimum of supervision and requires little or no review. Uses own initiative on matters without bringing them to the attention of the manager.

Qualifications: One year of specialized experience, which is experience that is directly related to the line of work of the position to be filled and which has equipped the applicant with the particular knowledge, skills, and abilities (KSAs) to successfully perform the duties of the position. These KSAs are as follows:

1. Ability to identify needed actions and plan, carry out, and make decisions to accomplish assigned workload.

2. Ability to coordinate varied administrative projects simultaneously.

3. Ability to interact with customers to identify needs and to achieve desired results.

4. Ability to convey nontechnical or administrative information to a variety of audiences in meetings, presentations, or briefings.

How to apply: You must apply online to receive consideration for this vacancy.

Civil Engineer (Highway)
Agency: Federal Highway Administration
Salary: $46,625 to $87,893
Location: Boise, Idaho

Duties: As a civil engineer, you will prepare reports and analyses on planning, design, construction, and maintenance proposals, projects, and programs; conduct field inspections of federal-aid projects; advise on problems and deficiencies, coordinate corrective actions, review and evaluate safety practices, procedures, and technologies; monitor projects to provide for cost containment and schedule adherence; evaluate projects in terms of structural and geometric design standards and applications, economic and environmental factors, maintenance and construction costs, traffic analysis and service, aesthetics, and appropriateness for the proposed highway system; review plans specifications and estimates (PS&E) for appropriate application of design standards and criteria, conformance with policy and regulations, eligibility for federal participation, traffic safety features, reasonableness of estimated unit prices, fulfillment of environmental commitments and proper standard and special specifications and contract provisions; review environmental documents for conformance with requirements; represent the FHWA in meetings, telephone contacts, public hearings, field reviews, visits with state DOT officials and other federal, state, and local agencies regarding assigned transportation program areas; participate on committees, task forces, or ad-hoc work groups (research, management improvement of state engineering practices, value engineering studies, special technical committees, etc.); provide advice and guidance and promotes agreement on general procedures, standards, and criteria, and application of policies and concepts on construction activities; perform or coordinates process reviews on construction activities; based upon the findings of the reviews, recommend improvements in the federal-aid process and product delivery.

Benefits: DOT recognizes the importance and encourages the use of telework. Telework supports departmental mission and performance goals and improves the department's capability to support homeland and national security requirements. Telework improves individual and organizational productivity; helps reduce highway congestion and mobile source emissions; serves as a recruitment and retention tool; helps maintain operations during emergency situations; and improves work life quality. This position has been identified as a telework-eligible position.

How to apply: Please complete all the steps in the online application process:

1. Register with USAJOBS, which includes creating a resume.

2. Select the vacancy announcement to which you wish to apply.

3. Complete the online DOT Careers in Motion core questions.

4. Generate fax cover sheets for supporting documentation.

5. Complete the online vacancy questions.

6. Fax in your supporting documentation.

Required documents: As this vacancy announcement is for an engineering position, which has an education requirement, you must provide a copy of your college transcript, Engineer-in-Training (EIT) certificate, or a copy of your Professional Engineer (P.E.) license unless you are currently in the engineering occupational series in the federal government. In this case, you may submit an official copy of your Notification of Personnel Action, SF-50 showing the Engineering series.

If you are a veteran and want to be considered as a five-point preference eligible, you must submit a copy of your Certificate of Release or Discharge From Active Duty, DD214. Your DD-214 must show the type of discharge and dates of active duty. If you are claiming 10-point preference eligible, you must submit a copy of your DD214; an Application for 10-point Veteran's Preference, SF15; and the proof of entitlement of this preference, which is normally an official statement, dated 1991 or later, from the Department of Veterans Affairs certifying to the present existence of the service-connected disability and indicating the percentage of your disability. Without this documentation, you will not receive veteran's preference.

Under merit promotion procedures, all current or former federal employees must submit a recent copy of their SF-50, Notification of Personnel Action, that verifies their eligibility for consideration under Merit Promotion procedures, your current grade, and the full performance level of your position.

If you are requesting concurrent consideration for this position based on eligibility under a special appointing authority, such as Schedule A, you must submit proof of this eligibility. If you are claiming CTAP/ICTAP eligibility under the Career Transition Assistance Program (CTAP) or the Interagency Career Transition Assistance Program (ICTAP), you must submit a copy of your most recent performance appraisal, proof of eligibility letter, and your most current SF-50 showing your position, grade level, and duty location no later than the closing date of the vacancy.

Please do not submit unrequested documentation. Resumes should only be submitted electronically as part of the application process and are not considered supplemental documents. Unless the vacancy announcement specifically asks for examples of work products, writing samples, letters of reference, pictures, or training certificates, do NOT submit them to the Automated Staffing Office. They will not be forwarded to the official making the selection for this vacancy.

Your application will not receive consideration without the required supporting documentation.

Maintenance Mechanic
Agency: Federal Aviation Administration
Salary: $26.60 to $31.08/hour
Location: Las Vegas, Nevada

Duties: The incumbent of this position performs major routine and emergency repair, evaluation, installation, and maintenance of structures, buildings, and grounds in the Air Traffic Organization including radar, communications, and navigational aid antenna systems. Incumbent performs electrical, carpentry, painting, and plumbing maintenance and repair work with limited or no direct supervision. Incumbent works from blueprints, sketches, or written or oral instructions.

Qualifications: This position requires the knowledge, skill, and ability in various trades of work (such as electrical, carpentry, and plumbing) to qualify for the position. On a separate sheet of bond paper, applicants must clearly demonstrate by appropriate experience and/or training that they are able to perform the duties of the position by responding to each of the following job elements:

★ **Ability to perform the duties of this position without more than normal supervision (screen out element).** This element assesses experience that demonstrates ability to perform complex work as a maintenance mechanic under minimum supervision with wide latitude for independent action evidenced by leader- or supervisory-type experience or high level of technical skill.

★ **Ability to maintain equipment, utilities, and physical structures.** This element measures your exhibited abilities in a variety of the building trades rather than in one basic journeyman skill. Although primary emphasis is placed on your abilities in electrical work, carpentry, and plumbing, it is important to show that you are a skillful maintenance person who can not only maintain facilities, but also construct them.

★ **Ability to use pertinent hand and power tools.** The ability to perform various building trades tasks is impacted by the ability to effectively employ pertinent tools. This element measures your familiarity with the tools utilized by this position.

★ **Ability to interpret project plans.** Following through complete construction projects or repairing and modifying existing facilities requires abilities in interpreting, reading, and, in some cases, sketching construction aids. This element measures your ability to utilize a variety of these aids, including project layouts, schematics, blueprints, and diagrams.

★ **Ability to use and maintain heavy equipment.** The incumbent of this position must possess a valid state driver's license. In addition to vehicles driven on streets and highways such as dump trucks, flat bed trucks, and pickup trucks, there is a requirement to operate equipment such as trenchers, forklifts, backhoes, and a mobile crane. The ability to perform routine and preventive maintenance on this equipment is also required.

★ **Ability to perform antenna tower maintenance.** The duties of this position require climbing antenna towers more than 300 feet high. This element measures your ability, experience, and willingness to perform inspections and maintenance on antenna towers 300 feet or more in height.

This position is covered by the Department of Transportation's Drug and Alcohol Testing Program. Any applicant tentatively selected for this position will be subject to drug screening.

Pipefitter

Agency: Saint Lawrence Seaway Development Corporation
Salary: $25.79 to $28.79/hour
Location: Massena, New York

Duties: Install, modify, maintain, and repair utility, supply, and disposal systems; fixtures, fittings, and equipment for sewage, water, gas, oil, compressed air, and vacuum systems; and water closets, water heaters, hydrants, valves, and pumps. Set up system routes, place and cut route openings, and determine the requirements for and install such things as expansion joints, pumps, pressure regulators, and gauges. Perform electric arc and gas welding of steels (carbon, alloy, and stainless) and aluminum in shop and field settings for repair and fabrication of piping, structures, and mechanical equipment. Operate and maintain water treatment and sewage treatment systems. Do routine maintenance and repair of mechanical, hydraulic, and pneumatic lock and facility machinery and equipment including auxiliary items such as air compressors, pumps, sandblasting machines, HVAC equipment, etc. Operate lock equipment from primary controls and from recesses for testing purposes. Machine small parts using portable or fixed machine tools such as small lathes or milling machines. Lay out, drill, and install rubber and wooden fenders; oil, grease, change filters, test, and troubleshoot machinery and equipment; rig equipment and machinery; place and maintain stoplogs and bulkheads; and repair and maintain HVAC equipment including lock furnaces, boilers, A/C units, etc.

Qualifications: Your application will be reviewed for knowledge, skills, and abilities in the following job elements:

1. Ability to do the work of the position without more than normal supervision where ability to do the common or complex tasks is prime.

2. Knowledge of equipment, assembly, installation, repair, etc.

3. Technical practices (theoretical, precise, artistic).

4. Ability to interpret instructions and specifications (includes blueprint reading).

5. Measurement and layout.

6. Troubleshooting.

You will be required to obtain (within 12 months of hire date) and maintain New York state certifications required to operate and maintain corporation water and wastewater treatment systems. You must currently possess or demonstrate the ability to successfully meet the requirements for all-position welding certification (within six months of date of hire) and may be periodically tested to assure that skill level is maintained.

You will be required to successfully complete a pre-appointment physical, which includes a functional capacity test that mimics the job movements and stressors of the essential functions of the position. You may be assigned to duties requiring the use of a respirator and will be fit-tested for a respirator upon entering the position. You must be clean-shaven for the initial fit-testing and for any future assignments requiring the wearing of the respirator.

Working conditions: Work requires frequent bending, reaching, stretching, climbing, and crouching. May work in tiring or uncomfortable positions for long periods. Sometimes performs strenuous work while standing, lying, or sitting. Frequently lifts and carries items weighing up to 40 or 50 pounds, and often puts forth similar effort in pushing, pulling, turning, and positioning parts, assemblies, equipment, and tools. Often lifts and moves heavier items with the assistance of other workers and with lifting devices.

Works both inside and outside. When inside, is frequently exposed to drafts, changing temperatures, and noise that is difficult to talk above. When outside, may sometimes work in bad weather, in mud or snow, and in wet or icy areas. Both inside and outside, is frequently exposed to irritation or discomfort from dust, heat, fumes, and from hard, damp floors or ground. Typically works on parts and systems that are dirty, oily, or greasy. Works from ladders, staging, man baskets, and rafts on/over water.

Is frequently exposed to the possibility of receiving cuts, burns, bruises, and sprains while repairing, positioning, and moving equipment. Is often exposed to the possibility of receiving burns and skin irritations from acid, fluids, and lubricants.

To reduce the dangers and irritations from these conditions, follows prescribed safety practices and uses safety equipment such as protective ear devices, hard hats, safety-toe shoes, respirators, fall protection, personal floatation devices, and protective clothing. Some of these safety items may be uncomfortable to wear or use and may be worn or used for long periods.

Railroad Safety Specialist
Agency: Federal Railroad Administration
Salary: $70,615 to $91,801
Location: Multiple locations throughout the United States

Job summary: This is a telecommuting position that requires you to be located conveniently to an airport from which to travel to other points in the United States, can be efficiently performed, considering levels of air service, prevailing air fares, and the proximity of the duty station to the airport. This position is perfect for a mid-level professional who has experience in rail failure analysis, rail flaw detection systems, and nondestructive testing of rail components; has received their Ultrasonic Level I certification; is mission-focused and likes to travel; and is looking for great health benefits and job security.

Duties: Analyzing the advances in the field of railway rail inspection and maintenance procedures for their effect on safety and recommending changes to federal railroad safety standards and policies based on those analyses. Performing on-site inspections, investigations, and/or evaluations to determine the effectiveness of railroad programs that address the inspection, maintenance, and replacement of rail. Providing oversight into the capabilities of various detection systems, the level of training and experience of test car operators, and the adequacy of the defect verification process employed by the test car operator. Developing and implementing safety practices to be used by FRA track inspectors who perform rail internal inspection observations. Providing guidance and assistance to FRA and state railroad track safety inspectors in the safe methods for performance of work on and about railroad track and structures. Conducting investigations of railroad industry implementation of federal and standard industry policies and guidelines governing the safety and integrity of railroad rail and components. Maintaining continuous overview of the application of the federal and standard industry policies and guidelines governing the safety and integrity of railroad rail and components by the railroad industry. Initiating and maintaining contact with officials of railroad corporations, labor organizations, federal and other government agencies and railroad suppliers within or affecting the FRA region to exchange information and views on significant railroad safety issues. Assisting individual railroads, railroad industry associations, and railroad labor organizations in the preparation and presentation of training programs and materials in the subject field of railroad rail inspection and management. Preparing written reports of contacts and committee activities to inform other FRA employees of the status of issues and to maintain a written record of agency positions on those issues. Accompanying FRA inspectors performing routine or special investigation activities to assess agency conformance with established guidelines and directives and the effectiveness of agency railroad safety enforcement programs. Supporting senior technical staff of the Office of Safety in responding to questions and recommendations presented formally to FRA by the Congress, National Transportation Safety Board, and other agencies, organizations, and individuals concerned with railroad rail and components. Conducting, leading, or participating in investigations of railroad accidents and incidents when directed, providing expertise in the areas of railroad rail and components and preparing or supporting the determination of the cause and the accident report.

Department of the Treasury

1500 Pennsylvania Avenue NW
Washington, DC 20220
202-622-2000

★ Web site: http://www.treas.gov/

★ Job vacancies: http://jobsearch.usajobs.opm.gov/a9trep.asp

★ How to apply: http://www.treas.gov/organization/employment/appInfoSite.html

★ Career information: http://www.treas.gov/organization/employment/

★ Strategic plan: http://www.treas.gov/offices/management/budget/strategic-plan/

The Department of the Treasury promotes economic prosperity and ensures the financial security of the United States. This department is responsible for a wide range of activities such as advising the president on economic and financial issues, encouraging sustainable economic growth, and fostering improved governance in financial institutions. The Department of the Treasury operates and maintains systems that are critical to the nation's financial infrastructure, such as the production of coin and currency, the disbursement of payments to the American public, revenue collection, and the borrowing of funds necessary to run the federal government. This department works with other federal agencies, foreign governments, and international financial institutions to encourage global economic growth, raise standards of living, and, to the extent possible, predict and prevent economic and financial crises. The Department of the Treasury also implements economic sanctions against foreign threats to the United States, identifies and targets the financial support networks of national security threats, and improves the safeguards of our financial systems. It employs more than 103,600 people.

Selected Treasury Agencies

The **Bureau of Engraving and Printing** (BEP) designs, prints, and finishes all of the nation's paper currency and many other security documents, including White House invitations, military identification cards, and postage stamps. It also is responsible for advising and assisting federal agencies in the design and production of other government documents that, because of their innate value or for other reasons, require security or counterfeit-deterrence characteristics. BEP is the largest producer of security documents in the United States, producing a wide range of documents at both its Washington, DC, and Fort Worth, Texas, facilities. Employment opportunities include administrative support, police officers, security specialists, chemists, engineers, and attorneys. BEP employs more than 2,100 workers.

★ Web site: http://www.moneyfactory.com/

★ Receive job information via e-mail: http://www.moneyfactory.gov/hr/section.cfm/95

★ How to apply: http://www.moneyfactory.gov/hr/section.cfm/98

★ Career information: http://www.moneyfactory.gov/hr/index.cfm/12

The **Internal Revenue Service** (IRS) collects the proper amount of tax revenue at the least cost to the public by efficiently applying the tax law with integrity and fairness. (It cost taxpayers 44 cents for each $100 collected by the IRS.) As the largest of the Department of the Treasury's bureaus, the IRS employs more than 101,000 people and has an operating budget of more than $10 billion. In 2007, the IRS collected nearly $3 trillion in revenue and processed more than 235 million tax returns.

★ Web site: http://www.irs.gov/

★ Student information: http://jobs.irs.gov/student.html

★ Career information/how to apply: http://jobs.irs.gov/home.html

In recent history, circulating coin production has varied between 11 billion and 20 billion coins annually. The **U.S. Mint** produces an adequate volume of circulating coinage for the nation to conduct its trade and commerce. The Mint designs and manufactures domestic bullion and foreign coins as well as commemorative medals and other items. The Mint also distributes U.S. coins to the Federal Reserve banks and maintains physical custody and protection of the country's silver and gold assets. There are Mint facilities in Washington, DC; Philadelphia, Pennsylvania; Fort Knox, Kentucky; Denver, Colorado; San Francisco, California; and West Point, New York. The Mint employs approximately 1,800 workers.

★ Web site: http://www.usmint.gov/

★ Internships and student programs: http://www.usmint.gov/about_the_mint/careers/index.cfm?action=Recruiting

★ Career information: http://www.usmint.gov/about_the_mint/careers/

Other Agencies in the Department of the Treasury

Alcohol and Tobacco Tax and Trade Bureau

http://www.ttb.gov/

Bureau of the Public Debt

http://www.publicdebt.treas.gov/

Community Development Financial Institutions Fund

http://www.cdfifund.gov/

Financial Crimes Enforcement Network

http://www.fincen.gov/

Financial Management Service

http://www.fms.treas.gov/

Office of Terrorism and Financial Intelligence

http://www.treas.gov/offices/enforcement/index.html

Office of the Comptroller of the Currency

http://www.occ.treas.gov/

Office of Thrift Supervision

http://www.ots.treas.gov/

Treasury Inspector General for Tax Administration

http://www.treas.gov/tigta/

Sample Job Vacancies

Accountant
Agency: Internal Revenue Service
Salary: $86,927 to $113,007
Location: Washington, DC

Duties: Serves as a senior accountant in the Chief Financial Officer (CFO) area responsible for preparation of agency-wide financial reports and statements, administrative general ledger and subsidiary ledger maintenance, analysis of accounts, and adjusting and closing entries. Provides support to the annual financial statement audit. Ensures that the service's financial systems, operations, and reports meet the requirements of law and regulation. Applies accounting theories, concepts, principles, and standards to the financial activities of the IRS. Reviews and interprets federal legislation, rules, standards, and regulations pertaining to accounting and financial management. Analyzes and evaluates agency-wide accounting operations, policies, procedures, and systems for compliance with standards and internal controls. Provides high-level technical support to the financial statement audit. Reviews existing systems for revisions and recommends modifications to systems design, as necessary (systems modernizations). Responds to Congressional, Treasury Inspector General for Tax Administration (TIGTA), and GAO reports. Determines corrective actions needed. Ensures corrective actions are implemented. Applies accounting principles, theories, and practices in new or novel ways where no precedents exist.

Qualifications: Applicants must have a bachelor's degree in accounting or a degree in a related field such as business administration, finance, or public administration or an equivalent combination of accounting experience, college-level education, and training that provided professional accounting knowledge. In addition, all applicants must possess one full year of specialized experience.

You must be a U.S. citizen to qualify for this position. Before you can be appointed into this position, you will need to successfully complete a background security investigation You will be required to do some travel one to five nights per month.

How you will be evaluated: You will be evaluated to determine if you meet the minimum qualifications required and to determine the extent to which your application shows that you possess the knowledge, skills, and abilities associated with this position. You must separately address each of the knowledge, skills, and abilities (KSAs) listed. In addressing your knowledge, skills, and abilities, you should discuss your experience, education, and accomplishments and provide examples explaining how often you used these skills, the complexity of the knowledge you possessed, the level of the people you interacted with, the sensitivity of the issues you handled, and so on. A well-written narrative statement provides you the opportunity to put your best foot forward by highlighting your strong points, which can help improve your chances for being selected.

Individual Taxpayer Advisory Specialist
Agency: Internal Revenue Service
Salary: $30,772 to $40,005
Location: Vacancies in multiple duty locations

Job summary: Please note that this announcement is for current and future vacancies. One or more positions may be filled using this vacancy announcement. This vacancy is announcing permanent career or career-conditional vacancies as well as term appointments. A term appointment is an appointment that is not to exceed 13 months, with the option of extending that appointment for up to a total of four years. Term appointments at the IRS may be converted to career-conditional positions after the completion of two years of continuous service. In addition, some of these vacancies may offer a seasonal work schedule. A seasonal work schedule involves full-time work for a certified period of time; that is, the seasonal work schedule will encompass a six-month or more work season with periods of nonpaid, nonwork time. All vacancies are eligible for full benefits. You will be asked to indicate your interest in seasonal and term positions in the occupational questionnaire. Most positions are anticipated to be full-time permanent or full-time seasonal.

There is a current need for a bilingual individual (Spanish) in Harlingen, Texas, and Richland, Washington. Bilingual positions require the ability to speak, read, and understand Spanish both orally and in writing. Applicants must be fluent in Spanish and will be required to pass a formal bilingual assessment, which will require an oral translation from English to Spanish and Spanish to English as well as a written translation from English to Spanish and Spanish to English. If you are able to speak, read, and understand fluently another language(s), please indicate that both on your resume and when completing the questionnaire.

Duties: Individual taxpayer assistance specialists in the Wage and Investment Operating Division are responsible for providing basic advice, technical and procedural information, and customer service to a variety of taxpayers and/or their representatives through face-to-face meetings. They are also responsible for resolving taxpayer account, payment, filing, and notices issues; facilitating the resolution of some examination and collection issues of wage and investment taxpayers; protecting taxpayer rights; and promoting compliance in accordance with tax laws and regulations.

Qualifications: In order to be qualified for this position, you must meet one of the following criteria:

A. A bachelor's degree.

B. At least three years of general experience (at least one year of which is equivalent to the GS-4 level in the federal service) that demonstrated a general knowledge of business practices and basic accounting principles.

C. A combination of education as described in letter A and specialized experience as described in letter B that is equivalent to 100 percent of the qualifications requirements. To compute this, first determine your qualifying experience as a percentage of the experience required in letter B. Second, determine your undergraduate education as a percentage of the education required in letter A. Then add the two percentages together. The total must equal at least 100 percent to qualify.

In order to be appointed to this job, you must be able to pass a pre-employment structured interview so that your customer service and oral communication skills can be assessed. Fingerprints will be required as part of the pre-employment process. The IRS policy will not allow individuals to enter on duty in any position until FBI fingerprint results, and, if applicable, case disposition information are received and reviewed. There will be no exceptions to this policy. Applicants also will be required to go through a Personal Identity Verification (PIV) process that requires two forms of identification from the Form I-9; one must be a valid state or federal government-issued picture identification.

To be selected for this position, you must be in compliance with tax laws.

Industrial Equipment Repairer
Agency: Financial Management Service
Salary: $21.45 to $24.11/hour
Location: Philadelphia, Pennsylvania

Duties: The incumbent serves as an Industrial Equipment Repairer in the Printing and Wrapping Section of the Payment and Mail Operations Branch. The check wrapping system is a complex, high-speed system that makes wrappings from a paper web that is continuously fed through the system and simultaneously wraps checks and inserts into the wrappings at a speed of up to 590 cycles per minute.

The incumbent will be required to set up, test, operate, maintain, troubleshoot, and repair the check wrapping system, including the unwind stand, printing section, patcher section, side flap knife section, bottom scorer and seal scorer section, bridge section, and the folder section. The unwind stand unwinds the paper web and controls tension to the paper. The printing section accomplishes outside printing on the wrapping. The patcher section applies score lines along sides of the web and cuts window openings. When required, this section also applies adhesive around window openings, feeds and cuts patches from a glassine web and applies the patches over the window opening. The side flap knife section cuts the side flap contours of the wrapping. The bottom scorer and seal scorer section applies the score lines where the bottom and seal of the wrapping will be folded during a subsequent step in the process. The bridge section feeds checks from a feed hopper, prints the signature on checks, feeds paper and card inserts from three insert feeders, feeds booklets from a booklet feeder, collates and inserts the pack of checks and inserts into the wrapping as the wrapper bottom is being folded. The folder section severs the blank wrapper from the web, folds the bottom of the wrapping, applies adhesive to the side flaps, folds the side flaps, applies adhesive to the seal flap, folds the seal flap, and stacks the wrapped checks and related inserts on a motorized conveyor. The work is performed in a noisy area, requires standing for periods of up to eight hours a day, and involves stooping, bending, and reaching.

Qualifications: Candidate must be a U.S. citizen. If selected, you must have a successfully adjudicated background investigation appropriate to the position, be eligible for a Personal Identity Verification (PIV) credential, and maintain PIV credential eligibility during your employment.

The employee must frequently lift and carry parts (such as gears, bearings, and valves) weighing over 50 pounds to and from system components. (The core shaft itself, which must be placed within the paper web approximately three times daily, weighs about 65 pounds.) He/she must frequently push and pull on component parts such as cylinders and rollers while repairing them, exerting forces up to 30 pounds. Work involves about 25 percent walking, climbing, balancing, stooping, kneeling, crouching, and crawling and about 75 percent reaching, handling, feeling, and standing. The employee is required to work fixed shifts and rotate between the first shift (7:00 a.m. to 3:30 p.m., Monday through Friday) and the second shift (3:00 p.m. to 11:30 p.m., Monday through Friday). This may include requirements to work on weekends, holidays, and before and/or after scheduled shift work. If selected for this position, you will be required to submit a signed statement certifying your availability to work rotating shifts and weekends.

Internal Revenue Agent

Agency: Internal Revenue Service
Salary: $30,772 to $73,329
Location: Many vacancies throughout the nation

Duties: We are filling three types of revenue agents under this vacancy announcement. A short description of each position is found below.

As an Internal Revenue Agent in the Small Business/Self-Employed Division (Examination), you will

★ Examine and audit individual, business, and corporate tax returns to determine correct federal tax liabilities.

★ Conduct examinations relating to compliance with technical requirements imposed by the Internal Revenue Code.

★ Interact with taxpayers, tax attorneys, and certified public accountants.

As an Internal Revenue Agent in the Small Business/Self-Employed Division (Bank Secrecy Act) (BSA), you will

★ Conduct compliance examinations on certain categories of financial institutions and nonfinancial trades or businesses in order to identify, detect, and deter money laundering whether it is in furtherance of a criminal enterprise, terrorism, tax evasion, or other unlawful activity.

★ Determine if certain financial institutions or nonfinancial trades or businesses properly register, maintain records, and file reports required by the anti-money laundering statutes and regulations.

As an Internal Revenue Agent in the Tax Exempt and Government Entities (TE/GE) Division you will

★ Apply your professional accounting skills in conducting examinations of employee plans, exempt organizations, and government entities.

★ Conduct examinations or make determinations on pension plans to ensure compliance with the pension plan provisions of the Internal Revenue Code.

★ Be involved in significant education and outreach activities.

★ Interact with pension trustees, individual taxpayers, pension attorneys, certified public accountants, enrolled agents, and other pension practitioners.

★ Make determinations that tax-exempt entities (including religious, charitable and educational organizations) meet the tax law requirements applicable to them.

IRS Internal Revenue Agents are required to conduct appointments at the taxpayer's location to discuss tax matters with taxpayers and/or their representatives.

How you will be evaluated: If you are eligible and tentatively qualified for this position based upon your responses to the application questions, you will receive an e-mail message directing you with additional information within 7 to 10 business days. This information will include additional instructions to the online assessment process. This electronic information will include directions for accessing the assessment Web site and a user log-in with password. The online job simulation measures the following Internal Revenue Agent competencies: decision making, interpersonal skills, and accounting knowledge. The online simulation takes about 45 minutes to complete. If you pass the online assessment, you will be placed into a tentative category and move on to the second part of the hiring process, the interview. Candidates will be interviewed in category order with applicable veterans' preference.

Research Chemist

Agency: Bureau of Engraving and Printing
Salary: $71,100 to $113,007
Location: Washington, DC

Duties: Applies scientific knowledge, improvements, or discoveries to the solution of defined or specific problems with production materials and finished products (printing inks, paper, packaging materials, electroplating products, etc.) in support of Bureau of Engraving and Printing (BEP) manufacturing operations. Studies the composition, structure, properties, interactions, and performance of materials or products. Conducts planned experiments or studies of materials and products, both routine and non-routine in nature, by utilizing state-of-the-art analytical techniques and procedures including spectroscopy and chromatography. Applies broad knowledge and experience in developing new and/or improving test methods and procedures for analyzing simple and complex materials and products used in currency manufacturing and other products. Participates and/or takes a leadership role in task forces involved in the troubleshooting of technical problems. Reviews and evaluates the requirements for analytical instruments, test methods and procedures, and reference and calibration standards. Works with resident chemical microscopist, ink chemists, and other personnel in conducting experiments or studies of significant importance to the agency or customers. Reviews and evaluates technical literature, agency and industry publications, and relevant data from laboratory and industry studies as well as studying the latest trends in the graphic arts printing and technology field. Provides leadership in maintaining the calibration program for laboratory instruments and devices. Serves as Contracting Officer Technical Representative (COTR) for materials and service contracts for laboratory equipment and so on. Performs other duties as assigned. Duties will require shift work and possible travel.

Qualifications: The applicant must have obtained a bachelor's degree in chemistry from an accredited college or university (or related field, such as physical science, life science, or engineering) that included 24 semester hours in chemistry, supplemented by course work in mathematics through differential and integral calculus, and at least 6 semester hours of physics. Exposure to and/or experience in working at the research level is highly desirable.

You must be a U.S. citizen to qualify for this position. After appointment, you will be subject to random testing for illegal drug use. You will need to successfully complete a background security investigation before you can be appointed into this position. You will be required to do some travel. You may need to stand for prolonged periods on concrete floors and walk over rough and uneven terrain.

Department of Veterans Affairs

810 Vermont Avenue NW
Washington, DC 20420
202-273-4800

★ Web site: http://www.va.gov/

★ Job vacancies: http://jobsearch.usajobs.opm.gov/a9va.asp

★ Career information: http://www.va.gov/jobs/

★ How to apply: http://www.va.gov/JOBS/hiring/applying.asp

★ Strategic plan: http://www1.va.gov/op3/docs/VA_2006_2011_Strategic_Plan.pdf

The Department of Veterans Affairs (VA) operates programs to benefit veterans and members of their families. Benefits include compensation payments for disabilities or death related to military service; pensions; education and rehabilitation; home loan guaranty; burial; and a medical care program incorporating nursing homes, clinics, and medical centers. The VA is made up of three organizations that administer veterans programs: the Veterans Health Administration, the Veterans Benefits Administration, and the National Cemetery Administration. Each organization has field facilities and a central office component. The VA is the second largest of the 14 cabinet departments, with more than 250,000 employees. Among the many professions represented in the vast VA workforce are physicians, nurses, counselors, statisticians, architects, computer specialists, and attorneys.

Selected VA Agencies

The **National Cemetery Administration** (NCA) operates 125 national cemeteries in the United States and territories, together with oversight/management of 33 soldiers' lots, confederate cemeteries, and monument sites. The mission of NCA is to honor our nation's veterans with a final resting place and commemorate their service to our nation.

★ Web site: http://www.cem.va.gov/

The **Veterans Benefits Administration** (VBA) provides information, advice, and assistance to veterans, their dependents, beneficiaries, representatives, and others applying for VA benefits. It also cooperates with the Department of Labor and other federal, state, and local agencies in developing employment opportunities for veterans and referral for assistance in resolving socioeconomic, housing, and other related problems. Major benefits include veterans' compensation, veterans' pension, survivors' benefits, rehabilitation and employment assistance, education assistance, home loan guaranties, and life insurance coverage.

★ Web site: http://www.vba.va.gov/VBA/

The **Veterans Health Administration** (VHA) provides hospital, nursing home, domiciliary care, and outpatient medical and dental care to eligible veterans of military service in the Armed Forces. It conducts both individual medical and health-care delivery research projects and multi-hospital

research programs, and it assists in the education of physicians and dentists and with training of many other health care professionals through affiliations with educational institutions and organizations.

The VHA operates more than 160 hospitals, with at least one in each of the 48 contiguous states, Puerto Rico, and the District of Columbia. It conducts more than 10,000 research projects at 115 VA medical centers, and its career development program provides young scientists an opportunity to develop skills as clinician-researchers. VHA provides care at more than 1,400 sites throughout the country, employs a staff of 204,000, and maintains affiliations with 107 academic health systems. More than 65 percent of all physicians in the United States today have trained in VA facilities.

★ Web site: http://www1.va.gov/health/

★ Job vacancies: http://www.vacareers.va.gov/

Other VA Agencies

Board of Veterans' Appeals

http://www.va.gov/vbs/bva/

Center for Minority Veterans

http://www1.va.gov/centerforminorityveterans/

Center for Veterans Enterprise

http://www.vetbiz.gov/

Center for Women Veterans

http://www1.va.gov/womenvet/

Employment Discrimination Complaint Adjudication

http://www.va.gov/orm/oedca.asp

Sample Job Vacancies

Cemetery Caretaker
Agency: National Cemetery Administration
Salary: $14.79 to $17.26/hour
Location: Portland, Oregon

Duties: Performs jobs requiring mainly manual skills and physical strength. Performs a variety of tasks, such as operating small tractors and riding lawn mowers; transplanting shrubs; digging graves to the proper level; cutting and removing sod; tamping and leveling dirt using hand and power tools; digging and squaring graves using pneumatic equipment, picks, and shovels; assisting in lifting and placing casket-lowering devices; loading and unloading materials; aligning headstones; cleaning and clearing cemetery grounds of debris using power trimmers, chainsaws, axes, shovels, rakes, blowers, and vacuums; weeding, mulching, and applying fertilizer; pruning shrubs and low-level dead branches; removing snow and ice; cleaning headstones using sprayer and hand brush; and cleaning service and administrative areas. Performs other related duties as assigned.

May be required to work Monday through Friday 8:00 a.m. to 4:30 p.m. to include occasional weekends. Due to the mission of the National Cemetery, the cemetery cannot be closed for more than two consecutive days at any given time. Additionally, when a federal holiday falls on a Monday or Friday, staff may be required to work on that holiday or a Saturday. All staff is required to work Memorial Day each year. Staff will be required to work overtime, weekends, and holidays when necessary to meet the needs of the cemetery. Occasionally staff may be called back to the facility to perform emergency overtime work.

Qualifications: Your background must demonstrate work involved in interment activities, including layout and excavation of new gravesites and reopening occupied gravesites, which requires extreme caution to avoid damage to previously interred containers. The work requires moderate effort in maneuvering large vehicles and in hooking up heavy equipment attachments to tractors. This position requires the incumbent to lift weights up to 100 pounds on a recurring basis. Items weighing greater than 50 pounds will be lifted with assistance. Most of the work involves twisting, climbing, lifting, bending, crouching, kneeling, leaning, stretching, bouncing, sitting, standing, stooping, and carrying. Administrative functions are performed both indoors in an office setting and outdoors because the incumbent attends committal services during any kind of weather conditions. Incumbent is exposed to heat, cold, wind, dirt, dust, mud, and water in the performance of the duties of this position. In addition, when operating vehicles, the incumbent drives in all types of weather and traffic and is exposed to the possibility of accidents.

Licensed Practical Nurse (Geriatrics)
Agency: Veterans Health Administration
Salary: $34,300 to $44,589
Location: Oklahoma City, Oklahoma

Duties: The incumbent of this position performs typical LPN duties as assigned as well as triage, initial assessments, medication refills, etc. He/she must be self-directed and require minimal supervision to get his/her work accomplished as well as preplanning and carrying out all assignments. Incumbent also provides nursing support to HBPC (Home Based Primary Care) patients. Incumbent also prepares/administers, oral, rectal, sub Q, IM, and topical medications according to written or verbal order or by established policy and protocol in a timely manner. He/she also uses appropriate techniques for completing and administering injections. Must inventory and order medical supplies as needed for HBPC program. Position incumbent also observes, identifies, and responds to changes in patient's behavior or reaction to treatment plan by providing emotional support or intervening to prevent a problem and notifying provider of such changes. This person will also provide patient and family education regarding disease condition, procedures, medication, and tests as well as health maintenance. Further, this person will document all teaching and the patient's reaction to the teaching and involve family and significant others in teaching activities. Incumbent must notify provider of changes in status of patients. He/she will screen patients who call-in with acute non-urgent problems, such as vomiting, urinary frequency, or incontinence, and notify provider/RN. Additionally, this person will also send/take specimens to the lab if obtained on a home visit. Incumbent will also manage schedules to include B12 injections, immunizations, medication planner set-up, and nurse follow-up for blood pressure checks, repeat labs, etc. This includes, but it is not limited to, scheduling patients in the computer, notifying patients of any changes in medications, following protocols for injections, and completing encounter forms for each visit.

Qualifications: In accordance with VA Qualification Standards, candidates must meet the following requirements. They must be citizens of the United States. (Noncitizens may be appointed when it is not possible to recruit qualified citizens.) They must be graduates of an approved school of practical or vocational nursing. (Health care education in the military service or training in the military service that is accepted by the licensing body in the jurisdiction in which the individual is licensed as qualifying for full LPN/LVN licensure will be accepted as meeting the education requirements for VHA employment.) They also must have full, active, current, and unrestricted licensure as a licensed practical or vocational nurse in a state, territory, or commonwealth (such as Puerto Rico) of the United States or District of Columbia. Applicants who meet the licensure requirement are considered fully qualified for GS-3.

Additional requirements are an ability in leadership, judgment, and decision-making; verbal and written communication skills; strong, positive interpersonal/customer service skills; integrity; dependability; ability to function independently with minimal supervision; ability to function as a self-directed, productive team member and adapt readily to varying patient care needs and fluctuation in workload; and the ability to work flexible hours as required.

For GS-4, six months of nursing experience is required. For GS-5 and above, one year of nursing experience equivalent to at least the next lower grade level is required. Qualifying experience includes nursing care work in a hospital, outpatient clinic, nursing home, or other supervised medical, nursing, or patient care facility that provided a practical knowledge of human body structure and sterile techniques and procedures, performing such duties as providing pre- and post-operative patient care; observing, recording, and reporting changes in behavior of mentally ill patients; providing reassurance and encouragement to mentally ill patients; assisting surgeons and registered nurses in operating room activities, including passing instruments, maintaining sterile conditions, and draping and positioning patients; and setting up and operating special medical equipment and apparatus.

Medical Records Technician
Agency: Veterans Health Administration
Salary: $22,999 to $56,210
Location: Chillicothe, Ohio

Duties: Assigns codes using the International Classification of Diseases, Ninth Revision, Clinical Modification (ICD-9-CM), Current Procedural Terminology (CPT-4), and HCPCS codes to describe diagnosis, surgical procedure, and special therapy or procedure. Uses standard medical records references. Independently codes a wide variety of medical diagnostic, therapeutic, and surgical procedures. Codes diseases and causes of injury. Codes stages of disease using International Classification of Diseases for Oncology. Maintains quality control of case-finding, abstracting, coding, and follow-up procedures. Codes complicated medical records having diagnostic, surgical, and therapeutic procedures that are identified as difficult to classify. Uses specialized procedures and methods to correct or amend records. Reviews records to obtain data and compiles, abstracts, and analyzes data. Collects core data from patient's records, including demographic characteristics, diagnostic procedures, diagnoses, and stage and extent of disease. Ensures that data is reported accurately and in correct format.

Qualifications: Two years of experience that demonstrates the applicant's ability to perform the work, or successful completion of an associate's degree with a major field of study in medical record technology/health information technology that was accredited by the American Health Information Management Association (AHIMA) at the time the program was completed, or an equivalent combination of experience and education.

You must be a U.S. citizen to qualify for this position. After appointment, you will be subject to random testing for illegal drug use. You will need to successfully complete a background security investigation before you can be appointed into this position. You must meet time-in-grade restrictions by the closing date of this announcement. Applicants for this position must pass a pre-employment medical examination.

How you will be evaluated: You will be evaluated based upon the question responses you provide during a structured interview. In responding to structured interview questions, you should be sure to cite specific examples of experience, explain exactly what you did, and describe the outcome.

How to apply: Mail your application so it will be postmarked by the closing date. Hand-delivered applications must be received by the closing date. Please do not apply online. Be sure your application includes VA Form 10-2850c, OF 306, a complete resume of experience, official college transcripts, and any veterans' preference documentation.

Occupational Therapist
Agency: Veterans Health Administration
Salary: $50,411 to $70,618
Location: Memphis, Tennessee

Duties: Incumbent performs a variety of duties including: evaluating, developing, and implementing comprehensive treatment plans for patients with complex disabilities following diagnoses such as stroke, orthopedic problems/surgery, spinal cord injury, cardiopulmonary complications, polytrauma, traumatic brain injury, and geriatric-related conditions. Patients are seen on an outpatient and inpatient basis.

Qualifications: Graduation from a baccalaureate degree program in occupational therapy or a post-baccalaureate certificate program recognized by the American Occupational Therapy Association (AOTA) or the Committee on Allied Health, Education, and Accreditation of the American Medical Association is required. Graduates of foreign occupational therapy training programs meet the education requirement if they have graduated from a degree or equivalent program recognized by the AOTA. The individual must have passed the Certification Examination for Occupational Therapists Registered OTR, which is administered by the National Board for Certification in Occupational Therapy. The individual must meet the physical requirements for the position as determined by satisfactory results of a physical examination and must be proficient in spoken and written English.

You must be a U.S. citizen to qualify for this position. After appointment, you will be subject to random testing for illegal drug use. You will need to successfully complete a background security investigation before you can be appointed into this position.

Other information: This job is being filled by an alternative hiring process and is not in the competitive civil service. When promotion potential is shown, the agency is not making a commitment and is not obligated to provide future promotions to you if you are selected. Future promotions will be dependent on your ability to perform the duties at a higher level, the continuing need for an employee assigned to the higher level, and administrative approval. You must submit all required information by the closing date. If materials are not received, your application will be evaluated solely on the information available and you may not receive full consideration or may not be considered eligible. The materials you send with your application will not be returned. If you fax your application, we will not consider it. Send only those materials needed to evaluate your application. Please do not place your application in a notebook or binder. You will be required to serve a probationary period of one year.

How to apply: Applicants must submit the following materials: Application for Associated Health Occupations (VA Form 10-2850c); complete resume or C.V.; three letters of reference; official college transcripts; copy of current, full, and unrestricted license; OF-306, Declaration for Federal Employment (required only for applicants outside of VA Memphis); performance appraisals (submit most recent from VA or other federal or private sector employment); and SF-50, Notification of Personnel Action (required only from current or former federal employees; submit most recent action showing highest grade/step held; former federal employees should submit a copy of their separation personnel action). Veterans who are not current employees of VA Memphis must submit a DD-214 documenting their total military service and a SF-15, Application for 10-Point Veteran Preference, and required documentation if they are claiming 10-point veteran preference.

Non-mailed applications must be received by the Memphis VA Medical Center by 4:30 p.m. Central time on the closing date as listed on this announcement. Mailed applications must be postmarked by the closing date and received no later than five calendar days after the closing date. Applications received by government fax or in government postage paid envelopes will not be accepted and will be returned to the applicant. The entire application package will become a part of the vacancy announcement file and will not be filed in the individual's Official Personnel Folder (OPF). Application forms cannot be copied by Human Resources Management Service and will not be returned to you. You should keep a copy of your application package for your future use in applying for other positions. Failure to comply with the application procedures may result in an applicant receiving less than full credit in the evaluation process. Mail or bring your complete application package to the VA medical center.

Pharmacy Technician

Agency: Veterans Health Administration
Salary: $30,772 to $44,589
Location: San Antonio, Texas

Duties: Performs as general, all-around, nonprofessional assistant to the pharmacist. Must be capable of working efficiently and accurately, independent of supervision. Receives, reads, sorts, and interprets prescriptions and determines kind, strength, and dosage of drugs to be dispensed. Correlates instructions on the prescription with pharmacy policy. Generates labels and processes prescriptions by obtaining correct stock and counting or measuring correct amount of medication in proper container. Performs computer functions, including using input/output techniques, exercising proper security requirements with patient data or other sensitive information, and operating various kinds of computer equipment (visual display terminals and printers). Receives phone calls in a tactful and helpful manner from physicians, dentists, nurses, other professional staff members, patients, and volunteers regarding patient information. Also answers specific questions about drug availability or other limited information, referring therapeutic questions to the pharmacist. Monitors stock levels of drugs and office supplies, stores and/or transports incoming orders, and removes outdated or deteriorated items and prepares them for disposal. Maintains work area in a clean, neat orderly manner. Complies with safety and environmental rules and regulations for safe job performance. Uses and maintains personal protective equipment when required and provided. Promptly reports all accidents/illnesses to supervisor. Notifies supervisor of all unsafe or unhealthful conditions in the workplace and works to eliminate such conditions. Represents pharmacy services in a professional manner that focuses on the needs of the patient and not on personal or competing agendas. Instills confidence and trust with supervisors, peers and subordinates by providing timely and quality service. Meets established time frames and deadlines in area of responsibility. Provides professional and technical advice, support and assistance to all customers with a view towards accomplishing the service mission (that is, customer service). Interacts with a wide variety of staff and demonstrates sensitivity to and an understanding of their needs by taking ownership of a problem and adopting the customer's needs as their own. Maintains certification in good standing (as applicable).

Incumbent will work irregular tours of duty, including holidays and weekends, when required. As a representative of the Pharmacy Service, incumbent must project a positive attitude towards duties and responsibilities at all times. Customers are treated in a professional manner, with tact, courtesy, and respect. Relationships with supervisors, co-workers and others within the organization must be consistently courteous and cooperative in nature and overall contribute to the effective operation of the service. Performance must demonstrate the ability to adjust to change or work pressure in a pleasant manner; handle differences of opinion in a businesslike fashion; follow instructions conscientiously; and function as a team member, helping the group effort where possible.

How to apply: Applicants must submit the following:

1. Complete VA Form 10-2850c (Application for Associate Health Occupations) or resume.

2. Responses to the rating factors.

3. OF-306 (Declaration for Federal Employment).

4. If you are claiming veterans' preference, please provide a copy of your DD-214(s), documenting your type of discharge and periods of service. If you are claiming 10 point veterans' preference, please submit Application for 10 Point Veteran Preference (SF-15) with the required documentation.

5. Status applicants with career or career-conditional status or reinstatement eligibility must submit a copy of their Notification of Personnel Action (SF-50B) showing competitive status.

If you are submitting a resume, it must include the announcement number, position title, pay plan, occupational series and grade, your full legal name and complete mailing address, daytime and evening telephone numbers with area code, country of citizenship, and Social Security number. For experiences most relevant to the position, include name and address of employer, job title, starting and ending dates (month and year), average hours worked per week, supervisor's name and telephone number, and a description of your duties. If a past position was with the federal government, state the occupational series, grade or pay level, position title, and dates held. Indicate whether we may contact your current supervisor. For all colleges/universities attended, provide name, location, and dates of attendance. Specify type and date of degree awarded, if any. Describe training, honors, awards, recognition, license, or certification relevant to the position.

If you choose to submit a resume, you are certifying that, to the best of your knowledge and belief, all of the information on and attached to the resume is true, correct, complete, and made in good faith. You are certifying that you understand that false or fraudulent information on or attached to the resume may be grounds for not hiring you or for firing you after you begin work and may be punishable by fine or imprisonment. You are also certifying that you understand that any information given may be investigated.

Social Worker
Agency: Veterans Health Administration
Salary: $54,594 to $70,843
Location: Chico, California

Duties: The goal of the Readjustment Counseling Service Vet Center is to establish and maintain an outreach program to assist those eligible veterans (WWII, Korean War, Vietnam era, Lebanon, Grenada, and Panama conflicts, Persian Gulf War and GWOT), who have failed to make adequate psychosocial adjustment and re-entry into civilian life. The incumbent is the recognized expert within the community on the assessment and treatment of Post Traumatic Stress Disorder (PTSD) and family issues and will serve as case manager for clients of the Vet Center and conduct interviews and counseling with clients and their family members and provide psychological assessment and treatment. Additional responsibilities include bereavement counseling and sexual trauma and/or family counseling. The incumbent will provide psycho-diagnosis testing and psychological assessment to those clients who display clinically severe or unusual psychological disturbances. The incumbent personally conducts any or all of the following therapy programs: stress management, individual, group, conjoint and family therapy, biofeedback, relaxation training and other therapeutic intervention strategies and develops comprehensive treatment plans for adjustment/readjustment. The incumbent participates in conjoint emergency treatment with medical facility mental health personnel. The incumbent will maintain appropriate records and charting information necessary to ensure an accurate portrayal of the client's activities, condition, and progress in the program and will evaluate client records on a recurring basis to assess the current condition and progress. The incumbent serves as case manager and provides case consultation and assistance to the readjustment counseling specialists/technicians on highly complex cases and provides crisis intervention, stabilization, and follow-up.

Qualifications: All candidates must possess a license or certified at the master's level to independently practice social work in a state. VA may waive the licensure and/or certification requirement for persons who are otherwise qualified, pending completion of state prerequisites for examination. VA social workers who are not licensed at the time of appointment must be licensed or certified at the master's level within three years of their appointment as a social worker or one year from the day they meet the full requirement of the state for licensure or certification, whichever is longer. Those who fail to obtain state licensure or certification within the required time frames must be removed from the GS-185 Social Worker series. This may result in termination of employment. Note: Persons, who were permanently employed as social workers, GS-185 series, in VHA on or before August 14, 1991, do not have to satisfy the licensure and/or certification requirements, unless they leave this job series.

Candidates must also have a master's degree in social work from a school of social work accredited by the Council on Social Work Education. A list of college courses and hours or a copy of college transcript(s) must be submitted with your application package. If selected for this vacancy, you will be required to submit official transcripts prior to appointment.

In addition to meeting all basic requirements, candidates must have one year of professional social work experience, equivalent to the GS-9 grade level, under qualified social work supervision. This experience must have been in a clinical setting and must have demonstrated the potential to perform advanced assignments independently. Clinical social work experience obtained prior to completion of the requirements for the master's degree in social work is not qualifying. A doctoral degree in social work from a school of social work may be substituted for the required one year of professional social work experience in a clinical setting.

Applicants must meet all eligibility and qualification requirements within two weeks of the closing date of this announcement. Applicants for this position also must pass a pre-employment medical examination.

You must be a U.S. citizen to qualify for this position. You must submit to a drug test and receive a negative drug test before you can be appointed into this position. You will need to successfully complete a background security investigation before you can be appointed into this position.

Domestic Policy Council

Executive Office Building
Washington, DC 20504
202-456-1414

★ Web site: http://www.whitehouse.gov/dpc/index.html

The Domestic Policy Council (DPC) coordinates the domestic policy-making process in the White House and offers policy advice to the president. The DPC also works to ensure that domestic policy initiatives are coordinated and consistent throughout federal agencies. DPC monitors the implementation of domestic policy, and represents the president's priorities to other branches of government. Approximately 20 people are employed here.

Environmental Protection Agency

1200 Pennsylvania Avenue NW
Washington, DC 20460-0001
202-272-0167

★ Web site: http://www.epa.gov/

★ Job vacancies: http://www.epa.gov/careers/search.html

★ Student and fellowship information: http://www.epa.gov/careers/stuopp.html

★ How to apply: http://www.epa.gov/careers/apply.html

★ Career information: http://www.epa.gov/careers/

★ Research Triangle Park (RTP): http://www.epa.gov/rtp/

★ RTP jobs: http://www.epa.gov/rtp/employment/vacancy_announcements/rtpvacancy.htm

★ Strategic plan: http://www.epa.gov/ocfo/plan/plan.htm

The Environmental Protection Agency (EPA) protects human health and safeguards the natural environment (air, water, and land) upon which life depends. EPA develops and enforces regulations that implement environmental laws enacted by Congress, supports state environmental programs through grants, performs environmental research at laboratories around the country, sponsors voluntary environmental partnerships and programs that work to prevent pollution and conserve energy, and works to further environmental education.

EPA employs approximately 18,100 people across the country, including its headquarters in Washington, DC, 10 regional offices, and more than a dozen labs. EPA's staff are highly educated and technically trained; more than half are engineers, scientists, and policy analysts. In addition, a large number of employees are legal, public affairs, financial, information management, and computer specialists.

Selected EPA Agencies

The **American Indian Environmental Office** (AIEO) coordinates the agency-wide effort to strengthen public health and environmental protection in Indian country, with a special emphasis on building tribal capacity to administer their own environmental programs.

★ Web site: http://www.epa.gov/indian/

The **Office of Prevention, Pesticides, and Toxic Substances** (OPPTS) plays an important role in protecting public health and the environment from potential risk from toxic chemicals. It promotes pollution prevention and the public's right to know about chemical risks. It evaluates pesticides and chemicals to safeguard people and animals. Top priorities include dealing with emerging issues like endocrine disruptors and lead poisoning prevention.

★ Web site: http://www.epa.gov/oppts/

The **Office of Solid Waste and Emergency Response** (OSWER) provides policy, guidance, and direction for the agency's solid waste and emergency response programs. It develops guidelines for the land disposal of hazardous waste and underground storage tanks; provides technical assistance to the government to establish safe practices in waste management; and administers the Brownfields program, which supports state and local governments in redeveloping and reusing potentially contaminated sites. It also manages the Superfund program, which is designed to respond to abandoned and active hazardous waste sites and accidental oil and chemical releases as well as encourage innovative technologies to address contaminated soil and groundwater.

★ Web site: http://www.epa.gov/swerrims/

The mission of the **Office of Water** is to ensure that drinking water is safe and to restore and maintain oceans, watersheds, and their aquatic ecosystems in order to protect human health; support economic and recreational activities; and provide a healthy habitat for fish, plants, and wildlife.

★ Web site: http://www.epa.gov/OW/

Other EPA Agencies

History Office

http://www.epa.gov/history/

Office of Administration and Resources Management

http://www.epa.gov/oarm/

Office of Air and Radiation

http://www.epa.gov/oar/

Office of Compliance and Enforcement

http://www.epa.gov/compliance/

Office of Environmental Information

http://www.epa.gov/oei/

Office of Environmental Justice

http://www.epa.gov/compliance/environmentaljustice/

Office of International Programs

http://www.epa.gov/oia/

Office of Research and Development

http://www.epa.gov/ORD/

Science Policy Council

http://www.epa.gov/osa/spc/

Sample Job Vacancies

Biologist
Agency: Office of Prevention, Pesticides, and Toxic Substances
Salary: $41,210 to $65,531
Location: Arlington, Virginia

Duties: The position is entry level and developmental in nature at GS-7/9 levels. At the full performance level (GS-13), the incumbent, under the direction of a branch chief, provides advice, guidance, and support for the development of national guidelines, regulations, policies and procedures. The incumbent is responsible for reviewing applications for registration and petitions for tolerance and evaluating the levels of difficulty of each review. The incumbent gathers and assembles data for meetings with registrants, industry representatives, scientific and legal representatives, and OPP staff and managers concerning administrative and technical aspects of pesticide registrations, reregistrations, and related activities. In performing these reviews, the incumbent is required to apply a knowledge and understanding of policies and procedures in skillfully reviewing product labels, formula, and related data. The primary difference between grade levels is the degree of supervision, the level of training and guidance provided, and the complexity of assignment. This position has no extramural resources management responsibilities.

Qualifications: For the GS-7 level, at least one year of directly related experience comparable in difficulty and responsibility to the GS-5 level in the federal government is required. Examples of directly related experience are collecting basic data from field investigations, preparing samples, making observations on biological conditions, assisting in data entry and routine data analysis, and searching published technical sources for information on designated topics and preparing summaries for reference of others. For the GS-9 level, at least one year of directly related experience comparable in difficulty and responsibility to the GS-7 level in the federal government is required. Examples of directly related experience are assisting in planning, organizing, or implementing scientific investigations; performing data analyses on portions of larger investigations; and participating in organizing and interpreting biological, ecological, pathological, public use, or other pertinent research information.

Applicants may also qualify on the basis of education alone. For the GS-7, one full year of graduate level education or superior academic achievement in biological sciences, agriculture, natural resource management, chemistry, or related disciplines appropriate to the position is required. For the GS-9, a master's or equivalent graduate degree, or two full years of progressively higher level graduate education leading to such a degree, in one of the related disciplines is required.

The occupational questionnaire is designed to assess your ability to demonstrate the following competencies:

1. Ability to communicate scientific or technical information to industry, the general public, government agencies, and other stakeholders.

2. Knowledge of the Pesticides, Toxics, and Prevention Regulatory Program and regulatory testing equipment for industrial or pesticide chemicals.

3. Knowledge in developing, interpreting, and implementing objective-related environmental activities.

4. Ability to provide customer service in a timely, efficient, and accurate manner.

Travel, transportation, and relocation expenses will not be paid by the agency. Any travel, transportation, and relocation expenses associated with reporting for duty in this position will be the responsibility of the selected candidate. The selectee will be required to complete a confidential Financial Disclosure Form, OGE Form 450, prior to entering on duty and annually thereafter.

This position has been designated as low risk. The person selected for this position is subject to a favorable pre-appointment background investigation and must successfully pass a (full field or limited) background investigation.

All males born in 1960 or later (who are selected for appointment) must certify that they have met registration requirements under the Selective Service Law prior to appointment.

Overnight travel is required for five nights per month.

How to apply: Resume and application questions for this vacancy must be received online via the USAJOBS Web site before midnight Eastern time on the closing date of this announcement. If you fail to submit a complete online resume, you will not be considered for this position. Paper applications will not be accepted and requests for extensions will not be granted.

All veterans must submit a copy of their DD 214 or documentation of qualifying service or receipt of a qualifying campaign badge or medal to claim veteran's preference. Veterans claiming 10-point preference must also submit an SF 15 and its supporting documentation.

As this is a position with a positive education requirement, you must provide a copy of your school/college transcripts or a list of courses including course title, credit hours, and grade regardless of your current employment status. If you do not provide proof of your education, your application will be rated ineligible. Only education from an accredited college or university recognized by the Department of Education is acceptable to meet positive education requirements. Education completed in foreign colleges or universities may be used to meet the requirements for this position if you can show that the foreign education is comparable to that received in an accredited educational institution in the United States. It is the responsibility of the applicant to provide such evidence by the closing date of the announcement. Your claim of college-level education may be checked against federal government and/or accrediting organization databases.

Note: USAJOBS recently implemented a feature that permits you to upload certain documents to your account. Please note at this time that the Environmental Protection Agency is not accepting online attachment documents. Instead, you must fax or e-mail your documents. Make sure that the vacancy announcement number is annotated on your documents. These documents must be received by the closing date of this vacancy announcement.

Engineering Technician

Agency: Office of Research and Development
Salary: $43,519 to $62,486
Location: Research Triangle Park, North Carolina

Duties: At the full performance level, the incumbent organizes, schedules, and conducts complex emissions measurements from stationary sources, including combustors and engines; operates and maintains pilot-scale combustors, including associated air pollution control equipment; operates and maintains Continuous Emission Monitors (CEMs); operates sampling trains; performs tests in an open-burn test facility or on various combustors tested on-site to evaluate performance and to measure or monitor air pollutant emissions; designs and modifies apparatus for specific mechanical and emission experiments; coordinates the determination of combustors and air pollution control systems and correlates results with others in industry and other branches of the government; performs calculations with test data, operates computer and mini-computer systems, and designs and modifies simple computer programs as needed; assists in and coordinates design of automatic data acquisition system for recording emission data and combustor/Air Pollution Control System (APCS) operation; troubleshoots technical problems in the performance of emission experiments; and resolves problems in combustors/APCS and sampling system operation and in analytical equipment.

The primary difference between grade levels is the degree of supervision, the level of training and guidance provided, and the complexity of assignments. This position has no extramural resources management duties.

Qualifications: GS-09 applicants may qualify on the basis of education alone with two full years of graduate education or a master's degree that is directly related to the work of the position. Otherwise, at least one year of specialized experience comparable in difficulty and responsibility to the next lower grade level in the federal government is required. Examples of occupations that may have provided qualifying specialized experience include draftsperson, surveying technician, construction estimator, physical science technician, or mathematical technician. Experience in a trade or craft may be credited as specialized experience when the work provided intensive knowledge of engineering principles, techniques, methods, and precedents. Examples are trade positions with substantial developmental, test, or design responsibilities such as a planner and estimator who analyzed designs for production purposes or an instrument or model maker who performed design or development work on fabricated devices.

The occupational questionnaire is designed to assess your ability to demonstrate the following competencies:

★ Ability to operate combustion facilities.

★ Ability to utilize CEMs for the collection of combustions emissions data using standardized EPA stationary source test methods.

★ Skill in applying EPA stationary source test methods.

★ Ability to use spreadsheet computer programs and engineering equations to generate data summaries in scientific formats.

★ Ability to apply mechanical and electronic principles when assembling and using specialized measurement and combustion test apparatus.

Benefits and other information: Join EPA in protecting human health and the environment and enjoy many work life quality options including flexible work schedules, telecommuting, fitness centers, career and personal development, leave, retirement programs, health benefits, group life insurance and long term care insurance programs, biweekly pay schedule, and transit subsidy. Note that all EPA employees are required to have federal payments made by direct deposit.

More than one position may be filled from this announcement. If selected, applicants will be subject to a one-year probationary period.

Your application contains information subject to the Privacy Act. This information is used to determine your qualifications for employment. The use of this information is authorized under Title 5 USC, Sections 3302 and 3361.

EPA provides reasonable accommodations to applicants with disabilities. If you need a reasonable accommodation for any part of the application and hiring process, please call the vacancy contact, prior to the closing date of this announcement. The decision on granting reasonable accommodations will be on a case-by-case basis.

EPA is an equal opportunity employer. Selection for this position will be based solely on merit without regard to race, color, religion, age, gender, national origin, political affiliation, disability, sexual orientation, marital or family status or other differences.

Applicants selected for Federal employment will be required to complete a "Declaration of Federal Employment," (OF-306), prior to being appointed in order to determine their suitability for federal employment and to authorize a background investigation. Failure to answer all questions truthfully and completely or providing false statements on the application may be grounds for not hiring an applicant or for dismissing an employee who has already started to work and may be punishable by fine or imprisonment in accordance with U.S. Code, Title 18, Section 1001.

Federal law requires all employers to verify the identity and employment eligibility of all persons hired to work in the United States. This employer will provide the Social Security Administration (SSA) and, if necessary, the Department of Homeland Security (DHS) with information from each new employee's Form I-9 to confirm work authorization. If the government cannot confirm that you are authorized to work, this employer is required to provide you with written instructions and an opportunity to contact SSA and/or DHS before taking adverse action against you, including terminating your employment.

Employers may not use E-Verify to pre-screen job applicants or to reverify current employees and may not limit or influence the choice of documents presented for use on the Form I-9. In order to determine whether Form I-9 documentation is valid, this employer uses E-Verify's photo screening tool to match the photograph appearing on some permanent resident and employment authorization cards with the official U.S. Citizenship and Immigration Services' (USCIS) photograph. If you believe that your employer has violated its responsibilities under this program or has discriminated against you during the verification process based upon your national origin or citizenship status, please call the Office of Special Counsel.

Promotion is based upon the following criteria: the employee meets the basic qualification requirements (time-in-grade and specialized experience) for the next higher grade level; the employee has demonstrated the ability to perform at the next higher grade level; and their performance appraisal at time of review was at least fully successful.

IT Auditor
Agency: Office of Inspector General
Salary: $60,989 to $113,007
Location: Washington, DC

Job summary: Applications will be accepted from all U.S. citizens. In addition to competitive referral lists, separate referral lists will be generated for candidates who are eligible under merit promotion procedures. You are eligible under merit promotion procedures if you meet one of the following criteria: all federal employees with career or career-conditional appointments in the competitive service; former federal employees with reinstatement eligibility based on previous career or career-conditional appointments in the competitive service; displaced federal employees requesting special priority selection consideration under the Career Transition Assistance Plan (CTAP) and the Interagency Career Transition Assistance Program (ICTAP); veterans who are preference eligibles or who have been separated under honorable conditions after three years or more of continuous service; individuals eligible for VRA appointments; and individuals with disabilities. You must submit your SF 50 and/or DD 214 in order to be considered under merit promotion procedures. One or more positions may be filled using this vacancy announcement.

Duties: Serves as an Information Technology (IT) auditor for the U.S. Environmental Protection Agency, Office of Inspector General. Is responsible for performing IT audits surrounding EPA's system development, IT investments, enterprise architecture, information security (application and general controls), or other information resources management-related areas. Provides advice and guidance on federal and EPA policies, strategic plans, and associated processes. Ensures that IT requirements are in compliance with federal and EPA organizational policies, standards, and procedures and that controls are adequately incorporated into the systems. Works with outside auditors to help reconcile discrepancies and to develop plans to review EPA policies, standards, processes, and procedures to assess, monitor, report, escalate, and remediate IT risk- and compliance-related issues. Researches, analyzes, reports, and recommends strategies for achieving and maintaining compliance with required federal mandates and resolves findings or discrepancies in existing audit efforts.

Qualifications: All applicants must meet the basic requirement of the position. This requirement may be met by an undergraduate degree in accounting or in a related field such as business administration, finance, or public administration that included or was supplemented by 24 semester hours of accounting (may include up to six semester hours in business law). This requirement also may be met by at least four years of experience in accounting or a combination of accounting experience, college-level education, and training that provided professional accounting knowledge.

To meet minimum qualification requirements at the GS-11 level, applicants must have at least one full year of experience (equivalent to the GS-9 level in the federal service) performing the following duties: planning, coordinating and conducting audits, studies and analyses of organizations and information technology systems; writing reports; developing data gathering instruments; conducting special studies; performing pre-evaluation testing; conducting briefings; and developing recommendations for action. Completion of three full years of progressively higher education toward a Ph.D. or a Ph.D. in accounting, auditing, or another field that is directly related to this position can also be used to meet this requirement. Applicants can also use a combination of specialized experience and graduate education that, when combined, are equivalent to 100 percent of the qualification requirements. Only graduate education in excess of the first two years may be used in this calculation. To compute this, first determine your total qualifying experience as a percentage of the experience required; second, determine your graduate education as a percentage of the education required; and then add the two percentages together. The total must equal at least 100 percent to qualify.

Mathematical Statistician
Agency: Office of Water
Salary: $60,989 to $95,026
Location: Washington, DC

Duties: Selects, uses, and adapts a variety of mathematical statistical methods and concepts to define problems in statistical terms, formulate overall statistical concepts, perform statistical calculations using standard statistical computer packages, and evaluate findings to water-related and environmental issues. The statistical methods may be fairly complex and sophisticated and based upon incumbent's familiarity with the advanced literature. The incumbent is responsible for the selection and application of such statistical techniques and demonstrates originality and resourcefulness in developing systems and procedures for statistical assignments. The incumbent also interprets statistical findings and provides recommendations to project teams and subject matter experts. Provides statistical expertise for data collection activities. This support is generally provided at each step of the statistical process: initiation, planning, execution, analysis, interpretation, and final presentation. Assesses statistical properties (precision, accuracy, interlaboratory and intralaboratory) of chemical analytical methods. Reviews analytical method test results to evaluate the reliability and accuracy of the test methods and draws inferences and conclusions. The performance of these methods is a critical element in monitoring and enforcement programs. Evaluates the validity of primary and secondary data sources to address the issues with the necessary quality, precision, and accuracy. Selects and implements a statistical approach to determine the quality, adequacy, and limitations of databases to address the questions raised by subject matter specialists (such as engineers, chemists, biologists, environmental scientists). Writes detailed and comprehensive reports summarizing the statistical analyses, data reviews, results, and conclusions/recommendations. Also briefs project team and managers on the results of the statistical analyses and evaluation of data. Consults and coordinates with other statisticians and subject-matter experts within EPA and outside the agency. About 20 percent of work time will be spent performing extramural resources management related duties.

Qualifications: At GS-11 level, at least one year of specialized experience comparable in difficulty and responsibility to the GS-09 level in the federal government is required. Examples of specialized experience are performing recurring or continuing complex mathematical statistical studies; and evaluating the validity of smaller, less-complex scientific studies; and assisting in the development reports-based statistical analyses. A Ph.D. or equivalent doctoral degree or three full years of progressively higher level graduate education leading to such a degree can substitute for this experience at this level. If you are applying under this provision, a copy of your official transcript must be received by the closing date of this announcement listing the type of degree held.

At the GS-12 level, at least one year of specialized experience comparable in difficulty and responsibility to the GS-11 level in the federal government is required. Examples of specialized experience are performing statistical work, such as sampling, collecting, computing, and analyzing statistical data; using a variety of complex mathematical and statistical techniques to initiate, develop, and evaluate data; and experience analyzing factual mathematical and statistical information, to recognize and evaluate significant and critical factors, to solve complex problems or advise others on the solution of such problems or to draw rational inferences based on statistical data, and to prepare comprehensive and publishable reports.

The assessment questionnaire is designed to assess your ability to demonstrate the following knowledge, skills, abilities, and/or competencies:

★ Ability to perform statistical studies

★ Ability to develop statistical methods

★ Ability to communicate orally

★ Skill in written communication

In addition to experience, applicants must have a degree that included 24 semester hours of mathematics and statistics, of which at least 12 semester hours were in mathematics and 6 semester hours were in statistics. Alternatively, applicants can have at least 24 semester hours of mathematics and statistics, including at least 12 hours in mathematics and 6 hours in statistics and appropriate experience or additional education. Courses acceptable toward meeting the mathematics course requirement must include at least four of the following: differential calculus, integral calculus, advanced calculus, theory of equations, vector analysis, advanced algebra, linear algebra, mathematical logic, differential equations, or any other advanced course in mathematics for which one of these was a prerequisite. Courses in mathematical statistics or probability theory with a prerequisite of elementary calculus or more advanced courses will be accepted toward meeting the mathematics requirements, with the provision that the same course cannot counted toward both the mathematics and the statistics requirement.

Because this position has a positive education requirement, proof of successful completion of required course work must be provided to determine whether you meet the basic qualification requirements for the position. Without this proof, your application will be rated ineligible. If selected for this position, you must provide an official copy of your school/college transcripts. Only education from an accredited college or university recognized by the Department of Education is acceptable to meet positive education requirements. Your claim of college level education may be checked against federal government and/or accrediting organization databases.

Equal Employment Opportunity Commission

131 M Street NE
Washington, DC 20507
202-663-4900

★ Web site: http://www.eeoc.gov/

★ Job vacancies, student jobs, and internships: http://www.eeoc.gov/soars/index.html

★ Strategic plan: http://www.eeoc.gov/abouteeoc/plan/index.html

The Equal Employment Opportunity Commission (EEOC) enforces laws that prohibit discrimination based on race, color, religion, sex, national origin, disability, or age in hiring, promoting, firing, setting wages, testing, training, apprenticeship, and all other terms and conditions of employment. EEOC conducts investigations of alleged discrimination; makes determinations based on gathered evidence; attempts conciliation when discrimination has taken place; files lawsuits; and conducts voluntary assistance programs for employers, unions, and community organizations. EEOC also has adjudicatory and oversight responsibility for all compliance and enforcement activities relating to equal employment opportunity among federal employees and applicants. It employs more than 2,200 personnel.

Executive Office of the President

The White House
1600 Pennsylvania Avenue NW
Washington, DC 20500
202-456-1414

★ Web site: http://www.whitehouse.gov/administration/eop/

Overseen by the White House chief of staff, the Executive Office of the President (EOP) consists of the immediate staff of the president of the United States, as well as multiple levels of support staff reporting to the president. Examples include the White House press secretary; the Office of Communications (including senior media relations personnel and presidential speechwriters); and White House–based presidential policy and legal advisors, including those focused on domestic, social, foreign, and national security policies. It employs approximately 1,700 people.

Export-Import Bank of the United States

811 Vermont Avenue NW
Washington, DC 20571
202-565-3946
800-565-3496 (toll-free)

★ Web site: http://www.exim.gov/

★ Job vacancies: http://www.exim.gov/about/jobs/current.cfm

★ Career information: http://www.exim.gov/about/jobs/jobs.cfm

★ Resume information: http://www.exim.gov/about/jobs/format.cfm

The Export-Import Bank of the United States (Ex-Im) is the official export credit agency of the United States. Ex-Im Bank's mission is to assist in financing the export of U.S. goods and services to international markets. Ex-Im Bank helps American exporters meet government-supported financing competition from other countries so that U.S. exports can compete for overseas business on the basis of price, performance, and service, and in doing so help create and sustain U.S. jobs. The bank also fills gaps in the availability of commercial financing for creditworthy export transactions. Ex-Im Bank does not compete with private sector lenders, but it provides export financing products that fill gaps in trade financing.

Ex-Im assumes credit and country risks that the private sector is unable or unwilling to accept. It also helps to level the playing field for U.S. exporters by matching the financing that other governments provide to their exporters. Ex-Im Bank provides working capital guarantees (pre-export financing); export credit insurance (post-export financing); and loan guarantees and direct loans (buyer financing). No transaction is too large or too small. On average, 85 percent of its transactions directly benefit U.S. small businesses.

Its board of directors consists of a president and chairperson, a first vice president and vice chair, and three other directors, all of whom are appointed by the president with the advice and consent of the Senate. In addition to its headquarters in Washington, the Export-Import Bank operates six regional offices and employs about 365 people in positions such as business development specialist, loan specialist, engineer (electronics, civil, mechanical, electrical, industrial, environmental, mining), economist, attorney-advisor, and resource manager (finance, accounting, human resources, information technology).

Farm Credit Administration

1501 Farm Credit Drive
McLean, VA 22102-5090
703-883-4000

★ Web site: http://www.fca.gov/

★ Job vacancies: http://jobsearch.usajobs.opm.gov/a9fl00.asp

★ Career information: http://www.fca.gov/about/careers.html

The Farm Credit Administration (FCA) provides American agriculture with a dependable source of credit. FCA ensures the safe and sound operation of the banks, associations, affiliated service organizations, and other entities that collectively comprise what is known as the Farm Credit System (FCS) and protects the interests of the public and those who borrow from Farm Credit institutions or invest in Farm Credit securities. In addition to credit, FCA provides banking services to agricultural producers and farmer-owned agricultural and aquatic cooperatives.

Major agency functions include conducting examinations of all system institutions; enforcing safe and sound banking practices, federal statutes, and FCA regulations; issuing and amending charters for system institutions; developing regulations; reviewing legal issues and resolving litigation; handling borrower-related issues and complaints; and administering the fiscal, personnel, and human resources of the agency. FCA employs approximately 260 people. The agency's headquarters are in McLean, Virginia. It has field examination offices in Bloomington, Minnesota; Dallas, Texas; Denver, Colorado; and Sacramento, California. FCS is a nationwide network of cooperatively organized banks and associations that are owned and controlled by their borrowers. It serves all 50 states and the Commonwealth of Puerto Rico.

Federal Communications Commission

445 Twelfth Street SW
Washington, DC 20554
888-225-5322 (toll-free)
202-418-0130

★ Web site: http://www.fcc.gov/

★ Job vacancies: http://www.fcc.gov/jobs/

★ Strategic plan: http://www.fcc.gov/omd/strategicplan/

The Federal Communications Commission (FCC) regulates interstate and foreign communications by radio, television, wire, satellite, and cable. It is responsible for the orderly development and operation of broadcast services and the provision of rapid, efficient nationwide and worldwide telephone and telegraph services at reasonable rates. FCC's responsibilities also include the use of communications for promoting safety of life and property and for strengthening the national defense.

The commission staff is organized by function. There are 7 operating bureaus and 10 staff offices. The bureaus' responsibilities include processing applications for licenses and other filings; analyzing complaints; conducting investigations; developing and implementing regulatory programs; and taking part in hearings. FCC employs approximately 1,800 people.

The FCC has 3 regional offices, 16 district offices, and 9 resident agent offices located across the United States. The FCC's jurisdiction covers the 50 states, the District of Columbia, and U.S. possessions.

Selected FCC Agencies

The **Media Bureau** develops, recommends, and administers the policy and licensing programs relating to electronic media, including cable television, broadcast television, and radio, in the United

States and its territories. The Media Bureau also handles post-licensing matters regarding direct broadcast satellite service.

★ Web site: http://www.fcc.gov/mb/

The **Public Safety and Homeland Security Bureau** develops, recommends, and administers the agency's policies pertaining to public safety communications issues, including 911 and E911, operability and interoperability of public safety communications, communications infrastructure protection and disaster response, and network security and reliability. The bureau also serves as a clearinghouse for public safety communications information and issues requiring emergency responses. It collaborates with the public safety community, industry, and other government entities to license, facilitate, restore, and recover communications services used by the citizens of the United States.

★ Web site: http://www.fcc.gov/pshs/

The **Wireless Telecommunications Bureau** handles nearly all FCC domestic wireless telecommunications programs, policies, and outreach initiatives. Wireless communications services include cellular telephone, paging, broadband PCS, and more. The bureau advises and makes recommendations to the FCC or acts for the FCC under delegated authority in all matters pertaining to the regulation and licensing of communications common carriers and ancillary operations (other than matters pertaining exclusively to the regulation and licensing of wireless telecommunications services and facilities).

★ Web site: http://wireless.fcc.gov/

Other FCC Agencies

Consumer and Governmental Affairs Bureau

http://www.fcc.gov/cgb/

Enforcement Bureau

http://www.fcc.gov/eb/

International Bureau

http://www.fcc.gov/ib/

Wireline Competition Bureau

http://www.fcc.gov/wcb/

Federal Deposit Insurance Corporation

550 Seventeenth Street NW
Washington, DC 20429
800-925-4618 (toll-free)
202-736-6000

★ Web site: http://www.fdic.gov/

★ Job vacancies: https://jobs1.quickhire.com/scripts/fdic.exe

★ Summer legal intern program: http://www.fdic.gov/about/legalinterns/index.html

★ Legal division honors program: http://www.fdic.gov/about/legalhonors/index.html

★ Division of Finance internship program: http://www.fdic.gov/about/dofinterns/index.html

★ Student employment information: http://www.fdic.gov/about/jobs/stuemp.html

★ How to apply for an FDIC job: http://www.fdic.gov/about/jobs/jobs_howtoapply.html

★ Career information: http://www.fdic.gov/about/jobs/index.html

★ Strategic plan: http://www.fdic.gov/about/strategic/index.html

The Federal Deposit Insurance Corporation (FDIC) promotes and preserves public confidence in U.S. financial institutions by insuring bank and thrift deposits up to the legal limit of $100,000; by periodically examining state-chartered banks that are not members of the Federal Reserve System for safety and soundness as well as compliance with consumer protection laws; and by liquidating assets of failed institutions to reimburse the insurance funds for the cost of failures. As banking has transformed into e-banking, the FDIC also analyzes Internet-related risk, explores the ramifications of wireless banking, and looks into the issues of technology interoperability.

The FDIC employs about 4,600 people. It is headquartered in Washington, DC, but conducts much of its business in six regional offices and in field offices around the country. It has 14 divisions or offices at its headquarters. Types of careers available at FDIC include bank examiners, compliance examiners, economists, financial analysts, information technology professionals, administrative personnel, and attorneys. The FDIC employs students as summer interns, assisting economists as research assistants. Ideal candidates for interns are students who are in the process of obtaining a degree in finance, economics, or statistics.

Sample Job Vacancies

Compliance Analyst
Agency: Division of Supervision and Consumer Protection
Salary: $59,741 to $107,774
Location: Multiple locations across the country

Job summary: The candidate selected will be offered a term appointment not to exceed two years, which may be extended to a maximum of four years based on management needs. Incumbent may be relocated to any duty location to meet management needs. This position requires very frequent overnight travel. FDIC employees should apply to the "FDIC Only Employees" announcement for this same vacancy.

Duties: Reviews loan samples for technical compliance with federal law. Evaluates the adequacy of board and management oversight of the compliance program and proposes corrective action. Participates in the evaluation of the Community Reinvestment Act (CRA) performance of financial institutions in accordance with current regulatory and corporate guidance, including small, intermediate, and large institutions as well as those with CRA special designations. Determines whether the defined assessment area complies with applicable law, rule, or regulation. Reviews public files of banks for completeness, including CRA public evaluation listing of bank services, map assessment area, loan application register, and a listing of branch locations by census tract, etc. Analysts may also be assigned to participate in investigations of applications where CRA protests or other significant compliance matters or problems exist. Assists in the development of the risk profile and scope memorandum and other reports and documents and analyzes, develops, and presents recommendations for appropriate corrective actions for identified program/policies weaknesses. Assists in evaluating the compliance management system for a financial institution, including policies, procedures, training, monitoring, auditing, and third-party arrangements. Meets with and interviews bank management and personnel to determine and assess their knowledge and understanding of current law and regulations and present relevant findings during the examination. Reviews loan samples for compliance with fair lending laws to determine whether the bank is discriminating on a prohibited basis in its treatment of customers. Determines whether a bank's policies and procedures discourage customers from certain groups from applying and whether there are loan disparities on a prohibited basis.

Qualifications: Applicants must have one year of specialized experience equivalent to the CG-9 level in the federal service; or have a Ph.D. or equivalent doctoral degree or three years of progressively higher level full-time graduate education leading to such a degree; or an LL.M. in a major field of study related to the line of work such as accounting, banking, business administration, commercial or banking law, economics, finance, marketing, or other fields related to the position. Specialized experience is defined as experience serving as an oversight auditor, internal auditor, insured financial institution consultant, or insured financial institution employee reviewing financial institutions for compliance with consumer regulations, CRA, and/or fair lending.

Only United States citizens and nationals (residents of American Samoa and Swains Island) are eligible for appointment to competitive service jobs. This is a moderate risk position, so a Minimum Background Investigation (MBI) is required. Candidates who are tentatively identified for appointment must meet suitability requirements for Federal employment prior to appointment. FDIC will request applicant to provide additional information, including a credit statement release, prior to making a formal offer of employment, as required by 12 CFR Part 336.

How you will be evaluated: Applicants will be evaluated using category-based rating instead of application of the "rule of three" (5 USC 3318(a)). The applicants' answers will be validated against information provided in their current performance appraisal (for FDIC employees) and in their resumes, including their paid or volunteer experience, education, training, and certifications. Qualified veterans will be placed ahead of nonpreference eligibles within each quality category instead of being assigned additional points.

Risk Management Examiner
Agency: Division of Supervision and Consumer Protection
Salary: $57,939 to $123,469
Location: Multiple locations across the country

Job summary: The range of pay shown is the basic pay for this position. Note that the pay is supplemented by locality adjustment reflecting differences between FDIC and non-federal cost-of-labor for each FDIC duty station. The locality adjustments for these duty locations range from a low of 3.11 percent to a high of 33 percent; the total salary would be the basic rate of pay plus supplemental locality adjustment.

Candidates selected for the mid-career examiner position in the FDIC will be placed in a career-conditional appointment in the competitive service. Mid-career examiners will be assigned to an FDIC field office and participate in a training program designed to achieve risk management or compliance commissioned examiner status. This training program may encompass formal classroom training, self-study, a technical evaluation, and/or work assignments located inside and outside of the employee's official duty station and/or territory.

Mid-career examiners must obtain a commission as an examiner in either risk management or compliance within 30 months of their initial appointment with the FDIC. If a mid-career examiner does not obtain a risk management or compliance commission within two years of reporting to the Division of Supervision and Consumer Protection, the candidate will be given a six-month extension period to become commissioned and will be issued a performance improvement plan during the extension period to perform tasks required for commissioning. If unsuccessful in achieving commissioned status after this six-month period, the candidate will be separated from the FDIC. A certification in a second discipline will be required when workload eases. The timeframe for obtaining the certificate will be determined at that time. The FDIC reserves the right to take any performance based or appropriate disciplinary or adverse action.

Duties: The incumbent is engaged primarily in bank examinations, the purpose of which is to determine the financial condition of the bank, evaluate its management, and determine its compliance with applicable laws and regulations. Such examinations require a careful appraisal and classification of assets; a comprehensive analysis of liabilities; accurate determination and analysis of capital; a studied review of dividend and charge-off policies, earnings trends, and future prospects; a review of trust department operations and policies; and full determination of all other factors and causes, unsafe and unsound practices, and violations of laws and regulations that have affected or may affect the condition and soundness of the institution under examination.

Determines whether there are inappropriate insider/affiliate dealings and whether bank practices and behaviors correspond with board-approved policies. Assesses management's ability and willingness to correct issues identified in formal or informal enforcement actions. Evaluates underwriting and credit administration practices (such as terms and structure of loans, including length, interest rate, conveyances, and pay terms) on loans. Assigns risk weightings to classified loans and completes loan line sheets based on loan analysis. Meets with management to discuss concerns regarding specific loans and file documentation. Evaluates the bank's conditions in other areas. Assesses the level and appropriateness of hedging activity and determines whether capital level is commensurate with the risk taken by the bank and whether the bank has an adequate allowance for loan and lease losses. Meets with bank management, boards of directors, attorneys, external auditors, and others to make recommendations regarding corrective action for deficiencies; to provide support for ratings; to inform bank management of potential enforcement actions; to answer questions; and to persuade bank management to take the corrective action recommended in the Report of Examination. Participates in formal training or self-study programs by attending seminars, conferences, and formal specialized training programs.

Qualifications: Applicants must possess one year of specialized experience equivalent to the CG-9 level in the federal service. Or applicants must have a Ph.D. or equivalent doctoral degree, three years of progressively higher level full-time graduate education leading to such a degree, or an LL.M. in the following major fields of study: accounting, banking, business administration, commercial or banking law, economics, finance, marketing, or other fields related to the position. Applicants also may qualify with a combination of both education and experience.

Under law, FDIC may not employ any person who has been convicted of any felony; been removed from, or prohibited from participating in the affairs of any insured depository institution pursuant to any final enforcement action by any appropriate federal banking agency; demonstrated a pattern or practice of defalcation regarding obligations to insured depository institutions; or caused a substantial loss, in an amount in excess of $50,000, to federal deposit insurance funds. FDIC employees, their spouses, and minor children are also prohibited from acquiring, owning, or controlling, directly or indirectly, a security of an FDIC-insured depository institution, or an affiliate of an FDIC-insured depository institution.

Other information: Financial institution examiners must maintain the highest personal ethical standards as provided in the FDIC's rules and regulations. Financial institution examiners must comply with the Supplemental Standards of Ethical Conduct for FDIC Employees, which, in part, prohibit them and their immediate families from accepting certain credit from state nonmember banks. All financial institution examiners are prohibited from the following:

1. Obtaining a loan or a line of credit from any insured state nonmember bank or its subsidiaries. Any extensions of credit held by the examiner, the examiner's spouse, or any dependent children are direct or indirect extensions of credit to the examiner. Exceptions: Loans for a primary residence are permissible. The examiner must not participate in any examination of that institution with which he holds the primary residence loan, and a "cooling off" period is required before negotiating a loan for a primary residence from any institution the examiner has examined. There are no restrictions on obtaining credit cards issued under the same terms and conditions available to the public from an insured state nonmember bank either within or outside of the field office of assignment.

2. Participating in any examination, or other matter, involving an insured depository institution or any person with whom the examiner has an outstanding loan or line of credit.

3. Performing any service for compensation with any bank, or for any officer, director, or employee thereof, or for any person connected therewith.

4. Disclosing any confidential information from a bank examination report except as authorized by law.

5. Soliciting or accepting any gift from a prohibited source or because of the examiner's official position.

How to apply: The first step is registering as a user of FDIC Careers and then responding to all of the vacancy questions. During registration, you will be required to establish a password. It is essential that you verify before noon of the closing date that you have access to your FDIC Careers account to ensure you are able to complete your application on time. If you are locked out of your account, you must contact careers@fdic.gov between 9 a.m. and 5 p.m., E.T. Monday-Friday. Each account is linked to a unique Social Security number; therefore, you cannot create a new account as a work-around to a lost password. Creating a false Social Security number or using another's is prohibited under 18 USC 1001.

We encourage you to review the resume that you load in FDIC Careers and update it to accurately reflect your current experience, providing specifics that will help us verify the responses provided to the vacancy questions. If you have rated yourself higher than is supported by your description of experience and/or education or your application is incomplete, you may be rated ineligible or your score may be lowered. You will be referred to the hiring officials for a duty location if your score places you among the best qualified who expressed interest in the location. You many elect to be considered for as many duty locations are you want, but you will be referred for no more than one site at a time.

Secretary

Agency: Division of Supervision and Consumer Protection
Salary: $51,945 to $82,665
Location: San Francisco, California

Duties: Receives and screens telephone and personal callers, referring matters to the appropriate staff member or handling them personally. Maintains the supervisor's calendar, schedules appointments and conferences (frequently without prior clearance), and arranges for participation of staff as necessary. Makes arrangements for travel, including transportation and hotel reservations, notifying places and people on the supervisor's itinerary of the visit and submitting travel vouchers and so on after the supervisor's return. Prepares reports and basic data for studies undertaken by the senior staff pertaining to regional banks, banking, and other matters in order to facilitate office operations. Types material from rough draft into final form by using an electric or automatic typewriter or a personal computer while ensuring correct grammar, spelling, and style. Reads incoming correspondence, replies to inquiries, handles routine matters personally, makes appropriate referrals, and follows up on responses. Drafts and sends routine correspondence for supervisor. Assembles and summarizes factual background materials for use in conferences. Maintains records for the immediate use of the deputy regional director, including files of confidential correspondence, region memoranda, and other such records as required. Respects and maintains the confidentiality inherent in the subject matter that the incumbent routinely encounters.

Qualifications: To qualify, you must have at least one year of experience performing office support duties equivalent to at least the Federal GS 6 level. Experience need not be gained in the federal service, but must be equivalent. Examples of qualifying experience include tracking activities and project completion; maintaining calendars; scheduling meetings; arranging conference rooms; arranging travel; receiving and placing telephone calls; assisting visitors; reviewing documents for grammar, punctuation, spelling, and formatting; using office software; and maintaining files and records.

How you will be evaluated: Applicants will be evaluated on responses to quality ranking factors described in vacancy questions. The applicants' answers will be validated against information provided in their resumes, including their paid or volunteer experience, education, training, and certifications. The score awarded will be augmented by additional points for applicants who are eligible for and claim veterans' preference.

Benefits: The FDIC offers a comprehensive package of employee benefits and work life programs. Some benefits are at no cost while others involve a premium or contribution, often on a pre-tax basis. Your type of appointment determines the benefits for which you are eligible. Benefits include the following:

★ Enrollment in the Federal Employees Retirement System.

★ Federal Thrift Savings Plan and FDIC 401(k) plan, both with employer matching funds.

★ Health and dependent care flexible spending accounts.

★ Federal and FDIC life insurance programs, federal health insurance, and FDIC dental and vision plans. For permanent appointments only, long-term disability insurance.

★ Thirteen paid sick leave days annually, including sick leave usage options for family-related reasons.

★ Ten paid holidays per year. Thirteen paid days of vacation for the first 3 years of federal service, increasing to 20 days for more than 3 to 15 years of service, and 26 days for more than 15 years of federal service.

★ Transit subsidy program for employees who commute via public transportation.

★ Work life programs and services, including teleworking, alternative work schedules, information and referral services and elder care support services.

★ Business casual dress code.

★ Clinical support services.

★ Supplemental pay and support for activated reserve and guard members.

Federal Election Commission

999 E Street NW
Washington, DC 20463
800-424-9530 (toll-free)
202-694-1100

★ Web site: http://www.fec.gov/

★ Job vacancies: http://www.fec.gov/pages/jobs/jobs.shtml

★ Strategic plan: http://www.fec.gov/pages/budget/fy2009/FECStrategicPlan2008-2013.pdf

The Federal Election Commission (FEC) ensures compliance by participants in the federal election campaign process. Its chief mission is to provide public disclosure of campaign finance activities and effect voluntary compliance by providing the public with information on the laws and regulations concerning campaign finance. The commission is made up of six members, who are appointed by the president and confirmed by the Senate. Each member serves a six-year term, and two seats are subject to appointment every two years. The FEC employs approximately 360 people.

Federal Housing Finance Agency

1700 G Street NW
Washington, DC 20552
866-796-5595

★ Web site: http://www.fhfa.gov/

★ Job vacancies: http://www.fhfa.gov/Default.aspx?Page=9

The Federal Housing Finance Agency (FHFA) was established by the Housing and Economic Act of 2008. The act merged the Office of Federal Housing Enterprise Oversight with the Federal Housing Finance Board and the GSE mission office of the U.S. Department of Housing and Urban Development. Its primary mission is ensuring the financial safety and soundness of Federal National Mortgage Association (Fannie Mae), the Federal Home Loan Mortgage Corporation (Freddie Mac), and the 12 Federal Home Loan (FHL) Banks. This agency employs examiners, economists, accountants, financial analysts, information technology specialists, and attorneys.

Fannie Mae is a government-sponsored enterprise (GSE) chartered by Congress to provide funds to and stabilize U.S. housing and mortgage markets. It doesn't directly loan money to home buyers. Instead, it works with bankers and mortgage brokers to make sure that they can offer home loans at affordable rates.

★ Web site: http://www.fanniemae.com

★ Career information: http:// www.fanniemae.com/careers/opportunities

Freddie Mac is also a GSE and has a similar mission to Fannie Mae. It also works through the secondary mortgage market.

★ Web site: http://www.freddiemac.com

★ Career information: http://www.freddiemac.com/careers/

The **Federal Home Loan Banks** were created in 1932 to improve the supply of funds to local lenders that, in turn, finance loans for home mortgages. The FHL Banks and their member-owners, which constitute the FHL Bank System, form a cooperative partnership that supports community-based financial institutions and facilitates their access to credit. The FHFA ensures that FHL Banks, which are privately capitalized, government-sponsored enterprises, operate in a safe and sound manner, carry out their housing and community development finance mission, and remain adequately capitalized and able to raise funds in the capital markets.

★ Web site: http://www.fhlbanks.com

As part of the FHL Bank System, the **Office of Finance** issues and services all debt securities for the FHL Banks while obtaining the most cost-effective terms possible.

★ Career information: http://www.fhlb-of.com/mission/aboutusframe.html

Federal Labor Relations Authority

1400 K Street NW
Washington, DC 20005
202-218-7770

★ Web site: http://www.flra.gov/

★ Job vacancies: http://www.flra.gov/hrd/hrd_job.html

★ How to apply: http://www.flra.gov/hrd/hrd_how.html

★ Career information: http://www.flra.gov/29-jobs.html

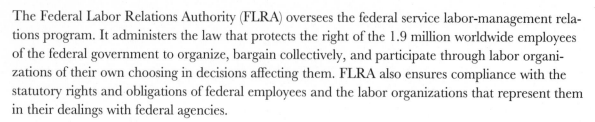

The Federal Labor Relations Authority (FLRA) oversees the federal service labor-management relations program. It administers the law that protects the right of the 1.9 million worldwide employees of the federal government to organize, bargain collectively, and participate through labor organizations of their own choosing in decisions affecting them. FLRA also ensures compliance with the statutory rights and obligations of federal employees and the labor organizations that represent them in their dealings with federal agencies.

FLRA employs approximately 130 people, about half of whom are in the Washington, DC, headquarters offices and the remainder of whom are divided among seven regional offices. The majority of FLRA employees are attorneys or labor relations specialists. FLRA consists of three major components: the Authority, the Office of the General Counsel, and the Federal Service Impasses Panel.

Federal Maritime Commission

800 North Capitol Street NW
Washington, DC 20573-0001
202-523-5707

★ Web site: http://www.fmc.gov/

★ Job vacancies: http://www.fmc.gov/bureaus/EmploymentOpportunities.asp

The Federal Maritime Commission (FMC) regulates shipping. It ensures that U.S. ocean-borne trades are open to all on fair and equitable terms and protects against concerted activities and unlawful practices. FMC protects U.S. commerce from restrictive rules and regulations of foreign shippers that have an adverse effect on U.S. shipping and investigates unfair practices of common carriers, terminal operators, and freight forwarders. It reviews tariff publications and regulates tariff rates, charges, classifications, rules, and regulations to ensure that they are just and reasonable. It also licenses U.S.-based international ocean transportation intermediaries, requires bonds of U.S. and foreign-based ocean transportation intermediaries, and issues passenger vessel certificates showing evidence of financial responsibility of vessel owners or charterers to pay judgments for personal injury or death or to repay fares for the nonperformance of a voyage or cruise. FMC employs approximately 100 people.

Selected FMC Agency

The **Bureau of Trade Analysis** (BTA) reviews agreements and monitors the activities of common carriers. It also reviews and analyzes service contracts, monitors rates of government-controlled carriers, reviews carrier-published tariff systems, and responds to inquiries or issues that arise concerning service contracts or tariffs. The BTA also is responsible for competition oversight and market analysis, focusing on activity that is substantially anti-competitive and market distorting. It is an expert organization on the economics of international liner shipping and maritime agreements, especially with respect to issues of competition and unfair trade practices as they may affect the interests of the shipping public and U.S. international trade.

★ Web site: http://www.fmc.gov/bureaus/bureau_of_trade_analysis/BureauofTradeAnalysis.asp

Other FMC Agencies

Bureau of Certification and Licensing

http://www.fmc.gov/bureaus/bureau_of_certification_and_licensing/
BureauofCertificationandLicensing.asp

Bureau of Enforcement

http://www.fmc.gov/bureaus/BureauofEnforcement.asp

Federal Mediation and Conciliation Service

2100 K Street NW
Washington, DC 20427
202-606-8100

★ Web site: http://www.fmcs.gov/internet/

★ Job vacancies: http://www.fmcs.gov/internet/itemDetail.asp?categoryID=41&itemID=17625

★ Mediator recruitment (PDF format): http://www.fmcs.gov/assets/files/HumanResources/
MED08.pdf

★ Strategic plan: http://www.fmcs.gov/internet/itemDetail.asp?categoryID=44&itemID=16348

The Federal Mediation and Conciliation Service (FMCS) assists labor and management in resolving disputes in collective bargaining contract negotiation through voluntary mediation and arbitration services. FCMS helps prevent disruptions in the flow of interstate commerce caused by disputes between labor and management by providing mediators to assist disputing parties in the resolution of their differences. It provides training to unions and management in cooperative processes to improve long-term relationships under the Labor Management Cooperation Act of 1978; provides alternative dispute resolution services and training to government agencies, including the facilitation of regulatory negotiations under the Administrative Dispute Resolution Act and the Negotiated Rulemaking Act of 1996; and awards competitive grants to joint labor-management committees to encourage innovative approaches to cooperative efforts.

In addition to administrative personnel, the FMCS primarily employs mediators. Stationed throughout the country, mediators perform duties in three major areas: collective bargaining mediation, relationship development training (preventive mediation), and outreach. Recruitment for mediators is continuous, with application materials available online. (Note the FMCS mediator recruitment site listed at the beginning of this description.) FMCS employs approximately 250 people.

Federal Mine Safety and Health Review Commission

601 New Jersey Avenue NW
Washington, DC 20001
202-434-9900

★ Web site: http://www.fmshrc.gov/

★ Strategic plan: http://www.fmshrc.gov/plans/strategicplan121907.htm

The Federal Mine Safety and Health Review Commission provides administrative trial and appellate review of legal disputes arising under the Federal Mine Safety and Health Amendments Act (Mine Act). The commission enforces these regulations by issuing citations, mine closure orders, and proposals for civil penalties issued for violations of the act or mandatory safety and health standards. The commission is concerned solely with the adjudication of disputes under the Mine Act, including the determination of appropriate penalties. It does not regulate mining or enforce the Mine Act. The commission was established as an independent agency to ensure its impartiality.

The commission consists of five members who are appointed by the president with the advice and consent of the Senate. The commission's headquarters and Office of Administrative Law Judges (OALJ) are co-located in Washington, DC, with an additional OALJ office in Denver, Colorado. Currently, the Commission has a budget of more than $7 million and a staff of 40 employees.

Federal Reserve System

Twentieth Street and Constitution Avenue NW
Washington, DC 20551
202-452-3000

★ Web site: http://www.federalreserve.gov/

★ Job vacancies: http://www.federalreserve.gov/careers/default.htm

★ Career information: http://www.federalreserve.gov/careers/careers.htm

★ Internships: http://www.federalreserve.gov/careers/internships.htm

★ Strategic plan: http://www.federalreserve.gov/boarddocs/rptcongress/default.htm#gpra

The Federal Reserve System (the Fed), the central bank of the United States, administers and formulates the nation's credit and monetary policy. Through its supervisory and regulatory banking functions, the Fed maintains the safety and soundness of the nation's economy, responding to the nation's domestic and international financial needs and objectives. Its major responsibility is in the execution of monetary policy. It also performs other functions, such as the transfer of funds, handling government deposits and debt issues, supervising and regulating banks, and acting as lender of last resort.

The Fed consists of the Board of Governors in Washington, DC; the 12 Federal Reserve Banks and their 25 branches and other facilities situated throughout the country; the Federal Open Market Committee; the Federal Advisory Council; the Consumer Advisory Council; the Thrift Institutions Advisory Council; and the nation's financial institutions, including commercial banks, savings and loan associations, mutual savings banks, and credit unions.

Selected Fed Agencies

The 12 **Federal Reserve Banks** operate under the general supervision of the Board of Governors in Washington, DC. Each bank has a nine-member board of directors that oversees its operations. Federal Reserve Banks generate their own income, primarily from interest earned on government securities that are acquired in the course of Federal Reserve monetary policy actions. A secondary source of income is derived from the provision of priced services to depository institutions, as required by the Monetary Control Act of 1980. Federal Reserve Banks are not operated for a profit, and each year they return to the U.S. Treasury all earnings in excess of Federal Reserve operating and other expenses.

★ Web site: http://www.federalreserve.gov/otherfrb.htm

Other Fed Agencies

Consumer Advisory Council

http://www.federalreserve.gov/aboutthefed/cac.htm

Federal Advisory Council

http://www.federalreserve.gov/generalinfo/adviscoun/fac.htm

Federal Open Market Committee

http://www.federalreserve.gov/monetarypolicy/fomc.htm

Federal Reserve Board

http://www.federalreserve.gov/aboutthefed/default.htm

Thrift Institutions Advisory Council

http://www.federalreserve.gov/generalinfo/adviscoun/tiac.htm

Federal Retirement Thrift Investment Board

1250 H Street NW
Washington, DC 20005
877-968-3778 (toll-free)
202-942-1600

★ Web site: http://www.frtib.gov/

★ Thrift savings plan: http://www.tsp.gov

★ Job vacancies: http://www.frtib.gov/personnel/index.html

The Federal Retirement Thrift Investment Board administers the Thrift Savings Plan, which provides federal employees the opportunity to save for additional retirement security. It is one of the smaller federal agencies, with just under 70 employees. The Thrift Savings Plan is a tax-deferred, defined contribution plan that was established as one of the three parts of the federal employees' retirement system. For employees covered under the system, savings accumulated through the plan make an important addition to the retirement benefits provided by Social Security and the system's basic annuity. Civil Service Retirement System employees and members of the uniformed services may also take advantage of the plan to supplement their retirement annuities.

Federal Trade Commission

600 Pennsylvania Avenue NW
Washington, DC 20580
877-FTC-HELP (877-382-4357—toll-free)
202-326-2222

★ Web site: http://www.ftc.gov/

★ Job vacancies: http://www.ftc.gov/ftc/oed/hrmo/jobops.shtm

★ Internships and student employment: http://www.ftc.gov/ftc/oed/hrmo/interns.shtm

★ Strategic plan: http://www.ftc.gov/opp/gpra/spfy06fy11.pdf

The Federal Trade Commission (FTC) works to ensure the smooth operation of the American free market system. It enforces federal consumer protection laws that prevent fraud, deception, and unfair business practices as well as federal antitrust laws that prohibit anticompetitive mergers and other business practices that restrict competition and harm consumers. In addition, the commission conducts economic research and analysis to support its law enforcement efforts and to contribute to the policy deliberations of Congress, the executive branch, other independent agencies, and state and local governments. FTC enforces the laws that prohibit business practices that are anti-competitive, deceptive, or unfair to consumers; promotes informed consumer choice and public understanding of the competitive process; and seeks to accomplish its mission without impeding legitimate business activity.

The FTC hires attorneys, economists, accountants, investigators, paralegals, and administrative support personnel, among others. It recruits annually for entry-level attorney positions. The Bureau of Competition generally employs the largest number of new law school graduates. The FTC employs more than 1,100 staff members, including more than 500 attorneys and 70 economists.

Selected FTC Agencies

The **Bureau of Consumer Protection** (BCP) protects consumers against unfair, deceptive, or fraudulent practices by enforcing a variety of consumer protection laws enacted by Congress, as well as trade regulation rules issued by the FTC. It investigates companies and industries, engages in litigation, makes rules, and educates consumers and businesses. The Bureau of Consumer Protection is divided into seven divisions: the Division of Advertising Practices, the Division of Enforcement, the Division of Financial Practices, the Division of Marketing Practices, the Division of Planning and Information, the International Division of Consumer Protection, and the Office of Consumer and Business Education. BCP provides oversight for the Do Not Call Registry.

★ Web site: http://www.ftc.gov/bcp/

★ Legal careers at BCP: http://www.ftc.gov/recruit

★ Summer law intern program: http://www.ftc.gov/bcp/lawclerk/index.shtm

★ Honors paralegal program: http://www.ftc.gov/ftc/oed/hrmo/hpp/index.shtm

Other FTC Agencies

Bureau of Competition

http://www.ftc.gov/bc/index.shtml

Bureau of Economics

http://www.ftc.gov/be/index.shtml

General Services Administration

1800 F Street NW
Washington, DC 20405
202-708-5082

★ Web site: http://www.gsa.gov/

★ Job vacancies: https://jobs1.quickhire.com/scripts/gsa.exe/runuserinfo?Haveusedbefore=5

★ Strategic plan: http://www.gsa.gov/graphics/admin/Strategic_Plan_2007.pdf

The General Services Administration (GSA) establishes policy for and provides economical and efficient management of government property and records, including construction and operation of buildings; procurement and distribution of supplies; utilization and disposal of real and personal property; transportation, traffic, and communications management; and management of the government-wide automatic data processing resources program. Eleven regional offices extend GSA's outreach to federal customers nationwide.

GSA has approximately 12,000 employees who provide valuable services to support other federal agencies and, in some cases, the general public. GSA support can include office space, equipment, supplies, telecommunications, and information technology. GSA also plays a key role in developing and implementing policies that affect many government agencies. To find out more about career opportunities and internships at the GSA, go to its home page and click the Careers link.

Selected GSA Agencies

The **Civilian Board of Contract Appeals** is responsible for resolving disputes arising out of contracts with the General Services Administration and other government agencies. The board also hears and decides requests for review of transportation audit rate determinations; claims by federal civilian employees regarding travel and relocation expenses; claims for the proceeds of the sale of property of certain federal civilian employees; and cases involving the Indian Self-Determination and Education Assistance Act and the Federal Crop Insurance Corporation. In addition, the board provides alternative dispute resolution services to executive agencies in both contract disputes that are the subject of a contracting officer's decision and other contract-related disputes. Although the board is located within GSA, it functions as an independent tribunal. (For information about internships, click the Legal Interns link on the left side of the board's home page.)

★ Web site: http://www.cbca.gsa.gov/

The **Federal Acquisition Service** (FAS) offers business, administrative, and mission-related solutions to customer agencies by providing innovative, compliant, and integrated solutions to acquisition challenges. It delivers excellent acquisition services that provide the best value in terms of cost, quality, and service. This includes acquisition of products and services and full-service programs in information technology, telecommunications, professional services, supplies, motor vehicles, travel and transportation, charge cards, and personal property use and disposal. The FAS provides a source for virtually every commercial product or service an agency might need at the best value possible. With a business volume topping $25 billion, the FAS offers more products and services than any commercial enterprise in the world. The FAS brings hundreds of thousands of federal customers together with more than 9,000 contractors.

★ Web site: http://www.gsa.gov/fas

Other GSA Agencies

Citizen Services and Communications (CSC)

http://www.gsa.gov/; click GSA Organization link, and then link to CSC

Office of Emergency Response and Recovery (OERR)

http://www.gsa.gov/; click GSA Organization link, and then click link to OERR

Office of Governmentwide Policy (OGP)

http://www.gsa.gov/ogp

Office of Small Business Utilization (OSBU)

http://www.gsa.gov/sbu

Office of the Chief Acquisition Officer (OCAO)

http://www.gsa.gov/chiefacquisitionofficer

Public Buildings Service (PBS)

http://www.gsa.gov/publicbuildingsservice

Regulatory Information Services Center

http://www.gsa.gov/risc

Sample Job Vacancies

Accounts Manager

Agency: Federal Acquisition Service
Salary: $73,100 to $95,026
Location: Washington, DC

Duties: Establishes, develops, and maintains effective working relationships with client agencies and interagency personnel. Together with Network Services Division (NSD) and General Services Administration (GSA) internal organizations, provides support as required and develops strategies designed to identify targets of opportunity for the provision of Federal Acquisition Service (FAS)/ National Capital Region (NCR) services to client agencies. Serves as an experienced writer/editor and project leader for a variety of internal and/or external communications projects. Is responsible for internal and/or external communications for all network product lines including collateral, Web sites, publicity, public relations, media outreach, and inquiry fulfillment. Plans, coordinates, and participates in forums, conferences, and seminars. Participates in activities hosted by Central Office, Public Buildings Service (PBS), FAS, and industry partners to keep current on latest programs and direction. Reviews, analyzes, and reports account status information and participates in periodic program management reviews. Conducts and/or participates in meetings and conferences to provide advice and assistance and makes effective and authoritative recommendations and proposals for solutions to routine problems/issues in support of the clients' mission-essential operations. Advises client agencies in interpreting the scope, terms, and conditions of GSA contracts and other related contractual documents. Maintains an up-to-date awareness of network services advances through consultation with colleagues and industry partners in order to communicate and recommend effective network solutions to client agencies.

Qualifications: In order to be considered qualified, applicants must demonstrate, in their resumes and responses to questions, at least one year of specialized experience equivalent to the GS-11 level in the Federal service. Specialized experience is experience providing technical advice, customer service, and project management for various projects in information technology (IT) and telecommunications. Such experience must demonstrate expert knowledge of telecommunications or IT and must have included experience in the design and acquisition of IT and/or telecommunications products and services.

How you will be evaluated: As part of the online application process, you will be asked a series of job-related questions that are designed to assess your possession of the following accounts manager knowledges, skills, and abilities:

★ Knowledge of laws, principles, policies, and practices of information technology (IT), network services and systems acquisition, and program management.

★ Ability to establish and maintain effective relationships with individuals and groups in the federal and private sector.

★ Ability to plan, organize, and manage critical aspects of a variety of acquisition functions and account management.

EEO statement: All applicants for federal employment receive consideration without regard to race, religion, color, national origin, sex, political affiliation, sexual orientation, age (with authorized exceptions) or any other nonmerit factor.

What to expect next: Once your complete application is received, an evaluation of your qualifications will be conducted to determine your ranking. The most highly qualified candidates will be referred to the hiring manager for further consideration and possible interview. You will be notified of the outcome. You also can check the status of your application online 24 hours a day through GSA Jobs. If you have questions about your rating, please submit your question in writing via e-mail or USPS mail to the contact listed in this announcement.

Appraiser

Agency: Public Buildings Service
Salary: $80,402 to $104,525
Location: Kansas City, Missouri

Duties: You will serve as the regional appraiser for the Heartland Region, Public Buildings Service (PBS) in the Portfolio Management Division. You will provide long-range planning and program oversight to all appraisal activities in the region, which is comprised of Missouri, Kansas, Iowa, and Nebraska. You will provide advice and counsel to the director of Portfolio Management, asset managers, and other directors and employees in PBS on both broad and specific realty problems in which the appraisal program and the evaluation of property are involved. As the regional appraiser, you will provide overall program leadership for the GSA regional appraisal program and develop program goals, objectives, and established standards. In addition, you will review procedures and operations to assure program effectiveness and adherence to standards, provide guidance on program requirements established by the central office, and provide administrative review and control of appraisal actions in the region.

Qualifications: Applicants must have at least one year of specialized experience equivalent to the GS-12 level or higher. Specialized experience is defined as preparing, reviewing, and analyzing complex and varied real estate appraisals for industrial or commercial property. Because of the complex nature of the appraisals, an applicant must be a state-certified general appraiser. In obtaining this certification, the appraiser has demonstrated and proven his/her ability to complete complex projects in conformance with the criteria established by the appraisal subcommittee of the Federal Financial Institution Examination Council and by the appraiser qualification board of the Appraisal Foundation.

If you are selected, you must serve a one-year probationary period (unless you are found to have previously satisfied this requirement), be able to make a direct deposit to a financial organization for your salary check, and have registered with the Selective Service (males born after 12/31/59). Applicants selected for employment will be required to complete a "Declaration of Federal Employment" (OF-306) prior to being appointed to determine their suitability for federal employment. Failure to answer all questions truthfully and completely or providing false statements on the application may be grounds for not hiring the applicant, dismissal after they begin work, and/or may be punishable by fine or imprisonment (U.S. Code, Title 18, Section 1001). If selected, you also will be required to complete OGE Form 450, Confidential Financial Disclosure Report, to determine if a conflict or an appearance of a conflict exists between your financial interest and your prospective position with GSA.

A background security investigation is required for all new appointments. Continued employment will be subject to successful completion of a background security investigation and favorable adjudication. Failure to successfully meet this requirement will be grounds for termination.

Federal law requires all employers to verify the identity and employment eligibility of all persons hired to work in the United States. The General Services Administration will provide the Social Security Administration (SSA) and, if necessary, the Department of Homeland Security (DHS), with information from each new employee's Form I-9, Employment Eligibility Verification, to confirm work authorization.

This position requires occasional travel. You will inspect all types of real property, including remote properties and properties containing hazardous materials, which will require protective equipment such as hardhats, boots, masks, goggles, or gloves.

How to apply: Applications will only be accepted through GSA's online application system, GSA Jobs. A brief description of the process is provided here, but for complete instructions and information on the application process, please read the instructions on the GSA Web site. The following steps must be completed by 11:59 p.m. Eastern time on the closing date of this announcement in order for your application to be considered for this vacancy:

1. Log into the GSA Jobs system or register if you have not previously done so.

2. Ensure that all information in your personal profile is current and complete.

3. Answer the vacancy-specific questions.

4. Submit the required supplemental documents.

GSA provides reasonable accommodations to applicants with disabilities. If you need a reasonable accommodation for any part of the application or hiring process, please notify the HR Office immediately. The decision on granting reasonable accommodation will be on a case-by-case basis.

Building Management Specialist

Agency: Federal Acquisition Service
Salary: $38,117 to $49,553
Location: Syracuse, New York

Duties: As a Building Management Specialist/Trainee, you will be located in the Property Management Division and will receive developmental assignments coordinated with individual coaching and formal classroom training in principles and application of federal property management. You will be responsible for progressively more difficult assignments, including work in regional and field offices. You will develop skills in working with building drawings, space assignment plans, and field inspection procedures and developing operating costs and other related management reports. You will be called upon to perform many varied administrative, technical and managerial duties.

Qualifications: You must have one of the following:

★ A bachelor's degree and superior academic achievement (have a GPA of 3.0 or higher, be ranked in the upper one-third of your class, or be a member of a national honor society).

★ One full year of graduate level study or a master's or higher degree (LL.B., J.D., LL.M., or Ph.D.) in business or public administration, industrial management, real estate management, architecture, engineering, economics, or a related field.

★ One year of specialized experience equivalent to the GS-5 level with responsibility in assisting with the planning, execution, and control of the management responsibilities of building management.

★ A combination of graduate education and specialized experience that is equal to one full year.

How to apply: To apply for this position, you must provide a complete application package, which includes your responses to the assessment questionnaire, your resume (must be limited to eight pages or less), transcripts (if you are using education to qualify), and veterans preference documentation (if you are requesting veterans preference). Please ensure that your resume contains your full name, address, phone number, and Social Security number. Please do not submit extra information.

Use Application Manager for convenience and quickest processing. Track your progress to a complete application package using the My Application Packages checklist and status displays in Application Manager. To verify uploaded documents have been processed, please wait one hour to ensure they have cleared the virus scan. You can verify that your uploaded documents are attached to your application by checking the Details tab of your Application Manager account.

What to expect next: Once the application process is completed in its entirety, a review of your application will be made to ensure you meet the job requirements. A review will be made of your responses to the occupational questionnaire and the documentation you submitted in your resume to support your responses. Applicants that are found among the most highly qualified may be referred to the hiring official for consideration. If, after reviewing your resume and/or supporting documentation, a determination is made that you have inflated your qualifications and/or experience, you may lose consideration for this position. You will receive notice via e-mail (or by mail if you didn't provide an e-mail address during the application process) once this process is completed (generally four to six weeks). If your name is referred to the hiring official, you may be contacted directly by that office for a possible interview.

Interdisciplinary Architect/Engineer
Agency: Public Buildings Service
Salary: $84,992 to $110,492
Location: Minneapolis, Minnesota

Job summary: At this time we are filling one vacancy, however additional vacancies may be filled from this announcement as needed. This position is interdisciplinary and may be filled in any of the following titles and series depending on the experience and educational background of the selectee. However, applicants should apply under primary vacancy code.

★ General Engineer, GS-801

★ Architect, GS-808

★ Civil Engineer, GS-810

★ Structural Engineer, GS-810

★ Mechanical Engineer, GS-830

★ Electrical Engineer, GS-850

Duties: Serves as the supervisor for an interdisciplinary team of architects, engineers, and technicians responsible for all technical matters related to the development and execution of an overall repair and alteration program for an assigned service center. Projects are for design, construction, alteration, remodeling, extension, repair, preservation, and improvement of government buildings, lease space, and related equipment and facilities. Determines personnel required to complete projects and the need for coordination with other architects or engineers and other personnel within GSA. Assembles design data and assigns tasks to appropriate personnel for completion. For contractual needs, the incumbent is involved in complete contracting procedures for architect-engineer firms, including the development of selection criteria, development of contract documents, possible selection of the architect-engineer firms, and contract negotiations for required design services. Coordinates and conducts detailed reviews of reports, surveys, drawings, specifications, estimates and amendments prepared by private architectural-engineering firms. Reviews work for compliance with specifications, technical accuracy, and adherence to applicable codes. Implements and schedules preconstruction conferences and progress and final inspections, and assigns subordinates to arrange and participate in these inspections and conferences. Interprets contract requirements; obtains, reviews, recommends, and processes proposals for contract modifications and costs; analyzes and makes recommendations on contractors' claims and contract requirements in dispute; and recommends approval or rejection of contractors' requests for extensions of contract completion time. Is responsible for the review and approval of equipment lists, material samples, and shop drawings submitted by contractors. Upon determining full project completion, recommends final settlement of contract. Maintains contact with those individuals or agencies participating in or affected by protect to exchange information and work out mutual problems. Prepares reports of the progress of projects assigned to the team. Acts as liaison between contractors and regional office to assure compliance with regional and central office directives.

Qualifications: For an architect (GS-808) position, applicants must possess a degree in architecture or related field. A combination of college-level education, training, and/or technical experience that furnishes a thorough knowledge of the arts and sciences underlying professional architecture and a good understanding, both theoretical and practical, of architectural principles, methods, and techniques and their applications to the design and construction or improvement of buildings is also acceptable.

For an engineer (GS-801, GS-810, GS-830, and GS-850) position, applicants must possess a degree in professional engineering from a school of engineering accredited by the Accreditation Board for Engineering and Technology (ABET). A combination of college-level education, training, and/or technical experience that furnished a thorough knowledge of the physical and mathematical sciences underlying professional engineering and a good understanding, both theoretical and practical, of the engineering sciences and techniques and their applications to one of the branches of engineering is also acceptable.

In addition to these basic requirements, candidates must possess one year of specialized experience equivalent to at least the GS-12 level in the federal service. Specialized experience is defined as experience in the design of construction projects and coordinating the activities of architects, engineers, tenant agencies, and construction contractors. Experience should also include directing all or large phases of a project.

This is a supervisory/managerial position. If selected for this position and you have not previously completed a supervisory or managerial probation period, you must complete a one-year supervisory or managerial probationary period. If you are a current federal employee, failure to complete the probationary period successfully can result in return to a former position or to a position of no lower grade and pay than the one vacated for the supervisory or managerial position.

Program Analyst

Agency: Office of the Regional Administrator
Salary: $50,408 to $65,531
Location: Washington, DC

Duties: Assists in the preparation of University for People (U4P) budgets, obtaining input from U4P staff and the director. Queries financial systems to provide information on the status of funds for the University for People. Reviews financial reports and ensures that costs are reported accurately, identifying discrepancies and errors, and initiating resolution and correcting actions. Assists the director in workload management. Acts as the branch focal point for all requests for services. Logs all requests, monitors due dates, and keeps the director appraised of project status. Coordinates University of People training between our clients and vendor providers. Coordinates and monitors associates' certification training. Coordinates and maintains the enrollment process for the U4P classes. Maintains certification as a government purchase cardholder. Maintains vendor information; researches sources and prices; purchases products, supplies, and services with director's approval; ensures accounting information is correctly entered into the financial system; reconciles purchase card account promptly; and maintains required supporting documentation. Maintains branch regulatory and technical resources and official division files. Maintains the branch electronic calendar, e-mail account, databases, public folders, and official bulletin board. Exercises initiative and independent judgment in accomplishing work assignments and in solving a variety of technical and administrative problems. Maintains and develops a good rapport with supervisors, employees, administrative and operating officials, customers, and others. Performs various other administrative duties in support of achievement of objectives.

Qualifications: In order to be considered qualified, applicants must demonstrate, in their resumes and responses to questions, at least one year of specialized experience equivalent to the GS-7 level in the federal service. Specialized experience may include assisting in research and investigation of new and improved business and management practices. A master's or equivalent graduate degree or two full years of progressively higher level graduate education leading to such a degree or LL.B. or J.D., if related, may substitute for specialized experience.

How you will be evaluated: No written test is required for this position. If you are found qualified for this position, you will receive a numerical rating (of 70–100 points) based on the quality of your experience demonstrated in your responses to the vacancy-specific questions, evaluated by an established rating schedule, and substantiated in your resume. Veterans' preference points will be added to a passing score only if the appropriate documentation is submitted. Applicants who have not submitted a resume in the GSA Jobs system and/or have not answered all of the vacancy questions will not be considered for this position. Note: Your responses must be substantiated by the resume submitted. If a determination is made that in responding to the vacancy questions you have rated yourself higher than is evident in your resume, experience, and/or education, your score may be manually adjusted by a human resources specialist.

As part of the online application process, you will be asked a series of job-related questions that are designed to assess your possession of the following program analyst knowledges, skills, and abilities:

★ Knowledge and understanding of the budget formulation process, funds management, procurement rules, and regulations

★ Ability to plan, organize, and prioritize work

★ Ability to analyze data, draw conclusions, and make findings and recommendations

Other information: GSA offers employees the opportunity to participate in an alternative work schedule program (AWS) for many positions. AWS includes both flexible work schedules and compressed work schedules.

GSA may pay a recruitment incentive to a newly appointed employee or a relocation incentive to a current employee. Determinations to pay incentives will be made on a case-by-case basis, subject to funding availability and documentation that the position is "difficult-to-fill." Before receiving any incentive, an employee must sign a written agreement to complete a specified period of employment. If an employee fails to complete the agreed-upon service period, the portion of the incentive attributable to the uncompleted period must be repaid to GSA.

Institute of Museum and Library Services

1800 M Street NW, Ninth Floor
Washington, DC 20036-5802
202-653-IMLS

★ Web site: http://www.imls.gov/index.shtm

★ Job vacancies: http://www.imls.gov/about/employment.shtm

The Institute of Museum and Library Services is the primary source of federal support for the nation's 122,000 libraries and 17,500 museums. The institute's mission is to create strong libraries and museums that connect people to information and ideas. The institute works at the national level and in coordination with state and local organizations to sustain heritage, culture, and knowledge; enhance learning and innovation; and support professional development. It employs approximately

65 people.

Inter-American Foundation

901 North Stuart Street, Tenth Floor
Arlington, VA 22203
703-306-4301

★ Web site: http://www.iaf.gov/

★ Internships: http://www.iaf.gov/about_iaf/iaf_jobs_en.asp?job_id=4

The Inter-American Foundation is an independent federal agency that supports social and economic development in Latin America and the Caribbean. It makes grants primarily to private, local, and community organizations that carry out self-help projects. It employs approximately 40 people.

International Boundary and Water Commission, United States and Mexico

4171 North Mesa Street, Suite C-100
El Paso, Texas 79902-1441
800-262-8857 (toll-free)

★ Web site: http://www.ibwc.state.gov/

★ Job vacancies: http://www.ibwc.state.gov/Employment_Opportunities/Index.html

★ Strategic plan: http://www.ibwc.state.gov/Files/FY06_Strategic_Plan.pdf

Established in 1889, the International Boundary and Water Commission (IBWC) has responsibility for applying the boundary and water treaties between the United States and Mexico and settling differences that may arise out of these treaties. The IBWC is an international body composed of the United States section and the Mexican section, each headed by an engineer-commissioner appointed by his or her respective president. The commission employs approximately 230 people.

International Joint Commission, Canada and the United States

2401 Pennsylvania Avenue NW, Fourth Floor
Washington, DC 20440
202-736-9024

★ Web site: http://www.ijc.org/en/home/main_accueil.htm

Canada and the United States created the International Joint Commission because they recognized that each country is affected by the other's actions in lake and river systems along the border. The two countries cooperate to manage these waters wisely and to protect them for the benefit of today's citizens and future generations. The commission employs approximately five people.

International Monetary Fund

700 Nineteenth Street NW
Washington, DC 20431
202-623-7000

★ Web site: http://www.imf.org/

★ Job vacancies: http://www.imf.org/external/np/adm/rec/vacancy.htm

★ Internships: http://www.imf.org/external/np/adm/rec/job/summint.htm

★ Research assistants program: http://www.imf.org/external/np/adm/rec/job/rap.htm

★ Career information: http://www.imf.org/external/np/adm/rec/job/joboppo.htm

The International Monetary Fund (IMF) is an international organization of 185 member countries. It was established to promote international monetary cooperation, exchange stability, and orderly exchange arrangements; to foster economic growth and high levels of employment; and to provide temporary financial assistance to countries to help ease balance of payments adjustments. To meet these objectives, it employs three main functions: surveillance, technical assistance, and lending. Surveillance is the regular dialogue and policy advice that the IMF offers to each of its members. Once a year, the IMF conducts in-depth appraisals of each member country's economic situation, and then discusses with the country's authorities the policies that are most conducive to stable exchange rates and growing a prosperous economy. The IMF provides technical assistance to help member countries strengthen their capacity to design and implement effective policies. Technical assistance is offered to member countries in fiscal policy, monetary policy, and macroeconomic and financial statistics. Finally, when a member country has balance of payment problems, the IMF provides financial assistance in the form of loans. The IMF employs about 2,596 people from 146 countries.

Selected IMF Agency

The **Joint Vienna Institute** is an international training institute located in Vienna, Austria. It offers a comprehensive program of seminars in specialized topics aimed at mid- and senior-level officials and private sector managers focusing primarily on practical policy issues relevant to economies in transition.

★ Web site: http://www.jvi.org/

Other IMF Agencies

Balkans Initiative

http://www.usip.org/balkans/

IMF Institute

http://www.imf.org/external/np/ins/english/index.htm

Joint Africa Institute

http://www.afdb.org/jai/

Regional Office for Asia and the Pacific

http://www.imf.org/external/oap/index.htm

Singapore Regional Training Institute

http://www.imfsti.org/

Legal Services Corporation

3333 K Street NW, Third Floor
Washington, DC 20007
202-295-1500

★ Web site: http://www.lsc.gov/

★ Job vacancies: http://www.lsc.gov/about/careers.php

★ Strategic plan: http://www.lsc.gov/about/strategicdirections20062010.php

The Legal Services Corporation (LSC) is a private, nonprofit corporation headed by an 11-member board of directors, appointed by the president and confirmed by the Senate. The corporation provides legal assistance for noncriminal proceedings to those who would otherwise be unable to afford it. As the main source of funding for civil legal aid, LSC provides grants to independent, local programs. In 2007, LSC funded more than 140 legal aid programs across the country and made grants to and contracts with individuals, firms, corporations, and organizations for the purpose of providing legal assistance to these clients.

Job vacancies posted on LSC's Web site are for its headquarters only. Legal Services Corporation grantee programs are private entities and conduct their own independent application and hiring process. As such, any individual with an interest in employment opportunities at one of the grantee programs should contact that program directly.

Merit Systems Protection Board

1615 M Street NW, Fifth Floor
Washington, DC 20419
202-653-7200

★ Web site: http://www.mspb.gov/

★ Job vacancies and internships: http://www.mspb.gov/sites/mspb/pages/Contact.aspx

The Merit Systems Protection Board (MSPB) protects federal employees against partisan politics and other prohibited personnel practices. More specifically, when an employee is separated from his or her position or suspended for more than 14 days, the employee can request that an administrative judge of MSPB conduct a hearing into the matter. In that hearing, the agency will have to prove that the action was warranted, and the employee will have the opportunity to present evidence that it was not. A decision of MSPB is binding unless set aside on appeal to federal court.

The board also reviews regulations issued by the Office of Personnel Management and has the authority to require agencies to cease compliance with any regulation that could constitute a prohibited personnel practice. It also conducts special studies of the civil service and other executive branch merit systems and reports to the president and the Congress on whether the federal work force is being adequately protected against political abuses and prohibited personnel practices.

The Merit Systems Protection Board is a successor agency to the United States Civil Service Commission. In addition to its headquarters in Washington, DC, MSPB has five regional and three field offices and employs more than 200 people.

National Aeronautics and Space Administration

300 E Street SW
Washington, DC 20546
202-358-0000

★ Web site: http://www.nasa.gov/

★ Job vacancies: http://www.nasajobs.nasa.gov/

★ Student internships, cooperative employment, and summer programs: http://www.nasajobs. nasa.gov/studentopps/employment/programs.htm

★ How to apply: http://nasajobs.nasa.gov/howtoapply/default.htm

★ Career information: http://www.nasa.gov/about/career/index.html

★ Astronaut recruitment: http://astronauts.nasa.gov/

★ Strategic plan: http://www.nasa.gov/news/budget/index.html

The National Aeronautics and Space Administration (NASA) conducts research for the solution of flight problems within and outside the Earth's atmosphere and develops, constructs, tests, and operates aeronautical and space vehicles. It conducts activities required for the exploration of space with manned and unmanned vehicles and arranges for the most effective utilization of the scientific and engineering resources of the United States with other nations engaged in aeronautical and space activities for peaceful purposes.

NASA employs approximately 18,500 people in more than 15 facilities around the country. The percentage of employees in each field is as follows:

★ Employees in the professional, scientific, or engineering fields (accounting, aerospace engineering, biology, computer engineering, computer science, general engineering, meteorology): 60 percent

★ Employees in administrative or managerial fields (administrative specialist, budget analyst, contract specialist, information technology specialist, public affairs specialist): 24 percent

★ Technical and medical support (electronics technician, engineering technician, meteorological technician) employees: 9 percent

★ Clerical and administrative support employees (accounting technician, clerk-typist, management assistant, office automation clerk, procurement clerk, secretary): 7 percent

★ Trades and labor employees (high-voltage electrician, instrument maker, model maker, utility systems repair): 1 percent

Selected NASA Agencies

The **Aeronautics Research Mission Directorate** (ARMD) improves airspace capacity and mobility, aviation safety, and aircraft performance while reducing noise, emissions, and fuel burn. It conducts cutting-edge, fundamental research in traditional and emerging disciplines to help transform the nation's air transportation system, and to support future air and space vehicles. ARMD researches solutions for increasing the capacity, efficiency, and flexibility of national airspace. The Ames Research Center, Dryden Flight Research Center, and Langley Research Center are divisions of ARMD.

★ Web site: http://www.aeronautics.nasa.gov/

The **Glenn Research Center,** in partnership with U.S. industries, universities, and other government institutions, develops critical systems technologies and capabilities that address national priorities. Their world-class research, technology, and capability development efforts are key to advancing the exploration of our solar system and beyond while maintaining global leadership in aeronautics. The Glenn team consists of more than 3,000 civil service employees and support service contractor personnel. Scientists and engineers comprise more than half of the workforce, and they are supported by technical specialists, skilled workers, and an administrative staff. The center is located in Cleveland, Ohio, and is a division of ARMD.

★ Web site: http://www.nasa.gov/centers/glenn/home/

★ Student opportunities and internships: http://www.nasa.gov/centers/glenn/education/index.html

The **Jet Propulsion Laboratory** (JPL) is managed for NASA by the California Institute of Technology and is NASA's lead center for robotic exploration of the solar system. It is responsible for the Spirit and Opportunity rovers that landed on Mars, the comet-chasing Stardust spacecraft, and the Cassini spacecraft set to explore Saturn. The JPL also manages NASA's Deep Space Network, an international network of antennas that supports communications between distant spacecraft and the Earth-based teams who manage them, and the Spitzer Space Telescope and Galaxy Evolution Explorer, which are capturing images of distant galaxies.

★ Web site: http://www.jpl.nasa.gov/

★ Job vacancies: https://careerlaunch.jpl.nasa.gov/; click View Job Postings

★ Student programs: https://careerlaunch.jpl.nasa.gov/college.html

★ Career information: https://careerlaunch.jpl.nasa.gov/

The **Office of Safety and Mission Assurance** (OSMA) assures the safety and enhances the success of all NASA activities through the development, implementation, and oversight of agency-wide safety, reliability, maintainability, and quality assurance policies and procedures. The Johnson Space Center, Kennedy Space Center, Marshall Space Flight Center, and Stennis Space Center are divisions of OSMA.

★ Web site: http://www.hq.nasa.gov/office/codeq/

The **Science Mission Directorate** (SMD) engages the nation's science community, sponsors scientific research, and develops and deploys satellites and probes in collaboration with NASA's partners around the world to answer fundamental questions requiring the view from and into space. SMD seeks to understand the origins, evolution, and destiny of the universe and to understand the nature of the strange phenomena that shape it. SMD organizes its work into four broad scientific pursuits: earth science, planetary science, heliophysics, and astrophysics. Each of these pursuits is managed by a division within the directorate, each having its own scientific sub-goals. The Goddard Space Flight Center is a division of this directorate.

★ Web site: http://nasascience.nasa.gov/

Other NASA Agencies

Exploration Systems Mission Directorate

http://www.nasa.gov/directorates/esmd/home/

Goddard Institute for Space Studies

http://www.nasa.gov/centers/goddard/home/

NASA Education

http://education.nasa.gov/home/index.html

Office of Space Operations

http://www.hq.nasa.gov/osf/

Sample Job Vacancies

Aerospace Technologist
Agency: John F. Kennedy Space Center
Salary: $56,411 to $104,525
Location: Kennedy Space Center, Florida

Duties: The selectee will serve as a senior electrical engineer responsible for research, analysis, specification planning, development, installation, test, modification, and use of control systems and electrical ground support equipment (GSE). As such, he or she will develop common PLC library functions for the Constellation GSE PLC control software; develop GSE control application software; provide engineering expertise and support to EGSE development teams; develop project documentation; and participate in requirement reviews, design reviews, acceptance and product reviews, safety reviews, test reviews, and concept and trade studies.

Qualifications: A bachelor's degree from an accredited college or university with major study in engineering, physical science, mathematics, life sciences, computer science, or other field of science.

Degrees in engineering technology are not considered to be qualifying for this position. Applicant must have one year of specialized experience equivalent to the next lower grade, which has equipped the applicant with the particular competencies needed to successfully perform the duties of the position. An example of qualifying specialized experience is experience in the design of complex control systems for ground support equipment.

How you will be evaluated: Resumes will be rated by an automated system (Resumix) that matches the competencies extracted from the candidate's resume to the competencies identified by the selecting official for the position. Candidates will be evaluated on the competencies they possess that are directly related to the duties of the job, as described in the announcement. Candidates should refer to NASA's Applicant Guide for assistance in developing a complete resume, because NASA will not accept separate KSA statements. Qualified candidates will be assigned to one of three quality levels based on the degree to which their competencies meet the duties required. A human resources specialist will validate the qualifications of those candidates eligible to be referred to the selecting official.

Other information: Any applicant tentatively selected for this position may be required to undergo a pre-employment background investigation. U.S. citizenship is required. As a condition of employment, male applicants born after December 31, 1959, must certify that they have registered with the Selective Service System, or are exempt from having to do so under the Selective Service Law. Any applicant tentatively selected for this position will be required to submit to screening for illegal drug use prior to appointment and will be subject to random drug tests while occupying the position. Travel and relocation expenses are not authorized. Selectee may be required to complete a financial disclosure statement.

Contract Specialist
Agency: NASA Shared Services Center
Salary: $46,625 to $84,913
Location: Stennis Space Center, Mississippi

Duties: Perform the day-to-day operations of the contracting activities required to support NASA Shared Services in accordance with NASA contracting and procurement functions and regulations. Process contractual and financial instruments such as service and supply contracts, small business innovative research contracts, grants, cooperative agreements, purchase orders and delivery orders. Conduct procurement analysis and research regarding regulations, troubleshoot procurement system issues, and prepare reports as assigned. Complete pre-award and post-award functions for contracts, grants, and orders for various requirements. Review purchase requests and prepare various types of solicitations, such as requests for quotations, invitations for bids, and requests for proposals. Review contractors' bids or proposals, including cost/price analysis to determine fair and reasonable price. Review grant recipient budgets for compliance with federal regulations. Negotiate and prepare and/or review and approve award documents, such as purchase orders, contracts, task orders, and delivering orders resulting in fixed-price or cost reimbursement-type contracts. Negotiate, review, and approve award of grants and cooperative agreements. Monitor contractor performance, negotiate changes, ensure compliance with contract terms and conditions, and close out contracts and orders.

Qualifications: Applicants must have completed a four-year course of study leading to a bachelor's degree with a major in any field or at least 24 semester hours in any combination of the following fields: accounting, business, finance, law, contracts, purchasing, economics, industrial management, marketing, quantitative methods, or organization and management. Employees who occupied GS-1102 positions on January 1, 2000 at grades 5 through 12 will be considered to meet the basic requirements for other GS-1102 positions up to and including the GS-12 level.

For the GS-9 grade level, applicants must have one year of specialized experience equivalent to the GS-7 level or two full years of progressively higher level graduate education or master's or equivalent graduate degree. Applicants also may qualify based on a combination of the experience and education requirements. Examples of qualifying specialized experience include the negotiation and administration of grants or contracts for services, materials, and equipment.

For the GS-11 grade level, applicants must have one year of specialized experience equivalent to the GS-9 level, a Ph.D. or equivalent doctoral degree in a related field, or three full years of progressively higher level graduate education leading to such a degree. Examples of qualifying specialized experience include pre-award and post-award contract functions and negotiation and administration of contracts or grants.

For the GS-12 grade level, applicants must have one year of specialized experience equivalent to the next lower grade. Examples of qualifying specialized experience include knowledge of contracting or grant/cooperative agreement principles, laws, statutes, regulations, and procedures applicable to pre-award and/or post-award actions or approval agreements.

Required documents: NASA's application process has been specifically developed to ensure that we ask you only for the information we absolutely need to evaluate your qualifications and eligibility. In order to apply for this position, you only need to submit your resume and answer the screening questions and supplemental information. No additional documentation is accepted at the time of application. In this way, we allow you to focus on preparing a resume that best describes your background and abilities. At a later point, the Human Resources Office may ask you to submit documentation to support statements made in your resume. For example, we may ask you to provide academic transcripts or proof of federal employment status. If you are claiming veterans' preference, we may ask you to submit proof of veterans' preference (DD-214 and, if claiming 10-point preference, SF-15 plus proof required by that form). If you fail to provide the required documents within the stated time period, we may withdraw a job offer and/or remove you from further consideration.

Engineering Tech

Agency: Langley Research Center
Salary: $46,625 to $73,329
Location: Hampton, Virginia

Duties: Interfaces with engineering and scientific customers and performs tasks under the direction of senior level technicians. Ensures compliance with branch, directorate, center, and agency policies, rules, and procedures. Provides technical assistance in problem investigations, troubleshooting, and issue resolution activities involving flight hardware, software, and associated ground support equipment and facilities. These duties require specialized and extensive knowledge of aircraft hardware and the unique test technologies required for integration with aircraft test plans. Serves as integration lead for special and/or advanced integration programs required to modify/update present aircraft and test systems capabilities for integration of test programs and test techniques. Conceptualizes the aircraft/test system modifications, develops requirements, defines the scope of the initial design, reviews and makes inputs to the designs, and oversees the construction and acceptance phases of the program. Designs and develops experimental research instruments, devices, or system components for projects with undefined or uncertain performance requirements, incomplete or conflicting data, or techniques or components that in combination or application differ from normal and documented uses. Plans, develops, and incorporates modifications and upgrades to experimental aircraft system components that allow expansion of capabilities and development of new technologies. Serves as an authoritative source of information and advice within the organization. Consults with management and planning personnel in preparing requirements and criteria for complex or high value projects for modification of aircraft and aircraft systems.

Position is subject to random drug testing and requires the applicant to pass a class three FAA equivalent flight physical. The incumbent can be required to fly as an alternate crew member on board the assigned aircraft during functional check flights and research flights.

Qualifications: Applicant must have one year of specialized experience equivalent to the next lower grade, which has equipped the applicant with the particular competencies needed to successfully perform the duties of the position. In addition to the specialized experience requirement, all candidates must be licensed and certified in FAA Airframe and Power-plant.

How to apply: This vacancy is being filled through NASA STARS, an automated staffing and recruitment system. NASA partners with USAJOBS in providing a seamless application process. Before you begin the application process, please read the vacancy announcement carefully and have all required information available. In order to be considered, you must submit a resume completed on the USAJOBS site. When completing your USAJOBS resume, please remember that NASA limits resumes to the equivalent of approximately six typed pages or approximately 22,000 characters including spaces. You will not be allowed to complete the application process if your resume is too long. Once you submit your resume to NASA, you will be asked to complete a short series of additional questions. You must finish the entire process in order to have a complete application package and receive consideration. Your answers will not be saved unless you finish the entire application. If you are a first-time applicant, we recommend that you review NASA's Applicant Guide to ensure that you are providing a complete resume. Failure to submit the supplemental data and a resume that contains all of the required information may result in loss of consideration for positions in which you are interested. All applications must be received no later than midnight Eastern time on the closing date of the announcement.

Physicist

Agency: Langley Research Center
Salary: $95,010 to $123,519
Location: Hampton, Virginia

Duties: This optical designer position will support the Climate Absolute Radiance and Refractivity Observatory (CLARREO) earth science mission. The foundation for CLARREO is the ability to produce irrefutable climate records through the use of exacting on-board traceability of the instrument accuracy. Spectral reflected-solar and emitted-infrared radiances and Global Positioning System (GPS) radio-occultation refractivities measured by CLARREO will be used to detect climate trends and to test, validate, and improve climate prediction models. The CLARREO mission will provide accurate, credible, and tested climate records that lay the groundwork for informed decisions on mitigation and adaptation policies that address the effects of climate change on society.

The incumbent will support a team of instrument managers and discipline engineers in the optical modeling, design, development, integration, test, and calibration of a suite of passive electro-optical remote sensing instruments. Initially, the position serves a key role in formulating instrument optical designs and in assessing technology readiness of the instrument optics by supporting initial trades, including material selection, mass, and cost, as well as initiating optical performance modeling studies. Conducts optical design to model, develop, deploy, and improve remote sensor-based instrumentation for airborne and space-based measurements of the Earth. Must be expert in the application of both geometrical and physical optics to design lenses, telescopes, and spectrometers capable of operating at various subsets of the electromagnetic spectrum from the ultraviolet to the far infrared. Must be expert in the areas of optical materials, metrology, tolerancing, and stray-light analysis in order to facilitate the optimization of the optical designs. Must be able to collaborate with mission scientists and systems engineers to trade and derive optical-system design requirements in order to meet the high-level science mission requirements. Must have broad enough technical background and previous instrument development experience to understand the optical design's impact on the other instrument subsystems, so as to be able to facilitate the optical analysis necessary to a remote-sensing instrument's overall Structural, Thermal, Optical Performance (STOP) analysis. Serves as an authoritative consultant, in the area of optical design and optical physics, for Earth science mission managers, scientists, systems engineers, and contractors. Proposes, defends, communicates, and documents solutions to optical engineering problems and trade studies associated with electro-optical systems, in general, and optical remote-sensing instrumentation, in particular.

Qualifications: Must have a bachelor's degree from an accredited college or university with major study in aeronautical engineering, aeronautics, aerospace engineering, astronautical engineering, astronautics, astronomy, astrophysics, biomedical engineering, ceramic engineering, ceramics, chemical engineering, chemistry, civil engineering, computer engineering, computer science, earth and planetary science, electrical engineering, electronics engineering, geology, geophysics, industrial engineering, materials engineering, materials science, mathematics (pure or applied), applied mechanics, engineering mechanics, mechanical engineering, metallurgical engineering, metallurgy, meteorology, nuclear engineering, nuclear engineering physics, oceanography, optical engineering, physics, Applied Physics, Engineering Physics, Space Science, Structural Engineering, Welding Engineering, or other appropriate physical science or engineering field. Degrees in engineering technology are not considered to be qualifying for this position. Note: Curriculum must include 30 semester hours of coursework in a combination of mathematics, statistics, and computer science. Of the 30 semester hours, 15 must be in any combination of statistics and mathematics that includes differential and integral calculus.

Applicant also must have one year of specialized experience equivalent to the next lower grade. Specialized experience also includes, but is not limited to, mastery of a range of specialized areas in optical physics, optical science, physics, applied physics, spectroscopy, and laboratory experimental and calibration techniques associated with these knowledge specialties sufficient to originate concepts and effect new developments applicable to emerging functions of a national magnitude and with long-term purposes. Must understand scientific objectives and translate scientific requirements into instrument optical-subsystem requirements. Must have broad enough technical background and previous instrument development experience to understand the optical design's impact on the other instrument subsystems. Must have expert knowledge in the areas of optical materials, metrology, tolerancing, and stray-light analysis in order to facilitate the optimization of the optical designs.

Resources Analyst

Agency: Goddard Space Flight Center
Salary: $60,989 to $79,280
Location: Prince George's County, Maryland

Duties: Identifies relationships between projected major program changes and the projected budget. Forecasts shortfalls and actions necessary to accommodate the changes. Prepares special analyses of fund expenditures as necessary. Evaluates the effect of cost and program changes on the budget execution process. Reviews and coordinates accounting records and prepares allocations and operating budgets. Monitors, tracks, and reports on program obligations. Conducts annual year-end closing activities and reconciles with accounting records. Analyzes proposed changes to internal operating programs and projected spending for those programs. Recommends actions to accommodate differences. Reviews and coordinates accounting documents that reflect relatively stable budget execution activities, such as obligations, payments, corrections, adjustments, receivables, apportionments, and allotments. Monitors, tracks, and reports on program obligations. Assures that program funding data is entered into the agency's financial management system correctly. Conducts annual year-end closing activities, and performs reconciliation with accounting, including contractor cost analysis and auditing. Reviews and performs cost analysis of contractor's financial management systems, making recommendations to procurement and accounting. Performs audits of contractor's financial reports. Prepares budget estimates for major substantive or administrative internal operating programs. Consolidates estimates into an integrated budget forecast. Analyzes and resolves issues related to the financial program aspects of a large organizational segment of the directorate. Prepares detailed analyses and estimates of annual funding needs for one or more future budget years. Provides to management procedural and regulatory guidance concerning the availability of or limitations on the use of funds. Performs operational budget execution duties. Performs studies and audits on control and use of funds throughout the year. Analyzes and forecasts usage of funds with in the areas assigned. Assures that obligations incurred and resulting expenditures of funds are in accordance with pertinent laws and regulations. Compiles and coordinates the presentation of materials for assigned budget area. Analyzes and evaluates the effects of program plans and budget issues.

Qualifications: For the GS-11 grade level, applicants must have one year of specialized experience equivalent to the GS-9 level in the federal service. Specialized experience is defined as assisting in analyzing and developing cost data for an operating program, assisting in preparing annual budget formulation documents, assisting in conducting cost studies, and consolidating financial data for reporting purposes. Or applicants may substitute a Ph.D. or equivalent doctoral degree in a related field or three full years of progressively higher level graduate education leading to such a degree. Applicants also may qualify based on a combination of these experience and education requirements.

What to expect next: Candidates for NASA positions are evaluated using our automated staffing and recruitment system, NASA STARS, which compares your skills and experience as described in your resume with the requirements of the position. If you are found to be a highly qualified candidate, you will be referred to the selecting official for further consideration. (In some cases, individuals with priority for special consideration must be considered and selected before other candidates.) Whether or not you are contacted for an interview depends upon the location of the position and the judg-

National Archives and Records Administration

700 Pennsylvania Avenue
Washington, DC 20408-0001
866-272-6272 (toll-free)

★ Web site: http://www.archives.gov/

★ Job vacancies: http://www.archives.gov/careers/jobs/

★ Internships: http://www.archives.gov/careers/internships/

★ Student information: http://www.archives.gov/careers/jobs/student.html

★ Volunteer information: http://www.archives.gov/careers/volunteering/

★ How to apply: http://www.archives.gov/careers/internships/about.html#apply

★ Tips and frequently asked application questions, including how to write KSAs: http://www.archives.gov/careers/resources/

★ Career information: http://www.archives.gov/careers/

★ Strategic plan: http://www.archives.gov/about/plans-reports/strategic-plan/

The National Archives and Records Administration (NARA) maintains, as archival records, the historically valuable records of the U.S. government, dating from the Revolutionary War era to the recent past. It preserves our nation's history by providing guidance and assistance to federal officials on the management of all federal records. The NARA determines the retention and disposition of records; stores agency records in records centers from which agencies can retrieve them; receives, preserves, and makes available permanently valuable federal and presidential records for use in research rooms, in its facilities, and via the Internet. The NARA provides oversight for archival facilities, including presidential libraries and public use donated materials that are determined by the archivist of the United States to have sufficient historical or other value to warrant their continued preservation by the U.S. government.

The NARA also establishes policies and procedures for managing U.S. government records. It assists federal agencies in documenting their activities, administering records management programs, scheduling records, and retiring noncurrent records. It arranges, describes, preserves, and provides access to the essential documentation of the three branches of government and publishes laws, regulations, presidential documents, and other public documents.

NARA also assists the Information Security Oversight Office, which manages federal classification and declassification policies, and the National Historical Publications and Records Commission, which makes grants to help nonprofit organizations identify, preserve, and provide access to materials that document American history. NARA has more than 30 sites across the country, including regional archives and records services facilities, presidential libraries, and three major buildings in the Washington, DC, area. NARA employs approximately 3,000 personnel, many of whom are historians and administrative staff.

Selected NARA Agencies

The presidential library system is currently made up of 13 presidential libraries. This nationwide network of libraries is administered by the **Office of Presidential Libraries** located in College Park, Maryland. These are not traditional libraries, but rather repositories for preserving and making available the papers, records, and other historical materials of U.S. presidents since Herbert Hoover.

Each presidential library contains a museum and provides an active series of public programs. When a president leaves office, NARA establishes a presidential project until a new presidential library is built and transferred to the government.

★ Web site: http://www.archives.gov/presidential_libraries/index.html

★ Presidential library locations: http://www.archives.gov/presidential-libraries/visit/

The **Office of Regional Records Services** operates 12 regional records services centers, plus the national personnel records center. These centers manage historically valuable records that are primarily of regional or local interest.

★ Web site: http://www.archives.gov/locations/regional-archives.html

The **Federal Records Centers** store and service noncurrent and certain active records of federal agencies.

★ Web site: http://www.archives.gov/frc/

The most often requested records are from the **National Personnel Records Center, Military Personnel Records** (NPRC-MPR), which is the repository of millions of military personnel, health, and medical records of discharged and deceased veterans of all services during the 20th century.

★ Web site: http://www.archives.gov/st-louis/military-personnel/

Other NARA Agencies

Information Security Oversight Office

http://www.archives.gov/isoo/

National Archives Trust Fund Board

http://www.archives.gov/about/laws/nara-trust-fund-board.html

National Historical Publications and Records Commission

http://www.archives.gov/grants/

Office of the Federal Register

http://www.archives.gov/federal-register/

Records Management

http://www.archives.gov/records-mgmt/

National Capital Planning Commission

401 Ninth Street NW, Suite 500
Washington, DC 20576
202-482-7200

★ Web site: http://www.ncpc.gov/

★ Job vacancies and internships: http://www.ncpc.gov/about/
pg.asp?p=employmentopportunities

The National Capital Planning Commission conducts planning and development activities for federal lands and facilities in the national capital region. The region includes the District of Columbia and all land areas within the boundaries of Montgomery and Prince George's counties in Maryland and Fairfax, Loudoun, Prince William, and Arlington counties and the city of Alexandria in Virginia.

The commission is composed of five appointed and seven ex officio members. Three citizen members, including the chairman, are appointed by the president; the other two members are appointed by the mayor of the District of Columbia. Presidential appointees include one resident each from Maryland and Virginia and one from anywhere in the United States, but the two mayoral appointees must be District of Columbia residents. The commission employs approximately 40 people.

National Council on Disability

1331 F Street NW, Suite 850
Washington, DC 20004
202-272-2004

★ Web site: http://www.ncd.gov/

The National Council on Disability (NCD) is an independent federal agency composed of members appointed by the president with the advice and consent of the Senate. The NCD provides advice to the president, Congress, and executive branch agencies to promote policies, programs, practices, and procedures that guarantee equal opportunity for all individuals with disabilities, regardless of the nature or severity of the disability, and to empower individuals with disabilities to achieve economic self-sufficiency, independent living, and inclusion and integration into all aspects of society. The council employs approximately 20 people.

National Credit Union Administration

1775 Duke Street
Alexandria, VA 22314-3428
703-518-6300

★ Web site: http://www.ncua.gov/

★ Job vacancies: http://jobsearch.usajobs.opm.gov/a9cu00.asp

★ Strategic plan: http://www.ncua.gov/ReportsAndPlans/plans-and-reports/index.html

The National Credit Union Administration (NCUA) charters, insures, supervises, and examines federal credit unions. Additionally, it insures savings in federal and most state-chartered credit unions across the country through the National Credit Union Share Insurance Fund (NCUSIF), a federal fund backed by the full faith and credit of the U.S. government. NCUA has five regional offices and an Asset Management and Assistance Center in Austin, Texas in addition to its headquarters in Alexandria, Virginia. NCUA has more than 940 employees.

National Economic Council

Executive Office Building
Washington, DC 20504
202-456-1414

★ Web site: http://www.whitehouse.gov/nec/index.html

The National Economic Council coordinates policy-making for domestic and international economic issues, coordinates economic policy advice for the president, ensures that policy decisions and programs are consistent with the president's economic goals, and monitors implementation of the president's economic policy agenda.

National Foundation on the Arts and the Humanities

1100 Pennsylvania Avenue NW
Washington, DC 20506-0001
202-682-5400 (NEA)
202-NEH-1121 (NEH)
202-606-8536 (IMLS)

The National Foundation on the Arts and the Humanities (NFAH) develops and promotes a broadly conceived national policy of support for the humanities and the arts in the United States and for institutions that preserve the cultural heritage of the United States. NFAH is comprised of the National Endowment for the Arts (NEA), the National Endowment for the Humanities (NEH), the Federal Council on the Arts and the Humanities, and the Institute of Museum and Library Services (IMLS). The Federal Council on the Arts and the Humanities assists the endowments in coordinating their programs and other activities with those of federal agencies.

Each endowment is advised on its respective grant making and related policies, programs, and procedures by its own national council, composed of the endowment chairman and other members appointed by the president and confirmed by the Senate. Members of Congress, appointed by the leadership of the House and the Senate, serve in an ex officio, nonvoting capacity on the National Council on the Arts.

Selected NFAH Agencies

The **National Endowment for the Arts** (NEA) supports excellence in the arts, both new and established, by bringing the arts to all Americans and providing leadership in arts and education. NEA is an independent agency of the federal government and is the nation's largest annual funder of the arts. NEA issues grants that support projects of artistic excellence in an effort to preserve and enhance the nation's cultural heritage. Grants are made to nonprofit arts organizations, units of state or local government (such as school districts and local arts agencies), and federally recognized tribal communities or tribes.

The NEA awards competitive fellowships to published creative writers and literary translators of exceptional talent and gives honorific fellowships to jazz masters and significant, influential master folk and traditional artists. The NEA also works in partnership with the 56 state and special juris-dictional arts agencies and their regional arts organizations to support projects that foster creativity, preservation, arts learning, and outreach to underserved communities. The NEA dedicates 40 per-cent of its program appropriation to this purpose. NEA also employs approximately 160 people.

Throughout the year, the NEA accepts interns in many of its offices. Internships offer a national overview of arts activities across the country. Interns work in assisting the staff with a variety of tasks related to the process of awarding federal grants.

★ Web site: http://www.nea.gov/about/

★ Job vacancies: http://www.nea.gov/about/Jobs/JobsMenu.html

★ Internships: http://www.nea.gov/about/Jobs/Internships.html

★ Strategic plan: http://www.nea.gov/about/Budget/index.html

The **National Endowment for the Humanities** (NEH) makes grants that support research, education, preservation, and public programs in the humanities. The grants target high-quality humanities projects in four funding areas: preserving and providing access to cultural resources, education, research, and public programs. NEH grants typically go to cultural institutions, such as museums, archives, libraries, colleges, universities, public television and radio stations, and to indi-vidual scholars. The agency is also a base supporter of its network of private, nonprofit affiliates, the 57 humanities councils in the United States. Each summer, NEH hosts undergraduate students from across the country as interns in various departments. Each intern is mentored by an NEH staff person and receives a stipend for 10 weeks of full-time work. NEH has approximately 160 full-time personnel.

★ Web site: http://www.neh.gov/

★ Job vacancies: http://www.neh.gov/whoweare/jobs.html

★ Internships: http://www.neh.gov/whoweare/NEH_Internships.html

★ Strategic plan: http://www.neh.gov/whoweare/strategicplan.html

The **Institute of Museum and Library Services** (IMLS) provides federal support for the nation's 122,000 libraries and 17,500 museums in order to connect people to information and ideas. The institute works at the national level and in coordination with state and local organizations to sustain heritage, culture, and knowledge; enhance learning and innovation; and support professional development.

In addition to providing distinct programs of support for museums and libraries, the IMLS encour-ages collaboration between these community resources. The institute's library programs help librar-ies use new technologies to identify, preserve, and share library and information resources across institutional, local, and state boundaries and to reach those for whom library use requires extra effort or special materials. Museum programs strengthen museum operations, improve care of collections, increase professional development opportunities, and enhance the community service role of museums. All IMLS competitive awards are reviewed by volunteer library and museum professionals. The IMLS employs approximately 160 people.

★ Web site: http://www.imls.gov/

★ Job vacancies and internships: http://www.imls.gov/about/employment.shtm

★ Volunteer grant reviewer information: http://www.imls.gov/reviewers/reviewers.shtm

National Labor Relations Board

1099 Fourteenth Street NW
Washington, DC 20570-0001
866-667-6572 (toll-free)
202-273-1000

★ Web site: http://www.nlrb.gov/

★ Job vacancies: http://jobsearch.usajobs.opm.gov/a9nlrb.asp

★ Student information: http://www.nlrb.gov/About_Us/Careers/job_descriptions_and_listings/ student_positions_law_and_non_-_legal.aspx

★ Honors program: http://www.nlrb.gov/About_Us/Careers/attorney_honors_program.aspx

★ Career information: http://www.nlrb.gov/About_Us/Careers/

★ Strategic plan: http://www.nlrb.gov/nlrb/shared_files/ reports/FY2007_StrategicPlan_FINAL.pdf

The National Labor Relations Board (NLRB) is vested with the power to prevent and remedy unfair labor practices committed by private sector employers and unions and to safeguard employees' rights to organize and determine whether to have unions as their bargaining representative. The agency has two major, separate components. The board itself has five members and primarily acts as a quasi-judicial body in deciding cases on the basis of formal records in administrative proceedings. The general counsel is independent from the board and is responsible for the investigation and prosecution of unfair labor practice cases and for the general supervision of the 34 NLRB field offices in the processing of cases.

A substantial number of jobs at the NLRB are for field attorneys and field examiners who work in the agency's regional, subregional, and resident offices located throughout the country and for attorneys who work for the board or the Office of the General Counsel in Washington, DC. In total, the NLRB employs more than 800 attorneys across the country in addition to 900 other professional, administrative, technical, and support staff.

National Mediation Board

1301 K Street NW, Suite 250 East
Washington, DC 20005
202-692-5000

★ Web site: http://www.nmb.gov/

★ Job vacancies: http://www.nmb.gov/whatsnew.html

★ Strategic plan: http://www.nmb.gov/documents/strategicplan2005-2010.pdf

The National Mediation Board maintains a free flow of commerce in the railroad and airline indus-tries by resolving labor-management disputes. The board also handles railroad and airline employee representation disputes and provides administrative and financial support in adjusting grievances in the railroad industry. The board employs approximately 1,700 people.

National Railroad Passenger Corporation (Amtrak)

60 Massachusetts Avenue NE
Washington, DC 20002
202-906-3000

★ Web site: http://www.amtrak.com/

★ Job vacancies: http://amtrak.teamrewards.net/TR_PublicWeb/

★ Job line: 1-877-AMTRAK1 (1-877-268-7251)

The National Railroad Passenger Corporation (Amtrak) operates intercity passenger trains at an average of 212 trains per day, serving more than 540 station locations in 46 states, over a system of approximately 21,000 route miles. Of this route system, Amtrak owns less than 1,000 track miles in the Northeast Corridor (Washington–New York–Boston; New Haven–Springfield; Philadelphia-Harrisburg) and several other small track segments throughout the country. Amtrak owns or leases its stations and owns its own repair and maintenance facilities. Amtrak employs a total workforce of approximately 19,000 and provides all reservation, station, and on-board service staffs, as well as train and engine operating crews.

Amtrak offers a year-long program to develop high potential, entry-level employees by providing skills and experiences to prepare them for leadership positions in both business and technical management within Amtrak Corporation. To qualify, you must have a B.A./B.S. in business admin-istration, transportation, logistics, industrial design, or civil, electrical, mechanical, or industrial engineering. To learn more about this program, visit Amtrak's home page, click on the Employment link, and then click the link to the Management Associate Program.

To find out about current job openings at Amtrak, call the Job Line. To apply for a job from the Job Line, write the specific job title and posting number on your resume and mail it to the appropri-ate address listed on the Job Line. Amtrak does not accept faxed resumes, and resumes without a job title or posting number will be returned. New jobs are added regularly, so make sure to check back often for the latest job opportunities.

National Security Council

The White House
Washington, DC 20502
202-456-1414

★ Web site: http://www.whitehouse.gov/nsc/

The National Security Council advises and assists the president on national security and foreign policies. The council also serves as the president's principal arm for coordinating these policies among various government agencies. The council works in conjunction with the National Economic Council. Approximately 60 people are employed here.

National Science Foundation

4201 Wilson Boulevard
Arlington, VA 22230
703-292-5111

★ Web site: http://www.nsf.gov/

★ Job vacancies: http://www.nsf.gov/about/career_opps/vacancies/

★ Student information: http://www.nsf.gov/about/career_opps/careers/student.jsp

★ Career information: http://www.nsf.gov/about/career_opps/

★ Strategic plan: http://www.nsf.gov/publications/pub_summ.jsp?ods_key=nsf0648

The National Science Foundation (NSF) promotes the progress of science and engineering by awarding grants, contracts, and fellowships that support research and education programs. Its major emphasis is on high quality, merit-selected research, the search for improved understanding of the fundamental laws of nature upon which our future well-being as a nation depends. Its educational programs are aimed at ensuring increased understanding of science and engineering at all educational levels and maintaining an adequate supply of scientists, engineers, and science educators to meet our country's needs.

NSF employs scientists, engineers, and educators in seven directorates on rotational assignment from academia, industry, or other eligible organizations to further the agency's mission of supporting the entire spectrum of science and engineering research and education. The most frequently used programs are the Visiting Scientist, Engineer, and Educator (VSEE) Program and the Intergovernmental Personnel Act (IPA) Program. NSF employs approximately 1,350 people.

Selected NSF Agencies

The **Directorate for Biological Sciences** promotes scientific progress in biology largely through grants to colleges, universities, and other institutions, especially in those areas where NSF has major responsibility. The foundation is the nation's principal supporter of fundamental academic research on plant biology, environmental biology, and biodiversity. Other divisions include integrative organismal biology, environmental biology, and molecular and cellular biosciences.

★ Web site: http://www.nsf.gov/dir/index.jsp?org=BIO

The **Directorate for Engineering** promotes the progress of engineering in order to enable the country's capacity to perform. The directorate sponsors programs in nanotechnology, biocomplexity, cyberinfrastructure, human and social dynamics, sensors and networks, and earthquake simulation. It administers the NSF's Small Business Innovation Research (SBIR) program.

★ Web site: http://www.nsf.gov/dir/index.jsp?org=ENG

Other NSF Agencies

Directorate for Computer and Information Sciences and Engineering

http://www.nsf.gov/dir/index.jsp?org=cise

Directorate for Education and Human Resources

http://www.nsf.gov/dir/index.jsp?org=EHR

Directorate for Geosciences

http://www.nsf.gov/dir/index.jsp?org=GEO

Directorate for Mathematical and Physical Sciences

http://www.nsf.gov/dir/index.jsp?org=MPS

Directorate for Social, Behavioral, and Economic Sciences

http://www.nsf.gov/dir/index.jsp?org=SBE

National Transportation Safety Board

490 L'Enfant Plaza SW
Washington, DC 20594
202-314-6000

★ Web site: http://www.ntsb.gov/

★ Job vacancies: http://jobsearch.usajobs.opm.gov/jobsearch.asp?jbf574=TB*&sort=rv&vw=d

★ Student internships and other career information: http://www.ntsb.gov/vacancies/listing.htm

★ Strategic plan: http://www.ntsb.gov/abt_ntsb/strategic-plan_2007-2012.pdf

The National Transportation Safety Board (NTSB) ensures that all types of transportation in the United States are conducted safely. The NTSB is an independent agency responsible for investigation of accidents involving aviation, highways, navigable waters, pipelines, and railroads in the United States (except aircraft of the armed forces and the intelligence agencies). The organization is also in charge of investigating cases of hazardous waste releases that occur from modes of transportation. The NTSB also conducts special investigations and safety studies and issues safety recommendations to prevent future accidents. During the past three decades, investigators have developed their own expertise in specialized areas and are often consulted by other safety professionals.

The NTSB consists of five members appointed by the president with the advice and consent of the Senate. The president designates two of these members as chairman (with Senate approval) and vice chairman of the board (no further approval needed). The NTSB conducts its own accident investigation training at the NTSB Academy, located on the campus of George Washington University in Ashburn, Virginia. The NTSB employs about 380 people across the country.

Nuclear Regulatory Commission

Washington, DC 20555-0001
301-415-7000

★ Web site: http://www.nrc.gov/

★ Entry and mid-level career positions: http://jobsearch.usajobs.opm.gov/a9nu00.asp

★ Special entry-level programs: http://www.nrc.gov/about-nrc/employment/careers.html#entrylevel

★ Student information: http://www.nrc.gov/about-nrc/employment/student-prog.html

★ Career paths: http://www.nrc.gov/about-nrc/employment/careers.html

★ Career advancement: http://www.nrc.gov/about-nrc/employment/salaries.html

★ Career information: http://www.nrc.gov/about-nrc/employment.html

★ Strategic plan: http://www.nrc.gov/reading-rm/doc-collections/nuregs/staff/sr1614/

Ranked the 2007 best place to work in the federal government (according to the Partnership for Public Service), the Nuclear Regulatory Commission (NRC) licenses and regulates civilian use of nuclear energy to protect public health and safety and the environment. The NRC also licenses the import and export of radioactive materials and participates in international nuclear activities, including multilateral and bilateral safety and security activities, and works closely with its international counterparts to enhance nuclear safety and security worldwide. The commission ensures that the civilian uses of nuclear materials and facilities are conducted in a manner consistent with public health and safety, environmental quality, national security, and antitrust laws. Most of the commission's effort is focused on regulating the use of nuclear energy to generate electric power. The commission makes rules and sets standards for these types of licenses. It also carefully inspects the activities of the people and companies licensed to ensure compliance with their safety rules.

The NRC is led by five commissioners, one of whom is the designated chairperson. The president appoints these commissioners for five-year terms. The NRC hires budget analysts; auditors; accountants; management analysts; program analysts; human resources specialists; contract specialists; secretaries and office automation assistants; attorneys; general, nuclear, mechanical, chemical, structural, electrical, environmental, materials, software, and human factors engineers; communications specialists; computer specialists; IT project managers; systems administrators; computer systems analysts; Web masters; information management specialists; investigators, analysts, and law enforcement specialists; chemists; nuclear physicists; radiation biologists; physical scientists; materials scientists; health physicists; geologists, hydrologists, and seismologists; security and safeguards analysts with physical, personnel, information, and operational security knowledge, as well as individuals with experience in the physical protection, surveillance, control, and accounting of nuclear material. The NRC employs approximately 3,700 people.

Selected NRC Agencies

The **Office of Investigations** develops policy, procedures, and quality control standards for investigations of licensees, applicants, and their contractors or vendors, including the investigations of all allegations of wrongdoing by other than NRC employees and contractors.

★ Web site: http://www.nrc.gov/about-nrc/organization/oifuncdesc.html

The **Office of Nuclear Reactor Regulation** is responsible for ensuring public health and safety through licensing and inspection activities at all nuclear power reactor facilities in the United States.

★ Web site: http://www.nrc.gov/about-nrc/organization/nrrfuncdesc.html

Other NRC Agencies

Advisory Committee on Reactor Safeguards

http://www.nrc.gov/about-nrc/organization/acrsfuncdesc.html

Advisory Committee on the Medical Uses of Isotopes

http://www.nrc.gov/about-nrc/regulatory/advisory/acmui.html

Atomic Safety and Licensing Board Panel

http://www.nrc.gov/about-nrc/organization/aslbpfuncdesc.html

Office of Enforcement

http://www.nrc.gov/about-nrc/organization/oefuncdesc.html

Office of Federal and State Materials and Environmental Management Programs

http://www.nrc.gov/about-nrc/organization/fsmefuncdesc.html

Office of Nuclear Material Safety and Safeguards

http://www.nrc.gov/about-nrc/organization/nmssfuncdesc.html

Office of Nuclear Regulatory Research

http://www.nrc.gov/about-nrc/organization/resfuncdesc.html

Office of Nuclear Security and Incident Response

http://www.nrc.gov/about-nrc/organization/nsirfuncdesc.html

Occupational Safety and Health Review Commission

1120 Twentieth Street NW
Washington, DC 20036-3457
202-606-5398

★ Web site: http://www.oshrc.gov/

★ Job vacancies: http://www.oshrc.gov/job_opportunities/job_opport.html

★ Strategic plan: http://www.oshrc.gov/strategic/strategic.html

Employers have the right to dispute any alleged job safety or health violation found during an inspection by the Department of Labor's Occupational Safety and Health Administration (OSHA), the penalties it proposes, and the time given to correct any hazardous situation. When such disagreements arise, the Occupational Safety and Health Review Commission (OSHRC) resolves them. The commission's principal office is in Washington, DC. Administrative law judges are also located in two regional offices.

Office of Administration

725 Seventeenth Street NW
Washington, DC 20503
202-456-2891

★ Web site: http://www.whitehouse.gov/oa/

The Office of Administration provides administrative services to all entities of the Executive Office of the President (EOP), including direct support services to the president of the United States. The services include financial management and information technology support, human resources management, library and research assistance, facilities management, procurement, printing and graphics support, security, and mail and messenger operations. The director of the organization oversees the submission of the annual EOP Budget Request and represents the organization before congressional funding panels. The Office of Administration employs about 230 people.

Office of Compliance

John Adams Building
110 Second Street SE, Room LA 200
Washington, DC 20540-1999
202-724-9250

★ Web site: http://www.compliance.gov/index.html

The Office of Compliance advances safety, health, and workplace rights in the U.S. Congress and the legislative branch. It provides an impartial dispute resolution process and investigates and remedies violations.

Office of the Director of National Intelligence

Washington, DC 20511
703-733-8600

★ Web site: http://www.dni.gov/

★ Job vacancies: http://www.intelligence.gov/0-community_vacancies.shtml

★ Student opportunities: http://www.intelligence.gov/3-student-opportunities.shtml

★ Career information: http://www.intelligence.gov/3-career.shtml

★ Academic Excellence Program: http://www.dni.gov/cae/index.htm

As head of the intelligence community, the Director of National Intelligence (DNI) oversees and coordinates the foreign and domestic activities of the intelligence community across the federal government. The DNI is responsible for overseeing and coordinating elements of the intelligence community and is the principal intelligence adviser to the president. The Office of the DNI has approximately 1,500 employees.

Office of Government Ethics

1201 New York Avenue NW, Suite 500
Washington, DC 20005-3917
202-482-9300

★ Web site: http://www.usoge.gov/

★ Job vacancies and rotational assignment program: http://www.usoge.gov/careers.aspx

The Office of Government Ethics prevents conflicts of interest on the part of government employees and resolves conflicts of interest that occur. In partnership with executive branch agencies and departments, the office fosters high ethical standards for employees and strengthens the public's confidence that the government's business is conducted with impartiality and integrity. The office is the principal agency for administering the Ethics in Government Act for the executive branch. It employs about 80 people.

Office of Management and Budget

Executive Office Building
725 Seventeenth Street NW
Washington, DC 20503
202-395-3080

★ Web site: http://www.whitehouse.gov/omb/

★ Job vacancies: http://www.whitehouse.gov/omb/recruitment/index_current.html

★ Internships: http://www.whitehouse.gov/omb/recruitment/internships.html

★ Career information: http://www.whitehouse.gov/omb/recruitment/index.html

★ Strategic plan: http://www.whitehouse.gov/omb/pubpress/2007/011007_strategic_plan.pdf

The Office of Management and Budget (OMB) assists the president in overseeing the preparation of the federal budget and supervising its administration in executive branch agencies. In helping to formulate the president's spending plans, OMB evaluates the effectiveness of agency programs, policies, and procedures; assesses competing funding demands among agencies; and sets funding priorities. OMB ensures that agency reports, rules, testimony, and proposed legislation are consistent with the president's budget and with administration policies. In addition, OMB oversees and coordinates the administration's procurement, financial management, information, and regulatory policies. In each of these areas, OMB's role is to help improve administrative management, to develop better performance measures and coordinating mechanisms, and to reduce any unnecessary burdens on the public.

OMB is a small agency of fewer than 500 professional and administrative staff. More than 90 percent of the staff hold career, rather than political, appointments. More than 70 percent of the staff are professionals, most with graduate degrees in economics, business and accounting, public administration and policy, law, engineering, and other disciplines. The OMB career staff members provide analyses on a full range of policy options to be considered by decision-makers. OMB's employees interact daily with high-level officials throughout government. OMB's work requires sharp analytical and quantitative skills; the ability to effectively present ideas and analyses both orally and in writing; and the ability to interact constructively with others, often under high pressure and tight deadlines. The environment in which OMB operates is fast-paced. Issues are diverse, cross-cutting, complex, politically sensitive, and frequently involve billions of dollars in resources. OMB's major occupations include management analyst, budget examiner, economist, budget preparation specialist, and legislative analyst.

Selected OMB Agencies

The **Office of Federal Financial Management** (OFFM) is responsible for the financial management policy of the federal government. OFFM responsibilities include implementing the financial management improvement priorities of the president and establishing government-wide financial management policies of executive agencies.

★ Web site: http://www.whitehouse.gov/omb/financial/index.html

The OFFM has two main branches. The **Financial Analysis and Systems Branch** ensures that federal financial programs are measuring and achieving intended results, eliminating inefficiencies and improprieties, and managing their financial activities in accordance with best practices.

★ Web site: http://www.whitehouse.gov/omb/financial/fia_branch.html

The **Financial Standards and Grants Branch** develops financial management policies for federal agencies and grant recipients; facilitates the development of timely, accurate, and useful financial information to support management decisions; and ensures accountability and effective customer service for federal grants programs.

★ Web site: http://www.whitehouse.gov/omb/financial/fin_branch.html

Other OMB Agencies

Office of E-Government and Information Technology

http://www.whitehouse.gov/omb/egov/index.html

Office of Federal Procurement Policy

http://www.whitehouse.gov/omb/procurement/index.html

Office of Information and Regulatory Affairs

http://www.whitehouse.gov/omb/inforeg/

Office of National AIDS Policy

Executive Office Building
725 Seventeenth Street NW
Washington, DC 20503
202-456-1414

★ Web site: http://www.whitehouse.gov/onap/aids.html

The Office of National AIDS Policy coordinates continuing domestic efforts to reduce the number of new infections of HIV/AIDS in the United States. Additionally, the office works to coordinate an increasingly integrated approach to the prevention, care, and treatment of HIV/AIDS. The office also emphasizes domestic and international efforts to combat HIV/AIDS.

Office of National Drug Control Policy

Executive Office of the President
750 Seventeenth Street NW
Washington, DC 20503
202-395-6700

★ Web site: http://www.whitehousedrugpolicy.gov/

★ Job vacancies: http://www.whitehousedrugpolicy.gov/about/employment_opportunities.html

★ Internships: http://www.whitehousedrugpolicy.gov/about/intern.html

The Office of National Drug Control Policy assists the president in establishing policies, priorities, and objectives in the National Drug Control Strategy. It provides budget, program, and policy recommendations on the efforts of National Drug Control Program agencies. The office has direct programmatic responsibility for the Drug-Free Communities Program, the National Youth Anti-Drug Media Campaign, the various programs under the Counter-Drug Technology Assessment Center, and the High Intensity Drug Trafficking Areas Program. The office employs approximately 100 people.

Office of Personnel Management

1900 E Street NW
Washington, DC 20415-0001
202-606-1800

★ Web site: http://www.opm.gov/

★ Job vacancies: http://jobsearch.usajobs.gov/a9opm.asp

★ USAJOBS: http://www.usajobs.gov/

★ Student jobs: http://www.studentjobs.gov/

★ Student educational employment: https://www.opm.gov/employ/students/

★ Scholarship for Service program: https://www.sfs.opm.gov/

★ Federal Career Intern Program (FCIP): http://www.opm.gov/careerintern/

★ Presidential Management Fellows Program: https://www.pmf.opm.gov/

★ Federal salaries and wages: http://www.opm.gov/oca/08tables/

★ New employee benefits: http://www.opm.gov/Insure/health/enrollment/new_employees.asp

★ Federal benefits: http://www.usajobs.gov/EI61.asp

★ Federal employment of people with disabilities: https://www.opm.gov/disability/index.asp

★ Veterans employment information: http://www.opm.gov/veterans/

★ Federal jobs by college major: http://media.newjobs.com/opm/www/usajobs/pdf/ei-23.pdf

★ Federal job information center: http://www.usajobs.gov/infocenter/

★ Career information: http://career.usajobs.opm.gov/

★ Strategic plan: http://www.opm.gov/strategicplan/

The Office of Personnel Management (OPM) provides guidance to agencies for operating human resources programs and ensures that the federal government has an effective civilian workforce. OPM supports government program managers in their human resources management responsibilities and provides benefits to employees, retired employees, and their survivors. OPM advises the president and federal agencies on human capital management and develops human resources policies, products, and services. OPM ensures federal compliance with merit system principles and personnel laws and regulations. It also assists agencies in recruiting, examining, and promoting people based on their knowledge and skills, regardless of their race, religion, sex, political influence, or other non-merit factors.

OPM provides leadership, direction, and policy for government-wide affirmative recruiting programs for women, minorities, individuals with disabilities, and veterans. It also provides leadership, guidance, and technical assistance to promote merit and equality in systemic workforce recruitment, employment, training, and retention. In addition, OPM gathers, analyzes, and maintains statistical data on the diversity of the federal workforce and prepares evaluation reports for Congress and

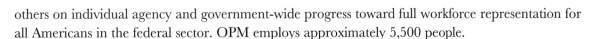

others on individual agency and government-wide progress toward full workforce representation for all Americans in the federal sector. OPM employs approximately 5,500 people.

OPM coordinates the temporary assignment of employees between federal agencies and state, local, and Indian tribal governments; institutions of higher education; and other eligible nonprofit organizations for up to two years, for work of mutual benefit to the participating organizations. It administers the Presidential Management Fellows Program, which provides two-year, excepted appointments with federal agencies to recipients of graduate degrees in appropriate disciplines. In addition, the Office of Personnel Management administers the Federal Merit System Standards, which apply to certain grant-aided state and local programs.

Selected OPM Agencies

Approximately 88 percent of all federal employees work outside the national capital region. Thus, federal programs have their impact largely through the actions of the regional and field representatives of the departments and agencies. **Federal Executive Boards** (FEBs) provide forums for communication and collaboration among federal agencies outside the Washington, DC, area. Under OPM's supervision and control, the 28 FEBs improve internal federal management practices and provide a central focus for federal participation in civic affairs in major metropolitan centers of federal activity. Each board is composed of heads of federal regional and field offices in its metropolitan area. A chairman is elected annually from among the membership to provide overall leadership to the board's operations. Committees and task forces carry out interagency projects consistent with the board's mission.

★ Web site: http://www.feb.gov/

Sample Job Vacancies

Emergency Operations Specialist
Agency: Center for Security and Emergency Actions
Salary: $50,408 to $95,026
Location: Washington, DC

Job summary: This position is perfect for a new or experienced mid to late career program manager who is looking for excellent benefits, including the potential for ongoing medical benefits after retirement. You will have the opportunity to influence the work with new ideas and ways of thinking, develop new and advanced skills, and impact an important public mission. We offer flexible work schedules and telework opportunities. OPM is just blocks from the Metro. Note that this announcement may be used to fill one or more vacancies. Relocation expenses will not be paid.

Key requirements: You must be a U.S. citizen. You must complete a single-scope background investigation. You must obtain and maintain Top Secret security clearance with SCI access. You also must submit to urinalysis test for illegal drugs.

Duties: Performs duties to maintain the situation room/command center in a state of operational readiness and awareness. Performs and oversees tasks that facilitate the command center's ability to interface with federal, state, civilian, military, and local emergency operations centers on government preparedness, disaster response, and other emergency matters. Monitors the National

Warning System (NAWAS) to ensure continuity of information flow and consistency with other sources of information. Develops, writes, and coordinates operations plans and checklists. Implements procedures that provide immediate, current information to elevated management positions for action decisions. Participates in scheduled and unscheduled exercises for continuity of operations. Assists in the coordination and implementation of agency security-related programs, as needed.

Qualifications: For the GS-9 level, you must have at least one year of specialized experience equivalent to the GS-7 level in the federal government. For the GS-11 level, you must have at least one year of specialized experience equivalent to the GS-9 level in the federal government. Specialized experience for both levels is experience in emergency planning and preparedness, organization, functions, and authorities in order to make recommendations and implement instructions, security techniques, practices, and methods of security programs. For the GS-12 level, you must have at least one year of specialized experience equivalent to the GS-11 level in the federal government. Specialized experience is experience in recognizing emergency situations, alerting appropriate authorities, recommending courses of action, formulating responses, and notifying appropriate organizations.

At the GS-09 or GS-11 grade level, you may substitute three full academic years of progressively higher level education or related Ph.D. or equivalent doctoral degree that demonstrates the knowledge, skills, and abilities required to perform the duties of an emergency operations specialist, such as making recommendations and implementing instructions, security techniques, practices, and methods. At the GS-12 grade level, there is no substitution of education for specialized experience.

How you will be evaluated: Upon receipt of your complete application package, a review of your application will be made to ensure you meet the basic qualification requirements. Next, your responses to the questionnaire and/or competency statements will be evaluated to determine the degree to which your skills match this position. The occupational questionnaire is designed to assess your ability to demonstrate the following competencies:

★ Knowledge of emergency planning and preparedness, organization, functions, and authorities in order to recognize emergency situations, alert appropriate authorities, recommend courses of action, formulate responses, and notify appropriate organizations.

★ Knowledge of communications and information systems, equipment, security regulations, and procedures.

★ Knowledge of operational concepts for emergency notification and alerting procedures for timely notification during potential or actual emergencies.

★ Ability to lead operations staff during emergency planning and implementation of decisions.

★ Ability to analyze emergency work situations/processes, identify problems, and recommend sound solutions.

★ Ability to effectively communicate orally and in writing.

How to apply: Submission of a resume alone is not a complete application. This position requires the completion of additional forms and/or supplemental materials. Failure to provide the required information and/or materials will result in your not being considered for employment. In addition to the online application (resume and responses to the questionnaire), you are required to submit the following forms:

★ Transcripts (if you are applying based on education)

★ SF-50 (or equivalent Notification of Personnel Action) if you are a current or former federal employee

★ Veterans preference documentation (DD-214 or equivalent, SF-15 and VA Letter, as appropriate) if you are claiming veterans preference

★ Interagency Career Transition Assistance Plan (ICTAP) documents, if you are applying for an ICTAP appointment

What to expect next: Once your complete application is received, we will conduct an evaluation of your qualifications and determine your ranking. The most highly qualified candidates will be referred to the hiring manager for further consideration and possible interview. We expect to make a selection within 45 workdays of the closing date of this announcement. You will be notified of the outcome.

Test Administrator

Agency: Office of Personnel Management
Salary: $13.18 to $17.13/hour
Location: Salina, Kansas

Duties: You will administer written tests using specific instructions for federal employment, including internal promotion tests for various federal agencies and the Armed Services Vocational Aptitude Battery Enlistment test for those wishing to enter into the military service. You also will administer Department of Defense student tests to high school students. You will be responsible for the security of test materials in your possession and will have to maintain inventory control and accountability of test materials. Sessions for written tests will range in size from 1 to 40 (enlistment and employment tests) and 1 to 250 (student tests) applicants. The various test sessions are conducted at locations such as federal office buildings, National Guard armories/reserve centers, high schools, international airports, and rented space. You will be required to drive to the test sites using your own private vehicle to transport test materials and conduct the test sessions. Mileage is reimbursed at the current government rate.

This is an intermittent position in the excepted service. Intermittent means that there are no guaranteed work hours per week. Work hours will be assigned on an "as-needed basis." This job will not lead to a full-time position. Therefore, if you are not willing to accept working on an "as-needed basis," do not apply for this job. Incumbent must complete three days of mandatory training before scheduled testing begins.

Qualifications: One year of general experience is required. General experience is one or more years of responsible clerical, office, or other work experience, such as teaching, that indicates the ability to orally present information to individuals or groups, the ability to handle administrative and clerical processes, and the ability to establish effective relationships with customers.

Your application will be rated and ranked on the following knowledges, skills, and abilities (KSAs):

★ Ability to conduct/administer written tests.

★ Knowledge of test security procedures.

★ Ability to communicate orally.

★ Ability to understand and follow written and oral instructions.

Successful completion of two years of education above the high school level or an associate's degree from an accredited business, secretarial, or technical school, junior college, or university is fully qualifying. To combine your education and experience, you must convert each to a percentage, and then add the percentages. The combined total of your percentage of education and experience must equal at least 100 percent in order to qualify.

To qualify for this position, you must be a U.S. citizen and reside within the local commuting area. You will be required to travel within a 100-mile radius of the duty location. You must possess a valid driver's license and provide own transportation. This position requires early morning travel. This position also requires periods of standing, walking, and sitting. You must be able to carry test material weighing an average of 10 to 35 pounds to and from examination location.

Your Social Security number (SSN) is requested under the authority of Executive Order 9397 to uniquely identify your records from other applicants' records that may have the same name. As allowed by law or presidential directive, your SSN is used to seek information about you from other employers, schools, banks, and others who may know you. Failure to provide your SSN on your application materials will result in your application not being processed.

Office of Science and Technology Policy

Executive Office of the President
725 Seventeenth Street, Room 5228
Washington, DC 20502
202-456-2800

★ Web site: http://www.ostp.gov/

★ Internships: http://www.ostp.gov/cs/Student_Volunteers

The Office of Science and Technology Policy serves as a source of scientific, engineering, and technological analysis and judgment for the president with respect to major policies, plans, and programs of the federal government. The office advises the president of scientific and technological considerations involved in areas of national concern, including the economy, national security, health, foreign relations, and the environment. It evaluates the scale, quality, and effectiveness of the federal effort in science and technology; provides advice and assistance to the president, the Office of Management and Budget, and federal agencies throughout the federal budget development process; and assists the president in providing leadership and coordination for the research and development programs of the federal government. The office employs approximately 30 people.

Office of Special Counsel

1730 M Street NW, Suite 218
Washington, DC 20036-4505
800-872-9855 (toll-free)
202-254-3600

★ Web site: http://www.osc.gov/

★ Job vacancies: http://www.osc.gov/oscjobs.htm

The Office of Special Counsel (OSC) investigates allegations of certain activities prohibited by civil service laws, rules, or regulations and litigates before the Merit Systems Protection Board. The primary role of OSC is to protect employees, former employees, and applicants for employment from prohibited personnel practices, especially reprisal for whistle-blowing. It employs more than 100 people.

Office of the United States Trade Representative

600 Seventeenth Street NW
Washington, DC 20508
202-395-3230

★ Web site: http://www.ustr.gov/

★ Internships: http://www.ustr.gov/Who_We_Are/USTR_Student_Internship_Program.html

The Office of the U.S. Trade Representative (USTR) is responsible for developing and coordinating U.S. international trade, commodity, and direct investment policy and overseeing negotiations with other countries. The head of USTR is the U.S. trade representative, a cabinet member who serves as the president's principal trade advisor, negotiator, and spokesperson on trade issues. USTR is part of the Executive Office of the President. Through an interagency structure, USTR coordinates trade policy, resolves disagreements, and frames issues for presidential decision. The U.S. trade representative also serves as vice chairperson of the Overseas Private Investment Corporation (OPIC), is a nonvoting member of the Export-Import Bank, and a member of the National Advisory Council on International Monetary and Financial Policies. The USTR employs approximately 230 people.

Office of the Vice President

The White House
1600 Pennsylvania Avenue NW
Washington, DC 20500
202-456-1414

★ Web site: http://www.whitehouse.gov/vicepresident/

The Office of the Vice President serves the vice president in the performance of the many detailed activities incident to his immediate office. The executive functions of the vice president include participation in cabinet meetings and, by statute, membership on the National Security Council and the Board of Regents of the Smithsonian Institution. The office employs about 20 people.

Organization of American States

1889 F Street NW
Washington, DC 20006
202-458-3000

★ Web site: http://www.oas.org/

★ Jobs, internships, and scholarships: http://www.oas.org/documents/eng/oporjobs.asp

The Organization of American States (OAS) brings together the nations of the Western Hemisphere to strengthen cooperation on democratic values, defend common interests, and debate the major issues facing the region and the world. The OAS is the region's principal multilateral forum for strengthening democracy, promoting human rights, and confronting shared problems such as poverty, terrorism, illegal drugs, and corruption.

Through decisions made by its political bodies and programs carried out by its General Secretariat, the OAS seeks to promote greater inter-American cooperation and understanding. All 35 independent countries of the Americas have ratified the OAS Charter and belong to the organization. Cuba remains a member, but its government has been excluded from participation in the OAS since 1962.

The principal parts of the OAS are the General Assembly, which is normally composed of the foreign ministers of the member states and meets at least once a year to decide the general action and policy of the organization; the Meeting of Consultation of Ministers of Foreign Affairs, which conducts ad hoc meetings to consider urgent matters of common interest or threats to the peace and security of the hemisphere; the Permanent Council, composed of ambassadors/permanent representatives at headquarters, which meets twice a month; the Inter-American Council for Integral Development; the Inter-American Juridical Committee; the Inter-American Commission on Human Rights; and the General Secretariat, which is the central and permanent organization, headquartered in Washington, DC.

The OAS has six specialized organizations that handle technical matters of common interest. They are the Pan American Health Organization (PAHO), the Inter-American Children's Institute (IIN), the Inter-American Commission of Women (CIM), Inter-American Indian Institute (III), Pan American Institute of Geography and History (PAIGH), and the Inter-American Institute for Cooperation on Agriculture (IICA).

Selected OAS Agencies

The **Pan American Health Organization** (PAHO) is an international public health agency with 100 years of experience in working to improve health and living standards of the countries of the Americas. It serves as the specialized organization for health of the Inter-American System. PAHO also serves as the Regional Office for the Americas of the World Health Organization and enjoys international recognition as part of the United Nations system.

PAHO is based in Washington, DC, and has scientific and technical experts at its headquarters, in its 27 country offices, and its 9 scientific centers, all working with the countries of Latin America and the Caribbean in dealing with priority health issues.

★ Web site: http://www.paho.org/

★ Job vacancies: http://www.paho.org/English/AM/HRM/RE/HRM-vacancies.htm

★ Fellowships: http://www.paho.org/Project.asp?SEL=TP&LNG=ENG&ID=241

The **Inter-American Institute for Cooperation on Agriculture** was founded as an institution for agricultural research and graduate training in tropical agriculture. In response to changing needs in the Americas, the institute gradually evolved into an agency for technical cooperation in the field of agriculture. The institute's purposes are to encourage, facilitate, and support cooperation among its member states to promote agricultural development and rural well-being.

★ Web site: http://www.iica.int/Eng/Pages/default.aspx

★ Job vacancies: http://www.iica.int/Eng/infoinstitucional/Pages/empleo.aspx

★ Center for Leadership in Agriculture: http://www.iica.int/Eng/dg/centroliderazgo/Pages/default.aspx

Other OAS Agencies

Columbus Memorial Library

http://www.oas.org/columbus/

Inter-American Children's Institute

http://www.iin.oea.org

Inter-American Commission of Women

http://www.oas.org/cim/default.htm

Inter-American Committee Against Terrorism

http://www.cicte.oas.org/Rev/en/

Inter-American Drug Abuse Control Commission

http://www.cicad.oas.org/en/default.asp

Leo S. Rowe Pan American Fund

http://www.oas.org/rowe/

Office of Humanitarian Mine Action

http://www.aicma.oas.org/

Overseas Private Investment Corporation

1100 New York Avenue NW
Washington, DC 20527
202-336-8400

★ Web site: http://www.opic.gov/

★ Job vacancies: http://www.opic.gov/about/jobs/index.asp

★ Internships: http://www.opic.gov/about/jobs/internship/index.asp

★ Strategic plan: http://www.opic.gov/about/reports/ocio_strategic_plan_2007_2011.pdf.pdf

The Overseas Private Investment Corporation (OPIC) helps U.S. businesses invest overseas and fosters economic development in new and emerging markets. OPIC promotes economic growth in developing countries and emerging markets by encouraging U.S. private investment in those nations. OPIC complements the private sector in managing the risks associated with foreign direct investment and supports U.S. foreign policy. By expanding economic development in host countries, OPIC-supported projects can encourage political stability, free market reforms, and U.S. best practices. OPIC projects also support U.S. jobs and exports. Because OPIC charges market-based fees for its products, it operates on a self-sustaining basis at no net cost to taxpayers. The OPIC staff consists of approximately 200 employees, all based in Washington, DC.

Panama Canal Commission

P.O. Box 526725
Miami, FL 33152-6725
507-272-7602

★ Web site: http://www.pancanal.com/

★ Job vacancies (information is available only in Spanish): http://www.pancanal.com/esp/hr/info-empleo.html

The Panama Canal Commission provides oversight to the Panama Canal Authority, which operates, maintains, and improves the Panama Canal to guarantee prompt, dependable, safe, and uninterrupted interoceanic transit. The commission is comprised of 11 members.

Peace Corps

1111 Twentieth Street NW
Washington, DC 20526
800-424-8580 (toll-free)
202-692-2000

★ Web site: http://www.peacecorps.gov/

★ Job vacancies (domestic): http://www.peacecorps.gov/index.cfm?shell=pchq.jobs.pcvac

★ Job vacancies (overseas): http://www.peacecorps.gov/index.cfm?shell=pchq.jobs.overseasOp

★ Job vacancies (headquarters): http://www.peacecorps.gov/index.cfm?shell=pchq.jobs.workingpc

★ Toll-free recruitment number: 1-800-424-8580

★ Professional medical opportunities: http://www.peacecorps.gov/index.cfm?shell=pchq.jobs.overseasop.medical

★ How to apply: https://www.peacecorps.gov/apply/now/index.cfm?&

★ Federal hiring process: http://pcitjobs.us/federal-hiring-process

★ Salary and benefits: http://www.peacecorps.gov/index.cfm?shell=pchq.jobs.workingpc.salary

★ Career information: http://www.peacecorps.gov/index.cfm?shell=pchq.jobs

The mission of the Peace Corps is to help the people of interested countries in meeting their need for trained men and women and to help promote better mutual understanding between Americans and people of other countries. The Peace Corps consists of a Washington, DC, headquarters; 11 area offices; and overseas operations in more than 73 countries, utilizing more than 8,000 volunteers at 68 posts.

To fulfill the Peace Corps mandate, men and women are trained for a 9- to 14-week period in the appropriate local language, the technical skills necessary for their particular job, and the cross-cultural skills needed to adjust to a society with traditions and attitudes different from their own. Volunteers serve for a period of two years, living among the people with whom they work and serving in six program areas: education, health and HIV/AIDS, environment, information technology, agriculture, and business development.

The most common international employment opportunities within the Peace Corps are Country Director (CD) and Associate Director (APCD). Occasionally, Peace Corps recruits MDs or DOs for Area Peace Corps Medical Officers for the Africa Region. There are 11 Peace Corps recruiting offices throughout the United States where staff identify and select the volunteers. One of the key positions in these offices is the regional recruiter. Peace Corps also seeks physicians, nurse practitioners, and physician assistants with independent practice experience for two-year contract positions overseas as Peace Corps Medical Officers (PCMOs). PCMOs provide health care, education, counseling, and manage the volunteer health care delivery system in the country of assignment. The Peace Corps employs approximately 1,100 people.

Selected Peace Corps Agencies

The **Peace Corps Office of Private Sector Initiatives** works with schools, civic groups, businesses, and neighborhood and youth organizations in the United States to facilitate their support of Peace Corps initiatives here and abroad.

★ Web site: http://www.peacecorps.gov/index.cfm?shell=resources.media.stories.opsi

Since its inception in 1989 by Paul D. Coverdell, **World Wise Schools** has helped more than one million U.S. students communicate directly with Peace Corps volunteers all over the world. Initially set up as a correspondence "match" program between volunteers and U.S. classes, World Wise

Schools has expanded its scope over the past 10 years by providing a broad range of resources for educators, including award-winning videos, teacher guides, classroom speakers, a newsletter, and online resources.

★ Web site: http://www.peacecorps.gov/wws/

Other Peace Corps Agencies

Fellows/USA

http://www.peacecorps.gov/index.cfm?shell=learn.whyvol.eduben.fellows

United Nations Volunteers

http://www.peacecorps.gov/index.cfm?shell=resources.former.unvol

Pension Benefit Guaranty Corporation

1200 K Street NW, Suite 12531
Washington, DC 20005-4026
800-400-7242 (toll-free)
202-326-4000

★ Web site: http://www.pbgc.gov/

★ Job vacancies: http://www.pbgc.gov/about/jobs.html

★ Strategic plan: http://www.pbgc.gov/docs/2008-2013strategicplan.pdf

The Pension Benefit Guaranty Corporation (PBGC) protects the retirement incomes of nearly 44 million American workers in 30,330 private-sector, defined benefit pension plans, including more than 1,600 multiemployer plans. A defined benefit plan provides a specified monthly benefit at retirement, often based on a combination of salary and years of service. PBGC is not funded by general tax revenues. It collects insurance premiums from employers that sponsor insured pension plans, earns money from investments, and receives funds from pension plans it takes over.

The PBGC consists of the secretaries of Labor, Commerce, and the Treasury. The secretary of Labor is chairman of the board. A seven-member advisory committee composed of two labor, two business, and three public members appointed by the president advises the agency on investment issues. The PBGC has approximately 850 employees with many different skills. PBGC staff includes accountants; actuaries; attorneys; auditors; budget, financial, and management analysts; computer, pension law, and public affairs specialists; and administrative personnel.

Selected PBGC Agency

The **Policy, Research, and Analysis Department** (PRAD) develops policy for PBGC's insurance programs and conducts related research and modeling. Policy activity encompasses legislative and regulatory analysis and proposal development related to benefit guarantees, employer liability, and premiums. Research addresses actuarial and financial issues to support policy development and involves modeling for forecasting purposes.

★ Web site: http://www.pbgc.gov/about/departments.html

Other PBGC Agency

Department of Insurance Supervision and Compliance

http://www.pbgc.gov/about/departments.html

President's Intelligence Advisory Board and Intelligence Oversight Board

Executive Office Building, Room 235
Washington, DC 20502
202-456-1414

★ Web site: http://www.whitehouse.gov/administration/eop/piab/

The President's Intelligence Advisory Board and Intelligence Oversight Board (PIAB) provides advice to the president concerning the quality and adequacy of intelligence collection, of analysis and estimates, of counterintelligence, and of other intelligence activities. The PIAB, through its Intelligence Oversight Board, also advises the president on the legality of foreign intelligence activities.

Postal Regulatory Commission

901 New York Avenue NW, Suite 200
Washington, DC 20268-0001
202-789-6800

★ Web site: http://www.prc.gov/

★ Job vacancies: http://www.prc.gov/prc-pages/about/hr/employment.aspx

The Postal Regulatory Commission develops and implements a modern system of postal rate regulation. The commission promulgates rules and regulations, establishes procedures, and takes other actions necessary to carry out its obligations. It considers complaints received from interested persons relating to postage rates and postal classifications and services. The commission also has certain reporting obligations, including a report on universal postal service and the postal monopoly. It is composed of five commissioners who are appointed by the president with the advice and consent of the Senate and one of whom is designated as chairman. The commission employs approximately 50 people.

Presidio Trust

P.O. Box 29052
34 Graham Street
San Francisco, California 94129
415-561-5300

★ Web site: http://www.presidiotrust.gov/

★ Job vacancies: http://www.presidio.gov/trust/jobs/

★ Career information: http://www.presidio.gov/trust/jobs/EmploymentInformation.htm

★ Strategic plan: http://www.presidio.gov/trust/plans.htm

The Presidio, a 1,491-acre site overlooking San Francisco Bay, had been a military post since 1776, when the Spanish established a post there. From 1846 until 1994, when it became part of the National Park Service, the Presidio served as a United States military base. It is now part of the 75,500-acre Golden Gate National Recreation Area (GGNRA), the world's largest national park in an urban area. The Presidio Trust was created in 1996 to manage the interior lands of the park. It has more than 330 employees.

Its mission is to preserve and enhance the natural, cultural, scenic, and recreational resources of the Presidio for public use in perpetuity and to achieve long-term financial sustainability. These efforts encompass the natural areas, wildlife, and native habitats of the park, as well as the historic structures and designed landscapes that make the park a National Historic Landmark District.

Railroad Retirement Board

844 North Rush Street
Chicago, IL 60611-2092
800-808-0772 (toll-free help line)
312-751-4500

★ Web site: http://www.rrb.gov/

★ Strategic plan: http://www.rrb.gov/strategicplan/2006/introduction.asp

The Railroad Retirement Board (RRB) administers comprehensive retirement-survivor and unemployment-sickness benefit programs for the nation's railroad workers and their families. To this end, the RRB employs field representatives to assist railroad personnel and their families in filing claims for benefits; examiners to adjudicate the claims; and information technology staff to maintain earnings records, calculate benefits, and process payments. The RRB also employs actuaries to predict the future income and outlays of the railroad retirement system, statisticians and economists to provide vital data, and attorneys to interpret legislation and represent the RRB in litigation. Internal administration requires a procurement staff, a budget and accounting staff, and personnel specialists. The inspector general employs auditors and investigators to detect any waste, fraud, or abuse in the benefit programs. The RRB employs approximately 1,000 people.

Securities and Exchange Commission

100 F Street NE
Washington, DC 20549
202-942-8088

★ Web site: http://www.sec.gov/

★ Career information: http://www.sec.gov/jobs.shtml

★ Internships: http://www.sec.gov/jobs/jobs_students.shtml

★ How to apply: http://www.sec.gov/jobs/jobs_apply.shtml

★ Applying via AVUE: https://www.avuedigitalservices.com/casting/agencyspecific/sec-sp/
eligQuest/summerPrograms.jsp

The Securities and Exchange Commission (SEC) provides protection for investors, ensures that securities markets are fair and honest, and, when necessary, provides the means to enforce securities laws through sanctions. The SEC protects investors and maintains fair, orderly, and efficient markets and facilitates capital formation. The SEC requires public companies to disclose meaningful financial and other information to the public, which provides a common pool of knowledge for all investors to use to judge for themselves whether a company's securities are a good investment.

The SEC also oversees other key participants in the securities world, including stock exchanges, broker-dealers, investment advisors, mutual funds, and public utility holding companies. Here again, the SEC is concerned primarily with promoting disclosure of important information, enforcing the securities laws, and protecting investors who interact with these various organizations and individuals. Crucial to the SEC's effectiveness is its enforcement authority. Each year the SEC brings 400 to 500 civil enforcement actions against individuals and companies that break the securities laws. Typical infractions include insider trading, accounting fraud, and providing false or misleading information about securities and the companies that issue them.

The SEC consists of five presidentially appointed commissioners, four divisions, and 19 offices. With approximately 3,500 staff, the SEC is small by federal agency standards. Headquartered in Washington, DC, the SEC has 11 regional and district offices throughout the country. It hires attorneys, accountants, securities compliance examiners, IT specialists, and economists, along with administrative and office support specialists.

Selected SEC Agency

The **Division of Corporation Finance** oversees corporate disclosure of important information to the investing public. Corporations are required to comply with regulations pertaining to disclosure that must be made when stock is initially sold and then on a continuing and periodic basis. The division's staff routinely reviews the disclosure documents filed by companies. The staff also provides companies with assistance interpreting the commission's rules and recommends to the commission new rules for adoption.

★ Web site: http://www.sec.gov/divisions/corpfin.shtml

Other SEC Agencies

Division of Enforcement

http://www.sec.gov/divisions/enforce.shtml

Division of Investment Management

http://www.sec.gov/divisions/investment.shtml

Division of Trading and Markets

http://www.sec.gov/divisions/marketreg.shtml

Office of Administrative Law Judges

http://www.sec.gov/about/offices/oalj.htm

Office of Compliance Inspections and Examinations

http://www.sec.gov/about/offices/ocie.shtml

Office of Economic Analysis

http://www.sec.gov/about/economic.shtml

Office of Information Technology

http://www.sec.gov/about/offices/oit.htm

Office of International Affairs

http://www.sec.gov/about/offices/oia.htm

Office of Investor Education and Advocacy

http://www.sec.gov/investor.shtml

Selective Service System

National Headquarters
Arlington, VA 22209-2425
703-605-4100

★ Web site: http://www.sss.gov/

★ Job vacancies: http://www.sss.gov/Vacancy%20Announcement%20Files/
Job%20Opportunities.htm

★ Become a high school registrar: http://www.sss.gov/registrar.htm

★ Volunteer as a local board member: https://www.sss.gov/localboardmembers/bminquiry.asp

★ Reserve forces officer information: http://www.sss.gov/rfo.htm

The Selective Service System (SSS) provides untrained manpower (young men) to the armed forces in an emergency and operates an Alternative Service Program during a draft for men classified as conscientious objectors. It is an independent agency within the executive branch of the federal government. The director of the Selective Service is appointed by the president and confirmed by the Senate.

The Selective Service System's structure consists of the national headquarters, the data management center, and three region headquarters. About 180 full-time employees, including 16 military officers, work in these locations. Also part of the Selective Service System is a field structure of 300 part-time military reservists and 56 civilian volunteer board members. In addition, the SSS has approximately 10,000 volunteers. Every state, the District of Columbia, and U.S. territories also have state directors. The Selective Service System's reservists, board members, and state directors serve part-time for the agency, remaining trained and ready to be called into service in the event of a draft. Registration is conducted at post offices within the United States, at U.S. embassies and consulates outside the United States, and online at http://www.sss.gov/.

Small Business Administration

409 Third Street SW
Washington, DC 20416
202-205-6600

★ Web site: http://www.sba.gov/

★ Job vacancies: http://www.sba.gov/, link to SBA Jobs at bottom of page

★ Internships: http://www.sba.gov/aboutsba/sbaprograms/oha/ OHA_INDEX_INTERNSHIPS.html

★ Strategic plan: http://www.sba.gov/idc/groups/public/documents/sba_homepage/ serv_strategic_plan_2006.pdf

The Small Business Administration (SBA) is an independent agency of the federal government designed to aid, counsel, assist, and protect the interests of small business concerns, to preserve free competitive enterprise, and to maintain and strengthen the overall economy of our nation. The SBA ensures that small business concerns receive a fair portion of government purchases, contracts, and subcontracts, as well as of the sales of government property; makes loans to small business concerns, state and local development companies, and the victims of floods or other catastrophes or of certain types of economic injury; and licenses, regulates, and makes loans to small business investment companies.

The SBA has 70 district and 10 regional offices. It offers a wide range of careers, including economic development specialist, business opportunity specialist, personnel specialist, criminal investigator, loan specialist, industrial specialist, contract specialist, procurement analyst, clerical and administrative support positions, accountant, auditor, economist, and attorney. It employs approximately 4,300 people.

Selected SBA Agencies

The **Office of Entrepreneurial Development** helps small businesses start, grow, and compete in global markets by providing training, counseling, and access to resources. It offers the following programs and resources: the Small Business Development Centers, SCORE, the Small Business

Training Network, the Office of Entrepreneurship Education, and the Office of Women's Business Ownership.

★ Web site: http://www.sba.gov/aboutsba/sbaprograms/ed/index.html

★ Small Business Development Centers: http://www.sba.gov/aboutsba/sbaprograms/sbdc/index.html

★ SCORE: http://www.score.org/

★ The Small Business Training Network: http://www.sba.gov/services/training/index.html

★ Office of Entrepreneurship Education: http://www.sba.gov/aboutsba/sbaprograms/oee/index.html

★ Office of Women's Business Ownership: http://www.sba.gov/aboutsba/sbaprograms/onlinewbc/index.html

The **Office of Government Contracting and Business Development** helps small, disadvantaged, and women-owned businesses build their potential to compete more successfully in a global economy. It administers the Office of Government Contracting, Business Development Centers, Business Information Centers, the Office of Technology, size standards, and the HUBZone program.

★ Web site: http://www.sba.gov/aboutsba/sbaprograms/gcbd/index.html

★ Office of Government Contracting: http://www.sba.gov/aboutsba/sbaprograms/gc/index.html

★ Office of Technology: http://www.sba.gov/aboutsba/sbaprograms/sbir/index.html

★ Size standards: http://www.sba.gov/services/contractingopportunities/sizestandardstopics/index.html

★ HUBZone program: https://eweb1.sba.gov/hubzone/internet/index.cfm

Other SBA Agencies

7(a) Lender Program

http://www.sba.gov/services/financialassistance/7alenderprograms/index.html

Financial Assistance

http://www.sba.gov/services/financialassistance/index.html

Investment Division

http://www.sba.gov/aboutsba/sbaprograms/inv/index.html

Office of Advocacy

http://www.sba.gov/advo/

Office of Credit Risk Management

http://www.sba.gov/aboutsba/sbaprograms/olo/index.html

Office of Disaster Assistance

http://www.sba.gov/services/disasterassistance/index.html

Office of Hearings and Appeals

http://www.sba.gov/oha/

Office of International Trade

http://www.sba.gov/oit

Office of Native American Affairs

http://www.sba.gov/aboutsba/sbaprograms/naa/index.html

Office of Surety Guarantees

http://www.sba.gov/osg

Office of the National Ombudsman

http://www.sba.gov/aboutsba/sbaprograms/ombudsman/index.html

Office of Veterans Business Development

http://www.sba.gov/aboutsba/sbaprograms/ovbd/index.html

Small Disadvantaged Business

http://www.sba.gov/aboutsba/sbaprograms/sdb/index.html

Sample Job Vacancies

Construction Analyst—Field Inspection Team
Agency: Office of Disaster Assistance
Salary: $38,117 to $73,329
Location: Many locations across the country

Job summary: Small Business Administration's Office of Disaster Assistance (ODA) is a highly motivated and diverse team that seeks talented people to help families and small businesses rebuild their lives after disasters. The Field Inspection Team is a group of fully qualified and trained SBA construction analysts who are available to respond to disaster emergencies anywhere in the continental United States, often within 48 hours or less. They conduct on-site damage assessments to personal, real, and business property that resulted from a catastrophe that was declared a disaster by the president or SBA. They determine the extent of the damage and estimate the cost of repair or replacement of damaged properties. Construction analysts work primarily in disaster-affected areas, but may work in an ODA center.

In order to respond quickly and efficiently to disaster victims, substantial compensated hours up to seven days a week and 12 to 14 hours a day may be required while on assignment. Travel will be for extended periods. Travel expenses are compensated based on SBA policy and federal regulations. In addition, employees may encounter hazardous working and/or living conditions, such as no water or electricity and/or minimal lodging facilities. Employees work on an intermittent work schedule.

This means that employees are in pay and duty status only when activated to respond to a disaster. When the disaster is over, employees return home in nonpay status until the next event when staff is needed to respond. For these positions, an employee's residence is considered his/her official duty station. The rate of pay will be based on the OPM Locality pay table that applies to the geographic location of the employee's residence. Benefits are not available for these positions.

Duties: Performs on-site inspections of rental, residential, and commercial properties to determine extent of damage and costs to repair and/or replace real property, vehicles, personal property, machinery, equipment, and other items. Schedules appointments with applicants, answers questions at the inspection site, and calculates the cost to replace or repair damaged items. Prepares worksheets using automated software and transmits data electronically. Higher-graded positions may involve working with businesses with multiple subsidiaries, apartment buildings, and condominium associations.

Qualifications: You may qualify based on experience, education, or a combination of both. To qualify for the GS-7 level, you must have at least one full year of specialized experience that is equivalent to the GS-5 grade level in the federal service. Specialized experience is experience working in the fields of construction, damage assessment, or engineering, which included all of the following: experience estimating quantity and cost of materials, labor, and equipment for constructing or repairing single-family homes; skill with computers sufficient to retrieve work assignments and to troubleshoot basic connectivity issues; practical knowledge of engineering techniques, methods, materials, and construction practices employed in conventional housing; and knowledge of national building codes and building restrictions. To qualify for the GS-9 level, you must have at least one full year of specialized experience that is equivalent to the GS-7 grade level in federal service. Specialized experience is experience as described for GS-7, except you must also have experience with multiple-family structures. To qualify for the GS-11 level, you must have at least one full year of specialized experience that is equivalent to the GS-9 grade level in federal service. Specialized experience is experience as described for GS-7, except you must also have experience with multiple-family structures, multiple-story residential or commercial buildings, and machinery and equipment, such as specialized medical equipment.

Your education must have been obtained an accredited college or university with major study in architecture, engineering, building construction, or another field related to this position. For GS-7, you must have one full year of graduate-level education or a bachelor's degree in one of the one of the listed majors with superior academic achievement. For GS-9, you must have a master's or equivalent graduate degree or two full years of progressively higher level graduate education leading to such a degree. For the GS-11, you must have a Ph.D. or equivalent doctoral degree or three full years of progressively higher level graduate education leading to such a degree.

How to apply: To apply for this position, you must provide a complete application package, which includes your responses to the assessment questionnaire, your resume, and any other documents specified in the Required Documents section of this job announcement. Use Application Manager for convenience and quickest processing. Track your progress to a complete application package using the My Application Packages checklist and status displays in Application Manager.

Student Temporary Employment Program Worker
Agency: Small Business Administration
Salary: $9.57 to $23.74/hour
Location: Many locations across the country

Job summary: The Small Business Administration (SBA) is seeking to hire summer students under the Student Temporary Employment Program (STEP). The STEP provides maximum flexibility to both the student and manager because the nature of the work does not have to be related to the student's academic or career goals. The STEP is designed to integrate the students' educational studies with a wide range of clerical, administrative, professional, and/or technical experiences that support the agency's mission.

Duties: The position(s) to be filled involve performing clerical duties for the SBA at various grade levels. At the GS-1 level, incumbent will sort mail or other documents into obvious categories according to specific guides or instructions and perform simple typing work not requiring the services of a qualified typist. Typing, if performed, is limited to such things as typing labels or other brief information on file tabs and index cards. The incumbent will also perform simple tabulating or counting of documents or other items received or dispatched. In conjunction with other clerical duties, the incumbent may also for part of the time perform routine repetitive messenger work by collecting and delivering mail and other papers on a small pre-determined route and in accordance with specific directions or schedule.

At the GS-2 level, the incumbent will perform routine clerical work not requiring any specialized training or experience; receive and direct telephone callers and/or visitors to the appropriate office staff members as well as provide routine answers regarding basic agency functions; receive and route incoming mail and documents; assemble and prepare packages for special mailings, such as Federal Express, by typing labels and attaching preprinted address labels for mailing; assist with the preparation and printing of routine correspondence and memorandum in final format, filing, and copying of various materials; perform routine automated assistance by transmitting and receiving electronic messages; and provide clerical support for group and/or team projects.

At the GS-3 level, the incumbent will perform routine clerical work not requiring any specialized training or experience; receive calls and visitors and refer them to appropriate staff members and/or provide general information about the office; assist staff members of the office with carrying out program-related activities, such as preparing correspondence, requesting information, and compiling survey studies and documents by gathering, reproducing, and arranging selected information; assemble information packages and materials to be used by the office staff members; and assist staff members with maintaining and updating office files.

At the GS-4 level, the incumbent will perform general clerical work not requiring any specialized training or experience. In addition, the incumbent will perform light typing not requiring the services of a qualified typist, such as labels for folders or internal mail distribution. The incumbent also will receive calls and visitors to the office and refer them to appropriate staff members; provide inquirers of the office with a limited amount of information, such as identifying staff members; receive and route mail and, when necessary, follow mail distribution assignments to route specific mailings and mail pickups; reproduce requested copies of memoranda, correspondence, and various other materials for the staff of the office; and assist the office staff in performing a variety of duties, such as distribution of supplies and equipment and hand-carrying specific letters, memoranda, and express mail packages.

At the GS-5 level, the incumbent will perform a variety of research assignments, which may entail gathering information when needed for special projects; draft routine replies to general public and Congressional correspondence; perform various technical assignments in support of office staff; gather facts for routine reports; and extract data from prescribed sources and compile and present results for review by higher level specialists.

At the GS-6 level, incumbent will develop methods for coordinating and preparing administrative reports and multiple uses of the data; use computer software to type or revise various letters, memos, and forms; standardize formatting of word processing documents; correct grammar, spelling, and punctuation in documents; refer questions regarding content to originator; adjust spacing of columns and tables for good appearance and clarity; and perform other office support duties, including acting as timekeeper, scheduling meetings, filing documents, sending and distributing mail, copying and maintaining office supplies and equipment, and answering phone calls and routing calls to the appropriate staff.

At the GS-7 level, incumbent will use desktop publishing software to prepare varied news releases, brochures, reports, and publications highlighting the activities of the office; use word processing and graphics software to prepare reports and briefing documents; use spreadsheet software to maintain the unit's fiscal records; use project management software to track the status of a number of projects assigned to the unit; and perform complex office automation duties requiring different approaches and methods. These duties may include using different word processing packages to edit lengthy and complicated technical reports and resolving incompatibility problems in transferring text from one software package to another when menu options or specific software instructions are not available.

Qualifications: To apply for the student temporary employment program, candidates must be at least 16 years of age at the time of appointment (those under the age of 18 must obtain and submit a work permit); be currently enrolled on at least a half-time basis (determined by the particular school or university) in an accredited high school, technical, or vocational school or a two- or four-year college, university, or graduate or professional school; be enrolled in an academic, vocational, or technical program leading to a degree, diploma, or certificate. Transcripts are required. Here are the requirements for each level:

★ **GS-1 positions:** No education or experience is required at this grade level.

★ **GS-2 positions:** Have completed high school or equivalent or have three months of general clerical work experience.

★ **GS-3 positions:** Have one year of education beyond high school or six months of general clerical work experience.

★ **GS-4 positions:** Have completed two years of education beyond high school or have one year of general clerical work experience.

★ **GS-5/6 positions:** Have completed a four-year course of study leading to a bachelor's degree or have three years progressively responsible work experience.

★ **GS-7 positions:** Have one-year of graduate study or one-year of specialized work experience equivalent to the GS-5/6 grade level.

General experience is progressively responsible clerical, office, or other work that indicates the ability to acquire the knowledge and skills needed to perform the duties of the job to be filled.

Specialized experience is experience that equipped the applicant with the particular knowledge, skills, and abilities (KSAs) to perform successfully the duties of the position and that is typically in or related to the position to be filled.

How you will be evaluated: Employment in the Student Temporary Employment Program (STEP) is a noncompetitive appointment. There is no testing, rating, or ranking of applicants for this program. Eligibility for appointment is based on applicant meeting the basic qualification requirements for the position.

Smithsonian Institution

1000 Jefferson Drive SW
Washington, DC 20560
202-622-1000

★ Web site: http://www.smithsonian.org

★ Job vacancies: http://www.sihr.si.edu/ or http://www.sihr.si.edu/jobs.cfm

★ Internships: http://intern.si.edu/

★ Horticultural internship program: http://www.gardens.si.edu/horticulture/res_ed/intern/intern3.htm

★ Anacostia Museum volunteers and internships: http://anacostia.si.edu/Volunteers.htm

★ Smithsonian Institution Traveling Exhibition Service internships: http://www.sites.si.edu/interns/internships.htm

★ Smithsonian Tropical Research Institute fellowship program: http://www.stri.org/english/education_fellowships/fellowships/index.php

★ Office of Policy and Analysis internships: http://www.si.edu/opanda/internships.html

★ Fellowship information: http://www.si.edu/ofg/

★ Research and study opportunities: http://www.si.edu/ofg/resopp.htm

★ How to apply: http://www.sihr.si.edu/howtoapply.html

★ Volunteer information: http://www.smithsonian.org/Encyclopedia_SI/volunteer/start.htm

★ Strategic plan: http://www.si.edu/opanda/docs/SIStrategicPlan2006to2011.pdf

As the world's largest museum and research complex, the Smithsonian Institution includes 16 museums and galleries, the National Zoo, and research facilities in several states and the Republic of Panama. It holds more than 143 million artifacts and specimens in its trust for the American people. The Smithsonian is dedicated to public education, national service, and scholarship in the arts, sciences, history, and culture. It was created by the Organic Act of August 10, 1846, to carry out the terms of the will of British scientist James Smithson (1765–1829), who in 1826 had bequeathed his entire estate to the United States "to found at Washington, under the name of the Smithsonian Institution, an establishment for the increase and diffusion of knowledge among men."

The Smithsonian, with more than 4,800 employees and nearly 6,000 volunteers at facilities in six states, the District of Columbia, and the Republic of Panama, requires a variety of skills to support its operations. It employs crafts people in virtually every trade to maintain and restore the historic buildings; horticulturalists and gardeners to design and maintain the grounds and display gardens; administrative and support staff to manage human resources, contracts, accounting, and finance; engineers and architects to oversee the design of new facilities and manage construction and renovation projects; scientists to do basic and applied research in a wealth of scientific disciplines as varied as astronomy, anthropology, botany, ecology, mineral sciences, earth sciences, and veterinary medicine; and historians, art historians, and archivists to collect and interpret the nation's history. There are also a variety of positions that are unique to the museum world, such as museum director, curator, conservator, and exhibit designer.

Selected Smithsonian Agencies

The **Archives of American Art** contains the nation's largest collection of documentary materials reflecting the history of visual arts in the United States. On the subject of art in America, it is the largest archives in the world, holding more than 16 million documents. The Archives gathers, preserves, and microfilms the papers of artists, craftsmen, collectors, dealers, critics, and art societies. These papers include manuscripts, letters, diaries, notebooks, sketchbooks, business records, clippings, exhibition catalogs, transcripts of tape-recorded interviews, and photographs of artists and their work.

★ Web site: http://www.aaa.si.edu/

★ Internships, fellowships, and volunteer information: http://www.aaa.si.edu/about/internship_volunteer_and_fellowship_opportunities.cfm

The **John F. Kennedy Center for the Performing Arts** is the only official memorial in Washington, DC, to President Kennedy. Since its opening in 1971, the center has presented a year-round program of the finest in music, dance, and drama from the United States and abroad. Visitor services are provided by the Friends of the Kennedy Center volunteers. Free performances are given every day on the Millennium Stage in the Grand Foyer. The center employs approximately 45 people.

★ Web site: http://www.kennedy-center.org/

★ Job vacancies: http://www.kennedy-center.org/jobs/

★ Fellowships, internships, and international training programs: http://www.kennedy-center.org/education/artsmanagement/

★ Volunteer information: http://www.kennedy-center.org/support/volunteers/

The **National Air and Space Museum,** the most popular of the Smithsonian museums, memorializes the development and achievements of aviation and space flight. It collects, displays, and preserves aeronautical and space flight artifacts of historical significance as well as documentary and artistic materials related to air and space. Among its artifacts are full-size planes, models, and instruments.

Highlights of the collection include the Wright brothers' *Flyer*, Charles Lindbergh's *Spirit of St. Louis*, a moon rock, and Apollo spacecraft. The exhibitions and study collections record human conquest of the air from its beginnings to recent achievements. The principal areas in which work is concentrated include flight craft of all types, space flight vehicles, and propulsion systems.

★ Web site: http://www.nasm.si.edu

★ Job vacancies: http://www.nasm.si.edu/getinvolved/employment/

★ Internships and fellowships: http://www.nasm.si.edu/getinvolved/internfellow.cfm

★ Explainers program for young adults: http://www.nasm.si.edu/getinvolved/explainers/

★ Volunteer information: http://www.nasm.si.edu/getinvolved/volunteer/

The **National Gallery of Art** houses one of the finest collections in the world, illustrating Western man's achievements in painting, sculpture, and the graphic arts. The collections, beginning with the thirteenth century, are rich in European old master paintings and French, Spanish, Italian, American, and British eighteenth- and nineteenth-century paintings; sculpture from the late Middle Ages to the present; Renaissance medals and bronzes; Chinese porcelains; and about 90,000 works of graphic art from the twelfth to the twentieth centuries. To expand visitors' appreciation for this collection, the National Gallery of Art offers the Micro Gallery, which is the most comprehensive interactive multimedia computer system in any American art museum. Thirteen computers enable visitors to see in magnified detail nearly every work of art on display in the permanent collection and provide access to information about artists, geographic areas, time periods, pronunciations (with sound), and more. The National Gallery of Art employs approximately 800 people.

★ Web site: http://www.nga.gov/

★ Job vacancies: http://jobsearch.usajobs.opm.gov/a9nga.asp

★ Internships and fellowships: http://www.nga.gov/education/interned.shtm

★ Volunteer information: http://www.nga.gov/education/volunteer.shtm

★ Career information: http://www.nga.gov/resources/employ.shtm

The **National Museum of American History** inspires a broader understanding of the United States and its people. In that capacity, the museum provides learning opportunities, stimulates the imagination of visitors, and presents challenging ideas about the nation's past. The museum's exhibits provide a unique view of the American experience. Emphasis is placed upon innovative individuals representing a wide range of cultures who have shaped our heritage and upon science and the remaking of our world through technology.

Exhibits draw upon strong collections in the sciences and engineering, agriculture, manufacturing, transportation, political memorabilia, costumes, musical instruments, coins, armed forces history, photography, computers, ceramics, and glass. Classic cars, icons of the American presidency, First Ladies' gowns, the Star-Spangled Banner flag, Whitney's cotton gin, Morse's telegraph, the John Bull locomotive, Dorothy's ruby slippers from *The Wizard of Oz,* and other American icons are highlights of the collection.

★ Web site: http://www.americanhistory.si.edu/

★ Job vacancies: http://www.americanhistory.si.edu/getinvolved/careers.cfm

★ Internships: http://www.americanhistory.si.edu/getinvolved/internprog.cfm

★ Fellowships: http://www.americanhistory.si.edu/getinvolved/fellowindex.cfm

★ Volunteer information: http://www.americanhistory.si.edu/getinvolved/volunteerprog.cfm

The **National Museum of Natural History** is dedicated to understanding the natural world and the place of humans in it. The museum's permanent exhibits focus on human cultures, Earth sciences, biology, and anthropology, with the most popular displays featuring gemstones such as the Hope diamond, dinosaurs, insects, marine ecosystems, birds, and mammals.

The museum's encyclopedic collections comprise more than 125 million specimens, making the museum one of the world's foremost facilities for natural history research. The museum's four departments are anthropology, mineral sciences, paleobiology, and systematic biology. Doctorate-level staff researchers ensure the continued growth and value of the collection by conducting studies in the field and laboratory.

★ Web site: http://www.mnh.si.edu/

★ Internships: http://www.nmnh.si.edu/rtp/other_opps/internintro.html

★ Fellowships: http://www.nmnh.si.edu/rtp/other_opps/fellowintro.html

★ Volunteer information: http://www.mnh.si.edu/getinvolved/volunteer.htm

The **National Zoological Park** encompasses 163 acres along Rock Creek Park in northwest Washington, DC. Established in 1889, the zoo is developing into a biopark with live animals, botanic gardens, and aquaria and artworks with animal themes. The collection today has animals ranging in size and diversity from leaf-cutter ants to giraffes. Research on genetics, animal behavior, and reproductive studies has given the National Zoo a leadership role among the nation's conservation institutions.

The National Zoo maintains its own security police similar to the Smithsonian Police. The National Zoological Park Police, which consists of 50 full-time and part-time officers, has concurrent jurisdiction over the zoo with the U.S. Park Police and the Washington, DC, Metropolitan Police Department.

★ Web site: http://nationalzoo.si.edu/

★ Job vacancies and internships: http://nationalzoo.si.edu/Audiences/JobSeekers/

★ Volunteer information: http://nationalzoo.si.edu/Support/Volunteer/default.cfm

★ Strategic plan: http://nationalzoo.si.edu/AboutUs/FuturePlans/StrategicPlan.pdf

Smithsonian Institution Libraries include more than one million volumes (among them 40,000 rare books) with strengths in natural history, art, science, humanities, and museology. Many volumes are available through interlibrary loan.

★ Web site: http://www.sil.si.edu/

Other Smithsonian Agencies

Anacostia Community Museum

http://anacostia.si.edu/

Architectural History and Historic Preservation Division

http://www.si.edu/oahp/

Center for Folk Life and Cultural Heritage

http://www.folklife.si.edu

Cooper-Hewitt National Design Museum

http://cooperhewitt.org/

Freer Gallery of Art and Arthur M. Sackler Gallery

http://www.asia.si.edu

Hirshhorn Museum and Sculpture Garden

http://www.hirshhorn.si.edu

Horticulture Services Division

http://www.gardens.si.edu/

Museum Conservation Institute

http://www.si.edu/mci/

National Museum of African American History and Culture

http://www.nmaahc.si.edu/

National Museum of African Art

http://www.nmafa.si.edu

National Museum of the American Indian

http://www.nmai.si.edu

National Portrait Gallery

http://www.npg.si.edu

National Postal Museum

http://postalmuseum.si.edu/

Office of Exhibits Central

http://oecexhibits.si.edu/

Office of International Relations

http://www.si.edu/intrel/

Scientific Diving Program

http://www.si.edu/dive/

Smithsonian American Art Museum and Renwick Gallery

http://americanart.si.edu/

Smithsonian Astrophysical Observatory

http://sao-www.harvard.edu/sao/

Smithsonian Environmental Research Center

http://www.serc.si.edu/

Smithsonian Institution Archives

http://siarchives.si.edu/

Smithsonian Institution Traveling Exhibition Service

http://www.sites.si.edu/

Smithsonian Marine Station

http://www.sms.si.edu/

Smithsonian Tropical Research Institute

http://www.stri.org/

Woodrow Wilson International Center for Scholars

http://www.wilsoncenter.org

Sample Job Vacancies

Animal Keeper
Agency: National Zoological Park
Salary: $20.65 to $24.08
Location: Washington, DC

Duties: Performs a variety of duties that ensure the proper care, feeding, exhibition, and propagation of a collection of wild and exotic animals, many of which are rare and endangered. Receives, inspects, stores, prepares, and issues food and dietary supplements, forage, and bedding materials. Monitors animals for symptoms of illness, injuries, or other unusual conditions and reports observations. Connects with visitors regarding animal natural history, conservation programs, natural habitats, status of animals in the wild, care and feeding of animals, and other topics of interest. Assists professional and scientific personnel in carrying out studies of animal collections.

Qualifications: You may be assigned to any eight-hour shift. Animal keepers are essential employees and are subject to be called at any time, including weekends, holidays, and for critical or emergency situations. You may be assigned to a unit within the departments of Animal Programs, Nutrition, or Animal Health, may rotate between Animal Programs and the Commissary as part of a training program, or may be reassigned to one of the three animal care departments. Temporary duty at the Conservation Research Center in Front Royal, Virginia, may be included as part of training in specific husbandry techniques for staff whose permanent duty station is Washington, DC. Your overall experience and training must indicate that you have the minimum knowledge, skills, abilities needed to perform the duties of this position. There is no substitution of education for experience for this position.

The work requires the ability to lift and carry materials weighing up to 100 pounds. The work also requires extended periods of standing, walking, bending, and stooping. The work is performed indoors and outdoors in all weather conditions. You may be exposed to dust and to unpleasant odors and noises from the animals and to cleaning solutions and other chemicals. You must receive immunizations to guard against zoological diseases and may be subject to regular medical screening.

How you will be evaluated: The online questionnaire will evaluate your experience and/or training that address the following job elements:

★ Ability to do the work of an animal keeper (exotic, rare, and/or endangered animals) without more than normal supervision (this is the screen-out element).

★ Ability to use hand and mechanical tools used in the care of animals and constructing exhibits.

★ Ability to interpret unusual behavior, symptoms of illness, and injury of rare, exotic, and/or endangered animals and ability to record observations in writing, such as keeping records and making reports.

★ Knowledge of animal nutrition and feed materials sufficient to prepare and issue food, recommend adjustments in diets, and ensure quality of food.

★ Ability to handle rare, exotic, and/or endangered animals in a safe and nonstressful manner and ability to follow proper animal care procedures in feeding, cleaning enclosures, capturing, and transporting.

★ Knowledge of the behavior patterns of wild, exotic, and/or endangered species.

★ Ability to check purchase orders to verify accuracy of deliveries and enter data into automated records systems.

If you do not meet the screen-out element, you will be rated ineligible. If you are found eligible for this position, you will receive a final numerical rating between 70 and 100 points based on an established rating schedule. Scores are augmented by veterans' preference points. The human resources office will certify enough names from the highest ranking eligibles to permit the selecting official to consider at least three names for each vacancy. Veterans have preference and must be selected before any nonpreference candidate who is lower on the referral list unless a valid objection is sustained.

If you have not submitted a resume in the USAJOBS system and/or have not answered all of the vacancy questions, you will not be considered for this position. Note: Your responses must be substantiated by the resume submitted. If a determination is made that in responding to the vacancy questions you have rated yourself higher than is evident in your resume, your score/status may be adjusted by a human resources specialist.

Audiovisual Operator

Agency: The Smithsonian Institution
Salary: $16.62 to $19.40
Location: Washington, DC

Who may be considered: All qualified candidates may apply including individuals with a disability. This is an open continuous announcement. When you apply, your resume will be active in our candidate inventory for 90 days. If you would like to be considered after 90 days, you must update and resubmit your application for reconsideration.

Attention: Due to the high volume of applications received, we are unable to confirm receipt of online application packages, including faxed documentation. Automated e-mail messages are proof of receipt for all application materials.

Duties: Performs A/V installation, design, support, consultation on repair, transportation, and technical operation services. Performs a variety of functions relative to audiovisual operations, including sound system design, audiovisual equipment exhibit installation and support, consultation, repair, contractor selection and monitoring, equipment transportation, and operation.

Qualifications: Your overall experience and training must indicate that you have the minimum knowledge, skills, and abilities needed to perform the duties of this position. There is no substitution of education for experience for this position. You must be able to identify sounds above 80 decibels; distinguish colors and shades of colors; move, lift, and transport equipment weighing up to 100 pounds (often up several flights of stairs) to projection booths and to facilities on and off the National Mall; endure long periods of standing; and climb ladders.

How you will be evaluated: Selection will be made from among those candidates who demonstrate the highest potential to perform work as determined by ratings on the following elements:

★ Ability to do the work of the position without more than normal supervision. This includes setting up, operating, and adjusting one or more of the following: a portable public address system with separate audio mixer, equalization, amplifier, and four speakers on stands; large-screen video playback or computer video connection to adjust registration on a CRT-based video data/video projector; digital video recording; projector; or 16 mm and 35 mm silent and sound motion picture projectors and screens. (This is the screen-out element. Applicants who are not rated satisfactory or potentially satisfactory on the screen-out element will not be rated on the remaining elements.)

★ Knowledge of related work practices (includes keeping things neat, clean, and in order).

★ Knowledge of technical practices (theoretical, precise, artistic).

★ Knowledge of materials used in the audiovisual operator trade.

★ Ability to operate equipment with dexterity and safety.

Other information: A background investigation is required for appointment. If you make a false statement in any part of your application, you may not be hired and/or you may be terminated after you begin work. All employees are required to participate in direct deposit/electronic funds transfer for salary payments. Relocation expenses will not be paid.

Visitor Services Assistant
Agency: National Museum of the American Indian
Salary: $33,269 to $43,251
Location: Washington, DC

Duties: The visitor services assistant is responsible for facilitating visitation to the National Museum of the American Indian by creating a welcoming environment for all visitors to the museum. He/she will direct line queues both inside and outside the museum; provide visitor orientation prior to entry; answer questions concerning the museum regarding exhibits, education, membership, and location of shops and restrooms; answer questions about the surrounding area including directions to other museums and parking; and distribute museum guides, brochures, and maps. The incumbent will also facilitate access to the museum's two theaters; answer questions; introduce films; maintain attendance records; and provide crowd control. The incumbent is expected to exercise appropriate sensitivity with respect to the museum's exhibits, programs, and Native American points of view in performing his/her duties.

Qualifications: Applicants must have qualifying education, experience, or a combination of education and experience. Qualifying education is the successful completion of education four years above the high school level in any field for which high school graduation or the equivalent is the normal prerequisite. This education must have been obtained in an accredited business, secretarial, or technical school, junior college, college, or university. Qualifying experience is one year of specialized experience (federal or other) that is equivalent to at least the GS-4 grade level in the federal government, performing the following duties: greeting customers, answering phones, and responding to visitor inquiries while displaying courtesy, tact, and politeness to others; dealing with difficult, hostile, or distressed customers; and working with culturally diverse groups. If you have less than the four years of education above the high school level and less than the amount of required experience, but have a combination of the type of education described and the type of experience described, you may meet the minimum requirements for the position.

What to expect next: When you apply for this announcement, your resume will be maintained in our candidate inventory and eligible applicants will be considered for vacancies that occur during the open period of this announcement. Only the highly qualified candidates from the current inventory of applicants will be referred to the selecting official for further consideration. You will receive an e-mail notifying you if you are eligible for further consideration under this announcement.

Please note that during the open announcement period, qualified applicants will be removed from the candidate inventory for this position if any of the following apply: if an applicant's resume expires in STARS, the Smithsonian's Automated Staffing System, and is not reactivated by the applicant within 60 days; if an applicant is selected from this announcement and accepts a position offered; if an applicant is selected from this announcement and declines a position offered; or if an applicant submits a written request to remove his/her application from consideration for this announcement.

Visual Information Specialist (Web Designer)
Agency: National Air and Space Museum
Salary: $60,989 to $79,280
Location: Washington, DC

Duties: Design, implement, and maintain overall graphic and visual interface design for the National Air and Space Museum Web site, computer interactives, and electronic displays. Create basic animation, effects, and interactions in Flash and work with programmer to integrate dynamic data into Flash applications. Optimize visual materials for broadest accessibility and ensure they are efficiently integrated into Web site or computer-based interactives while conforming to the museum guidelines, standards, and review procedures. Research design tools, techniques, and best practices to enhance museum Web presence, interactives, electronic displays, and other forms of electronic outreach. Work with museum staff to coordinate/prepare visual assets/designs and maintain and communicate visual presentation standards and best practices.

Qualifications: For Grade 11, you must have one year of specialized experience (federal or other) that is equivalent to at least the GS-9 grade level in the federal government performing the following duties: designing professional Web/new media graphics and visual interface (UI) for public Web site(s) utilizing Adobe software. Please fax in specific URLs to publicly accessible web sites that you have designed and describe your level of involvement in their design.

Alternatively, you can have a Ph.D. or equivalent doctoral degree in commercial art, fine arts, art history, industrial design, architecture, drafting, interior design, photography, visual communication, or other related fields or three full years of progressively higher level graduate education leading to such a degree. Such education must demonstrate the knowledge, skills, and abilities necessary to do the work. One academic year of graduate education is considered to be the number of credit hours that your graduate school has determined to represent one academic year of study. Such study may have been performed on a full-time or part-time basis. If you cannot obtain your graduate school's definition of one year of graduate study, 18 semester hours (or 27 quarter hours) should be considered as satisfying the requirement for one year of full-time graduate study.

If you have less than the full amount of education and less than the amount of experience described, but have a combination of the type of education and the type of experience described, you may meet the minimum requirements for the position. The total percentage of education and experience must equal at least 100 percent to qualify under this provision.

Credit will be given for appropriate unpaid work on the same basis as for paid experience. Part-time experience will be credited on the basis of time actually spent in appropriate activities. To receive credit for such experience, you must indicate clearly the nature of the duties and responsibilities in each position held and the average number of hours per week spent in such employment.

Are you using your education to qualify? You must provide transcripts or other documentation to support your educational claims.

How to apply: You must apply for this position online. Do not submit paper applications/resumes by mail, e-mail, or fax. You will be required to create an account and build a resume on www.usajobs.gov unless you previously established an account. You will also be asked to respond to assessment questions online.

Social Security Administration

6401 Security Boulevard
Baltimore, MD 21235-7775
800-772-1213 (toll-free)
410-965-1234

★ Web site: http://www.ssa.gov/

★ Job vacancies: http://jobsearch.usajobs.opm.gov/a9ssajob.asp

★ Student employment: http://www.ssa.gov/careers/students&grads.htm

★ How to apply: http://www.ssa.gov/careers/application.htm

★ Recruiting events: http://www.ssa.gov/careers/recruiting.htm

★ Human resources offices: http://www.ssa.gov/careers/nearestyou.htm

★ Career information: http://www.ssa.gov/careers/

★ Strategic plan: http://www.ssa.gov/asp/

The Social Security Administration (SSA) administers the country's social insurance programs, including retirement, survivors, and disability insurance programs, as well as the Supplemental Security Income program for people who are aged, blind, or disabled. SSA is responsible for studying the problems of poverty and economic insecurity among Americans and making recommendations on effective methods for solving these problems through social insurance. By agreement with the Department of Labor, SSA is involved in certain aspects of the administration of the black lung benefits provisions. SSA also assigns Social Security numbers to U.S. citizens and maintains earnings records for workers.

In addition to its headquarters in Baltimore, Maryland, SSA has more than 1,260 field offices, 140 hearing offices, 35 teleservice centers, 7 program service centers, and 10 regional offices all over the country. It employs more than 62,500 people in a variety of different areas. Examples of these include public contact positions (claims representative, claims authorizer, benefit authorizer, service representative, and teleservice representatives), information technology (software development, network services, systems analysis, Web development, and data management), law (staff attorneys, attorney-advisors, administrative law judges, and attorney-examiners), law enforcement (criminal investigators), and management/administrative and support positions (management analysts, budget analysts, human resource specialists, program analysts, staff assistants).

Selected SSA Agencies

The **Office of Disability Adjudication and Review** holds hearings and issues decisions as part of SSA's process for determining whether a person may receive benefits. Administrative Law Judges (ALJs) conduct hearings and issue decisions. The Appeals Council considers appeals from hearing decisions and acts as the final level of administrative review for the Social Security Administration.

★ Web site: http://www.ssa.gov/appeals/about_odar.html

★ Legal careers: http://www.ssa.gov/careers/legalcareers.htm

The **Social Security Advisory Board** (SSAB) is an independent, bipartisan board that advises the president, the Congress, and the commissioner of Social Security on matters related to the Social Security and Supplemental Security Income programs.

★ Web site: http://www.ssab.gov/

Other SSA Agencies

Office of Disability Programs

http://www.ssa.gov/disability/

Office of Employment Support Programs

http://www.ssa.gov/work/

Office of International Programs

http://www.ssa.gov/international/

Office of Program Development and Research

http://www.ssa.gov/disabilityresearch/

Office of the Chief Actuary

http://www.ssa.gov/OACT/

Sample Job Vacancies

Carpenter
Agency: Office of Facilities Management
Salary: $22.37 to $26.20/hour
Location: Woodlawn, Maryland

Job summary: In this important support position, you will perform a variety of carpentry work relating to alteration, repair, and maintenance of buildings and structures and the fabrication, repair, and maintenance of wooden or related products. This position is a mission-critical position. Employees will be required to be on call 24 hours a day. In the event of emergencies, employees may be called to work after hours and on weekends and holidays.

Duties: Plans and lays out work from blueprints, sketches, work orders, or oral instructions. Erects, alters, repairs, and/or removes partitions of wood, glass, metal, plastic, sheetrock, acoustical title, or related materials. Repairs or replaces wood or metal window framing, doors, baseboards, moldings, transoms, and panels. May duplicate or make new keys to fit the locks by code, impression, or duplicating machine. May set up coding systems involving varying types of locks and keyways. Installs window glass in window frames. Removes and replaces damaged sections of wood or tile flooring and stairways. Lays masonite, asphalt, rubber title, and inlaid linoleum. Sharpens saws and saw blades and other tools. Occasionally repairs office furniture and constructs bulletin boards and picture frames.

Qualifications: To qualify, you must demonstrate that you possess the skills and knowledge required to perform the duties of the position without more than normal supervision. Your qualifications will be evaluated on the basis of your level of knowledge, skill, or ability in the following specific elements:

★ Knowledge of carpentry equipment

★ Ability to use carpentry prints and drawings

★ Ability to follow directions in a carpentry shop

★ Knowledge of all materials used in carpentry

How you will be evaluated: Your resume and supporting documentation will be compared to your responses to the occupational questionnaire. The questionnaire is designed to capture the desired knowledge, skills, and abilities for this position. The evaluation you receive is based on your responses to the questionnaire and is a measure of the degree to which your background matches the knowledge, skills, and abilities required of this position. If you are eligible for veterans' preference, you will be given preference based on the documentation you submit.

Please ensure you answer all questions and follow all instructions carefully. Errors or omissions may affect your evaluation. When answering the questionnaire, remember that your experience and education are subject to verification by investigation. You may be asked to provide specific examples or documentation of experience or education as proof to support your answers, or you may be required to verify a response by a practical demonstration of your claimed ability to perform a task. If your application does not support your responses to the questionnaire, or if you are not able to provide verifying documentation on request, it may affect your evaluation or result in your name being removed from further consideration.

Case Technician (Legal Assistant)
Agency: Office of Disability Adjudication and Review
Salary: $27,504 to $34,300
Location: Harrisburg, Pennsylvania

Duties: Legal assistants (case technicians) provide a full range of clerical and technical support of administrative law judges and other technical/professional positions in the hearing office in processing cases filed under Titles II, XVI, and XVIII of the Social Security Act. These assistants review and analyze a wide variety of medical and legal documentation; request consultative examinations and medical records; schedule cases for hearings, which includes arranging for space, travel, and reimbursement; compose correspondence; examine and process attorney fees; respond to a wide range of inquiries from the public, legal and judicial officials, and federal, state, and local officials relating to the legal processing of the hearings and appeals program; maintain, review, and utilize a variety of data systems and use personal computers for word processing functions (typing decisions, data input, case tracking systems, and so on); and may assist the hearing office systems administrator in training support staff in the use of computers.

Qualifications: The GS-4 level requires one year of general experience. This experience must have been progressively responsible clerical, office, or other work that indicates the ability to acquire the knowledge and skills needed to perform the duties of this position. Examples of positions where such experience could be gained include a general office assistant or clerk, data entry clerk, file clerk, receptionist, operator, or student aide.

The GS-5 level requires one year of specialized experience equivalent to the GS-4 level. Specialized experience includes knowledge of legal, medical, and technical terminology; skill in effectively communicating policy and procedural matters to a wide range of individuals; and knowledge of office automation software and processing procedures in order to produce routine letters and reports. Examples of positions where such experience could be gained include secretary or clerical assistant in a medical or legal office or a hearing reporter.

The GS-6 level requires one year of specialized experience equivalent to the GS-5 level. Specialized experience includes demonstrated knowledge of legal, medical, and technical terminology; skill in effectively communicating medical or legal policy and procedural matters to a wide range of individuals; and knowledge of office automation software and processing procedures in order to develop complex letters and reports. Examples of positions where such experience could be gained include medical or legal secretary.

If you have no general or specialized experience, you may be able to qualify for this position based solely on your education. For GS-4, two years of education beyond the high school level can be substituted for the GS-4 general experience requirements. For GS-5, completion of a four-year degree from an accredited college or university can be substituted for the GS-5 specialized experience requirements. (Only the junior and senior years of coursework may be substituted for specialized experience).

How to apply: Applying for this position requires three steps:

1. Submission of a resume.

2. Completion of the occupational questionnaire.

3. Submission of any supporting documentation, such as a DD-214, Veterans Administration letter, or educational transcripts.

First, you will be required to complete and submit a USAJOBS resume. After you have submitted the resume, you will enter Application Manager. If you have an Application Manager account, you will be prompted to log in. If not, you may create an account and log in or select the option to apply for a job without using an account. After you enter the vacancy identification number in the appropriate box, you will be directed to the questionnaire. Please complete all parts of the assessment questionnaire. After you submit the assessment questionnaire, you will have the opportunity to upload any supporting documents or additional resume items. If you complete all steps successfully, an automated receipt will be sent to your e-mail account.

Electronic applications (entire application package) must be completely received by midnight Eastern Standard Time on the closing date of the announcement. Due to our security procedures, we will not accept any applications submitted via e-mail. Applications received in this manner will be considered ineligible. E-mail addresses are listed only for inquiries about the position or the application process. In order to be considered, applicants must apply online or submit a hard copy via fax.

Contact Representative (Teleservice Representative)
Agency: Social Security Administration
Salary: $32,718 to $40,527
Location: Auburn, Washington

Duties: Contact representatives (teleservice representatives) provide assistance to the public, via telephone, answering a wide variety of questions by interviewing individuals, investigating situations, and resolving problems. Using multiple computer systems and applications, they access, interpret, and apply technical information, including a variety of policies, procedures, laws, and regulations, to resolve issues related to Social Security programs. Contact representatives (teleservice representatives) utilize a comprehensive knowledge of SSA programs, as well as related federal and state programs, to perform independent analysis and problem solving. Strong computer navigation skills are a necessity because a majority of the work is completed by utilizing multiple computer systems and applications in order to successfully meet customer needs.

Qualifications: For the GS-5 level, you must have 52 weeks of specialized experience equivalent to the GS-4 level. Specialized experience at this level is experience providing straightforward factual information that involves basic interpretation and application of policies and guidelines related to a complex technical or regulatory program. You can substitute successful completion of a four-year course of study (120 semester hours or 180 quarter hours) leading towards a bachelor's degree or completion of a bachelor's degree from an accredited college or university for this experience. You also can combine specialized experience and education to meet the minimum qualification requirements for the position at the GS-5 grade level. You would need to have a combination of junior and/or senior level college courses and a portion of the specialized experience that when prorated and combined equal 100 percent of the requirement for qualifying. For example, six months of specialized experience (50 percent) and completion of the junior year of college (50 percent).

For the GS-6 level, you must have 52 weeks of specialized experience equivalent to the GS-5 level. Specialized experience at this level is experience in applying and interpreting complex, technical, or regulatory laws, rules, regulations, or written guidelines and explaining these requirements to a variety of individuals. For the GS-7 level, you must have 52 weeks of specialized experience equivalent to the GS-6 level. Specialized experience at this level is experience interpreting, applying and explaining complex laws, regulations, and written guidelines (for example, federal, state, or county laws or private sector equivalent) in order to resolve problems and provide advice/guidance about program policies, benefits, or entitlements. There is no substitution of education for the GS-6 or GS-7 grade levels.

Note: Part-time work is prorated in crediting experience (for example, if you work 20 hours per week for a 12-month period, you will be credited with 6 months of experience). Your resume must indicate both a beginning and ending date and the number of hours worked per week for each position you've held. Your beginning and ending dates must include a month and year, and you should not use a range of hours to indicate the number of hours per week you worked.

After basic eligibility determination, applicants will be referred to management to undergo a telephone assessment interview. Applicants must pass this assessment in order to be found fully qualified for this position and receive further consideration for selection. The interview will cover typical situations that might be encountered on the job. Candidates must demonstrate qualities such as clarity of speech, ability to listen, ability to establish confidence and put others at ease, and the ability to organize and express thoughts clearly. Candidates must also demonstrate the ability to read, interpret, and apply written material. If you do not pass the telephone assessment interview, you will not qualify for the job. If you have previously taken and passed the telephone assessment interview, please submit a copy of your notice as verification.

How you will be evaluated: The following knowledge, skills, and abilities (KSAs) are necessary to perform the duties of the position:

★ Ability to communicate orally with individuals from various socio-economic backgrounds and intellectual levels in order to explain and provide information on SSA laws, rules, regulations, and procedures and to obtain information from claimants/third parties in order to determine benefits and entitlements

★ Ability to interpret and apply laws, regulations, and operating procedures in order to determine eligibility for SSA program entitlements and continuing eligibility, to provide information to claimants, and to make appropriate referrals

★ Ability to process work in a computer environment in order to meet customer needs

★ Ability to use reasoning to analyze issues in order to make decisions and resolve problems

★ Ability to organize, prioritize, and process a large volume of work within established deadlines

Your resume and supporting documentation will be compared to your responses to the occupational questionnaire. The questionnaire is designed to capture the desired KSAs for this position. The evaluation you receive is based on your responses to the questionnaire and is a measure of the degree to which your background matches the KSAs required of this position.

State Justice Institute

1650 King Street, Suite 600
Alexandria, VA 22314
703-684-6100

★ Web site: http://www.statejustice.org/

The State Justice Institute is a private, nonprofit corporation that furthers the development and improvement of judicial administration in the state courts. The institute is supervised by a board of directors consisting of 11 members appointed by the president with the advice and consent of the Senate.

Tennessee Valley Authority

400 West Summit Hill Drive
Knoxville, TN 37902-1499
865-632-2101
202-898-2999

★ Web site: http://www.tva.gov/

★ Job vacancies: https://jobs.tva.com/pljb/tva/external/applicant/index.jsp

★ Internships and co-ops: http://www.tva.com/employment/intern_coop.htm

★ Operations and maintenance training programs: http://www.tva.com/employment/ops_maint/index.htm

★ Career information: http://www.tva.gov/employment/

★ Strategic plan: http://www.tva.gov/abouttva/pdf/gpra2005.pdf

The Tennessee Valley Authority (TVA) conducts a unified program of resource development for the advancement of economic growth in the Tennessee Valley region. The authority's program of activities includes flood control, navigation, electric power production and transmission, recreation improvement, water supply, water quality, environmental stewardship, and economic development. TVA is a wholly owned government corporation responsible for managing the nation's fifth-largest river system and the area's resources, working to protect the environment through clean air and water initiatives and fostering a healthy economy in the Tennessee Valley. The TVA is America's largest public power company, with 31,658 megawatts of dependable generating capacity spread over 80,000 square miles in seven southeastern states and 12,000 employees. TVA's power facilities include 11 fossil (coal-fired) plants, 29 hydroelectric dams, three nuclear plants, six combustion turbine plants, a pumped-storage facility, and 18 green power sites that employ wind turbines, methane gas, and solar panels and 17,000 miles of transmission lines. Through 158 locally owned distributors, TVA provides power to nearly 8.6 million residents in the Tennessee Valley. It operates a national laboratory for environmental research that focuses on the cleanup and protection of land, air, and water resources. It also participates in economic and community development programs by providing technical assistance in industrial development, waste management, tourism promotion, and community preparedness.

Sample Job Vacancies

Business Support Rep Intern
Agency: Tennessee Valley Authority
Salary: Competitive
Location: Nashville, Tennessee

Job summary: This role will support internal and external communication and marketing objectives and further define the processes needed to make TVA more competitive. The primary responsibility of this role is to gather data and documents from multiple sources in multiple departments in the agency and compile in one electronic location. Other administrative responsibilities will apply. Some regional travel will apply.

Duties: Typical duties may include the performance of a variety of day-to-day transactions independently within assigned functional area(s). Ensure proper classification, storage, retention, and disposal of organizational records. Serve as organizational representative/contact for office and personal communication equipment (copiers, fax machines, pagers, cellular phones, telecommunications equipment, and so on). Ensure/coordinate entry of required data/schedules into various information and business reporting systems. Format and retrieve standard and nonstandard reports from various business systems. Identify and resolve discrepancies found in data used to make business decisions. Perform procurement and materials management functions as required by organization including following contractual agreements and requisitioning and receiving goods and services. Serve as the coordination point for activities supporting the full range of work in assigned functional areas. Provide orientation or training in assigned functional areas.

Qualifications: You must be enrolled as a junior or senior full-time student in an accredited institution with studies toward a B.S. degree in business, computer science, and/or engineering. You must have the computer skills necessary to complete assigned tasks using programs in the Microsoft Office Suite such as Excel, PowerPoint, and Word. Web design experience also could be useful in this role.

You also need to have the following skills and proficiencies:

★ Knowledge of business systems, procedures, and practices for assigned functional areas

★ Ability to select, apply, and explain procedures for assigned functional areas

★ Knowledge of key organization contacts for coordination of multifunctional areas

★ Ability to organize and plan effectively

★ Ability to meet deadlines

★ Ability to access, retrieve, and format data using various business systems and produce standard and nonstandard reports

How to apply: Applying for a job is a three-step process:

1. Create an account on the TVA site. Creating an account is TVA's way of collecting information such as your resume and contact information.

2. Submit your resume online.

3. Apply for each job that is of interest to you.

Electrical Engineer
Agency: Tennessee Valley Authority
Salary: Competitive
Location: Spring City, Tennessee

Duties: Plans, schedules, conducts, or coordinates detailed phases of electrical engineering work in a part of a major project or in a total project of moderate scope. Performs work that involves conventional electrical engineering practice but may include a variety of complex features, such as conflicting design requirements, unsuitability of conventional materials, and difficult coordination requirements. As a fully competent electrical engineer in all conventional experience aspects of the subject matter of the functional area of the assignments, plans and conducts work requiring judgment in the independent evaluation, selection, and substantial adaptation and modification of standard techniques, procedures, and criteria. Devises new approaches to problems encountered. Provides procurement and field engineering, including walk downs, modifications/maintenance, and testing support. May supervise or coordinate the work of multidiscipline engineers, drafters, technicians, and others who assist in specific assignments.

Qualifications: Bachelor's degree in electrical engineering or other related engineering degrees from an accredited curriculum, plus appropriate continuing education. Minimum of four years' experience in a power plant or industrial environment. Licensed professional engineer is desirable. Membership in professional and technical societies is desirable. Must be able to obtain and maintain unescorted nuclear plant access and S-3 and S-4 medical qualifications when applicable. Must be able and willing to assume "on-call" rotational assignments that may include 24 hour-a-day, 7 day-a-week availability. Must be willing and medically able to work rotating shifts and maximum over-time permitted by NPG procedures during peak periods. Must be able and willing to travel to plant locations as required when performing assigned tasks and, as necessary, to be temporarily assigned to a field location. Must have demonstrated proficiency in electrical engineering as evidenced by completion of post-graduate engineering education and experience.

United Nations

First Avenue at 46th Street
New York, New York 10017
212-963-1234

★ Web site: http://www.un.org

★ Job vacancies: https://jobs.un.org/Galaxy/Release3/vacancy/vacancy.aspx?lang=1200

★ Internships: http://www.un.org/Depts/OHRM/sds/internsh/index.htm

★ Volunteer information: http://www.unv.org/

★ Career information: https://jobs.un.org/Galaxy/Release3/VacancyFM/VacancyFM.aspx?lang=1200

The United Nations (UN) provides the means to help resolve international conflicts and formulate policies. It maintains international peace and security; develops friendly relations among nations; achieves international cooperation in solving international problems of an economic, social, cul-tural, or humanitarian character and in promoting respect for human rights. The UN is a center for harmonizing the actions of nations in the attainment of these common ends. The principal organs of the UN are the General Assembly, the Security Council, the Economic and Social Council, the Trusteeship Council, the International Court of Justice, and the Secretariat.

At the UN, all the member states—large and small, rich and poor, with differing political views and social systems—have a voice and a vote in this process. The UN consists of 192 member states, of which 51 are founding members. All UN member states are represented in the General Assembly, the "parliament of nations," which meets to consider the world's most pressing problems. Each member state has one vote. The assembly cannot force action by any state, but its recommendations are an important indication of world opinion and represent the moral authority of the community of nations.

The Security Council has primary responsibility for maintaining international peace and security. The council may convene at any time, whenever peace is threatened. There are 15 council mem-bers. Five of these (China, France, the Russian Federation, the United Kingdom, and the United States) are permanent members. The other 10 are elected by the General Assembly for two-year terms. Decisions of the council require nine yes votes. The council can take measures to enforce its decisions, such as imposing economic sanctions or an arms embargo. On rare occasions, the council has authorized member states to use "all necessary means," including collective military action, to see that its decisions are carried out. Under the charter, all member states are obligated to carry out the council's decisions.

The Economic and Social Council, under the overall authority of the General Assembly, coordinates the economic and social work of the United Nations and the UN family of organizations. The council has 54 members, elected by the General Assembly for three-year terms. The council's subsidiary bodies meet regularly and report back to it. The Commission on Human Rights, for example, monitors the observance of human rights throughout the world. Other bodies focus on such issues as social development, the status of women, crime prevention, narcotic drugs, and environmental protection. Five regional commissions promote economic development and cooperation in their respective regions.

The Trusteeship Council was established to provide international supervision for 11 trust territories administered by seven member states and ensure that adequate steps were taken to prepare the territories for self-government or independence. By 1994, all trust territories had attained self-government or independence. Its work completed, the Trusteeship Council now consists of the five permanent members of the Security Council. It has amended its rules of procedure to allow it to meet as and when the occasion may require.

The International Court of Justice, also known as the World Court, is the main judicial organ of the UN. Consisting of 15 judges elected jointly by the General Assembly and the Security Council, the court decides disputes between countries. Participation by states in a proceeding is voluntary, but if a state agrees to participate, it is obligated to comply with the court's decision. The court also provides advisory opinions to the General Assembly and the Security Council upon request. The court is located in The Hague in The Netherlands.

The Secretariat carries out the substantive and administrative work of the UN as directed by the General Assembly, the Security Council, and the other organizations. At its head is the secretary-general, who provides overall administrative guidance. The Secretariat consists of departments and offices with a total staff of some 8,900 under the regular budget and a nearly equal number under special funding. They are drawn from some 170 countries. Duty stations include UN Headquarters in New York, as well as UN offices in Geneva, Vienna, Nairobi, and other locations.

The International Monetary Fund, the World Bank, and 12 other independent organizations known as "specialized agencies" are linked to the UN through cooperative agreements. These agencies, among them the World Health Organization and the International Civil Aviation Organization, are autonomous bodies created by intergovernmental agreement. They have wide-ranging international responsibilities in the economic, social, cultural, educational, health, and related fields. Some of them, such as the International Labor Organization and the Universal Postal Union, are older than the UN itself.

In addition, a number of UN offices, programs, and funds (such as the Office of the UN High Commissioner for Refugees [UNHCR], the UN Development Program [UNDP], and the UN Children's Fund [UNICEF]) work to improve the economic and social condition of people around the world. They report to the General Assembly or the Economic and Social Council.

All these organizations have their own governing bodies, budgets, and secretariats. Together with the United Nations, they are known as the UN family or the UN system. Together, they provide technical assistance and other forms of practical help in virtually all economic and social areas.

Selected UN Programs and Funds

The **United Nations Children's Fund** (UNICEF) advocates for the protection of children's rights to help meet their basic needs and help them reach their full potential. It is committed to ensuring special protection for the most disadvantaged children, victims of war, disasters, extreme poverty, all forms of violence, and exploitation, and those with disabilities and aims, through its country programs, to promote the equal rights of women and girls and to support their full participation in the political, social, and economic development of their communities. UNICEF works for the benefit of the world's children in five broad areas: child protection, girls' education, HIV/AIDS prevention and care, immunization, and early childhood health and education.

★ Web site: http://www.unicef.org

★ Job vacancies: http://www.unicef.org/about/employ/index_currentvacancies.html

★ Internships: http://www.unicef.org/about/employ/index_internship.html

★ Volunteer information: http://www.unicef.org/about/employ/index_volunteers.html

★ Young professional program: http://www.unicef.org/about/employ/index_ypp.html

★ How to apply: http://www.unicef.org/about/employ/index_apply.html

★ Employment qualifications: http://www.unicef.org/about/employ/index_qualifications.html

★ Career information: http://www.unicef.org/about/employ/index_careers.html

The concerns of developing countries over the international market, multinational corporations, and great disparity between developed nations and developing nations led to the creation of the **United Nations Conference on Trade and Development** (UNCTAD). The UNCTAD aims to integrate developing countries into the world economy. It performs research, policy analysis, and data collection; provides technical assistance to developing countries; and serves as a forum for intergovernmental discussions related to trade and development. The UNCTAD is located in Switzerland and has 400 staff members and an annual regular budget of approximately $50 million, with $25 million of extrabudgetary technical assistance funds.

★ Web site: http://www.unctad.org/

★ Job vacancies: http://www.unctad.org/Templates/Page.asp?intItemID=1652&lang=1

★ Internships: http://www.unctad.org/Templates/Page.asp?intItemID=2106&lang=1

The mission of the **Office of the United Nations High Commissioner for Human Rights** (OHCHR) is to promote and protect the human rights guaranteed under international law. OHCHR alerts governments and the world community to the daily reality that these standards are too often ignored or unfulfilled and seeks to be a voice for the victims of human rights violations everywhere. OHCHR presses the international community to take the steps that can prevent violations, including support for the right to economic development. OHCHR is located in Switzerland and has 1,000 Geneva-based staff and a budget of $120 million.

★ Web site: http://www.ohchr.org/english/

★ Job vacancies: http://www.ohchr.org/EN/AboutUs/Pages/WorkStudyOpportunities.aspx

★ Strategic plan: http://www.ohchr.org/Documents/Press/SMP2008-2009.pdf

The **United Nations High Commissioner for Refugees** (UNHCR) protects and supports refugees at the request of a government or the UN itself and assists in their voluntary repatriation, local integration, or resettlement to a third country. UNHCR strives to ensure that everyone can exercise the right to seek asylum and find safe refuge in another state. In more than five decades, the agency has helped an estimated 50 million people restart their lives. Today, a staff of around 6,300 people in more than 110 countries continues to help some 32.9 million persons.

★ Web site: http://www.unhcr.org/cgi-bin/texis/vtx/home

★ Job vacancies: http://www.unhcr.org/admin/3ba1d4794.html

★ Internships: http://www.unhcr.org/admin/3b8a31f94.html

★ Junior professional officer program: http://www.unhcr.org/admin/ADMIN/484e8d364.pdf

★ How to apply: http://www.unhcr.org/admin/ADMIN/3bb43985a.html

★ Career information: http://www.unhcr.org/admin/3ba1bdcb7.html

★ Strategic plan: http://www.unhcr.org/publ/PUBL/4889a2372.pdf

UN-HABITAT, the **United Nations Human Settlements Program,** promotes socially and environmentally sustainable towns and cities with the goal of providing adequate shelter for all. UN-HABITAT's programs help policy-makers and local communities address human settlement and urban issues and find workable, lasting solutions. It's headquartered at the UN office in Nairobi, Kenya.

★ Web site: http://www.unchs.org/

★ Job vacancies: http://www.unhabitat.org/list.asp?typeid=12&catid=4

★ Internships: http://www.unon.org/; link to Internship, bottom of page

The **United Nations Research Institute for Social Development** (UNRISD) is an autonomous UN agency that researches contemporary problems affecting global trends in social development. UNRISD research has been guided by two core values: that every human being has a right to a decent livelihood and that all people should be allowed to participate on equal terms in decisions that affect their lives. The challenge for research is not only to reinforce and help operationalize these values, but also to expose the extent to which they are ignored.

UNRISD is a small organization with around 20 full time staff members (professional and administrative), based in Geneva. Members of professional staff are supported by approximately 6–10 research analysts per year who are recruited for a limited period of time, depending on the exigencies of any given project at any given time.

★ Web site: http://www.unrisd.org/

★ Job vacancies: http://www.unrisd.org/; link to About UNRISD, The Institute & Vacancies, Working at UNRISD.

Other UN Entities

Joint United Nations Program on HIV/AIDS

http://www.unaids.org/en/

United Nations Capital Development Fund

http://www.uncdf.org/english/index.php

United Nations Democracy Fund

http://www.un.org/democracyfund/index.htm

United Nations Development Fund for Women

http://www.unifem.org/

United Nations Development Program

http://www.undp.org/

United Nations Environment Program

http://www.unep.org/

United Nations Institute for Disarmament Research

http://www.unidir.org/

United Nations Institute for Training and Research

http://www.unitar.org/

United Nations International Research and Training Institute for the Advancement of Women

http://www.un-instraw.org/

United Nations Interregional Crime and Justice Research Institute

http://www.unicri.it/

United Nations Office for Partnerships

http://www.un.org/partnerships/

United Nations Office for Project Services

http://www.unops.org/

United Nations Office on Drugs and Crime

http://www.unodc.org/

United Nations Population Fund

http://www.unfpa.org/

United Nations Relief and Works Agency for Palestine Refugees in the Near East

http://www.un.org/unrwa/

United Nations System Staff College

http://www.unssc.org/web/

United Nations University

http://www.unu.edu/

World Food Program

http://www.wfp.org/

Sample Job Vacancies

Administrative Officer
Agency: Office of Central Support Services
Salary: $89,982 to $118,209
Location: New York, New York

Duties: The incumbent acts as the team leader of the General Administration Team. He or she will manage the staff and activities of the team, which includes registry operation, bid openings, file and record management, and data entry for management of various reporting system and other administrative tasks. He or she will also administer the division's requirements for communication equipment and service, office equipment, service and supplies, and office space. The incumbent provides assistance in the management of financial resources of the division. He or she will conduct analysis of financial resource requirements; collect data and draft proposals for the division's budgetary requirements under regular budget and support account for peacekeeping operations; monitor and control budgetary allocations through regular reviews; provide effective monitoring reports and data; identify deviations from plans and propose corrective measures; produce budget performance reports and process IMDIS data entry; and establish and maintain a set of sound policies, procedures, standards, and tools that are consistent with UN policy and practice in order to ensure proper accounting, financial management, and control. The incumbent provides assistance in the management of human resources of the division. He or she will provide assistance in classification of posts, construction of vacancy announcements, selection of candidates, and review of contractual status and future contractual arrangements of staff; review and provide assistance in processing staff travel requirements; monitor implementation of performance appraisal system and financial disclosure program; provide assistance in appointment of consultants, interns, and other experts; and develop reports on a wide range of human resource management issues. He or she will also provide advice to others on human resources administration, financial administration, and management information issues and practices.

Qualifications: Advanced university degree (master's degree or equivalent), preferably in business administration, public administration, human resources management, finance, or a related field is required. A first-level university degree with a combination of qualifying experience may be accepted in lieu of the advanced university degree. Also required is at least seven years of progressively responsible experience in administration, human resources, finance, or a related field. Experience in the United Nations system is required. Experience in and knowledge of the United Nations procurement activities are desirable. English and French are the working languages of the United Nations Secretariat. For this post, fluency in oral and written English is required; knowledge of a second official UN language is an advantage. Proficiency in the utilization of Microsoft Office (Word, Excel, and PowerPoint) and IMIS or similar financial and human resource management system is required.

The applicant should also possess the following competencies:

★ Professionalism: has knowledge of programming, budgeting, and financial management. Has knowledge of procurement policy and procedural issues; the UN system, organization, and inter-relationships; UN human resources policies, procedures, practices, regulations, and rules; and UN financial rules and regulations. Takes responsibility for incorporating gender perspectives and ensuring the equal participation of women and men in all areas of work.

★ Planning and organizing: develops clear goals that are consistent with agreed strategies; identifies priority activities and assignments; adjusts priorities as required; allocates appropriate amount of time and resources for completing work; foresees risks and allows for contingencies when planning; monitors and adjusts plans and actions as necessary; and uses time efficiently.

★ Client orientation: considers all those to whom services are provided to be clients and seeks to see things from the clients' point of view; establishes and maintains productive partnerships with clients by gaining their trust and respect; identifies clients' needs and matches them to appropriate solutions; monitors ongoing developments inside and outside the clients' environment to keep informed and anticipate problems; keeps clients informed of progress or setbacks in projects; meets timeline for delivery of products or services to client.

★ Communication: speaks and writes clearly and effectively; listens to others, correctly interprets messages from others and responds appropriately; asks questions to clarify, and exhibits interest in having two-way communication; tailors language, tone, style, and format to match audience; and demonstrates openness in sharing information and keeping people informed.

Team Assistant

Agency: Department of Management
Salary: $44,726 to $63,010
Location: New York, New York

Duties: Provide general office support services to help ensure the smooth functioning of an organizational unit. Use standard word processing package to produce a variety of routine correspondence, reports, tables, charts, and graphs in accordance with institutional standards. Proofread documents for grammatical and typographical accuracy. Maintain calendar/schedules and monitor changes and communicate relevant information to appropriate staff inside and outside the immediate work unit. Review, record, route and/or process mail or other documents; gather pertinent background material; and track and monitor follow-up action as required. Maintain files (both paper and electronic) and databases for work unit. Perform basic data entry and management functions. Perform a variety of administrative duties (leave recording, meeting organization, reservations, office supply and equipment orders). Operate and maintain a variety of office equipment in the performance of basic office functions, such as photocopier, fax machine, printer, and scanner. Perform other duties as assigned.

Qualifications: Must have high school diploma or equivalent. Must have passed the United Nations Administrative support Assessment Test (ASAT) in English at New York Headquarters. Experience in general office support or related area is desirable. English and French are the working languages of the United Nations Secretariat. For this post, fluency in oral and written English is required. Knowledge of another official UN language is desirable. Good computer skills and proficiency in standard computer applications for e-mail, word processing, spreadsheets, and Internet are desirable.

The applicant should also possess the following competencies:

★ Professionalism: shows pride in work and in achievements. Is conscientious and efficient in meeting commitments, observing deadlines, and achieving results. Is motivated by professional rather than personal concerns. Shows persistence when faced with difficult problems or challenges. Remains calm in stressful situations. Is committed to implementing the goal of gender equality by ensuring the equal participation and full involvement of women and men in all aspects of work.

★ Planning and organizing: plans own work to meet designated deadlines.

★ Communication: has good communication (spoken and written) skills, including the ability to draft routine correspondence.

★ Teamwork: demonstrates good interpersonal skills and ability to establish and maintain effective working relations with people in a multicultural, multiethnic environment with sensitivity and respect for diversity and gender.

How to apply: All applicants are strongly encouraged to apply online as soon as possible after the vacancy has been posted and well before the deadline stated in the vacancy announcement. To start the application process, applicants are required to register by opening a My UN account. Online applications will be acknowledged where an e-mail address has been provided. If you do not receive an e-mail acknowledgement within 24 hours of submission, your application may not have been received. In such cases, please check the status of your application online and resubmit the application, if necessary.

Note: The United Nations does not charge a fee at any stage of the recruitment process (application, interview meeting, processing, training, or any other fees). The United Nations does not concern itself with information on bank accounts.

United States African Development Foundation

1400 I Street NW, Suite 1000
Washington, DC 20005
202-673-3916

★ Web site: www.usadf.gov

★ Job vacancies: http://www.usadf.gov/employment.html

★ Strategic goals: http://www.usadf.gov/goals.html

The United States African Development Foundation (USADF) promotes the participation of Africans in the economic and social development of their countries. For more than 25 years, USADF has helped grassroots groups and individuals in Africa help themselves by providing the resources they need to advance their own efforts to promote economic and social development. It is an independent public corporation that enables grassroots groups to generate increased incomes through productive enterprises that expand the overall economic production capacity and increase the economic security of their families and communities. The foundation employs approximately 30 people.

United States Agency for International Development

1300 Pennsylvania Avenue NW
Washington, DC 20523-1000
202-712-0000

★ Web site: http://www.usaid.gov/

★ Job vacancies: http://www.usaid.gov/careers/gscover.html

★ Foreign service: http://www.usaid.gov/careers/fs.html

★ Fellows program: http://www.usaid.gov/careers/fellows/

★ Student internships and volunteer programs: http://www.usaid.gov/careers/studentprograms.html

★ Employment reference guide: http://www.usaid.gov/careers/guidnew.html

★ USAID mission directory: http://www.usaid.gov/locations/missiondirectory.html

★ USAID mission Web sites: http://www.usaid.gov/missions/

★ Employment FAQs: http://www.usaid.gov/careers/cpfaqn.html

★ The work of USAID: http://www.usaid.gov/our_work/

★ Career information: http://www.usaid.gov/careers/

★ Strategic plan: http://www.usaid.gov/policy/coordination/stratplan_fy07-12.html

The U.S. Agency for International Development (USAID) administers U.S. foreign economic and humanitarian assistance programs worldwide. It is the principal U.S. agency to extend assistance to countries recovering from disaster, trying to escape poverty, and engaging in democratic reforms. Under the foreign policy guidance of the secretary of state, USAID supports long-term and equitable economic growth and advances U.S. foreign policy objectives by supporting: economic growth, agriculture, and trade; global health; and democracy, conflict prevention, and humanitarian assistance. It provides assistance in five regions of the world: Sub-Saharan Africa, Asia, Latin America and the Caribbean, Europe and Eurasia, and the Middle East. USAID has field offices around the world. It works in close partnership with private voluntary organizations, indigenous organizations, universities, American businesses, international agencies, other governments, and other U.S. government agencies. USAID has working relationships with more than 3,500 American companies and more than 300 U.S.-based private voluntary organizations. USAID employs approximately 2,500 people worldwide.

Selected USAID Agencies

The **Bureau for Africa** provides assistance to 47 countries in Africa, and USAID currently has 23 bilateral missions there. In addition, three regional missions support activities in countries with a limited USAID presence. These regional missions also manage programs that aim to strengthen selected African regional institutions and organizations in order to improve their capacity to contribute to Africa's development in an environment of stability and security.

Central to USAID's assistance programs in Africa are four new initiatives: governing justly and democratically (including the women's justice and empowerment initiative), investing in people (including AIDS relief, malaria initiative, education, and Congo Basin conservation), economic growth, including an initiative to end hunger in Africa, and humanitarian assistance.

USAID provides support to African nations to strengthen democratic institutions, professionalize security forces, and promote key reforms. It provides significant funding to African countries experiencing the most serious effects of HIV/AIDS. It is expanding the malaria prevention and treatment program. USAID supports training of new teachers and provides textbooks and scholarships for children. It supports water and sanitation development through the Congo Basin Forrest Partnership. USAID is working to develop programs and policies that open up African markets to agricultural trade, improve economic infrastructure, support small-scale farmers, provide safety nets to the most vulnerable groups, and incorporate technological advances. It facilitates increased cross-border, regional, and international trade. USAID seeks to raise awareness and support for improved African disaster preparedness, mitigation, and response capacity.

★ Web site: http://www.usaid.gov/locations/sub-saharan_africa/

The **Bureau for Democracy, Conflict, and Humanitarian Assistance** works to promote democracy, resolve conflicts, and provide humanitarian assistance to those in need. In the area of democracy, it seeks to strengthen the rule of law, promote competitive elections, develop a politically active civil society, and encourage more transparent and accountable governments. In the area of humanitarian assistance, it runs a variety of programs that provide assistance to victims of foreign disasters, displaced children and orphans, those disabled by conflict in need of prosthetics, and victims of torture. In the area of conflict, it is examining how its longer-term assistance in the areas of democracy and governance, economic growth, agriculture, the environment, and health can help reduce tensions before conflict occurs or build a more sustainable peace once conflict ends.

★ Web site for the Office of Democracy and Governance: http://www.usaid.gov/our_work/democracy_and_governance/

★ Web site for the Office of Conflict Management and Mitigation: http://www.usaid.gov/our_work/cross-cutting_programs/conflict/

★ Web site for humanitarian assistance: http://www.usaid.gov/our_work/humanitarian_assistance/

The **Bureau for Economic Growth and Trade** works to support the efforts of low-income countries to improve the levels of income their citizens enjoy as well as with farmers, scientists, businesses, and local communities in an effort to increase production and profit, including agricultural output.

★ Web site for economic growth and trade: http://www.usaid.gov/our_work/
economic_growth_and_trade/

★ Web site for agriculture: http://www.usaid.gov/our_work/agriculture/

Other USAID Agencies

Bureau for Asia

http://www.usaid.gov/locations/asia_near_east/

Bureau for Europe and Eurasia

http://www.usaid.gov/locations/europe_eurasia/

Bureau for Global Health

http://www.usaid.gov/our_work/global_health/

Bureau for Latin America and the Caribbean

http://www.usaid.gov/locations/latin_america_caribbean/

Bureau for Policy and Program Coordination

http://www.usaid.gov/policy/

Bureau for the Middle East

http://www.usaid.gov/locations/middle_east/

United States Commission on Civil Rights

624 Ninth Street NW
Washington, DC 20425
202-376-7700

★ Web site: http://www.usccr.gov/

★ Job vacancies, internships, student programs: http://www.usccr.gov/jobs/jobs.htm

★ Strategic plan: http://www.usccr.gov/pubs/Strategicweb.pdf

The Commission on Civil Rights collects and studies information on discrimination or denials of equal protection of the laws because of race, color, religion, sex, age, disability, national origin or in the administration of justice in such areas as voting rights, enforcement of federal civil rights laws, and equal opportunity in education, employment, and housing. The commission makes findings of fact but has no enforcement authority. The commission evaluates federal laws and the effectiveness of government equal opportunity programs. It also serves as a national clearinghouse for civil rights information. It employs about 45 people.

United States Election Assistance Commission

1225 New York Avenue NW, Suite 1100
Washington, DC 20005
866-747-1471 (toll-free)
202-566-3100

★ Web site: http://www.eac.gov/index_html1

★ Job vacancies: http://www.eac.gov/about/employment

The U.S. Election Assistance Commission (EAC) is an independent, bipartisan commission charged with developing guidance to meet the Help America Vote Act of 2002 (HAVA) requirements, adopting voluntary voting system guidelines, and serving as a national clearinghouse of information about election administration. EAC also accredits testing laboratories and certifies voting systems, as well as audits the use of HAVA funds. It employs approximately 350 people.

United States Holocaust Memorial Museum

100 Raoul Wallenberg Place SW
Washington, DC 20024-2126
202-488-0400

★ Web site: http://www.ushmm.org/

★ Job vacancies: http://jobsearch.usajobs.opm.gov/a9ushmm.asp

★ Volunteering and internships: http://www.ushmm.org/museum/volunteer_intern/volunteer/

★ Strategic plan: http://www.ushmm.org/museum/mission/StrategicPlan.pdf

The United States Holocaust Memorial Museum is America's national institution for the documentation, study, and interpretation of Holocaust history. The museum's primary mission is to advance and disseminate knowledge about the Holocaust, to preserve the memory of those who suffered, and to encourage visitors to reflect upon the moral and spiritual questions raised by the events of the Holocaust as well as their own responsibilities as citizens of a democracy.

Chartered by a unanimous Act of Congress in 1980 and located adjacent to the National Mall in Washington, DC, the museum strives to broaden public understanding of the history of the Holocaust through multifaceted programs, such as exhibitions; research and publication; collecting and preserving material evidence, art, and artifacts relating to the Holocaust; annual Holocaust commemorations known as Days of Remembrance; distribution of educational materials and teacher resources; and public programming designed to enhance understanding of the Holocaust and related issues, including those of contemporary significance. It employs approximately 200 people.

United States Institute of Peace

1200 Seventeenth Street NW, Suite 200
Washington, DC 20036
202-457-1700

★ Web site: http://www.usip.org

★ Career information and job vacancies: http://www.usip.org/jobs/index.html

★ Internships: http://www.usip.org/fellows/ra.html

★ Fellowships: http://www.usip.org/gf.html

The United States Institute of Peace is an independent, nonpartisan federal institution created by
Congress to promote the prevention, management, and peaceful resolution of international conflicts.
The institute promotes research, policy analysis, education, and training on international peace and
conflict resolution. The institute has an array of programs, including research grants, fellowships,
professional training, education programs from high school through graduate school, conferences
and workshops, library services, and publications.

United States International Trade Commission

500 E Street SW
Washington, DC 20436
202-205-2000

★ Web site: http://www.usitc.gov/

★ Job vacancies: http://jobsearch.usajobs.opm.gov/tc00.asp

★ Career information: http://www.usitc.gov/employment/employment.htm

★ Strategic plan: http://www.usitc.gov/ext_relations/about_itc/strategic_plan_03_08.pdf

The U.S. International Trade Commission (ITC) is an independent, quasi-judicial federal agency
established by Congress with a wide range of trade-related mandates. ITC is headed by six commissioners, who are supported by a permanent staff of roughly 360 career employees. Under its
fact-finding authority, the ITC exercises broad investigative powers on matters related to trade. The
ITC is also called upon by both the legislative and executive branches of government to provide
information on trade and competitiveness issues to both government organizations and the public.
In its adjudicative role, the ITC makes determinations with respect to certain unfair trade practices,
including illegal practices in merchandise trade and violations of intellectual property rights.

The ITC provides oversight for a number of functions. In countervailing duty and antidumping
investigations, the ITC works in concert with the U.S. Department of Commerce. Commerce determines whether the alleged subsidies or dumping are actually occurring, and the ITC determines
whether the U.S. industry is materially injured by reason of the dumped or subsidized imports. The
ITC also assesses whether U.S. industries are being seriously injured by fairly traded imports and

can recommend to the president that relief be provided to facilitate positive adjustment to import competition.

Through its research program, the ITC conducts objective studies on many international trade matters and has an extensive library of international trade resources called the National Library of International Trade, which is open to the public. The ITC frequently holds public hearings as part of its investigations and studies. It makes determinations in investigations involving unfair practices in import trade, mainly involving allegations of infringement of U.S. patents and trademarks by imported goods. If it finds a violation of the law, the ITC may order the exclusion of the imported product from the United States. Finally, the ITC is responsible for continually reviewing the Harmonized Tariff Schedule of the United States (HTS), a list of all the specific items that are imported into and exported from the United States, and for recommending modifications to the HTS that it considers necessary or appropriate.

United States Postal Service

475 L'Enfant Plaza SW
Washington, DC 20260
800-ASK-USPS (800-275-8777—toll-free)
202-268-2000

★ Web site: http://www.usps.gov/

★ Mail processing jobs: http://www.usps.com/employment/, link to Mail Processing Jobs

★ Sales and marketing jobs: http://www.usps.com/employment/, link to Sales and Marketing Jobs

★ Employment requirements: http://www.usps.com/employment/employrequirements.htm

★ Career information: http://www.usps.com/employment/

★ Strategic plan: http://www.usps.com/strategicplanning/2006-2010.htm

The United States Postal Service (USPS) provides mail processing and delivery services to individuals and businesses within the United States. Led by the postmaster general, USPS is committed to serving customers through the development of efficient mail-handling systems and operates its own planning and engineering programs. It also protects the mail from loss or theft and apprehends those who violate U.S. postal laws.

USPS has approximately 750,000 career employees and handles about 207 billion pieces of mail annually. In addition to the national headquarters, there are area and district offices supervising approximately 38,000 post offices, branches, stations, and community post offices throughout the United States. USPS is the only federal agency whose employment policies are governed by a process of collective bargaining under the National Labor Relations Act.

Selected USPS Agencies

The **Office of Strategic Planning** (OSP) focuses on the future of the Postal Service. Its mission is to support the postmaster general in assessing the business and political environment and to assist senior management in the development of strategic goals, objectives, performance measures and indicators, and annual targets.

★ Web site: http://www.usps.com/strategicplanning/welcome.htm

The **U.S. Postal Inspection Service** is the federal law enforcement agency that has jurisdiction in criminal matters affecting the integrity and security of the mail. Postal inspectors enforce more than 200 federal statutes involving mail fraud, mail bombs, child pornography, illegal drugs, and mail theft, as well as being responsible for the protection of postal employees.

★ Web site: http://postalinspectors.uspis.gov/

United States Trade and Development Agency

1000 Wilson Boulevard, Suite 1600
Arlington, VA 22209-3901
703-875-4357

★ Web site: http://www.ustda.gov/

★ Job vacancies: http://www.ustda.gov/about/jobopps.asp

★ Internships: http://www.ustda.gov/about/internships.asp

★ Strategic plan: http://www.ustda.gov/otherinfo/USTDAStrategicPlan2008_2012.pdf

The U.S. Trade and Development Agency (USTDA) advances economic development and U.S. commercial interests in developing and middle-income countries in Asia, Europe and Eurasia, Latin America and the Caribbean, Middle East, North Africa, South Asia, and Sub-Saharan Africa. USTDA is the foreign assistance agency that delivers its program commitments through overseas grants, contracts with U.S. firms, and the use of trust funds at several multilateral development bank groups. The projects supported by USTDA activities represent strong and measurable development priorities in host countries and offer opportunities for commercial participation by U.S. firms. Public and private sector project sponsors in developing and middle-income countries request USTDA support to assist them in implementing their development priorities. The USTDA employs about 45 people.

White House Office

1600 Pennsylvania Avenue NW
Washington, DC 20500
202-456-1414

★ Web site: http://www.whitehouse.gov/

★ Job information: https://app2.whitehouse.gov/ppo/

★ Internships: http://www.whitehouse.gov/government/wh-intern.html

★ Fellows program: http://www.whitehouse.gov/fellows/

The White House Office serves the president in the performance of the many detailed activities incidental to his immediate office. The staff of the president facilitates and maintains communication with the Congress, the individual members of the Congress, the heads of executive agencies, the press and other information media, and the general public. The various assistants to the president assist the president in such matters as he may direct. The White House Office employs about 430 people, according to the Office of Personnel Management. The Executive Residence at the White House staff employs approximately 90 people.

White House Military Office

Executive Office Building
725 Seventeenth Street NW
Washington, DC 20503
202-456-1414

★ Web site: http://www.whitehouse.gov/whmo/

The White House Military Office oversees all military operations aboard Air Force One on presidential missions worldwide. WHMO units include the White House Communications Agency, Presidential Airlift Group, White House Medical Unit, Camp David, Marine Helicopter Squadron One, Presidential Food Service, and the White House Transportation Agency.

Part III

Special Federal Job Opportunities

317

CHAPTER 7

Special Federal Job Opportunities for Veterans

If you're a military veteran, Uncle Sam wants you. This time, though, you can leave the uniforms in your closet because Uncle Sam wants you dressed in civvies for your new career as a civilian government employee. If you meet certain criteria, you'll receive hiring preference for many federal job openings, eligibility for special hiring programs open only to veterans, and preference if your agency has layoffs (in government jargon they're called *reductions in force*).

Of course, the rules regarding veterans' programs, like most government rules, are extremely complex. We'll explore the highlights in this chapter—the information you really need to know if you're a veteran.

What Is Veterans' Preference?

Veterans' preference has existed for nearly 150 years, back to the days of the Civil War. Recognizing that people who serve in the nation's armed forces make sacrifices, Congress has tried to ensure that veterans who seek federal jobs are not penalized for their time in military service. Veterans' preference recognizes the economic loss suffered by citizens who have served in the military, restores veterans to a favorable competitive position for federal employment, and acknowledges the larger obligation owed to veterans who suffered disabling wounds. Veterans' preference is intended to give eligible veterans an extra assist in getting a job with the government and in keeping it in the event of a reduction in force.

How does veterans' preference work? In Chapter 3, you learned that all federal job applicants receive a score based on an evaluation of their education and experience or performance on a required test. Qualifying veterans who meet the requirements for a federal job are awarded extra points in their scores.

Veterans get 5 or 10 points added to their score depending on their circumstances, pushing them above candidates who have similar backgrounds but haven't served in the military. Because, in most cases, federal agencies are limited to considering the three candidates with the highest scores, the extra points veterans receive can tip the selection process in their favor.

Veterans' preference applies to permanent and temporary jobs in the competitive and excepted services of the executive branch. It does not apply to positions in the senior executive service or in the legislative and judicial branches *unless* the positions are in the competitive service, such as jobs at the Government Printing Office.

Who Qualifies for Veterans' Preference?

It's probably easiest to start by listing who is *not* eligible for veterans' preference:

★ Veterans who did not receive an honorable or general discharge when they left military service

★ Military retirees at the rank of major, lieutenant commander, or higher unless they are disabled veterans

★ Members of the National Guard and Reserves who went on active duty only for training purposes

Qualifications for a 5-Point Preference

Five points are added to the score of a veteran who served in one of the following situations:

★ During a war.

★ During the period from April 28, 1952, through July 1, 1955.

★ For more than 180 days, any part of which occurred after January 31, 1955, and before October 15, 1976.

★ During the Gulf War from August 2, 1990, through January 2, 1992.

★ For more than 180 consecutive days, other than for training, any part of which occurred during the period beginning September 11, 2001, and ending on the date prescribed by presidential proclamation or by law as the last day of Operation Iraqi Freedom.

★ In a campaign or expedition for which a campaign medal was authorized. This includes El Salvador, Grenada, Haiti, Lebanon, Panama, Somalia, and Southwest Asia.

Qualifications for a 10-Point Preference

Ten points are added to the score of applicants who match one of the following descriptions:

★ A veteran who served any time and who has a present service-connected disability or is receiving compensation, disability retirement benefits, or a pension from the military or the Department of Veterans Affairs. Individuals who received a Purple Heart qualify as disabled veterans.

★ A spouse of certain deceased veterans who has not remarried.

★ A spouse of a veteran who is unable to work because of a service-connected disability.

★ The mother of a veteran who died in service or who is permanently and totally disabled.

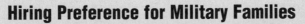

Hiring Preference for Military Families

To lessen the employment and career interruptions of spouses who relocate with their active duty husbands and wives, the Department of Defense offers the Military Spouse Preference (MSP) program. Through this program, eligible military spouses can receive a hiring preference when applying for Department of Defense jobs in the general location where their spouses are stationed. Dependents of active duty personnel can receive hiring preference for government jobs under the Family Member Preference Program.

How Is Veterans' Preference Applied?

Veterans' preference is applied in a variety of ways depending on the type of job, the number of points the applicant receives, and other circumstances:

★ For scientific and professional positions in grades GS-9 and higher, all candidates (both veterans and nonveterans) are ranked by their overall score. Applicants who qualify for veterans' preference receive a 5- or 10-point boost in their scores, depending on the nature of their preference, but these applicants do not receive any other special consideration in hiring.

★ For all other positions, the names of veterans who qualified for a 10-point preference and who have a compensable, service-connected disability of 10 percent or more are placed ahead of the names of all other eligible candidates. The names of other veterans who qualified for a 10-point preference, veterans who received a 5-point preference, and nonveterans are then ranked by their overall score.

★ Examinations for certain jobs are only open to applicants who qualify for veterans' preference as long as such applicants are available. The jobs include custodian, guard, elevator operator, and messenger.

★ People who qualify for a 10-point preference may apply for any federal jobs subject to competition where a nontemporary appointment has been made within the previous three years.

★ A person who is unable to apply for an open competitive job because of military service may apply after the position's closing date.

In the last two situations, interested veterans should contact the agency that announced the position for further information.

The Veterans' Preference Advisor

The Department of Labor has created a handy online Veterans' Preference Advisor that helps veterans determine the preference to which they're entitled, the benefits associated with the preference, and the steps necessary to file a complaint if a federal agency fails to provide the required benefits. Using the system simply requires clicking on the applicable answers to some questions. The Veterans' Preference Advisor is available at http://www. dol.gov/elaws/vetspref.htm.

You may wonder whether veterans actually receive the preferences to which they are entitled. Several years ago veterans groups raised concerns about whether veterans who applied for federal jobs received the required preferences. In response to these concerns, OPM launched a study in 2000 that found that veterans usually receive proper consideration in federal hiring. But the OPM study did find some problems:

★ Over the previous two years, some government agencies had hired approximately 8,000 lawyers and 95,000 student trainees without a clear understanding of how to apply veterans' preferences.

★ Officials in many offices that were part of the excepted service, rather than the competitive service, incorrectly believed they did not have to comply with veterans' preferences laws and rules.

★ The hiring of disabled veterans was "very uneven" among government agencies and "most managers were unaware of specific initiatives by their agency to hire disabled veterans," the report said.

What Special Hiring Programs Are Available for Veterans?

Many veterans enter the federal workforce through special hiring programs that seek to recruit veterans. In government-speak, these programs are called "special appointing authorities for veterans." Several different programs exist. All are optional for federal agencies, so a specific agency may or may not use particular programs. The following sections describe two of these programs.

Veterans' Recruitment Appointment

The largest hiring program for veterans is the Veterans' Recruitment Appointment (VRA), under which agencies can hire an eligible veteran without competition. The veteran must meet the basic qualification requirements for the job and must have served on *active duty*, not been placed on active duty for training purposes only.

Agencies can use the VRA to fill jobs at any grade through General Schedule 11 (GS-11) or the equivalent. VRA applicants are hired under excepted appointments to positions that are otherwise in the competitive service. After two years of satisfactory performance, the agency must convert the veteran to a normal competitive service appointment.

Once VRAs are hired, they're treated like any other competitive service employee and may be promoted, reassigned, or transferred. VRA hires who have less than 15 years of education must complete a training program established by the agency.

Veterans who have received either an honorable or general discharge are eligible for VRA if they meet one of the following criteria:

★ They are disabled.

★ They served on active duty in the armed forces during a war or in a campaign or expedition for which a campaign badge has been authorized.

★ While serving on active duty in the armed forces, they participated in a United States military operation for which an Armed Forces Service Medal was awarded.

★ They have been separated from active duty within the past three years.

★ They received an honorable or general discharge after three or more years of continuous active service.

Note that veterans who claim eligibility on the basis of service in a campaign or expedition for which a medal was awarded must have the campaign badge or medal.

To apply for VRA, veterans should directly contact the personnel office at the federal agency where they are interested in working to find out more about VRA opportunities. Additional information about VRA is also available online at http://www.usajobs.gov/EI4.asp.

Program for Veterans with Disabilities

Another program provides special benefits to veterans who have disabilities of 30 percent or more. These veterans can be hired under temporary or term appointments for any job where they meet the requirements. Unlike the VRA program, there is no grade limitation. After demonstrating satisfactory performance, the veteran may be converted at any time to a normal competitive service appointment.

To apply for this program, veterans should contact the personnel office at the federal agency where they want to work to inquire about opportunities. As part of the hiring process, veterans must submit a copy of a letter dated within the previous 12 months from the Department of Veterans Affairs or the Department of Defense certifying that they receive compensation for a service-connected disability of 30 percent or more.

Two Online Guides to Special Hiring Programs

Two publications by the Office of Personnel Management describe other special hiring programs for veterans. The "VetsInfo Guide" (http://www.opm.gov/veterans/html/vetsinfo.asp) is aimed at veterans, while the longer and more detailed "VetGuide" (http://www.opm.gov/veterans/html/vetguide.asp) is aimed at federal personnel specialists and managers.

How Do You Find a Federal Job If You're a Veteran?

The most effective method for finding a federal job is to contact the personnel office at the agency where you're interested in working to ask about opportunities. If you qualify for one of the special hiring programs for veterans, be sure to mention this.

If you don't know which agency you want to work for, you may want to start your job search by contacting the agencies that hire the most veterans. Veterans currently fill about 25 percent of all executive branch jobs. Not surprisingly, the majority of veterans in the federal government work in civilian jobs at agencies that are part of the Department of Defense. The Department of the Army employs 17.4 percent of all veterans in the federal government, the Department of the Navy 15 percent, the Department of the Air Force 13.2 percent, and other Defense Department agencies 6.3 percent, according to the latest statistics available.

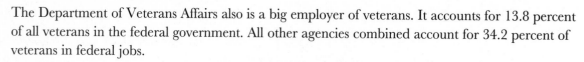

The Department of Veterans Affairs also is a big employer of veterans. It accounts for 13.8 percent of all veterans in the federal government. All other agencies combined account for 34.2 percent of veterans in federal jobs.

Outside the Departments of Defense and the Veterans Affairs, some of the federal agencies that have the highest percentages of veterans on their staffs include the Department of Energy, the Department of Justice, and the Department of Transportation. Chapter 6 lists contact information for all of these agencies.

Another job search method is to look for job openings at USAJOBS, the official job site for the federal government. You can access USAJOBS online at http://www.usajobs.gov. (We discuss how to use USAJOBS in detail in Chapter 2.) USAJOBS has a section devoted to helping veterans obtain federal employment under the Veterans tab. This section provides tools to determine your veteran's preference status, information on federal benefits, and information on federal programs. The required form for verifying your veteran's preference is located here. There is also an easy-to-use comparison of federal jobs to military jobs with links to current federal job openings.

Note that being a veteran does not guarantee you a federal job—it just improves your chances of getting one. You still must meet the job's basic qualification requirements to be considered. For more information on veterans and federal jobs, go online to http://www.usajobs.gov/EI3.asp or http://www.opm.gov/veterans/html/vetguide.asp.

CHAPTER 8

Special Federal Job Opportunities for People with Disabilities

The federal government serves as a model for all employers in abiding by equal employment opportunity legislation, which protects current and potential employees from discrimination based on race, color, religion, sex, national origin, disability, or age. While making an effort to have a workforce as diverse as the nation's civilian labor force, the federal government also makes a special effort to recruit and accommodate persons with disabilities. This chapter provides an overview of the issues of interest to federal job applicants who have disabilities.

What Constitutes a Disability?

The Americans with Disabilities Act of 1990 makes employment discrimination based on disability a civil rights offense. The 2008 Amendments provide broader protections for disabled workers.

But what does the government consider to be a disability? The Rehabilitation Act of 1973, which protects executive branch applicants and employees against employment discrimination based on disability, defines a person with a disability as someone who has a physical or mental impairment that substantially limits one or more of the person's major life activities, has a history of such an impairment, or is perceived by others as having such an impairment.

A "physical or mental impairment" means one of the following:

★ Any physiological disorder, condition, cosmetic disfigurement, or anatomical loss affecting one or more systems such as neurological, musculoskeletal, special sense organs, cardiovascular, reproductive, digestive, respiratory, genito-urinary, hemic and lymphatic, skin, and endocrine

★ Any mental or psychological disorder, such as mental retardation, organic brain syndrome, emotional or mental illness, and specific learning disabilities

Examples of "major life activities" include caring for yourself, performing manual tasks, walking, seeing, hearing, speaking, breathing, learning, concentrating, and working.

The Rehabilitation Act also requires federal agencies to provide reasonable accommodation for known physical or mental limitations of applicants and employees, unless doing so would cause "undue hardship." In addition, Executive Order 13164, which was issued on July 26, 2000, requires federal agencies to develop written procedures for providing reasonable accommodation.

If you've looked at some federal job announcements, you've probably seen statements similar to the following:

> "This agency provides reasonable accommodation to applicants with disabilities where appropriate."

> "If you need reasonable accommodation for any part of the application and hiring process, notify the agency. Determinations on requests for reasonable accommodation will be made on a case-by-case basis."

Reasonable accommodation "is any change to a job, the work environment, or the way things are usually done that allows an individual with a disability to apply for a job, perform job functions, or enjoy equal access to benefits available to other individuals in the workplace," according to a publication from the Office of Personnel Management.

Accommodations can range from providing application forms in alternative formats such as large print or Braille to providing a sign language interpreter for someone who is deaf. The government must pay for the accommodations. Note that applicants or employees with disabilities are responsible for making their needs known. For example, if you're applying for a federal job but have a disability that makes it impossible for you to type, you must alert the agency as soon as possible if you cannot fill out the online resume builder that it requires.

What Special Hiring Authorities Apply to People with Disabilities?

Over the last decade, people with various types of disabilities have consistently constituted about 7 percent of the federal workforce. This has translated into the government employing between 120,000 and 145,000 people with disabilities annually. The majority of people with disabilities who work for the federal government were hired in open competitions by applying through vacancy announcements.

However, some people with disabilities, whether physical or mental, qualify for special federal hiring authorities where they do not have to compete with other applicants. These hiring authorities are not widely advertised, so people with disabilities must be aggressive in pursuing them.

These hiring authorities cover people with mental retardation, people with severe physical disabilities, people with psychiatric disabilities, disabled veterans who are enrolled in a Department of Veterans Affairs training program, and veterans who are 30 percent or more disabled. (Chapter 7 provides more information about hiring authorities that relate to veterans who are disabled.) Note that agencies are not required to use these special hiring authorities.

Applicants with disabilities frequently apply for consideration under OPM's Schedule A hiring authority. This authority can be used to hire them on a trial basis. After two years of successful performance, they can be noncompetitively converted to a permanent appointment in the competitive service. If that does not happen, they may remain on the excepted service appointment.

If you wish to be considered under a special hiring authority, you must contact a counselor at either your state vocational rehabilitation agency or, if you're a veteran, at the Vocational Rehabilitation and Employment Service at the Department of Veterans Affairs. The counselor will prepare and review the necessary documents.

Ask the counselor to give you a "certification" statement that

★ Verifies that you have a severe disability and are therefore eligible under the Schedule A special hiring authority.

★ States that you are able to perform the duties of the job for which you're applying.

★ Lists any needed reasonable accommodation.

Once you have the certification statement, you have two options:

1. You can send an application and the certification to the Selective Placement Coordinator at the agency where you'd like to work.

2. You can contact the person at the agency who handles the Selective Placement program (it's sometimes called the Disability Employment program).

Selective Placement Program Coordinators

Selective Placement program coordinators can help match your core skills, along with any needed reasonable accommodations, with available jobs. You'll find them in either the human resources department or the Equal Employment Opportunity office of each federal agency. A directory of Selective Placement program coordinators at federal agencies is available online at http://apps.opm.gov/sppc_directory.

Sometimes the certification is done in two steps. The first step is a letter from the counselor certifying that you are disabled and eligible for employment under the special hiring authority. This type of certification is sufficient for an applicant to be considered for any job.

The second step occurs after you have been tentatively selected for the position. It requires a second letter that must state the counselor has evaluated the job tasks and determined you are able to perform the essential duties of the position. The letter also must state what reasonable accommodations, if any, are sought.

To be hired, you must meet all basic qualification requirements for the job. You also must be able to perform the job's essential functions, either with or without reasonable accommodation. In determining whether you can perform the job's functions, the hiring agency must conduct an individualized assessment. The agency cannot exclude from consideration an entire group of people with a particular disability.

More Federal Resources on Disabilities

More information about federal employment of people with disabilities is available from the Office of Personnel Management at http://www.opm.gov/disability/index.asp. Another useful site is DisabilityInfo.gov (http://www.disabilityinfo.gov), which is a gateway to federal information and resources about disabilities. Lastly, the USAJOBS site has a page about federal job opportunities for people with disabilities at http://www.usajobs.gov/EI11.asp.

CHAPTER 9

Special Federal Job Opportunities for Students

The federal government offers more internship and employment opportunities for students and recent college graduates today than ever before. Some of the internships lead directly into good federal jobs, and acceptance of some job offers results in the government paying up to $60,000 toward your college loans.

That's right: Up to *$60,000* in debt vanishes.

The purpose of this chapter is to highlight some of the largest programs for students and point you in the right direction so you can get information about the rest.

Opportunities for High School and College Students

In an effort to meet future employment needs, the federal government offers a variety of programs designed to attract talented students to careers in public service. Students in these programs gain on-the-job experience and a better understanding of how the federal government works in addition to earning academic credit or a paycheck. The following sections outline the major types of programs that are offered.

Student Volunteer Service

Federal agencies and departments offer unpaid training opportunities to students in high school and college. These opportunities provide work experience related to a student's academic program. The program allows students to explore career options as well as develop personal and professional skills. As a student volunteer, students are exposed to the federal work environment and will learn about the missions and responsibilities of various federal agencies and departments.

Some of the benefits of volunteering in the Student Volunteer Service include the following:

★ Career exploration early in academic studies

★ Exposure to new and emerging occupations and professions

★ Academic credit (determined by the academic institution)

★ Work experience that will enhance your ability to obtain paying jobs in the future

To participate as a student volunteer, you must be enrolled at least half-time in one of the following types of schools:

★ An accredited high school or trade school

★ A technical or vocational school

★ A junior or community college

★ A four-year college or university

★ Any other accredited educational institution

For more information, contact the personnel office at the federal agency or department for which you wish to work. The Defense (Army, Air Force and Navy), Commerce, Health and Human Services, Interior, Justice, State, Treasury, and Veterans Affairs departments have utilized the largest number of student volunteers. You can find telephone numbers for federal agencies in your telephone directory under "U.S. Government." Part II of this book also lists URLs and phone numbers for these agencies. For further information, visit your school's guidance, career counseling, job placement, or internship office. You also can go online to http://www.usajobs.gov/EI20.asp.

Internships

Just like with the private sector, an internship with the federal government is a great way to obtain some work experience, check out a place where you may later want to work, and get your foot in the door for future job openings. Internships are invaluable, especially in today's tight job market.

When many people think about federal internships, the place that comes immediately to mind is Washington, DC. Each year thousands of young people descend on Washington to participate in government internships. You shouldn't forget, however, that internship opportunities also exist at many local and regional offices of federal agencies throughout the country. Wherever you intern with the federal government, you'll end up with an impressive experience to list on your resume—even if you don't end up working for the government.

Any federal office where you apply for an internship will ask you questions, and you need to ask some questions of your own to try to ensure, as much as possible, that you'll have a worthwhile experience. Most offices try hard to make sure you learn as much as possible during your internship, but a few simply chain interns to fax and photocopy machines for their entire stays.

Before accepting an internship, you should ask questions such as:

★ What will my primary duties be as an intern?

★ What will a typical day be like?

★ How many other interns do you expect will work at your office during my stay?

Many young people gravitate toward Congress for their internships. It's useful to keep in mind, however, that agencies throughout the federal government—the Smithsonian Institution, the Library of Congress, and the Environmental Protection Agency, to name just a few—also offer internships.

For example, the State Department uses close to 1,000 interns annually, split evenly between positions in the United States and positions at U.S. embassies in foreign countries. The department seeks students with a broad range of majors, including business, public administration, social work, economics, information management, journalism, and biological and engineering sciences, as well as majors directly related to international affairs. Applicants must be U.S. citizens in good academic standing, and must qualify to receive a Secret or Top Secret clearance. (For more information, go to http://www.careers.state.gov/students/.)

White House Internship Program

The White House Internship Program provides interns with a unique opportunity to observe government officials and gain practical knowledge about the daily operations of the White House. Interns work in a variety of White House offices, including communications, legislative affairs, presidential correspondence, public liaison, and scheduling, among others. Internships are unpaid and cannot exceed 90 days in length. Applicants must be U.S. citizens, enrolled in a college or university, and willing to undergo a security clearance prior to working at the White House. For more information, go online to http://www.whitehouse.gov/about/internships/.

Federal agencies and departments usually post information about internship programs on their Web sites. Internship information is sometimes included under a broad category such as "Employment" or "Jobs" at a Web site. In Part II of this book, listings for specific agencies include the URL for their internship page if one is available.

Student Temporary Employment Program (STEP)

The STEP, another name for a temporary internship with a federal agency, is a great way for students to be exposed to the government. STEP positions are paid positions that can range from a summer job to a position that lasts as long as the student is in school. It is not necessary for the work to be related to the student's academic major, which allows the student to gain experience in a variety of fields. Students enrolled in high school, a two-year or four-year college or university, a technical or vocational school, or a graduate program are eligible to apply. The program requires that the student be a U.S. citizen. For more information, view http://www.opm.gov/employ/students/intro.asp.

Student Career Experience Program (SCEP)

SCEP positions, which are for undergraduate and graduate students, are substantive internships in federal agencies. The work must be related to the student's area of study and requires the agency to have a formal commitment with the student's institution.

Most positions are paid, and the student may also receive academic credit. If the student successfully completes 640 hours of work, he or she can be appointed to a permanent position without going through the traditional hiring process. This program requires its students to be U.S. citizens. For more information, see http://www.usajobs.gov/EI14.asp.

Opportunities for Recent Graduates

If you already have an undergraduate degree, the federal government wants you to consider putting that degree to work in public service. The following sections describe federal programs aimed at attracting the best and brightest college graduates. Note that Appendix A lists federal job titles that correspond to different college majors. This list is a good starting point in the search for a federal job.

The Federal Career Intern Program (FCIP)

The Federal Career Intern Program is designed to help agencies attract outstanding undergraduate and graduate students to a variety of entry-level positions (GS-5, 7, 9). These jobs are two-year, full-time commitments and are not short-term internships. Upon successful completion of the program, participants may be eligible for permanent placement within an agency. Individuals interested in Career Intern opportunities should contact the specific agency directly. Agencies control their own FCIP hiring process and may restrict the selection pool to certain schools. For more information, go to http://www.opm.gov/careerintern/.

Presidential Management Fellows (PMF) Program

The highly competitive Presidential Management Fellows (PMF) Program is an excellent way for graduate students who are committed to leading and managing public policies and programs to launch a career in the federal government. These two-year positions start at GS-9 and can move to GS-11 in the second year. During this time, Fellows have the opportunity to complete rotational assignments and receive extensive training. Upon completion of the program, fellows are eligible for appointment to permanent federal jobs and promotion to GS-12.

The application deadline for this program is in early fall, and applicants must be nominated by their schools. To find out more, view http://www.pmf.opm.gov/ or http://www.usajobs.opm.gov/EI18.asp.

The Emerging Leaders Program

Many agencies run their own programs in addition to participating in government-wide efforts such as the Presidential Management Fellows Program. For example, the Emerging Leaders Program at the Department of Health and Human Services provides two-year internships for graduate students that can lead to permanent employment. For more information, go to http://hhsu.learning.hhs.gov/ELP/.

Student Loan Repayment Program

If you're like most college students and have tens of thousands of dollars in college loans to repay, Uncle Sam may be able to help. As an incentive to attract top candidates or to retain excellent employees, agencies can agree to repay up to $10,000 in federally insured student loans for an employee in a calendar year, with total payments capped at $60,000 for each employee. In return, the employee must sign an agreement promising to work for the agency for a minimum of three years.

The penalty for breaking that promise to work for three years is stiff. If you leave the agency at any time during the three-year period, you must reimburse the agency for every penny that it paid toward your loans. There's only one exception: If you transfer to another federal agency and your service agreement does not specifically require repayment upon a transfer. But your new agency is not obligated to continue the financial support.

The student loan repayment program is in its infancy, but it's growing as agencies realize the program's power as an incentive. According to the most recent data, the 33 participating agencies repaid more than $42 million in student loans for 6,619 employees. That was a big jump from 2002, when the 16 participating agencies repaid a little more than $3.1 million in student loans for 690 employees. Since the program's inception, the State Department has been its biggest user. In fiscal year 2007, the department repaid more than $3.7 million in loans for 626 employees.

Agencies are not required to participate in the student loan repayment program, and those that do are largely free to make their own rules. For example, they may extend the required period of service beyond the three years established by law. More information about the program, including a list of participating agencies, is available at http://www.opm.gov/oca/PAY/StudentLoan/index.asp.

Other Helpful Information Links for Students

Studentjobs.gov (at http://www.studentjobs.gov) is a one-stop portal for a range of employment opportunities within the federal government for students in high school, college, and graduate school. As a subset of the USAJOBS site, Studentjobs.gov is set up in much the same way. (Refer to Chapter 2 for information on how to use this site.) For example, you can click on the Search Jobs tab to find positions for students. Once you create an account, you can log in on the My Studentjobs tab and create a resume in the online resume builder. (See Chapter 3 for information on how to write a competitive federal resume.) Studentjobs.gov also provides links to student employment pages for a wide variety of agencies on the Agency Info tab.

Another helpful Web site is e-Scholar at http://www.studentjobs.gov/e-scholar.asp. This OPM Web site publicizes educational opportunities that are available to students from high school through graduate school.

Here are some additional online sources of information of interest to students:

★ AmeriCorps: http://www.usajobs.gov/EI21.asp

★ Federal Employment Overseas: http://www.usajobs.gov/EI10.asp

★ Federal Occupational Groups: http://www.usajobs.gov/EI12.asp

★ Federal Student Internship Programs: http://www.usajobs.opm.gov/EI-13.asp

★ Peace Corps: http://www.usajobs.gov/EI17.asp

★ Summer Employment: http://www.usajobs.gov/EI19.asp

Part IV

Appendixes

Federal Jobs by College Major

No matter what your college major might be, the federal government has a job for you. Look through this list until you find your major, and then look under it for the types of jobs that may be available. But keep three things in mind:

★ The jobs listed under each major are usually examples, not an all-inclusive list.

★ If you don't have a college degree, in many cases work experience in the field is just as good.

★ If you're looking for an administrative job, you often can qualify with a degree in any academic major.

Any Major

Administrative Officers

Air Traffic Controllers

Civil Rights Analysts

Claims Examiners

Contract Representatives

Contract Administrators

Environmental Protection

General Investigators

Internal Revenue Officers

Logistics Managers

Management Analysts

Paralegal Specialists

Personnel Occupations

Public Affairs

Supply Managers

Writers and Editors

Accounting

Accountants

Auditors

Contract Specialists

Financial Administrators

Financial Institution Examiners

Financial Managers

Government Accountability Office Auditors

Intelligence Specialists

Internal Revenue Agents

Agriculture

Agricultural Commodity Graders

Agricultural Engineers

Agricultural Management Specialists

Agricultural Market Reporters

Agricultural Marketing Specialists

Agricultural Program Specialists

Foreign Agriculture Affairs Specialists

Soil Conservationists

Soil Scientists

Agronomy

Agricultural Management Specialists

Agronomists

Soil Conservationists

Soil Scientists

Anthropology

Anthropologists

Management Analysts

Museum Curators

Museum Specialists

Program Analysts

Archeology

Archeologists

Museum Curators

Museum Specialists

Architecture

Architects

Construction Analysts

Construction Control Inspectors

Landscape Architects

Naval Architects

Program Analysts

Arts, Fine and Applied

Arts Specialists

Audio-Visual Production Specialists

Exhibits Specialists

General Arts and Information Specialists

Illustrators

Photographers

Recreation and Creative Arts Therapists

Visual Information Specialists

Astronomy

Astronomers and Space Scientists

Geodesists

Aviation

Air Navigators

Air Safety Investigators

Air Traffic Controllers

Aircraft Operators

Aircrew Technicians

Aviation Safety Inspectors

Biology

Entomologists

Fishery Biologists

General Biological Scientists

Government Accountability Office Evaluators

Microbiologists

Range Conservationists

Wildlife Biologists

Zoologists

Botany

Agronomists

Botanists

Forestry Technicians

Geneticists

Horticulturists

Plant Pathologists

Plant Physiologists

Plant Protection and Quarantine Specialists

Range Conservationists

Business

Budget Analysts

Business and Industry Specialists

Commissary Store Managers

Contract Specialists

Government Accountability Office Analysts

Government Accountability Office Evaluators

Import Specialists

Internal Revenue Officers

Miscellaneous Administrative and Programs Specialists

Quality Assurance Specialists

Trade Specialists

Cartography

Cartographers

Cartographic Technicians

Geodetic Technicians

Chemistry

Chemical Engineers

Chemists

Consumer Safety Officers

Environmental Engineers

Food Technologists

Health Physicists

Intelligence Specialists

Toxicologists

Communications

Communications Specialists

Public Affairs Specialists

Technical Writers and Editors

Telecommunications Managers

Writers and Editors

Computer Science

Computer Programmers

Computer Specialists

Information Technology Specialists

Management Analysts

Program Managers

Corrections

Correctional Institution Administrators

Correctional Officers

Program Analysts

Counseling

Chaplains

Education and Vocational Training Specialists

Educational Services Specialists

Equal Opportunity Compliance Specialists

Personnel Specialists

Psychologists

Psychology Aides and Technicians

Social Service Aides and Assistants

Social Service Representatives

Vocational Rehabilitation Specialists

Criminal Justice/Law Enforcement

Border Patrol Agents

Criminal Investigators

Game Law Enforcement Agents

Government Accountability Office Evaluators

Internal Revenue Officers

Police Officers

United States Marshals

Dietetics and Nutrition

Dietitians

Food Technologists

Nutritionists

Economics

Actuaries

Budget Analysts

Contract Specialists

Economists

Financial Analysts

Financial Institution Examiners

Government Accountability Office Evaluators

Loan Specialists

Trade Specialists

Transportation Industrial Analysts

Education

Education and Training Specialists

Education and Vocational Training Specialists

Educational Program Specialists

Educational Services Specialists

Employee Development Specialists

Instructional Systems Specialists

Public Health Educators

Training Instructors

Vocational Rehabilitation Specialists

Electronics Technology

Communications Specialists

Electronics Mechanics

Electronics Technicians

Patent Examiners

Employee/Labor Relations

Contractor Industrial Relations Specialists

Employee Relations Specialists

Hearing and Appeals Specialists

Labor Management Relations Examiners

Labor Relations Specialists

Mediators

Salary and Wage Administrators

Workers Compensation Claims Examiners

Engineering (Any Specialty)

Aerospace Engineers

Biomedical Engineers

Civil Engineers

Computer Engineers

Electrical Engineers

Electronics Engineers

General Engineers

Industrial Engineers

Mechanical Engineers

Nuclear Engineers

English and Literature

Editorial Assistants

Management Analysts

Miscellaneous Administrative and Programs Specialists

Printing Specialists

Program Analysts

Program Managers

Public Affairs Specialists

Technical Writers and Editors

Writers and Editors

Environmental Studies

Ecologists

Environmental Health Technicians

Environmental Protection Assistants

Environmental Protection Specialists

Fish and Wildlife Refuge Managers

General Fish and Wildlife Administrators

Government Accountability Office Evaluators

Miscellaneous Administrative and Programs Specialists

Toxicologists

Epidemiology

Environmental Health Technicians

General Health Scientists

Industrial Hygienists

Microbiologists

Facilities Management

Commissary Store Managers

Correctional Institution Administrators

Distribution Facility and Storage Managers

Equipment Specialists

Facility Managers

General Facilities and Equipment Managers

Housing Managers

Industrial Property Managers

Production Controllers

Finance

Appraisers and Assessors

Budget Analysts

Financial Administrators

Financial Analysts

Financial Institution Examiners

Securities Compliance Examiners

Tax Examiners

Trade Specialists

Fish, Game, and Wildlife Management

Fish and Wildlife Refuge Managers

Fishery Biologists

Game Law Enforcement Agents

General Biological Scientists

General Fish and Wildlife Administrators

Soil Conservationists

Wildlife Biologists

Wildlife Rescue Managers

Food Technology and Safety

Consumer Safety Inspectors

Consumer Safety Officers

Dietitians and Nutritionists

Food Assistance Program Specialists

Food Technologists

Toxicologists

Foreign Language

Air Safety Investigators

Border Patrol Agents

Customs Inspectors

Equal Employment Opportunity Specialists

Foreign Affairs Specialists

Foreign Agricultural Affairs Specialists

Intelligence Specialists

Language Specialists

Forestry

Fish and Wildlife Refuge Managers

Foresters

General Fish and Wildlife Administrators

Management Analysts

Program Analysts

Soil Conservationists

Geography

Cartographers

Geographers

Geology

General Physical Scientists

Geodesists

Geologists

Hydrologists

Oceanographers

Geophysics

General Physical Scientists

Geophysicists

Health

Environmental Health Technicians

General Health Scientists

Health Physicists

Health System Administrators

Health System Specialists

Industrial Hygienists

Public Health Programs Specialists

Safety and Occupational Health Management Specialists

History

Archives Technicians

Archivists

Exhibits Specialists

Historians

Intelligence Specialists

Management Analysts

Miscellaneous Administrative and Programs Specialists

Museum Curators

Program Analysts

Home Economics

Consumer Safety Officers

Food Technologists

Horticulture

Agricultural Marketing Specialists

General Biological Scientists

Horticulturists

Plant Physiologists

Plant Protection and Quarantine Specialists

Hospital Administration

Administrative Officers

General Health Scientists

Health System Administrators

Health System Specialists

Hospital Housekeepers

Public Health Programs Specialists

Human Resource Management

Apprenticeship and Training Representatives

Employee Relations Specialists

Equal Employment Opportunity Specialists

Military Personnel Management Specialists

Personnel Management Specialists

Personnel Staffing Specialists

Position Classification Specialists

Hydrology

Environmental Engineers

Environmental Protection Specialists

Fish and Wildlife Refuge Managers

General Fish and Wildlife Administrators

Hydrologists

Program Analysts

Industrial Management

Business and Industry Specialists

Equipment Specialists

Industrial Hygienists
Industrial Property Managers
Industrial Specialists
Management Analysts
Production Controllers
Program Analysts
Property Disposal Specialists
Quality Assurance Specialists

Insurance

Crop Insurance Administrators
Miscellaneous Administrative and Programs Specialists
Program Analysts
Social Insurance Administrators
Social Insurance Claims Examiners
Unemployment Insurance Specialists

International Relations

Foreign Affairs Specialists
Foreign Agricultural Affairs Specialists
Intelligence Specialists
International Relations Workers
Language Specialists
Public Affairs Specialists
Trade Specialists

Journalism

Agricultural Market Reporters
Printing Specialists
Program Analysts
Public Affairs Specialists
Technical Writers and Editors
Writers and Editors

Law

Administrative Law Judges
Attorneys
Hearing and Appeals Specialists
Legal Instruments Examiners
Paralegal Specialists
Patent Attorneys
Tax Law Specialists

Law Enforcement

Alcohol, Tobacco, and Firearms Inspectors
Border Patrol Agents
Criminal Investigators
Customs Inspectors
Game Law Enforcement Agents
Immigration Inspectors
Inspections, Investigations, and Compliance Specialists
Police Officers
United States Marshals

Liberal Arts/Humanities

Contact Representatives
Customs Inspectors
Education Services Specialists
Equal Opportunity Compliance Specialists
Management Analysts
Personnel Management Specialists
Program Analysts
Social Insurance Claims Examiners
Veterans Claims Examiners

Library Science

Librarians
Library Technicians
Medical Record Librarians
Technical Information Services

Management

Administrative Officers

Logistics Management Specialists

Management Analysts

Manpower Development Specialists

Miscellaneous Administrative and Program Specialists

Program Analysts

Support Services

Management Information Systems

Computer Science Specialists

Computer Specialists

Financial Managers

Logistics Management Specialists

Management Analysts

Miscellaneous Administrative and Programs Specialists

Operations Research Analysts

Program Analysts

Program Managers

Marketing

Agricultural Marketing Specialists

Bond Sales Promotion Representatives

Business and Industry Specialists

Contract Specialists

Inventory Management Specialists

Packaging Specialists

Property Disposal Specialists

Supply Specialists

Trade Specialists

Mathematics

Actuaries

Cartographers

Computer Science Specialists

Mathematical Statisticians

Mathematicians

Operations Research Analysts

Statisticians

Medical Support

Diagnostic Radiological Technicians

Medical Instrument Technicians

Medical Record Technicians

Medical Technicians

Nuclear Medicine Technicians

Pathology Technicians

Therapeutic Radiological Technicians

Meteorology

General Physical Scientists

Meteorologists

Natural Resource Management

Fish and Wildlife Administrators

General Biological Scientists

Program Analysts

Wildlife Biologists

Wildlife Refuge Managers

Nursing

Nurses

Physicians' Assistants

Park and Recreation Management

Foresters

Management Analysts

Outdoor Recreation Planners

Park Rangers

Recreation and Creative Arts Therapists

Recreation Specialists

Pharmacy

Consumer Safety Inspectors

Consumer Safety Officers

Pharmacists

Pharmacologists

Physical Education

Corrective Therapists

Outdoor Recreation Planners

Program Analysts

Recreation Aides and Assistants

Recreation and Creative Arts Therapists

Recreation Specialists

Sports Specialists

Physical Science

General Physical Scientists

Metallurgists

Physicists

Physics

Astronomers and Space Scientists

General Physical Scientists

Geodesists

Geophysicists

Health Physicists

Hydrologists

Oceanographers

Patent Examiners

Physicists

Political Science/ Government

Archivists

Budget Analysts

Foreign Affairs Specialists

Government Accountability Office Analysts

Historians

Miscellaneous Administrative and Program Specialists

Program Analysts

Public Affairs Specialists

Social Scientists

Psychology

Educational Services Specialists

Employee Development Specialists

Government Accountability Office Evaluators

Personnel Management Specialists

Personnel Staffing Specialists

Position Classification Specialists

Psychologists

Recreation and Creative Arts Therapists

Public Administration

Budget Analysts

Employee Development Specialists

Employee Relations Specialists

Government Accountability Office Evaluators

Housing Managers

Management Analysts

Manpower Development Specialists

Miscellaneous Administrative and Program Specialists

Program Analysts

Public Utilities Specialists

Public Health

Environmental Health Technicians

Food Assistance Program Specialists

Food Inspectors

Health System Administrators

Health System Specialists

Industrial Hygienists

Public Health Educators

Public Health Programs Specialists

Social Insurance Administrators

Veterans Claims Examiners

Public Relations

Contact Representatives

Foreign Affairs Specialists

Foreign Agricultural Affairs Specialists

Public Affairs Specialists

Purchasing

Business and Industry Specialists

Commissary Store Managers

Contract Specialists

Purchasing Specialists

Real Estate

Building Managers

Business and Industry Specialists

Contract Specialists

Housing Managers

Realtors

Rehabilitation Therapy

Corrective Therapists

Manual Arts Therapists

Occupational Therapists

Physical Therapists

Prosthetic Representatives

Rehabilitation Therapy Assistants

Social Work

Food Assistance Program Specialists

Psychology Aides and Technicians

Recreation Specialists

Social Science Aides and Technicians

Social Scientists

Social Service Aides and Assistants

Social Service Representatives

Social Workers

Sociology

Program Analysts

Social Science Aides and Technicians

Social Scientists

Social Service Aides and Assistants

Social Service Representatives

Sociologists

Statistics

Actuaries

Computer Science Specialists

Mathematical Statisticians

Operations Research Analysts

Program Analysts

Statisticians

Transportation Industry Analysts

Surveying

Geodesists

Land Surveyors

Systems Analysis

Computer Science Specialists

Computer Specialists

Government Accounting Office Information Technology Analyst

Management Analysts

Miscellaneous Administrative and Programs Specialists

Program Analysts

Theology

Chaplains

Program Analysts

Social Workers

Transportation

Cargo Schedulers

Highway Safety Specialists

Marine Cargo Specialists

Traffic Management Specialists

Transportation Industry Analysts

Transportation Loss/Damage Claims Examiners

Transportation Operators

Transportation Specialists

Travel Assistants

Zoology

Animal Scientists

Physiologists

Zoologists

APPENDIX B

Sample Federal Job Vacancy Announcement

Although federal vacancy announcements are usually quite long, don't be intimidated by them. A vacancy announcement explains the job opening, its location, salary, required qualifications, and more. Vacancy announcements also tell you exactly how to apply and the deadline for your application materials. (For a clear explanation of the main parts of an announcement, refer to Chapter 3.) To prepare you for your first encounter with a federal vacancy announcement, we've reproduced the complete text for one that appeared on the USAJOBS Web site. (We did not modify the agency contact information. Just keep in mind that the announcement will have expired by the time you read this information.) Note that some sections on vacancy announcements may not apply to you. Most announcements include sections on veterans' preference, which is preferential hiring for qualified veterans; the Career Transition Assistance Program (CTAP), which is preferential hiring for federal employees whose jobs have been eliminated; and merit promotion procedures, which are application instructions for current federal employees. Skip these sections if they do not apply to you. However, you must make absolutely certain that you are qualified to apply for a vacancy. If you are not qualified, your application will not be considered. Announcements also include equal opportunity statements, information for applicants with disabilities who need assistance, and sometimes admonitions to tell the truth on applications. So take a deep breath, take your time, and read through the following announcement.

Department: Department of Veterans Affairs

Agency: Veterans Health Administration

Job Announcement Number: VZ-09-CRO-212986

Overview

Management Analyst

SALARY RANGE: 48,753.00 - 63,384.00 USD per year

OPEN PERIOD: Friday, October 17, 20XX to Thursday, October 23, 20XX

SERIES & GRADE: GS-0343-09

POSITION INFORMATION: Full Time Career/Career Conditional

DUTY LOCATIONS: 1 vacancy - Braintree, MA

WHO MAY BE CONSIDERED: United States Citizens

Job Summary

Vacancy Identification Number (VIN): VZ212986 (include on all documents)

Be a member of a team providing compassionate health care to veterans.

The Department of Veterans Affairs is an employer of choice as a center of excellence in patient care, education, and research. We value trust, respect, commitment, compassion, and excellence; we value you. For more information on the Department of Veterans Affairs, go to http://www.va.gov.

NOTE: In order to view and/or print the entire announcement, please scroll to the bottom of this page and click on Print Preview; then Print. Otherwise, you may miss important instructions on how to apply for this position.

Applicant Checklist

Please use this checklist to ensure compliance with all application requirements. We recommend that you print a copy of this checklist for reference while completing your application package. Detailed instructions of the application process are included after the checklist. Be sure to read and follow the instructions carefully.

_____ Responses to the Assessment Questionnaire (see Step 1).

_____ Resume (see Step 2 for the information you should include on your resume) or Optional Application for Federal Employment (OF-612).

_____ If you are faxing your documentation, the United States Government Application Cover Page must be used in order to link your documents with your online questionnaire. Failure to provide this cover page—or the use of a different cover page—will prohibit your documentation from being processed (see Step 3 for URL).

_____ If a particular level of education/certification is required OR if you are asking us to qualify you based upon your education, you must submit a copy of your college transcript or an appropriate course listing (see Step 3).

_____ Veterans must provide a _legible_ copy of DD-214(s) showing all dates of service as well as character of service (honorable, general, etc.). Note: More than one DD-214 may be needed to show all dates of service. You will be given preference based on the information you submit with your application (see Step 3).

_____ Disabled veterans and other veterans eligible for 10-point preference must also submit an SF-15 (version August 20XX) with required proof as stated on the form (see Step 3). 10-point preference will be given only when proper documentation is submitted.

_____ An OF-306, Declaration for Federal Employment (version dated January 20XX or later), must be submitted prior to appointment. You may include this form as part of your application documents. It is available at http://www.opm.gov/forms/pdf_fill/of0306.pdf.

Key Requirements

★ Please refer to the "Qualifications" section of this vacancy announcement.

★ You must be a U.S. citizen to apply for this job.

★ This announcement may be used to fill one or more vacancies.

Duties

Major Duties

This position is in the Business Model Development section of the Allocation Resource Center (ARC) located in Braintree, MA. The Allocation Resource Center is responsible to the Associate Chief Financial Officer (ACFO) for the Veterans Equitable Resource Allocation (VERA) Model. The center is responsible for the integrity of the model outcomes, including the design, implementation, and production of management information that supports the VERA system. This job includes the review, the evaluation, the maintenance and the improvements to this system that are responsible for the distribution of 90 percent of VHA resources. In this position, you will serve as a management analyst.

Duties of this position: You will work self-sufficiently and on teams to accomplish tasks that are directed to this section. You will learn effective techniques and use a robust set of skills to accomplish a wide range of ongoing tasks that are critical to the Center's smooth operation. Specific duties include, but are not limited to, the following.

Customer Service and Reports

The information the center deals with directly affects budgets throughout the agency and there is urgency to all the requests from customers. You will use management information to answer a wide range of these questions and are expected to use all the resources at the Center to assist in fulfilling these requests.

Financial Model Analysis

You will serve as an active participant in supporting the CFO's VERA system. You will turn data into information that the executives of the organization can use to make critical decisions. You will provide analytical staff support for a variety of projects with which the Center is involved using the data embedded in the VERA system.

Application Programming

You will be responsible for several specific pieces of the VERA model inputs including the modeling, creation and validation of these components. You will work with senior staff to ensure that all model factors reflecting policy changes are incorporated. You will maintain the procedures and documentation that produce the vital information that is embedded in the VHA VERA model and have the ability to make modifications that will reflect policy changes as determined by VHA leadership. You will focus on computer applications used to produce clinically relevant data analyses emphasizing financial issues.

Data Management

You will access a wide range of data from a variety of systems and must be capable of managing data within a database environment. You will develop data models, know the data definitions, acquire the data, and perform data validation for specific data sets that support information that helps with explanation of VHA budgets. You will create data tables, populate them, and give appropriate access to the data to members of the ARC staff.

RELOCATION EXPENSES AND/OR INCENTIVES ARE NOT AUTHORIZED

Qualifications and Evaluation

Qualifications

EXPERIENCE: Must possess at least one (1) full year of Specialized Experience that equipped you with the knowledge, skills, and abilities to perform the duties of this position. This experience must have been equivalent to at least the GS-7 level in Federal service.

Examples of Specialized Experience include: analyzes, gathers, and organizes data to be used in making recommendations and recognizing solutions; uses database management programs to produce clinically relevant data; communicates effectively orally and in writing with people from a variety of backgrounds; organizes and plans your own work; turns data into information that is used to make critical decisions; applies knowledge of data collection, analysis and manipulation of computerized data sources in a healthcare environment; applies knowledge of health care industry practices and techniques with specific focus on reimbursement and funding methods such as financial management, workload measures, and quality of care issues; applies working knowledge of database management languages such as ORACLE SQL in a UNIX-like environment; and extracts a wide range of health related management information and recommends or modifies the content and format as necessary to accomplish the work of a healthcare organization. Note: Evidence of this specialized experience must be supported by detailed documentation on your resume or OF-612. Also provide work experience information such as hours per week, salary, and starting/ending dates of employment (month and year format) to establish one (1) full year of Specialized Experience.

OR

EDUCATION: Must possess at least two (2) full years of successfully completed graduate education OR a master's degree OR your LL.B. or J.D., directly related to the work of the position. One year of full-time graduate education is considered to be the number of credit hours that the school attended has determined to represent 1 year of full-time study. Part-time graduate education is creditable in accordance with its relationship to a year of full-time study at the school attended (transcripts required).

OR

COMBINATION OF EXPERIENCE AND EDUCATION: Must possess equivalent combinations of successfully completed graduate education and Specialized Experience directly related to the work of the position, as outlined above (i.e.: Six (6) months Specialized Experience and one (1) full year of successfully completed graduate education directly related to the work of the position). (Transcript required.)

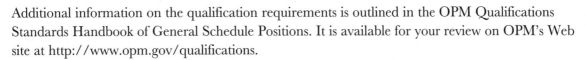

Additional information on the qualification requirements is outlined in the OPM Qualifications Standards Handbook of General Schedule Positions. It is available for your review on OPM's Web site at http://www.opm.gov/qualifications.

APPLICANTS PLEASE NOTE: Education must be accredited by an accrediting institution recognized by the U.S. Department of Education in order for it to be credited towards qualifications (particularly positions with a positive education requirement). Therefore, applicants must report attendance and/or degrees from only these schools. Applicants can verify accreditation at the following Web site: www.ed.gov/admins/finaid/accred/index.html. All education claimed by applicants will be verified by the appointing agency accordingly.

Foreign Education: To receive credit for education completed outside the United States, you must show proof that the education has been submitted to a private organization that specializes in the interpretation of foreign educational credentials and such education has been deemed at least equivalent to that gained in conventional U.S. education programs.

REQUIREMENTS (Failure to comply may be grounds for withdrawal of an offer of employment, or dismissal after appointment):

★ Applicants must meet any physical, language, license or degree requirements.

★ Applicants must be citizens of the United States.

★ Applicants tentatively selected for certain designated positions may be subject to a random drug screening for illegal drug use. Applicants who refuse to be tested will be denied employment.

★ New appointees may be subject to a probationary period.

★ New appointees will be subject to a background investigation to determine suitability.

★ An OF-306, Declaration for Federal Employment (version dated January 20XX), must be submitted prior to appointment. This form is available at www.opm.gov/forms/pdf_fill/of0306.pdf.

How You Will Be Evaluated

Please ensure you answer all questions and follow all instructions carefully. Errors or omissions may affect your evaluation. When answering the questionnaire, remember that your experience and education are subject to verification by investigation. You may be asked to provide specific examples or documentation of experience or education as proof to support your answers, or you may be required to verify a response by a practical demonstration of your claimed ability to perform a task.

Benefits and Other Information

Benefits

The Department of Veterans Affairs offers a comprehensive benefits program that you can customize for your individual medical and financial needs. In addition to traditional "dollars and cents" benefits, we offer a range of benefits to help you balance life with the VA to life outside of work. For additional information about the many benefits of a career with the VA, please visit our "Benefits at a Glance" Web page at http://www.va.gov/jobs/job_benefits/benefits.asp.

Other Information

Area of consideration: All citizens of the United States of America. Applications received under this announcement will be rated under competitive procedures in accordance with Office of Personnel Management examining regulations. [The Human Resources (HR) Office for the facility with this vacancy may be accepting applications separately under one or more special employment authorities, such as: Veterans Recruitment Appointment (VRA); Veterans Employment Opportunity Act (VEOA); hiring compensably disabled veterans with ratings of 30 percent or greater; hiring persons with disabilities; or reinstatement to, or transfer within, the Federal government. If so, you may find a separate announcement covering one or more of these special authorities on http:// www.usajobs.opm.gov/. You may also contact the facility's HR Office directly to inquire if applications are being accepted under any of the special authorities for which you are eligible.]

For a fact sheet explaining how Federal jobs are filled, click on http://www.usajobs.opm.gov/ EI55.asp.

Priority consideration: Individuals who have special priority selection rights under the Agency Career Transition Assistance Program (CTAP) or the Interagency Career Transition Assistance Program (ICTAP) must be well qualified for the position to receive consideration for special priority selection. CTAP and ICTAP eligibles will be considered well qualified if they attain an eligibility rating of 90.0 or higher, not including points for veterans' preference, from the facility with the vacancy.

Federal employees seeking CTAP/ICTAP eligibility must submit proof that they meet the requirements of 5 CFR 330.605 (a) for CTAP and 5 CFR 330.704 for ICTAP. This includes a copy of the agency notice, a copy of their most recent Performance Rating and a copy of their most recent SF-50 noting current position, grade level, and duty location. Please annotate your application to reflect that you are applying as a CTAP or ICTAP eligible.

Filling additional vacancies: If additional vacancies for this position occur within 90 days, this announcement may be used without reannouncement.

How to Apply

PLEASE NOTE:

★ It is your responsibility to insure that all application materials are received by 11:59 p.m. Eastern Standard Time on the closing date of the announcement (Thursday, October 23, 20XX) in order to be considered. We cannot be responsible for incompatible software, illegible fax transmissions, interruptions in Internet service, etc.

★ You must submit a complete application package. Failure to provide complete information may result in your not receiving consideration for this position.

★ You must submit your assessment questionnaire online (through Application Manager) or on OPM Form 1203-FX (and faxed). Do not send printouts of your Application Manager Questionnaire Answers. If you fax your application and/or documentation, please keep a copy of your fax transmittal receipt for future verification, if necessary.

★ If you upload your documents using Application Manager, do not fax the same documents. To verify that your uploaded documents have been processed, please wait one hour to ensure they have cleared the virus scan. You can then verify that your uploaded documents are attached to your application by checking the Details tab of your Application Manager account (https:// applicationmanager.gov) for this vacancy announcement. Your documents will display under the Details tab in the Document area.

★ You will not be contacted for additional information. do not contact our offices for verification of receipt or status reports—we do not provide this information.

★ Your application materials will not be returned. Do not submit original documents that you may need in the future.

★ Your application must be completed online or faxed. This office does not accept applications by electronic mail (e-mail), regular mail, or in person.

Applying for This Position Is as Easy as 1, 2, 3...

Just by following three steps, you will submit a complete application package and receive consideration for this position. Be sure to follow the steps carefully and complete all three. Each step is described in detail below.

1. Your responses to the Assessment Questionnaire (which may be completed electronically or on the OPM Form 1203FX and faxed)

2. Your resume or OF-612 (which may be completed electronically, uploaded, or faxed)

3. Other documents specified in this job announcement (which may be uploaded or faxed)

Use *Application Manager* for convenience and quickest processing. Track your progress to a *Complete* Application Package using *My Application Packages* checklist and status displays in Application Manager. Your Application Package status must be *Complete* by 11:59 p.m. EST on Thursday, October 23, 20XX.

Step 1

Complete and submit the Assessment Questionnaire. The questionnaire must be completed and submitted in order to receive consideration for this position.

PLEASE NOTE: We highly encourage you to complete the Assessment Questionnaire online as it is the most efficient way to process your responses. Using paper application forms may delay the processing of your application. If you are unable to complete the Assessment Questionnaire online, go to STEP 3 of this announcement and refer to the alternatives described under "Alternative Methods for Completing the Application Package."

You must provide responses to all required questions. Be sure to double-check your application before submission and click on SUBMIT when it is complete. Your application is not transmitted to us until you submit it.

To complete your Assessment Questionnaire online, click the following link:

Online Questionnaire

or enter https://ApplicationManager.gov. You can save your work and come back later. Return to Application Manager at any time by simply going back to this Web address.

The Assessment Questionnaire must be completed and submitted by 11:59 p.m. EST on Thursday, October 23, 20XX.

ASSESSMENT QUESTIONNAIRE

Social Security Number

Enter your Social Security Number in the space indicated. Providing your Social Security Number is voluntary; however, we cannot process your application without it.

Vacancy Identification Number

VZ212986

1. **Title of Job**

   Management Analyst

2. **Biographic Data**

3. **E-Mail Address**

   Please enter your e-mail address in the space provided. If you do not provide an e-mail address you may not receive a notice of your results.

4. **Work Information**

   If you are applying by the OPM Form 1203-FX, leave this section blank.

5. **Employment Availability**

   If you are applying by the OPM Form 1203-FX, leave this section blank.

6. **Citizenship**

   Are you a citizen of the United States?

7. **Background Information**

   If you are applying by the OPM Form 1203-FX, leave this section blank.

8. **Other Information**

   If you are applying by the OPM Form 1203-FX, leave this section blank.

9. **Languages**

   If you are applying by the OPM Form 1203-FX, leave this section blank.

10. **Lowest Grade**

    Enter the lowest grade (09) you will accept for this position.

11. **Miscellaneous Information**

    If you are applying by the OPM Form 1203-FX, leave this section blank.

12. **Special Knowledge**

    If you are applying by the OPM Form 1203-FX, leave this section blank.

13. **Test Location**

If you are applying by the OPM Form 1203-FX, leave this section blank.

14. **Veteran Preference Claim**

15. **Dates of Active Duty - Military Service**

16. **Availability Date**

If you are applying by the OPM Form 1203-FX, leave this section blank.

17. **Service Computation Date**

If you are applying by the OPM Form 1203-FX, leave this section blank.

18. **Other Date Information**

If you are applying by the OPM Form 1203-FX, leave this section blank.

19. **Job Preference**

If you are applying by the OPM Form 1203-FX, leave this section blank.

20. **Occupational Specialties**

The specialty code(s) for this position is (are): 001 Management Analyst

21. **Geographic Availability**

The location code(s) for this position is (are): 0130 Braintree, MA

22. **Transition Assistance Plan**

23. **Job-Related Experience**

If you are applying by the OPM Form 1203-FX, leave this section blank.

24. **Personal Background Information**

If you are applying by the OPM Form 1203-FX, leave this section blank.

25. **Occupational/Assessment Questions**

Select the appropriate answer to each of the following questions based on your current level of education and/or experience that demonstrates your ability to perform the duties of this position.

1. EXPERIENCE: Do you possess at least one (1) full year of Specialized Experience that equipped you with the knowledge, skills, and abilities to perform the duties of this position? This experience must have been equivalent to at least the GS-7 level in federal service. Examples of Specialized Experience include: analyzes, gathers, and organizes data to be used in making recommendations and recognizing solutions; uses database management programs to produce clinically relevant data; communicates effectively orally and in writing with people from a variety of backgrounds; organizes and plans your own work; turns data into information that is used to make critical decisions; applies knowledge of data collection, analysis and manipulation of computerized data sources in a healthcare environment; applies knowledge of health care industry practices and techniques with specific focus on

reimbursement and funding methods such as financial management, workload measures, and quality of care issues; applies working knowledge of database management languages such as ORACLE SQL in a UNIX-like environment; and extracts a wide range of health related management information and recommends or modifies the content and format as necessary to accomplish the work of a healthcare organization. (Evidence of this specialized experience must be supported by detailed documentation of duties performed in positions held on your resume or OF-612. You will also need to provide work experience information such as hours per week, salary, and starting/ending dates of employment (month and year format) to establish you have one (1) full year of Specialized Experience at the required grade level).

   A. Yes

   B. No

2.   EDUCATION: Do you possess at least two (2) full years of successfully completed gradu-ate education OR a master's degree OR your LL.B. or J.D., directly related to the work of the position? One year of full-time graduate education is considered to be the number of credit hours that the school attended has determined to represent 1 year of full-time study. Part-time graduate education is creditable in accordance with its relationship to a year of full-time study at the school attended (transcripts required).

   A. Yes

   B. No

3.   COMBINATION OF EXPERIENCE AND EDUCATION: Do you possess equivalent combinations of successfully completed graduate education and Specialized Experience directly related to the work of the position, as outlined above? (i.e.: Six (6) months Specialized Experience and one (1) full year of successfully completed graduate education directly related to the work of the position.) (Transcript Required)

   A. Yes

   B. No

KSA #1- The following statements refer to your ABILITY TO GATHER, ORGANIZE, AND ANALYZE PERTINENT DATA TO BE UTILIZED TO MAKE RECOMMENDATIONS AND RECOGNIZE SOLUTIONS.

For each task in the following group, choose the statement from the list below that best describes your experience and/or training. Please select only one letter for each item.

   A- I have not had education, training or experience in performing this task.

   B- I have had education or training in performing the task, but have not yet performed it on the job.

   C- I have performed this task on the job. My work on this task was monitored closely by a supervisor or senior employee to ensure compliance with proper procedures.

   D- I have performed this task as a regular part of a job. I have performed it independently and normally without review by a supervisor or senior employee.

E- I am considered an expert in performing this task. I have supervised performance of this task or am normally the person who is consulted by other workers to assist them in doing this task because of my expertise.

4. Performs data collection, analysis and manipulation of computerized data sources in a healthcare setting.

5. Applies knowledge of healthcare industry practices and techniques with specific focus on reimbursement and funding methods such as financial management, workload measures, and quality of care issues.

6. Turns data into information that executives can use to make critical decisions.

7. Provides analytical staff support for a variety of projects.

8. Participates in studies and evaluations.

9. Validates your work and the work of others.

10. Ensures the reliability of the information produced.

KSA #2- The following statements refer to your KNOWLEDGE OF DATABASE MANAGEMENT PROGRAMS.

11. Accesses a wide range of data from a variety of systems.

12. Manages data within a database environment.

13. Provides data driven information.

14. Works with spreadsheets.

15. Explains the budget, data definitions, validation techniques, data acquisition and data modeling.

KSA #3- The following statements refer to your SKILL IN ACCESSING COMPUTER APPLICATIONS USED TO PRODUCE CLINICALLY RELEVANT DATA.

16. Applies good working knowledge of database management languages such as ORACLE SQL in a UNIX-like environment.

17. Learns new programming languages and tools with ease.

18. Extracts a wide range of health related management information and recommends or modifies the content and formats as necessary to accomplish the work of an organization.

19. Responsible for several specific pieces of a database model input.

20. Models, creates, and validates database model components.

21. Maintains procedures that produce data information.

22. Makes modifications that reflect policy changes as determined by leadership.

23. Focuses on computer applications used to produce clinically relevant data analyses.

24. Emphasizes financial issues.

KSA #4- The following statements refer to your ABILITY TO PLAN AND ORGANIZE YOUR OWN WORK UNDER CONDITIONS WHERE PRIORITIES CAN CHANGE FREQUENTLY.

25. Works effectively independently and on teams to accomplish tasks.

26. Carries out assignments independently.

27. Establishes and meets objectives.

28. Plans projects and resolves conflicts.

29. Integrates related projects.

30. Produces reports or memos.

31. Uses good judgment and deductive skills.

KSA #5- The following statements refer to your ABILITY TO EFFECTIVELY COMMUNICATE ORALLY WITH INDIVIDUALS OR GROUPS FROM A VARIETY OF BACKGROUNDS WITH DIVERGENT OPINIONS.

32. Uses management information to answer a wide range of questions.

33. Keeps higher level management staff informed of progress, potential problems and controversial matters.

34. Contacts visitors from other agencies as well as other health care professionals in related fields.

35. Contacts program and technical persons throughout the agency.

KSA #6- The following statements refer to your ABILITY TO EFFECTIVELY COMMUNICATE IN WRITING WITH INDIVIDUALS OR GROUPS FROM A VARIETY OF BACKGROUNDS WITH DIVERGENT OPINIONS.

36. Takes a complex problem and produces written analysis backed by data analysis and clinical integrity.

37. Communicates work with other persons in writing.

38. Creates standard reports.

39. Handles information that affects the budget.

40. Processes requests from customers.

You must now complete and submit additional application materials (by Thursday, October 23, 20XX) as required by this vacancy announcement via uploading or faxing this information. To fax application materials, refer to the instructions in *Alternative Methods for Completing the Application Package* after Step 3 of this vacancy announcement.

Step 2

Submit your choice of a Resume or an OF-612 - Optional Application for Federal Employment available at www.opm.gov/forms/pdf_fill/of612.pdf. We must receive a complete resume or OF 612 in order to determine your qualifications for this position.

Your resume must include the following information:

★ **Vacancy Information**: Announcement Number (VZ212986), Position Title (Management Analyst), and grade (09/09)

★ **Personal Information:**

Your full legal name and mailing address

Day and Evening telephone numbers including area code

Country of citizenship

Social Security number

★ **Work experience** (NOTE: You must include the following information in order to receive credit for your experience):

Name and address of employer.

Your job title.

The beginning and ending month and year of your employment.

The average hours worked per week. Full-time work is considered to be 35-40 hours of work per week. Part-time experience will be credited on the basis of time actually spent in appropriate activities. Applicants wishing to receive credit for such experience must indicate clearly the number of hours a week spent in such employment.

Your supervisor's name and phone number (indicate if we may call your supervisor).

A description of your duties that is sufficiently detailed to document the level of your experience. If the position is (was) with the federal government (military or civilian), state the series and grade or pay grade (rank) and the date of last promotion.

★ **Education:** Name, location, and dates of attendance for colleges attended (if required). Type and date of degree received (if any).

★ **Other**: Training, license(s), or certification(s) relevant to the position.

Do not submit letters of recommendation, performance appraisals, position descriptions, examples of your work, etc. This additional information will not be forwarded to the hiring facility.

Step 3

Submit other required application materials, as applicable.

★ If you are using education to qualify, you must submit copies of college transcripts or a course listing that identifies for each course completed: the college or university, semester or quarter hours earned, grade, and grade-point average received.

★ If you are applying for veterans' preference, you must submit evidence of eligibility, such as: DD-214 (Certificate of Release or Discharge from Active Duty), or Standard Form 15 (Application for 10-Point Veterans' Preference version dated August 20XX), and the proof requested on the form. For Access to DD214 and military records click on this link - Military Information. To print a copy of the SF15 go to www.opm.gov/forms/pdf_fill/sf15.pdf. Veterans preference will not be given unless proper documentation is submitted with your application materials.

Submitting Documents

If you upload your documents using Application Manager, do not fax the same documents. To verify uploaded documents have been processed, please wait one hour to ensure they have cleared the virus scan. You can verify that your uploaded documents are attached to your application by checking the Details tab of your Application Manager account https://applicationmanager.gov for this vacancy announcement. Your documents will display under the Details tab in the Document area.

Faxed documents will take 2-3 business days to process. To fax documents, you must use the United States Government Application Cover Page. Print the pre-populated cover page on the upload documents screen of Application Manager or you may click this link http://staffing.opm.gov/pdf/usascover.pdf to print a blank copy of the cover page. When faxing documents, follow the procedures outlined below.

★ You may submit multiple documents for the same vacancy announcement using one cover page.

★ Include the eight-character Vacancy Identification Number: VZ212986.

★ Provide your Social Security number and full name in the spaces provided or we will not be able to associate your document(s) with the rest of your application.

★ Place the cover page on top of the document(s) you are faxing.

★ Fax your cover page and documents to 1-478-757-3144.

Faxed documents submitted with missing information will not be processed. The following will prevent your documents from being processed:

★ Not using the United States Government Application Cover Page mentioned above

★ Missing, incomplete, or invalid Vacancy Identification Number

★ Missing or incomplete Social Security Number or name

Note: If you have documents in your Application Manager account from a previous vacancy announcement they can be opened, copied and saved then reused as an upload file for this vacancy. Uploading your documents will speed the processing of your application for this announcement.

Be sure to complete all THREE STEPS of the application process described above in order to submit a complete application package and receive consideration for this position.

Alternative Methods for Completing the Application Package

To complete the Assessment Questionnaire manually, you will need a copy of the questionnaire answer sheet, referred to as the Occupational Questionnaire- OPM Form 1203-FX, which can be obtained electronically at http://www.opm.gov/forms/pdf_fill/opm1203fx.pdf, or by calling USAJOBS at 703-724-1850 and following the instructions given, or by visiting the Human Resources Management Service of the VA Medical Center at the duty location.

You will also need a copy of the vacancy announcement to use as a guide in answering the questions. You must provide responses to all required questions. Some questions may request an additional written response to support your answer, such as "Please explain or provide additional information to support your response to the above question." When additional information is requested, please provide your answer(s) on a separate sheet of paper with the corresponding questionnaire number indicated, and type or print your answers legibly. You may omit any sections marked "optional" and be sure to double-check your application before submission. Note: The questionnaire answer sheet is six pages long. All six pages must be submitted even when the number of questions does not exceed Page 5. In this case, please complete the top of Page 6 with your Social Security number and the vacancy ID number.

You may submit the Form 1203-FX, resume, and any supporting documents by fax.

If you are faxing a Form 1203-FX, do not use a separate cover sheet. Simply make sure the Form 1203-FX is on top of any other documents you are faxing.

If you are faxing any documents without the Form 1203-FX on top, you must use the United States Government Application Cover Page. Print the pre-populated cover page on the upload documents screen of Application Manager, or you may click this link (http://staffing.opm.gov/pdf/usascover. pdf) to print a blank copy of the cover page. When faxing documents, follow the procedures outlined below:

★ Place the cover page on top of documents being faxed.

★ Include the eight-character Vacancy Identification Number VZ212986.

★ Provide your Social Security number and full name in the spaces provided, or we will not be able to associate your document(s) with the rest of your application.

★ Place your documents in the following order: United States Government Application Cover Page, resume or OF-612 (Optional Application for Federal Employment), and other required application materials.

★ You may submit multiple documents for the same vacancy announcement using one cover page.

Fax your cover page and documents to 1-478-757-3144.

Feed all documents into your fax machine top first so that we receive them right-side up. If you fax your documents using any other cover page, you may not receive consideration.

Mailed, e-mailed, or hand-delivered applications will not be accepted. If you are unable to upload your documents after completing the Occupational Questionnaire online, you may fax your documents (resume, transcripts, etc.) as instructed above.

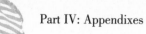

Required Documents

All of the government forms mentioned in the above statements can be downloaded from the following Web address: www.opm.gov/forms or obtained at the Human Resources Management Office of the duty station.

Contact Information:

VHA Nationwide DEU-TOP
Phone: 785-350-1543
Fax: 478-757-3144
TDD: 800-877-8339
E-mail: HRCDEUJKR@va.gov

What to Expect Next

Your resume and supporting documentation will be compared to your responses to the Assessment Questionnaire. The questionnaire is designed to capture the desired knowledge, skills, and abilities for this position. The evaluation you receive is based on your responses to the questionnaire and is a measure of the degree to which your background matches the knowledge, skills, and abilities required of this position.

If your application does not support your responses to the questionnaire, or if you are not able to provide verifying documentation, it may affect your evaluation or result in your name being removed from further consideration.

If you are eligible for veterans' preference, you will be given preference based on the documentation you submit. Please see the "Veterans Information" section of this announcement for details.

This office will not contact you to discuss missing or illegible documents.

Once your qualifications have been evaluated, your application will be assigned a numeric score. Candidates will be ranked in score order with appropriate points added for veterans' preference.

An electronic notification letter will be sent to applicants who provide an e-mail address. If you do not provide an e-mail address, you will receive a notification letter via the U.S. Postal Service. Normal processing time is four to six weeks. This office is responsible for initial evaluation only. Facilities are responsible for contacting eligible applicants thereafter.

For questions about this job:

VHA Nationwide DEU-TOP
Phone: (785)350-1543
Fax: (478)757-3144
TDD: 800-877-8339
E-mail: HRCDEUJKR@va.gov
USAJOBS Control Number: 1356071

APPENDIX C

Sample Federal-Style Resumes and KSAs

As we explain in Chapter 3, you can't use your regular resume when applying for a federal job. Your standard resume can serve as the basis for your federal-style resume, but the government requires more information. Federal-style resumes may run two to five pages because of the information that's required and/or that you have the option to include. You can format your federal-style resume (paper) any way you like. You can take advantage of a paper resume's flexibility by choosing a format that highlights your strengths. If you are a recent graduate, for example, you might place education before work experience. The only limitation when applying for a federal job is that you must list jobs in reverse chronological order, so start with your most recent job. Each page should include the vacancy announcement number and your name and Social Security number. Keep in mind that these are general guidelines. You should always follow the instructions given in the How to Apply section of the vacancy announcement.

In the past few years, more federal agencies want job applications to be made online. In these instances, the agency sometimes offers a fax option. As you decide how to submit your application package, it is worth considering how to position yourself in the most advantageous manner. First impressions count, so you want to consider the person reading your application package. Faxes have a tendency to blur your words and to leave some of your words illegible. A prudent person will make a choice that presents their application in the most competitive manner.

Following are examples of federal-style paper resumes and an electronic/scannable resume from USAJOBS. We have also included sample responses to knowledge, skills, and abilities statements (KSAs). These statements are typically found in the Qualifications and Evaluations section of vacancy announcements or in the form of questions as part of an online application. For more information about writing federal resumes and KSAs, see Chapter 3.

Sample Resume 1

JOE SMITH
100 Fishers Lane, Rockville, MD 20853
(H) 301-555-0555 * (W) 202-100-0000 * jsmith@hotmail.com

Social Security No: 123-45-6789
Highest grade: N/A

Country of citizenship: United States
Veterans' preference: No

Position applied for: Legislative Aide
Announcement number: DHSHQYR08-1467

SUMMARY OF QUALIFICATIONS

Experienced Capitol Hill staffer with more than eight years working with two senators.
Proven effectiveness in government and constituent affairs.
Recognized for solid public policy background.
Strong research and writing skills; demonstrated ability to coordinate large-scale events.
Highly motivated self-starter known for strong follow-through skills.

SPECIAL SKILLS

Advanced skills in database administration.
Computer proficiency includes: Microsoft Word, Excel, WordPerfect, Quorum, LexisNexis, Thomas, and Internet research.
Languages: fluent in English, conversant in Hindi, understand basic French.

EDUCATION

University of Chicago, Chicago, IL, Masters of Arts in Public Policy, 1996.
Researched urban policy issues with William Wilson, leading scholar of urban poverty.
Smith College, Northampton, MA, Bachelor of Arts in Government, 1993.

PROFESSIONAL EXPERIENCE

United States Senate, Washington, DC
Grade Level: N/A
Supervisor: Edward Forrester, 202-555-0000 (may be contacted)

Hours per week: 40

Office of Senator Richard Durbin	05/2000–Present
Legislative Aide	03/2003–Present
Legislative Correspondent, Governmental Affairs Committee	07/2001–03/2003
Legislative Correspondent	05/2000–07/2001

Worked closely with senator, staff, and legislative process to bring projects/ initiatives to fruition:
- Prepared preliminary drafts of bills; monitored progress of proposed and pending legislation.
- Provided senator with background information and statistics re high-profile issues (included daily briefings); advised senator on issues relating to arts, humanities, and postal services; evaluated and devised responsive legislative proposals.
- Conducted research using a wide range of sources; synthesized complex information.
- Advocated for constituents in their dealings with government agencies.

- Tracked legislation and assisted senior legislative staff with policy and issue research; analyzed how proposed legislation could affect constituency.
- Attended briefings and hearings; represented senator in meetings with constituents, lobbyists, and advocacy organizations, state agencies, and legislative offices.
- Drafted, revised, proofread, and typed congressional responses to constituent inquiries.

United States Senate, Washington, DC
Grade Level: N/A   Hours per week: 40
Supervisor: Jeffery Shorts (no longer there), 202-224-0000

Office of Senator Barbara Boxer   01/1999–05/2000
Coordinator of Internet Correspondence/Intern Coordinator
- Insured correspondence software system functioned properly.
- Supervised and selected intern teams comprised of 8–10 people.

MAJOR ACCOMPLISHMENT: Developed an Internet correspondence system that was described as "flawless" in a comprehensive constituent survey.

HIGHLIGHTS OF PREVIOUS EXPERIENCE

Public Relations Intern, Collaborations, Inc., Philadelphia, PA   08/1997–12/1998
- Coordinated community liaison event for a major constituent banquet.

Marketing Coordinator, Philadelphia Hospitality, Inc., Philadelphia, PA   01/1996–12/1996
- Implemented a customized database for the hospitality industry that is still in use.

Library Assistant, Museum of Broadcast Communications, Chicago, IL   03/1995–11/1995
Legislative Intern, Office of Senator Barbara Boxer, Washington, DC   Summer 1994
News Intern, WLKY-TV, Louisville, KY   Summers 1991&1992

Sample KSA

JOE SMITH
SSN: 123-45-6789
Job Announcement Number: DHSHQYR08-1467

<u>KSA</u>

1. Knowledge of the legislative process and the structure of Congress as they relate to jurisdiction over homeland security programs.

During my tenure as a Capitol Hill staffer initially working for Senator Boxer, and more recently working for Senator Durbin, I gained in-depth knowledge and understanding of the federal legislative process. My knowledge was acquired mostly through my work on the Governmental Affairs Committee and as a professional in the personal office of Senator Durbin.

My most noteworthy contribution took place as a legislative correspondent just after the 9/11 attacks when I worked on the Governmental Affairs Committee. At that time, the Governmental Affairs Committee provided oversight for domestic security matters, and the Department of Homeland Security had not yet been established. In response to the 9/11 tragedy, the Governmental Affairs Committee was convened and given a short turnaround time to develop legislation creating the new department. In those difficult and angst-ridden days, I worked closely with the staff director of the Governmental Affairs Committee to provide research and information for her to pass on to Senator Durbin. The following tools were crucial to my success: LexisNexis, Gartner, and Thomas. Senator Durbin used the information I provided to build a strong case for establishing the Department of Homeland Security.

Moreover, I worked closely with the committee as it prepared for hearings on Homeland Security. I attended committee markups where various bills relating to the establishment of the new Department of Homeland Security were being discussed and amended. The end result was the establishment of the Department of Homeland Security as we all now know it. Senator Durbin was pleased with the hard work of the committee and publicly thanked committee members from the Senate floor when the legislation to establish a new Department of Homeland Security was passed.

JOE SMITH

SSN: 123-45-6789
Job Announcement Number: DHSHQYR08-1467

<u>**KSA**</u>

2. Ability to use the Internet and subscription services to monitor and track the legislative process and activities of Congress and to conduct analytical research of legislative and policy matters.

As a legislative professional for Senator Durbin, I used Internet and subscription services to monitor and track legislative matters in such issue areas as homeland security, energy, environment, governmental affairs, housing, and postal matters. I used the Legislative Information Service (LIS), the Library of Congress Thomas Legislative search engine, and subscription services such as eenews.net and LexisNexis to assist senior legislative staff with policy and research in their issue areas. In addition, I analyzed and prepared memoranda on how proposed legislation could affect the constituency Senator Durbin was representing.

An example of my work took place when gasoline prices were extremely high during the summer of 2008. I researched the Internet and provided Senator Durbin background information and statistics comparing gasoline prices nationwide with gasoline prices in Illinois. My memorandum was reviewed by my immediate supervisor on Energy Issues and by Senator Durbin's legislative director. The senator was pleased with the content and with how easy it was to comprehend the information as I presented it. Senator Durbin subsequently requested that I provide daily briefings to keep him apprised about the fluctuation in gasoline prices.

JOE SMITH
SSN: 123-45-6789
Job Announcement Number: DHSHQYR08-1467

<u>KSA</u>

3. Skill in written communications to edit and develop responses to congressional correspondence concerning an organization's programs/policies, post hearing questions for the record, and review outgoing correspondence for correct grammar and conformance to guidelines.

Throughout my career as a legislative staffer, skill in written communication has been vital to my success. For the past six years, I have written and edited materials responsive to constituent correspondence in such subject areas as homeland security, agriculture, energy, environment, housing, and postal is sues. My strong written communication skills have enabled me to convey to constituents highly technical information about public policy issues in clear and understandable terms. As the legislative correspondent on homeland security issues, I responded to a high volume of constituent inquiries about the creation of a new Department of Homeland Security. I researched this issue thoroughly, attended relevant hearings, and wrote a detailed form letter to Illinois constituents providing information about the new department. This correspondence was reviewed and approved by the staff director on the Governmental Affairs Committee, as well as by Senator Durbin's legislative director and chief of staff. Furthermore, as a legislative correspondent on the Governmental Affairs Committee, I worked with the committee staff director to write Senator Durbin's opening statement and questions for the record on committee hearings such as "U.S. Postal Service: What Can Be Done to Ensure Its Future Viability?"

JOE SMITH

SSN: 123-45-6789

Job Announcement Number: DHSHQYR08-1467

KSA

4. Skill in effectively interacting with agency officials, congressional staff, and officials of other government agencies to exchange information, coordinate presentation materials, and schedule meetings.

As a legislative aide for Senator Durbin, I advocate for constituents in their dealings with government agencies and have developed effective working relationships with federal and state agency officials. For example, when Senator Durbin wanted the United States Postal Service (USPS) to issue a postage stamp commemorating the life of former Chicago Mayor Harold Washington, I scheduled a meeting with Postmaster General Potter and Senator Durbin and made sure to include the Illinois House delegation to discuss the stamp. After our meeting, the Postmaster General agreed to give Senator Durbin's request full and fair consideration. Additionally, I have worked with congressional staff in both the House and Senate in creating legislation and cosponsoring bills and resolutions in issue areas such as energy, the environment, homeland security, and postal issues. As a staffer on the Governmental Affairs Committee, I worked with other Senate staff and officials of other government agencies to schedule briefings and to discuss recent developments related to homeland security.

Sample Resume 2

SALLY JONES
9000 Decatur Place, Hyattstown, MD 20700
301-555-8237 (H) ✦ 301-555-0101 (C) ✦ sjones@hmail.com

Social Security No: 123-45-6789   Country of citizenship: United States
Highest grade: N/A   Veterans' preference: No

Position applied for: Logistics Management Specialist
Announcement number: ST-08-14

Security clearance: Secret level

PROFESSIONAL PROFILE

Professional with strong analytical and critical-thinking skills.
Highly motivated, articulate, self-starter, with strong leadership skills.
Traveled internationally to South Africa, Spain, and Mexico.

AREAS OF STRENGTH

Analyzing/ Problem Solving/ Negotiating/ Detail Oriented/ Quick Learner/ Team Player

SPECIAL SKILLS

DTRA databases; type 40+ WPM; proficient using Microsoft Word, Excel, PowerPoint, and Access, and
in using the Internet for research

EMPLOYMENT HISTORY

Agreement Analyst Specialist   4/2006–Present
Federal Management Systems, Inc., Washington DC, 20000
Grade level: N/A   Hours per week: 40
Supervisor: William Oldman, 202-555-2736 (may be contacted)
Provide international security, security assistance, military operations, defense strategy and
policy, military use of space, and defense trade data analysis for Department of State's Bureau
of Political and Military Affairs. Review approximately 20–30 proposals and proposal amendments
per day.

- Analyze technical and manufacturing data to ensure compliance of foreign exports and
  imports.
- Prepare correspondence and make recommendations for action.
- Examine records, reports, and documents to establish facts and detect discrepancies.
- Monitor investigations of suspected offenders to ensure they are conducted in accordance
  with constitutional requirements.
- Investigate applications for special licenses or permits, as well as alleged license or
  permit violations.
- Recommend legal or administrative action to protect government property.

SALLY JONES, 123-45-6789, ST-08-14   Page 2

Sales Manager   10/2003–4/2006
Gallery Nairobi, Largo, MD 20700
Grade level: N/A   Hours per week: 40
Supervisor: Weston Watson, 301 -555-0000 (may be contacted)
Managed and provided oversight for the sales of classic and eclectic art from African-influenced cultures in a company with two sites and $1.2 million in annual revenue.

- Directed, coordinated, and reviewed African American art sales activities.
- Managed three employees engaged in sales activities; reconciled daily cash receipts.
- Resolved customer complaints regarding sales and service.
- Conferred with potential customers regarding equipment needs and advised customers on types of equipment to purchase.

Intern   Summers 2000, 2001 & 2002
Maryland Parks and Planning, 1000 Merrimack Road, Langley Park, MD 20748
Grade Level: N/A   Hours per week: 40
Supervisor: Sandra Parker, 301-555-4500
Supplied staff support for managing Prince George's County community centers.

- Provided basic personnel office support duties such as photocopying, filing, organizing, shredding documents, and performing receptionist duties.
- Co-led adult and child recreational trips: skiing, whitewater rafting, and mountain biking.

SPECIAL AWARDS

Maryland Parks and Recreation Service Excellence Award, 2000

EDUCATION

Florida Agricultural and Mechanical University, Tallahassee, FL   1999–2004
Political Science major/ Education minor, 120 credit hours
Related Courses:
Introduction to Political Science, State and Local Government, American National Government, Budget and Fiscal Management

Sample Electronic/Scannable Resume 2

Sally Jones
9000 Decatur Place
Hyattstown, MD 20700
Mobile: 301-555-0101
Day phone: 301-555-8237
E-mail: sjones@hmail.com

Country of citizenship:	United States of America
Veterans' preference:	No
Registered for Selective Service:	Not applicable
Contact current employer:	Yes

WORK EXPERIENCE   **Federal Management Systems, Inc.**
Washington, DC US
4/2006 - Present
Hours per week: 40
Agreement Analyst Specialist
Provide international security, security
assistance, military operations, defense
strategy and policy, military use of space,
and defense trade data analysis for the
Department of State's Bureau of Political
and Military Affairs. Review approximately
20-30 proposals and proposal amendments per
day.

* Analyze technical and manufacturing data
to ensure compliance of foreign exports and
imports.
* Prepare correspondence and make
recommendations for action.
* Examine records, reports, and documents to
establish facts and detect discrepancies.
* Monitor investigations of suspected
offenders to ensure they are conducted in
accordance with constitutional requirements.
* Investigate applications for special
licenses or permits, as well as alleged
license or permit violations.
* Recommend legal or administrative action
to protect government property.
Contact supervisor: Yes
Supervisor's name: William Oldman
Supervisor's phone: 202-555-2736

Gallery Nairobi
Largo, MD US
10/2003 - 4/2006
Hours per week: 40
Sales Manager
Managed and provided oversight for the sales of classic and eclectic art from African-influenced cultures in a company with two sites and $1.2 million in annual revenue.
* Directed, coordinated, and reviewed African American art sales activities.
* Managed three employees engaged in sales activities; reconciled daily cash receipts.
* Resolve customer complaints regarding sales and service.
* Confer with potential customers regarding equipment needs and advise customers on types of equipment to purchase.
Contact supervisor: Yes
Supervisor's name: Weston Watson
Supervisor's phone: 301-555-0000

Maryland Parks and Planning
6/2000 - 8/2002
Langley Park, MD US
Hours per week: 40
Intern
Supplied staff support for managing Prince George's County community centers. Worked summers only.
* Provided basic personnel office support duties such as photocopying, filing, organizing, shredding documents, and performing receptionist duties.
* Co-lead adult and child recreational trips: skiing, whitewater rafting, and mountain biking.
Contact supervisor: Yes
Supervisor's name: Sandra Parker
Supervisor's phone: 301-555-4500

EDUCATION

Florida Agricultural and Mechanical University
Tallahassee, FL US

Some College Coursework Completed
120 Semester Hours
Major: Political Science
Minor: Education
Relevant Coursework, Licensures and Certifications:
Introduction to Political Science, State and Local Government, American National Government, Budget and Fiscal Management

JOB-RELATED TRAINING

Dealing Effectively on a Team, 5/2008
Government Budgeting, 6/2007
Conflict Resolution, 8/2006
Getting Along With Difficult People, 3/2005

AFFILIATIONS

Toastmasters, Intl.   Member

REFERENCES

Bobby Brown
Phone number: 310-555-1212
Reference type: Professional

Michael Jackson
Phone number: 310-555-1212
Reference type: Professional

Sean Combs
Phone number: 310-555-1212
Reference type: Personal

ADDITIONAL INFORMATION

SECURITY CLEARANCE
Secret level

SPECIAL SKILLS
DTRA databases; type 40+ WPM; proficient using Microsoft Word, Excel, PowerPoint, and Access, and in using the Internet for research

PROFESSIONAL PROFILE
Professional with strong analytical and critical-thinking skills.
Highly motivated, articulate, self-starter, with strong leadership skills.
Traveled internationally to South Africa, Spain, and Mexico.

AREAS OF STRENGTH
Analyzing/ Problem Solving/ Negotiating/ Detail Oriented/ Quick Learner/ Team Player

Sample KSA

SALLY JONES
SSN:123-45-6789
Job Announcement Number: ST-08-14

KSA

1. Ability to communicate orally and in writing.

In my current position as a contract analyst for the State Department, I review approximately 20–30 arms sales proposals and proposal amendments each day. An integral part of my review includes analyzing data from a variety of sources. I analyze and evaluate the data, which I then include in a report, and submit to my supervisor for final review. I prepare correspondence for a variety of recipients with a wide range of requirements and expectations. I prepare this correspondence by researching and reviewing source data and making recommendations for action. As a federal contractor, I am employed by the State Department as an agent for the government. Therefore, I am knowledgeable about federal regulations governing correspondence, and I utilize this knowledge in my work. I provide briefings to my supervisor on a weekly basis regarding the nature of the correspondence that I receive and develop. On occasion, I have been called upon to accompany my supervisor to director-level meetings. During a recent meeting, I was provided the opportunity to deliver aspects of the briefing to the director. My supervisor commented that I am "a deliberate and thoughtful speaker with excellent ability to relate to an audience."

In my prior position as a sales manager at an art gallery, I communicated with customers on a regular basis. In addition, I supervised three employees, which required daily and continuous communication, orally and in writing. Because of my ability in oral communication, I played a key role in helping the company achieve $1.2 million in annual revenue. The store's owner commended me on several occasions for my skill at personal salesmanship. In addition, several customers commented that they would not have bought the items they did without my listening and paying attention to their needs and ultimately recommending art that met their requirements.

Throughout my career and in all of my positions, I have been commended for my ability to communicate with a variety of audiences, ranging from children through adults. In my intern positions with Maryland Parks and Planning, I co-led numerous recreational trips with children and adults. In this role, I was called upon in numerous situations to give instruction to participants. I also provided updates to my supervisor.

Throughout college, I gave individual presentations as part of my coursework. I also participated as a member of a team on several projects, during which I provided oral and well as written reports. I have taken job-related training in teamwork, conflict resolution, and getting along with difficult people. In addition, I have been a member of Toastmasters International, an organization that provides members with the opportunity to develop their skills and ability in public speaking. In Toastmasters, I have honed my skills as a speaker, and I won several speech contests.

Helpful Web Sites for Federal Job Seekers

The Web is full of many sites that provide information on federal jobs. This appendix describes some of the most useful sites.

Air Force Civilian Employment

https://ww2.afpc.randolph.af.mil/resweb/

Information about civilian job opportunities with the Air Force is available at this site, which also has job listings.

Army Civilian Employment

http://www.cpol.army.mil/

This site describes working for the U.S. Army as a civilian and has job listings.

Careers in National Defense

http://www.go-defense.com/

The Department of Defense operates this site, which describes civilian career opportunities.

Central Intelligence Agency: Careers

https://www.cia.gov/careers/index.html

This site provides information about various career paths at the Central Intelligence Agency, lists job openings, and describes numerous programs for students. Because the CIA's work is classified and prospective hires are extensively screened, the application process can last more than a year.

Congressional Budget Office: Employment

http://www.cbo.gov/Employment/jobs.cfm

The Congressional Budget Office is a nonpartisan agency that produces policy analyses, cost estimates, and budget and economic projections for Congress. The site has information about working at the CBO and announcements about job openings at the agency.

Government Accountability Office: Employment Opportunities

http://www.gao.gov/careers/apply.html

The nonpartisan Government Accountability Office is often referred to as the investigative arm of Congress. Its Web site provides background about the agency and job listings.

Government Printing Office: Careers

http://www.gpo.gov/careers/jobs.htm

The Government Printing Office is part of the legislative branch. Its Web site has career information and announcements about job openings.

Library of Congress: Jobs and Fellowships

http://www.loc.gov/hr/employment/index.php?action=cMain.showJobs

This site provides information about working at the Library of Congress, which includes the Congressional Research Service. It also has listings for job vacancies.

National Security Agency: Careers

http://www.nsa.gov/careers/

Collecting signals intelligence is the primary job of the super-secret National Security Agency. Its Web site offers information about working at the agency, details about student programs, and job listings.

Navy Civilian Employment

https://chart.donhr.navy.mil/

Civilian jobs in the U.S. Navy are the focus of this site, which also has job listings.

Nuclear Regulatory Commission: Employment Opportunities

http://www.nrc.gov/about-nrc/employment/careers.html

Extensive information about working at the Nuclear Regulatory Commission, an independent agency that regulates the nation's nuclear power plants, is available at this site. It also features an online job application system.

OPM: Electronic Forms

http://www.opm.gov/Forms

Just about any form you'll ever need regarding federal employment is available through this page at the Office of Personnel Management's Web site.

OPM: Salaries and Wages

http://www.opm.gov/oca/08tables/

This site provides salary ranges for a variety of federal jobs, including locality pay.

OPM: Video Library

https://www.opm.gov/Video_Library/index.asp

The Office of Personnel Management offers numerous videos about federal employment and the benefits of working for the federal government. The videos discuss topics such as benefits for new federal employees; career development programs; and special employment programs for people with disabilities, military veterans, and students.

Peace Corps: Jobs

http://www.peacecorps.gov/jobs/

This site provides information about working at the headquarters of the Peace Corps in Washington, DC.

Studentjobs.gov

http://www.studentjobs.gov

Studentjobs.gov, which provides information about federal jobs for students, is an offshoot of USAJOBS. Its searchable database contains listings from USAJOBS of federal job openings that are available to students.

Today's Military: Careers

http://www.todaysmilitary.com/careers

The Department of Defense operates this site, which provides information about different types of careers available in the military.

USAJOBS

http://www.usajobs.gov

USAJOBS is the official jobs site for the federal government. It has a searchable database of tens of thousands of federal job openings, search agents that send you e-mail messages when jobs meeting your criteria are listed, an online resume builder that you can use to quickly apply for many federal jobs, and publications about working for the federal government.

The jobs database primarily lists executive branch positions, but it also lists some jobs in other branches of government and at independent agencies.

USAJOBS: Careers

http://career.usajobs.gov

This site helps users explore their career interests. Different sections help you find jobs for which you're best suited based on your interests, help you match your interests to specific jobs, provide descriptions and minimum qualification requirements for specific federal jobs, and match federal jobs to jobs in the private sector.

USAJOBS: Publications

http://www.usajobs.gov/faqs.asp

This page at USAJOBS offers dozens of publications about working for the federal government. They cover topics such as employment of noncitizens, employment opportunities for attorneys, federal employment overseas, federal qualification requirements, the hiring of postal employees, pay and benefits, and summer employment opportunities for students, among others.

U.S. Courts: Employment Opportunities

http://www.uscourts.gov/employment.html

This site is the best source for job listings in the judicial branch. It provides information about job vacancies at the U.S. Supreme Court and at various U.S. Courts of Appeals, U.S. District Courts, and U.S. Bankruptcy Courts around the country. However, note that the job listings are incomplete because individual courts may post vacancy announcements only on their own Web sites.

U.S. House of Representatives: Employment Opportunities

http://www.house.gov/cao-hr

This site is the key source for information about vacancies in staff jobs at the U.S. House of Representatives.

U.S. Postal Service: Employment

http://www.usps.com/employment

The U.S. Postal Service is an independent agency that operates its own employment system. This Web site provides details about the USPS hiring process and lists job openings.

U.S. Senate: Employment Opportunities

http://www.senate.gov/visiting/resources/pdf/seb.pdf

This is the site of the Senate Employment Bulletin, which lists jobs available in the U.S. Senate. Because Senate jobs are excepted service rather than competitive service jobs, they are not listed on the USAJOBS Web site.

Index

F

I

O

Q–R

T

© JIST Works